ON THE WITNESS STAND

WITH CONTRIBUTIONS BY:

Eugene Borgida
John C. Brigham
Helen J. Burns
Theodore Cross
Denise Dougherty
Howard E. Egeth
Ronald P. Fisher
R. Edward Geiselman
Heidi L. Holland
Saul M. Kassin
Jerome Kravitz
Elizabeth F. Loftus
David T. Lykken
Anne Maass

David P. MacKinnon
Roy S. Malpass
Michael McCloskey
David G. Miller
Kermit Netteburg
John A. Podlesny
William H. Putnam
David C. Raskin
Martin Reiser
Leonard Saxe
Marilyn Chapnik Smith
Janet Swim
Gary L. Wells
Stephen G. West

ON THE WITNESS STAND

Controversies In The Courtroom

EDITORS

Lawrence S. Wrightsman

Cynthia E. Willis

Saul M. Kassin

SAGE PUBLICATIONS
The Publishers of Professional Social Science
Newbury Park   Beverly Hills   London   New Delhi

Copyright © 1987 by Sage Publications, Inc.

For information address:

SAGE Publications, Inc.
2111 West Hillcrest Drive
Newbury Park, California 91320

SAGE Publications Inc.
275 South Beverly Drive
Beverly Hills
California 90212

SAGE Publications Ltd.
28 Banner Street
London EC1Y 8QE
England

SAGE PUBLICATIONS India Pvt. Ltd.
M-32 Market
Greater Kailash I
New Delhi 110 048 India

Printed in the United States of America

Library of Congress Cataloging-in-Publication Data

Main entry under title:

On the witness stand.

(Controversies in the courtroom ; v. 2)
Bibliography: p.
1. Witnesses—United States.   2. Evidence (Law)—United
States.   3. Psychology, Forensic.   I. Wrightsman,
Lawrence S.   II. Willis, Cynthia E.   III. Kassin, Saul M.
IV. Series.
KF8950.05.   1987   347.73'066   87-23373
ISBN 0-8039-3168-9   347.30766
ISBN 0-8039-2793-2 (pbk.)

Contents

Preface

Ever since 1908, with the publication of Hugo Musterberg's *On the Witness Stand*, psychologists and other social scientists have sought to understand the trial process. It is noteworthy that these first efforts concentrated on reactions to evidence. Even though Musterberg's early efforts were ignored for a number of decades, in the last twenty years there has been a renewed focus on reactions to different types of evidence. Psychological factors play a large role in judges' and jurors' reactions to many types of evidence, whether they be from eyewitnesses to a crime, from polygraphy tests that attempt to detect lying, or from victims' memories refreshed through hypnosis.

The purpose of this book is to highlight some of the controversies when psychologists and other social scientists study reactions to types of evidence and courtroom procedures. We have identified five aspects that, we believe, are justifiably titled as "controversial" because there remains, for each, a difference of opinion within disciplines or between disciplines. The five topics are lie detection and polygraph testing, refreshing witnesses' memory through hypnosis, the accuracy of eyewitnesses, the testimony of expert witnesses, and the use of cameras in the courtroom. We have selected, for reprinting, three articles for each section. Some of these articles are reviews of the literature; many are reports of empirical studies; and the remainder portray the opinions of experts in the field. Although a few were originally published in law reviews, the majority first appeared in psychological journals. Authors of these articles come from a variety of professions: clinical psychology, social psychology, experimental psychology, and journalism.

We have used several devices to increase the utility of the book as a learning aid. Each of the five sections contains an introduction and a summary written especially for this volume. The purposes of the introductions are to define the concepts under study, to place the articles in a historical perspective, and to orient the reader to the significant and relevant aspects of the reprinted articles that follow. The purposes of the summaries are to highlight the basic conclusions of the articles, to describe any more recent work on the issue, to attempt to resolve conflicting findings, and to identify unanswered questions. Original bibliographies have been retained so that readers can pursue the topic in more depth if they wish.

This book of readings has a multitude of uses. In conjunction with its companion volume, *In the Jury Box: Controversies in the Courtroom,* the material in this volume is appropriate for the increasing number of undergraduate courses on the psychology of the law or the psychology of the criminal justice system, because it reports empirical findings that are relevant to issues covered in these courses. A significant proportion of the coverage in such courses deals with such topics as the use of hypnosis to enhance the memories of crime victims, the accuracy of the testimony by eyewitnesses, the use of the polygraph, and the function of expert witnesses. Another potential use of this book is in law school courses on trial advocacy and similar courses that seek collections of empirical work of usefulness to the trial attorney. Scholars may find the compilation of recent articles from a variety of sources to be a useful resource for teaching and the generation of research ideas.

The editors wish to acknowledge the assistance of several people in the preparation of this book. Charles T. Hendrix, Executive Editor of Sage Publications, Inc., not only encouraged our pleas for a different approach to the psychology-and-law field, but he also provided the solutions necessary to get this and its companion volume published in a format congenial with the goals of the editors. Julie A. Allison assisted in the collection and preparation of articles for reprinting and typed introductions and summaries. We especially want to thank the authors and publishers of the selections for permission to reprint this material. Our understanding of the psychology of the trial process has been enriched by our reading of these articles and we are pleased to assist in providing an opportunity for others to do so, too.

> —*Lawrence S. Wrightsman*
> *Cynthia E. Willis*
> University of Kansas
>
> —*Saul M. Kassin*
> Williams College

SECTION I

LIE DETECTION
AND POLYGRAPH TESTING
Introduction

Imagine you have just graduated from college and are seeking positions in your chosen field. Imagine further that you have applied for a job, have completed the necessary forms, been given an interview, and are requested to undergo a polygraph test before final approval by the company. If you fail the polygraph assessment you will not be hired. Would you subject yourself to the polygraph test? *Psychology Today* (1984) readers were asked what their response would be, and 55% responded they would refuse the test, even if that meant losing their chances for employment.

Why would the readers of *Psychology Today* (1984) decline a polygraph test and forfeit a possible job? Apparently, their attitudes reflect a response to the controversy surrounding use of the polygraph to detect deception and the uncertainty of whether the polygraph's results are valid measures of guilt or innocence. In other words, does the polygraph measure what it is intending to measure, and should polygraph results be used as evidence of guilt or innocence? The purpose of this section is to provide an overview of the current controversy surrounding polygraph use and its potential as a criterion for establishing guilt or innocence.

As early as 1917, the use of physiological measures to detect deception of criminal suspects was suggested (Marston, 1917), and the polygraph was in use for most of the first half of this century. Even today all law enforcement agencies make use of the polygraph to provide information about guilt or innocence of criminal suspects (Raskin, 1981). Measures such as heart rate, respiratory rate, galvanic skin response (GSR), and blood pressure have all been used to measure changes in arousal which, in turn, are thought to be indicative of deception. In fact, the polygraph measures emotion through physiological arousal, and part of the controversy surrounding the polygraph's validity is whether such emotion is indicative of guilt or innocence.

More recently, the Department of Defense and other departments in the Executive Branch of the U.S. government have proposed the routine use of the polygraph to aid in hiring prospective employees and to eliminate espionage. Even the eminent legal scholar, John Henry Wigmore, once proposed allowing the jury to monitor witnesses' responses by installing a polygraph in the witness stand (Linehan, 1978). Moreover, it has been estimated that in 1983, 23,000 polygraph exams were conducted by the federal government and approximately one million such exams are administered in the United States every year (*Psychology Today*, 1984). Thus, the validity of the polygraph is a matter of importance, because its advocates purport that it can distinguish guilt from innocence. And it is thought the emotion measured through physiological arousal is different for innocent and guilty suspects, leading to indications of deceit.

The first chapter in this section, "The Validity of Polygraph Testing," by Leonard Saxe, Denise Dougherty, and Theodore Cross, is based on a report they completed for the Office of Technology Assessment (OTA) at the request of the House Committee on Governmental Operations. The purpose was to assist Congress in making informed decisions on possible legislative limitations on polygraph use, since the White House had sought its widespread application. The result is an overview of accumulated research evidence that investigates both the reliability and validity of polygraph testing in laboratory and field settings. Another benefit of the chapter is that it provides an introduction to different polygraph question techniques and testing procedures. Furthermore, the chapter offers a summary of the predictive value of both field setting experiments, which are designed to test the validity of the polygraph, and mock crime experiments, in which experimental subjects have actually taken part in a mock crime and their responses to the polygraph are examined.

David T. Lykken, author of the second chapter in this section, is a major critic of the use of the polygraph. His chapter centers around the reasonableness of the theory underlying the potential accuracy of the polygraph technique. Moreover, Lykken examines the scoring methods and design of the questions used by the proponents of the control question technique. He provides an insight into why the polygraph is invalid when polygraphers use global analysis (an analysis that includes all the known information about the suspect, including the suspect's demeanor during the testing). Finally, Lykken questions the accuracy rates claimed by polygraph studies, since he proposes that accurate detection of deception rates must be compared against rates that would be expected by sheer guessing or chance.

The title of the third chapter, "Truth and Deception: A Reply to Lykken," by David C. Raskin and John A. Podlesny, reflects its goal. It is a reply to Lykken's concerns involving the accuracy of the polygraph techniques and the questions raised concerning the validity of the theory behind the polygraph's utility. Specifically, Raskin and Podlesny address the theory underlying the polygraph with the use of the control question technique. This theory states that a guilty suspect will respond with greater autonomic responses (i.e., greater physiological responses to emotion) to the relevant questions than will an innocent suspect; it is assumed the latter subject will provide stronger responses to the control questions. The control questions are presumed to "deal with acts of the same general nature as those covered by the relevant questions" (p. 54). Innocent subjects know they are truthful in answering the relevant questions but not sure in answering the control questions, causing an increase in autonomic arousal to the control questions as compared to the relevant questions. Guilty suspects, on the other hand, would exhibit strong responses to both types of questions. The purpose then of the control question technique is to make positive identifications of innocent suspects.

The main issue for chapters 2 and 3 concerns the theory underlying the polygraph and whether that theory is valid. Also of concern is the accuracy of polygraph techniques. Does the polygraph provide information on deception? Chapter 1 provides an overview of the current research measuring the polygraph's validity and offers conclusions from a review of the literature. The various research strategies used to investigate the polygraph's accuracy are examined and a critique of polygraph research findings offered.

1

THE VALIDITY
OF POLYGRAPH TESTING
Scientific Analysis
and Public Controversy

LEONARD SAXE
DENISE DOUGHERTY
THEODORE CROSS
Boston University

Ever since use of physiological recordings to detect the deceptiveness of criminal suspects was proposed by Marston (1917), controversy over polygraphic "lie detector" tests has raged. Polygraph tests have been

Author's Note. Appreciation is expressed to the Office of Technology Assessment (OTA), John H. Gibbons, Director. OTA requested the authors conduct the study of polygraph validity and provided funds (to Boston University) for its completion. Thanks are also extended to members of the OTA scientific advisory panel, in particular, Edward Katkin, Chair. Denise Dougherty is currently a staff member at the Office of Technology Assessment and worked on final drafts of the report and this manuscript while at OTA. All opinions expressed here are those of the authors. Requests for reprints should be debated in the U.S. Congress, courtrooms, and in a plethora of scientific and nonscientific forums. Within scientific psychology, as outside, loyalists have arisen who either vigorously support or oppose use of polygraph tests. Although much of the public debate about polygraph tests focuses on ethical problems, at the heart of the controversy is validity—the relatively simple question of whether physiological measures can actually assess truthfulness and deception.

As had happened several other times, in 1983 the U.S. Congress conducted hearings concerning polygraph testing (cf. U.S. Congress, 1983) and considered legislation to limit its application. Congressional review was stimulated by administration proposals to expand significantly use of polygraph tests to prevent unauthorized disclosures of classified information and other official misconduct (see Brooks, 1985). An analysis of polygraph testing was conducted as part of these congressional deliberations and is described in this article. The analysis was developed for the congressional Office of Technology Assessment (OTA), and its goal was to provide an evenhanded assessment of current scientific knowledge about polygraph tests.

The study conducted for OTA was not a comprehensive "technology assessment," as characterizes OTA's work (cf. Saxe & Dougherty, in press). Rather, it was a narrowly focused study of the scientific issues concerning polygraph testing, and it served to review and synthesize available research evidence. To conduct the study, a comprehensive review of literature on polygraph testing was conducted. The review was supplemented by site visits and discussions with government officials and polygraph examiners. A scientific advisory panel was formed to aid the investigators, and information from a wide range of sources was sought. A literature review, meta-analysis, and theoretical analysis were incorporated, along with a survey and interviews. The resulting analysis attempted to blend a careful evaluation of data with an assessment and development of theory about the detection of deception.

The study found that although there is no such device as a lie detector per se, a number of approaches to inferring truth or deceptiveness have been developed based on physiological measurement. The type of approach used depends on the situation. Unfortunately, none of these approaches is foolproof. Whether a person is correctly identified as being truthful or deceptive depends largely on

addressed to Leonard Saxe, Center for Applied Social Science, Boston University, 195 Bay State Road, Boston, Massachusetts, 02215.

From *American Psychologist*, 1985, *38*(3), 355-366. Copyright 1985 by the American Psychological Association. Reprinted by permission of the publisher and authors.

the skill of the examiner and a number of characteristics and behaviors of the examinee. Neither available data nor theoretical analysis indicates that polygraph tests function as claimed by their proponents. Substantial numbers of both truthful and deceptive individuals may be misidentified through use of polgraph tests, and the tests can be "beaten." For most common use of polygraph testing there is not even rudimentary evidence to support such use, and reliance on polygraph testing to protect national security would appear to be very problematic. In this article, we describe how this conclusion was developed and explore the current controversy over polygraph testing.

The following analysis is intended to provide an objective description, to the extent that is possible, of current psychological knowledge of polygraph testing. Although there have been other recent attempts (see, in particular, Kleinmuntz & Szucko, 1984) to explicate the psychological theory and research that underlie the use of polygraph tests, this analysis is distinguished by its policy focus. It is rare that psychology and research evidence loom so large in policy deliberations. Many will probably wish that psychology might gain notoriety through other issues; nevertheless, polygraph tests are a psychological procedure and their use should be of central interest to psychologists as well as laypersons.

NATURE OF TESTS

The validity of polygraph examinations to detect deception has long been controversial, both within and outside psychology (cf. Lykken, 1981; Raskin, 1982; Waid & Orne, 1981, 1982). Polygraph examinations have been advocated as a way to ascertain guilt of criminal suspects and to exculpate innocent suspects. Increasingly, they are being used as part of the efforts by private firms to reduce employee theft and by the government to protect national security. Although their use is increasing dramatically, there are a host of questions about their accuracy, and it is not simple to sort out the conflicting claims.

Two problems with most discussions of polygraph testing are (a) polygraph testing is regarded as a monolithic technique and (b) in most lay discussions, the technology of the polygraph instrument, rather than the testing situation, is emphasized. Both are false impressions. A polygraph examination is a form of psychological testing (cf. Kleinmuntz & Szucko, 1982) and, as such, represents a set of interrogational techniques. Simple physiological changes (heart rate, breathing, electrodermal response) are assessed in reaction to a carefully structured set of questions. The pattern of autonomic arousal to these questions is used as the basis for inferring a subject's truthfulness or deception. Unfortunately, because there is no unique physiological response to deception (Lykken, 1981; Orne, 1975), interpretation of arousal is, in fact, a complex clinical task.

A number of techniques have been developed to structure questions asked in a polygraph examination. The choice of which technique to use depends on the nature of the test situation. Most important, different question procedures are used in "specific incident" investigations and screening situations. In a specific incident test, a suspect is questioned about particular facts of a crime; in screening, presumably honest individuals are asked broad questions about their past behavior. Variations in techniques are also related to the examiners' training, but such differences typically affect the way in which a technique is used rather than the choice of a specific technique. Described below are three major types of question procedures used in polygraph tests: the relevant/irrelevant technique (R/I), the control question test (CQT), and concealed information tests (CIT). Also described is the format of typical polygraph examinations. As will be shown the psychological conditions of a test, along with the type of question technique, have an important impact on the validity of polygraph tests.

Question Techniques

The central element of any polygraph examination is the test of a subject's responses to a set of questions. The purpose of most polygraph tests is to elicit physiological reactions to questions that are referred to as "relevant" questions and to compare these reactions with reactions that result when other questions are asked. Comparison questions are called either irrelevant or control questions depending on their function. Relevant questions are directly related to the focus of an investigation (e.g., the specific act involved in a theft) and can either be narrowly focused (e.g., "Did you take $500 from the cash drawer?") or broad (e.g., "Have you ever disclosed classified information to an unauthorized source?"). An irrelevant question is not related to the focus of the investigation and is believed to have little emotional impact (e.g., "Is your name . . . ?"). Control questions are similar to irrelevant questions in that they are not the focus of the investigation; however, they are assumed to be emotionally arousing. A fourth type, concealed information questions, is also used on occasion. Such items include details that only a person with direct knowledge of the situation would react to. The different types of questions result in distinct examination procedures.

Relevant/irrelevant. The R/I technique was the first standard method of polygraph questioning and was developed by Marston (1917). Although no longer used in most specific incident examinations, a variant of this technique is the basis for most screening tests. In a traditional R/I examination, relevant and irrelevant questions are interspersed. Deceptive subjects are assumed to have a significantly greater reaction to relevant questions than to irrelevant questions. An underlying assumption is that nondeceptive subjects will respond equivalently to all questions, because they do not fear questions about the relevant issue any more than irrelevant questions.

There are a number of well-recognized problems with the R/I technique (Lykken, 1981; Podlesny & Raskin, 1978; Raskin, 1982). The most important problem is that, because the intent of the questions is transparent, nondeceptive as well as deceptive subjects are likely to be more aroused to relevant than irrelevant questions. In addition, any drug or mental state that either heightens or depresses physiological reactions may yield false or inconclusive readings. Despite problems with the technique, however, it is still used (along with variants) because it is simple to employ. In situations in which the examiner does not have knowledge of the information that the subject may be trying to withhold, it may be the only available technique.

Control question test. The CQT is the most common question technique used in investigations of a specific issue. As in the procedure with R/I tests, CQTs use relevant questions that ask about situations such as crimes. Also, as with R/I tests, deceptive subjects in CQTs are assumed to show greater autonomic arousal to relevant than to other questions. The CQT, however, adds control questions designed to provoke arousal in nondeceptive subjects. Nondeceptive subjects are thought to show greater autonomic arousal to control questions than to relevant questions, and thus such questions are hypothesized to control for a subject's arousability. Where no clear difference emerges between relevant and control questions, the examination is judged inconclusive, and subjects may be retested.

Control questions must be skillfully constructed and are designed to cause nondeceptive subjects to be doubtful and concerned about whether they have actually told the truth in response to them. Such questions usually probe for past misdeeds similar to the crime being investigated, transgressions that polygraph examiners assume most people have committed (cf. Reid & Inbau, 1977). A control question might be, "Before the age of 25, did you ever steal anything from a place where you worked?" Control questions usually cover a long period of time in order to make subjects even more doubtful about the veracity of their answers.

Control questions are developed during part of a lengthy pretest interview. The examiner does not tell the subject that there is a distinction between relevant and control questions. Control questions are described as questions necessary to determine if the subject is the "type of person" who would commit an act such as the one being investigated (Raskin, 1982). The examiner stresses that the subject must be able to answer the questions completely ith a simple "yes" or "no" answer and that the polygraph will record any confusion, misgivings, or doubts. The situation is set up such that the subject is persuaded that the examiner wants the truth. In reality, however, the examiner wants the subject to experience considerable doubt about his or her truthfulness. According to Kircher and Raskin (1983), "Control questions are intentionally vague and extremely difficult to answer truthfully with an unqualified 'No'" (p. 7).

Concealed information tests. A third type of question procedure works on an entirely different premise than either the CQT or R/I. Instead of detecting deception about having committed a crime, per se, CITs aim to detect whether a suspect has information about a crime that only a guilty subject would have, such as details about the site of the crime or the means by which it was committed. Such CITs have been proposed as an alternative to CQT examinations (Kleinmuntz & Szucko, 1982; Lykken, 1974, 1981) but are not typically used by polygraph examiners in the field to ascertain the deceptiveness of a subject. One reason the use of CITs is limited is that the test is only possible to conduct when the examiner has substantial information about the situation under investigation that would not be known to innocent subjects.

Test Procedures

Not only is a polygraph test heavily dependent on the nature of the question technique used, but its validity is greatly affected by the conditions established by an examiner. Most of the time involved in an examination is spent in development of questions and review of procedures, which is called establishing a "psychological set" by texts on polygraph procedure (Barland & Raskin, 1973). A typical polygraph test used as part of a criminal investigation may take 3 to 4 hours. Less than 15 minutes of this time is actually spent obtaining physiological recordings. The bulk of test time is spent in a pretest interview and discussion before and after each of several polygraph charts are "run."

Pretest interview. Discussion prior to the conduct of an actual polygraph test has been considered an indispensable component of the examination (Mullenix & Reid, 1980; Reid & Inbau, 1977; Waid & Orne, 1981). The pretest interview provides subjects with information about the examination and helps to generate the psychological climate necessary to conduct testing. An important purpose of the examination is to persuade a subject that attempted deception "will be very obvious to the examiner" (Barland & Raskin, 1973, p. 424). The pretest interview has marked similarities to instructions given subjects in deception experiments (cf. Aronson & Carlsmith, 1968). The instructions are intended to place truthful subjects at ease and to increase anxiety in subjects who intend to be deceptive. The pretest also allows the examiner to assess the effect of special conditions that might affect the subject's physiological responsiveness. Thus, for example, subjects are typically queried (but not otherwise tested) about medical problems and their use of drugs.

In addition to establishing "psychological climate," the pretest interview focuses on discussion of the relevant issues to be tested (or the person's background, if a screening test), along with development and review of the questions to be used. In almost all polygraph examinations, the questions to be tested are reviewed beforehand. This is designed to ensure that the subject and examiner share a common understanding of each question and, in addition, to heighten the subject's fear of responding deceptively. Much of the success of the pretest interview depends on the subject's cooperation. If a subject is uncooperative, information necessary to construct both relevant and control questions cannot be obtained.

Stimulation tests. Polygraph examiners typically conduct what are known as stimulation ("stim") tests. Typically, stim tests are given immediately after the pretest or after the first chart (i.e., sequence of actual test questions). The most common stim tests are "number" or "card" tests. A subject is instructed to select, from a deck, a card that has a number, word, or suit on the back (Decker, 1978; Fingerhut, 1978). Sometimes, the cards are secretly marked so that the examiner is sure to know the correct answer (Reid & Inbau, 1977), although this is not currently done by federal examiners. Whether or not such markings are used, however, the test then proceeds in the same way as a CIT, and the examiner demonstrates the ability of the polygraph to detect the correct card, number, or suit.

The purpose of a stim test is to convince subjects of the accuracy of the polygraph examination. Stimulation tests are intended to reassure truthful subjects and provoke anxiety in deceptive subjects (cf. Barland, 1978). Their effect should be to increase differential responsivity of deceptive and nondeceptive subjects to different questions on the examination. Research suggests that stimulation tests may, indeed, increase the accuracy of polygraph tests (Bradley & Janisse, 1981; Senese, 1976).

Posttest. Interspersed among test questioning and measurement of physiological responses are opportunities for an examiner to review questions and to query subjects about their responses. At the end of the examination, the examiner will often make an assessment of whether a subject is being deceptive or nondeceptive. Different test techniques and circumstances lead to somewhat different examiner behavior. In many cases, the examiner will indicate a "diagnosis," and if a subject is thought to be deceptive, the examiner will attempt to elicit a confession. This may or may not be done directly and may be couched in terms of providing the subject with an opportunity to clarify his or her responses.

Summary

Polygraph tests are thus complex situations that employ structured question formats, physiological recording of reactions, and various situational inducements for a subject to be fearful of providing false answers. The accuracy of polygraph tests is highly dependent on the way in which the questions have been developed and the situation established by the examiner.

EVIDENCE FROM FIELD STUDIES

Controversy over the validity of polygraph tests has continued for over 60 years, escalating recently as use has dramatically increased. In the 1920s, questions about the validity of a crude polygraph test established a legal precedent (the "Frye" test) on admissibility of scientific evidence. The U.S. Congress, along with a host of state and foreign governments, has wrestled with the usefulness of polygraph evidence in criminal proceedings, their use by private employers, and the licensing and regulation of examiners. Each of these controversies focuses on the question of whether a polygraph examination actually identifies truthful and nontruthful individuals.

In recent years, controversy about polygraph tests has flared within psychology; most prominently, in a debate between Raskin at the University of Utah, and Lykken, at the University of Minnesota (see, e.g. Lykken, 1979; Podlesny & Raskin, 1978; Raskin & Podlesny, 1979). The debate has centered on interpretation of data, although the theoretical viability of polygraph tests has been an underlying aspect of the debate. Lykken claimed that from a theoretical as well as empirical vantage point, polygraph tests have not shown their value; Raskin, in contrast, based both on his own research and that of others, claimed that validity for certain uses has been established.

The scientific debate on polygraph test validity has been joined by other researchers and practitioners (cf. U.S. Department of Defense, 1984; Waid & Orne, 1982). The debate focuses on results of a small number of studies that have been conducted, most within the last 15 years, on the actual use of polygraph tests. These studies, referred to here as field studies, have a number of distinguishing characteristics. Field studies report actual uses of polygraph examinations conducted by professional examiners, use typical field polygraph techniques, and use some independent criterion to assess actual guilt or innocence.

The most difficult aspect of developing a field study is assessment of subjects' actual deceptiveness or nondeceptiveness. Although "ground truth" can never be known in an absolute sense, field studies described here use some systematic judgment of ground truth, independent of the polygraph examination. Such measures are typically based on judicial outcome, an expert panel, or confession.

Available Studies

There are, perhaps, 250 empirical reports of the validity of polygraph testing. Most such reports, however, do not include an independent assessment of ground truth and are case study reports of the known results from the use of the tests with a particular population. Only 10 of the available studies met the criteria established for field studies in the OTA review (U.S. Congress, 1983). It should be noted, however, that in some important respects these studies are not characteristic of the polygraph testing field. All 10 studies concern use of polygraph tests in specific incident criminal situations. No field studies examined the use of polygraph testing in screening or national security situations. In addition, almost all studies use variants of the CQT, even though it is a type of R/I test that is generally used in screening situations. The limited range of available studies reduces the external validity of findings.

The 10 studies included in our analysis of field studies are listed in Table 1. They include two studies conducted with military personnel (Bersh, 1969; P. O. Davidson, 1968) and several studies conducted by psychologists Barland and Raskin (1976). The largest group of studies has been reported by polygraph examiners from John Reid and Associates of Chicago, a leading private polygraph agency (Horvath &

TABLE 1.1
Characteristics of Field Studies

Study	Criterion	Types of cases
Bersh (1969)	Panel of legal professionals' assessment of investigative files	Criminal investigation/military personnel
Barland and Raskin (1976)	Panel of legal professionals' assessment of investigative files	Sex crimes, drug crimes, crimes of violence, crimes of financial gain, other crimes[a]
Raskin (1976)	Confession	Sex crimes, drug crimes, crimes of violence, crimes of financial gain, other crimes
Horvath and Reid (1971)	Confession	Theft, sexual misconduct, sabotage, bribery, criminal damage to property
Hunter and Ash (1973)	Confession	Theft, official misconduct, brutality, sexual assaults, homicide
Slowik and Buckley (1975)	Confession	Theft, industrial sabotage, drug abuse, rape
Wicklander and Hunter (1975)	Confession	Homicide, sexual assault, theft, official misconduct
Horvath (1977)	Confession	Crimes against persons, crimes against property
W. A. Davidson (1979)	Confession	Crimes against property/military personnel
Kleinmuntz and Szucko (1982)	Confession	Theft

Note: All studies use some version of control question technique.
a. Only 77 of 92 cases were analyzed as to type of crime.

Reid, 1971; Hunter & Ash, 1973; Slowik & Buckley, 1975; Wicklander & Hunter, 1975). The latter studies were drawn from records of criminal investigations and, for the most part, each study reports results of examinations on person-related crimes (e.g., sexual assault) and property crimes (e.g., theft).

Each study selected was coded for a number of variables, including the outcome of the study (number of correct, incorrect, and inconclusive decisions for guilty and innocent subjects) and such factors as the design (e.g., sample selection, attrition rate, base rate of guilt), type of crime, type of test, and characteristics of the examiner. Codings were made by two reviewers and relied on published sources and, in some cases, correspondence or other contact with the author(s).

Findings

To assess the basic question about validity, outcome frequencies for each category of guilt/decision correctness were converted to percentages, and means were calculated. As shown in Table 2, a great deal of variability exists across results of these studies. Correct guilty decisions ranged from 70.6% to 98.6%. Correct innocent detections were more variable, ranging from a low of 12.5% to a high of 94%. False negatives ranged from zero to 29%, whereas false positives ranged from zero to 75%. Inconclusives ranged from zero to 25%.

TABLE 1.2

Outcomes of Field Studies

		Guilty			Innocent			
	N	Correct	Incorrect	Inconclusive	Correct	Incorrect	Inconclusive	λ_b
Bersh (1969)[a]								
GQT unanimous[b]	68	96.9%	3.1%	NA	88.9%	11.1%	NA	0.84
ZOC unanimous[b]	89	89.5	10.5	NA	94.1	5.9	NA	0.82
Average unanimous	157	93.2	6.8	NA	91.5	8.5	NA	0.83
Majority (ZOC and GQT)	59	70.6	29.4	NA	80.0	20.0	NA	0.40
Horvath and Reid (1971)	40	85.0	15.0	0	90.5	9.5	0	0.76
Hunter and Ash (1973)	20	87.1	11.4	1.4	86.4	14.1	0	0.74
Slowik and Buckley (1975)	30	84.0	15.3	0.7	90.7	6.6	2.7	0.77
Wicklander and Hunter (1975)								
Polygraph & case material	20	98.6	1.3	0	86.6	8.3	5.0	
Polygraph alone		90.0	8.3	1.6	86.6	5.0	8.3	
Average		94.4	5.0	1.0	86.6	6.7	6.7	0.88
Horvath (1977)	56	77.1	22.9	0	51.1	48.9	0	0.28
W. A. Davidson (1979)	21	90.0	10.0	0	91.0	0	9.0	0.90
Raskin (1976)[c]	16	91.7	0	8.3	75.0	0	25.0	0.75
Barland and Raskin (1976)								
Criterion panel	64	91.5	0	8.5	29.4	52.9	17.6	0.29
Judicial outcome	41	90.9	0	9.1	12.5	75.0	12.5	0.13
Kleinmuntz and Szucko (1982)	100	75.0	25.0	0	63.0	37.0	0	0.38

a. Includes studies using unanimous or majority decisions by a panel as a criterion of ground truth.
b. The General Question Test (GQT) is a version of the R/I test and the Zone of Comparison Test (ZOC) is a type of CQT.
c. Includes only the outcome using numerical scoring.

A measure of predictive association (λ_b; Goodman & Kruskal, 1954) was calculated. This shows the proportional reduction in the probability of error gained by using the polygraph to predict deception. The results of this analysis indicated that across studies λ_b was .64. This can be interpreted to mean that, on average, in field studies polygraph test results reduced 64% of the error of chance prediction. For individual studies λ_b ranged from .13 to .90.

The use, however, of a single index of polygraph validity is probably inadequate, for reasons that both support and refute the usefulness of polygraph testing. In addition to the variability of the results, it should be recognized that there are only a small number of available studies and they are not necessarily representative of polygraph testing situations.

No significant relationships were found between the design and setting factors that were coded and the outcome of the examinations. This may well be related to the great variability in design and setting, especially relative to the small number of acceptable studies. Thus available field studies of polygraph CQTs appear to indicate that testing was better than chance at differentiating deceptive from nondeceptive subjects in certain criminal investigations. However, substantial false positive and negative rates were obtained in several investigations, and there were also a substantial number of cases in which no decision was made on the basis of polygraph tests.

In some ways, field study data are impossible to generalize. To cite one problem, in field studies polygraph charts are generally selected to create a 50% base rate of guilt (i.e., half the subjects are guilty and half innocent). Yet it is unclear how many suspects of a crime underwent polygraph examinations in the original investigations from which the charts were drawn. The greater the number of subjects polygraphed, the lower the base rate of guilt and the greater the number of incorrect identifications at a given rate of false positives. In addition, it is unclear whether there are important differences among studies where an independent assessment of ground truth is available and where such information cannot be obtained. Also problematic is the variability in accuracy rates across studies. This suggests that there are unknown factors, perhaps related to subjects, examiners, or the test situation, that influence the outcome of studies.

EVIDENCE FROM ANALOGUE STUDIES

A separate analysis was conducted on what were called "analogue studies." Analogue studies are investigations in which field methods of polygraph testing are used in simulations of crimes or other situations. Such studies investigate either mock crimes created by an experimenter (with the knowledge of subjects) or actual small crimes set up by the experimenter. Analogue studies are not actual criminal investigations, and subjects are usually aware that they are participants in polygraph research. The principal methodological advantage of analogue studies is that ground truth is known because in most cases, "guilt" and "innocence" are assigned to subjects. In addition, they provide more control of the polygraph situation and conditions of testing. Use of analogue studies as indicators of polygraph test validity, however, is potentially problematic because of external validity problems. The crime situation differs between actual and analogue polygraph examinations, as do the testing situation, training and background of examiners, and often the polygraph equipment used. In addition, demand characteristics in analogue studies may yield a somewhat different polygraph situation than would be found in field settings (Barland & Raskin, 1973).

Studies were only included as analogue studies if they employed actual field polygraph techniques and pertained to some actual use of polygraph testing. They were analyzed by the same methods used with the field studies. The studies selected that are analogues of the CQT are listed in Table 3. Because there were only two studies of R/I tests, the other questioning technique being debated, they were not analyzed as a group.

TABLE 1.3

Outcomes of Control Question Analogue Studies

		Guilty			Innocent			
	N	Correct	Incorrect	Inconclusive	Correct	Incorrect	Inconclusive	λ_b
Barland and Raskin (1975)	72	63.9%	8.3%	27.8%	41.7%	16.7%	41.7%	0.47
Podlesny and Raskin (1978)	40	69.0	16.0	15.0	91.0	4.0	5.0	0.75
Raskin and Hare (1978)	48	87.5	0	12.5	75.0	4.0	20.8	0.83
Rovner et al. (1978)	72	77.8	8.3	13.9	80.5	13.9	5.5	0.72
Kircher (1983)	100	60.0	4.0	36.0	76.0	2.0	22.0	0.72
Dawson (1980)	24	91.7	0	8.3	58.3	25.0	16.7	0.67
Bradley and Janisse (1981)	192							0.33
EDR		60.4	13.5	26.0	58.3	9.4	32.3	
Heart rate		35.4	20.8	43.8	33.3	19.8	46.9	
Szucko and Kleinmuntz (1981)[a]	30	71.3	28.7	NA[a]	49.3	50.7	NA[a]	0.22
Ginton et al. (1982)	15	100.0	0	0	84.6	15.4	0	0.00[b]
Honts and Hodes (1982a)								
No countermeasures	21	67.0	0.0	33.0	33.0	17.0	50.0	0.25
Countermeasures	19	58.0	5.5	36.6	NA	NA	NA	NA[c]
Honts and Hodes (1982b)[a]								
No countermeasures	38	84.2	0.0	15.8	31.6	15.8	52.6	0.05
Countermeasures	19	36.8	26.3	36.8	NA	NA	NA	NA[c]
Hammond (1980)	62	71.9	3.0	25.0	40.0	20.0	40.0	0.50

a. Examiners were not allowed to categorize an examination as inconclusive.
b. λ_b is a misleading statistic in this study because the base rate is skewed.
c. λ_b is not possible to calculate when only guilty or innocent subjects were used.

More analogue studies have been conducted with college students (Barland & Raskin, 1975; Bradley & Janisse, 1981; Honts & Hodes, 1982a, 1982b; Szucko & Kleinmuntz, 1981; Widacki & Horvath, 1978) than with other groups. This creates an external validity problem, in that students are likely to be less concerned with the outcome of the test and, in various ways, are different from typical polygraph examinees. Raskin (cited in U.S. Congress, 1983) noted that CQT experiments using students tended to have a lower accuracy rate than other studies. In their own research, Raskin and his colleagues have increasingly, used nonstudent paid volunteers as subjects (Kircher, 1983; Podlesny & Raskin, 1978; Rovner, Raskin, & Kircher, 1978). Even with these subjects, however, the experimental nature of the polygraph examinations and the lack of serious consequences raise questions about the external validity of these studies. Other analogue studies have tested specific hypotheses about the CQT polygraph examination on special populations or groups such as prisoners (Raskin & Hare, 1978), police candidates (Ginton, Daie, Elaad, & Ben-Shakhar, 1982), psychiatric patients (Hammond, 1980; Heckel, Brokaw, Salzberg & Wiggins, 1962) and actors recruited to use their skills to "beat" the polygraph (Dawson, 1980). Two of these studies (Ginton et al.; Heckel et al.) employed actual transgressions (relatively minor) that subjects were induced to commit or accused of committing.

Twelve analogue studies using CQT techniques were examined and included in the meta-analysis. Results for each of these studies are listed in Table 3. As with the field studies, there was a great deal of variability among the results. Correct guilty decisions ranged from

36.4% to 100%. Correct innocent decisions ranged from 31.6% to 91%. The range of false positives was 2% to 50.7%, whereas that of false negatives was 0% to 28.7% The mean λ_b for CQT analogue studies was .47. As with the field studies, the additional design and setting factors coded were not significantly related to outcome, with the variability and small number of studies again being problematic.

FACTORS AFFECTING POLYGRAPH EXAMINATION VALIDITY

The meta-analyses of field and analogue studies indicated that there is considerable variability in accuracy rates of polygraph examinations. Research suggests that there are several factors related to the situation of a polygraph examination that affect its validity and that could account for this variability. These factors are especially important to consider in light of proposed government expansion of polygraph tests, which would employ polygraph tests in new situations with different groups of examinees than have been previously studied. Such applications of polygraph testing may differ considerably from the applications for which the polygraph has been tested systematically. Thus it is necessary to focus on these additional factors that may affect validity, as well as on the tests themselves. Three primary factors affecting validity are characteristics of the polygraph examiner, the subject, and the setting. In addition, various countermeasures used to "beat" the polygraph can affect validity.

Examiner

An examiner's skill has long been recognized (Lykken, 1981; Orne, 1975; Raskin, 1981) to have an important effect on polygraph validity, and has often been used to explain differences in accuracy rates (Raskin & Podlesny, 1979). In recognition of the effects of examiner skill on results, an extensive array of training facilities now exists, offering different orientations to polygraph testing. On the basis of presently available data, it is not possible to determine whether types of training have an effect on outcome. A study by Raskin (1976) found that examiners who trained in schools that emphasize numerical scoring were significantly more accurate than other examiners (97.1% vs. 86.9%). It is difficult to determine, however, if training in numerical scoring is more efficient or if better examiners select such techniques. Examiner experience can also be an important determinant in the outcome of polygraph examinations (Horvath & Reid, 1971).

Subjects

Substantial attention has been devoted to subject characteristics. Several studies have examined the effect of psychopathy or level of socialization, the theory being that subjects high in psychopathy (or low in socialization) may differ in their pattern of physiological arousal in the polygraph examination. Significant relationships have been found in the laboratory between socialization and various measures of autonomic responsiveness (Barland & Raskin, 1975; Waid, 1976; Waid, Orne, & Wilson, 1979a, 1979b), suggesting that less socialized subjects are less electrodermally responsive and therefore less detectable. Other research, however, suggests no difference between psychopathic or undersocialized subjects and others (Raskin & Hare, 1978). Research on polygraph accuracy with other diagnostic groups is sparse, is of questionable methodological rigor, and has produced mixed results (Hammond, 1980; Heckel et al., 1962).

There is little research on the effect of intelligence or education level on validity. Intelligent subjects could theoretically escape detection more easily because they could better anticipate questions and employ countermeasures, or they could be more detectable because they understand the consequences better and so respond to relevant questions with heightened arousal (Barland & Raskin, 1975). Kugelmass (1967) and Barland and Raskin (1975) found no relationship between intelligence or education level and detectability, but the former study dealt only with a CIT. Interestingly, a separate analysis of the latter study (Raskin, 1976) found that the majority of false positives occurred among subjects who had college degrees.

Although evidence for ethnic differences in reaction to stress (Kugelmass & Lieblich, 1968; Sternbach & Tursky, 1965) suggests corresponding differences in detectability, effects of ethnic differences have not been tested with respect to polygraph examinations. Likewise, gender differences in detectability have not been found (Cutrow, Parks, Lucas, & Thomas, 1972; Honts & Hodes, 1982a, 1982b). A final individual difference among examinees that may affect validity is what Waid and Orne (1981) have called autonomic lability— consistent individual differences between subjects on level of autonomic arousal.

Setting

One theory underlying lie detection using a polygraph is that the fear of being detected and punished leads an individual to manifest a physiological reaction (Davis, 1961). This suggests, then, that settings in which individuals are more certain of being detected and in which the consequences are greatest will permit higher levels of detection. One component of subjects' concern that they will be detected is their belief in the efficacy of the instrument. Polygraph examiners usually try to enhance belief in efficacy through persuasion and the use of stim tests. Experimental studies of CITs in which subjects have been led to believe that the instrument was inoperative (Orne, Thackray, & Paskewitz, 1972; Thackray & Orne, 1968) have not yielded significant differences in detectability. A similar study (Waid, Orne, & Wilson, 1979a), however, which used a CQT and a more powerful manipulation (turning the instrument off while secretly recording with another instrument) significantly reduced detectability.

Social psychological research on the so-called bogus pipeline (cf. Jones & Sigall, 1971; Quigley-Fernandez & Tedeschi, 1978; Sigall & Page, 1972) suggests that subjects may often admit hidden thoughts if they believe that a lie detector device can detect them, even when the machine is a fake. Thus one practical effect of the polygraph setting is to induce subjects to confess, as they often do after having the polygraph procedure explained or being shown the results of the examination. Subjects often admit to past misdeeds during the pretest interview in personnel screening examinations (Barton, 1976; U.S. Central Intelligence Agency, 1980). Although it is probably an important factor in the detection of deception in the field and may influence anecdotal accounts of the accuracy of polygraph testing, the influence of the bogus pipeline effect on the the validity of polygraph examinations themselves has not been tested.

Countermeasures

Countermeasures are deliberate techniques used by deceptive subjects to avoid detection. They range from simple physical movement techniques, to so-called mental countermeasures, to the use of drugs and biofeedback techniques. There is a potentially large list of such countermeasures, and there are a number of plausible, but not yet validated, techniques to avoid deception.

Any physical activity that affects physiological response is a potential problem for interpretation of a polygraph chart. There is no question that physical measures, from tensing muscles, to biting the tongue, to squeezing toes, to shifting one's position can affect physiological responses. Physical countermeasures have been effective in reducing detectability in recent analogue studies (Honts & Hodes, 1982a, 1982b; Honts, Raskin, & Kircher, 1983). Although this is a potentially serious problem, Honts, Raskin, and Kircher reported that examiners were able to uncover 80% of the use of countermeasures.

The use of drugs to obscure differences between reactions to relevant and control questions is more difficult to detect, unless a urinalysis is conducted, as the Department of Defense is proposing (Stilwell, 1984). Subjects may be able to "beat" the polygraph test with drugs or at least obtain an inconclusive result. Meprobamate, for example, has been found to increase a subject's ability to avoid detection in one concealed information study (Waid, Orne, Cook, & Orne, 1981), whereas propanolol increased the number of inconclusives in a control question test study (Gatchel, Smith, & Kaplan, 1983), although it did not otherwise affect the error rate. On the other hand, neither diazepam nor methylphenidate were found to affect accuracy of detection in a CIT (Iacoco, Boisvenu, & Fleming, 1983).

Psychological interventions may also be used as countermeasures, although there is little research on the effects. In one study (Barland & Raskin, 1973), hypnotized subjects were not found to be less susceptible to detection, whereas in another study (Corcoran, Lewis, & Garver, 1978) biofeedback training was found to have a negative effect on test validity. Instructing subjects to control their thoughts during the examination was not successful in one experiment (Dawson, 1980), although this has not been studied with subjects who are knowledgeable about polygraph procedures. Having experienced prior polygraph examinations may help subjects avoid detection in a subsequent examination (Gustafson & Orne, 1965), although some evidence suggests that this occurs only if subjects are instructed how to "beat" particular types of polygraph tests (Rovner, Raskin, & Kircher, 1978). Manipulating subjects' belief in the instrument, a possible countermeasure, has yielded mixed results in its effect on detectability (Bradley & Janisse, 1981; Timm, 1979).

Overall, there seems to be at least limited evidence for the effectiveness of some types of countermeasures. Further research, however, is needed to determine their influence on the error rates in different polygraph techniques and to assess different methods of detecting their use.

CONCLUSIONS

Using psychological research data to answer public policy questions is inherently difficult. Neither policymakers who seek to utilize such data nor the researchers responsible for study designs have one another in mind. The communication problem between policymakers and researchers is made more difficult by the lack of clear standards to evaluate data and the nascent state of techniques to synthesize information across research studies. With polygraph testing, most of the usual problems of policy-relevant research are exacerbated.

Only recently have psychologists become centrally involved in the assessment of polygraph tests, and there is thus a paucity of methodologically appropriate research. In addition, there is no well-established theoretical base, and use of polygraph tests has far outstripped research efforts.

The most serious difficulty in the development of policy-relevant conclusions about polygraph testing is the lack of theory to explain results of testing. Theoretically, a polygraph test operates on a simple principle: that anxiety is related to lying. Yet, it is clear that anxiety has a host of causal factors and making attributions of deception is cognitively complex (cf. Ekman, 1985). It is for this reason that many scientists are skeptical about claims for polygraph testing.

Despite a priori grounds for ignoring much of the applied research on polygraph testing, the present analysis attempted to review this work as carefully as possible. What emerges is a picture that may seem overly complicated to laypersons, but is in fact relatively obvious from a psychological perspective (cf. Saxe, 1983). The data suggest that under certain conditions CQTs can detect deception at rates significantly better than chance, although the data also suggest that substantial rates of false positives, false negatives, and inconclusives are possible. What appear to be very important are the conditions of the test. These probably include, at a minimum, a narrowly focused question, an experienced examiner/investigator, and a subject who believes in the efficacy of the test. Many other conditions may also be necessary, and only a small number of these conditions can be controlled by an examiner.

There is, thus, no way to ensure that a polygraph test has provided any new information. Similar, perhaps, to eyewitness evidence that can be systematically biased (Loftus, 1979), polygraph tests are not infallible. Despite the aura of technology, they are relatively simple devices that rely on relatively simplistic inferences. Research evidence about polygraph tests obviously has a role, but cannot determine public use of such tests. Nevertheless, psychological thinking and research can do much to educate policymakers about the nature of the problem. Such was the case in this situation (cf. Brooks, 1985) and the debate still rages—in Congress, in courts, and in psychological journals. One can only hope that the debate is now more informed than before.

REFERENCES

Aronson, E., & Carlsmith, J. M. (1968). Experimentation in social psychology. In G. Lindzey & E. Aronson (Eds.), *The handbook of social psychology* (2nd ed., Vol. 2, pp. 1-79). Reading, MA: Addison-Wesley.

Barland, G. H. (1978). A fail-proof blind numbers test. *Polygraph, 7,* 203-207.

Barland, G. H., & Raskin, D. C. (1973). Detection of deception. In W. F. Prokasy & D. C. Raskin (Eds.), *Electrodermal activity in psychological research* (pp. 418-471). New York: Academic Press.

Barland, G. H., & Raskin, D. C. (1975). An evaluation of field techniques in detection of deception. *Psychophysiology, 12,* 321-330.

Barland, G. H., & Raskin, D. C. (1976). Validity and reliability of polygraph examinations of criminal suspects (Contract No. 75-N1-99-0001). Washington, DC: National Institute of Justice, Department of Justice.

Barton, M. (1976). *A study of the admissions made during pre-employment polygraph examinations (1964-1975) and their significance to the business community.* Unpublished master's thesis, Sam Houston State University.

Bersh, P. J. (1969). A validation study of polygraph examiner judgements. *Journal of Applied Psychology, 53,* 399-403.

Bradley, M. T., & Janisse, M. P. (1981). Accuracy demonstrations, threat and the detection of deception: Cardiovascular, electrodermal, and pupillary measures. *Psychophysiology, 18,* 307-314.

Brooks, J. (1985). Polygraph testing: Thoughts of a skeptical legislator. *American Psychologist, 40,* 348-354.

Corcoran, J. F. T., Lewis, M. D., & Garver, R. B. (1978). Biofeedback conditioned galvanic skin response and hypnotic suppression of arousal: A pilot study of their relation to deception. *Journal of Forensic Sciences, 23,* 155-162.

Cutrow, R. J., Parks, A., Lucas, N., & Thomas, K. (1972). The objective use of multiple physiological indices in the detection of deception. *Psychophysiology, 9,* 578-588.

Davidson, P. O. (1968). Validity of the guilty-knowledge technique: The effects of motivation, *Journal of Applied Psychology, 52,* 62-65.

Davidson, W. A. (1979). Validity and reliability of the Cardio Activity Monitor. *Polygraph, 8,* 104-111.

Davis, R. C. (1961). Physiological responses as a means of evaluating information. In A. D. Biderman & H. Zimmer (Eds.), *The manipulation of human behavior* (pp. 142-169). New York: Wiley.

Dawson, M. E. (1980). Physiological detection of deception: Measurement of responses to questions and answers during countermeasure maneuvers. *Psychophysiology, 17,* 8-17.

Decker, R. E. (1978). The Army simulation test: A control procedure. *Polygraph, 7,* 176-178.

Ekman, P. (1985). *Telling lies.* New York: W. W. Norton.

Fingerhut, K. R. (1978). Use of the stimulation test in preemployment testing. *Polygraph, 7,* 185-188.

Gatchel, R. J., Smith, J. E., & Kaplan, N. M. (1983). *The effect of propanolol on polygraphic detection of deception.* Unpublished manuscript.

Ginton, A., Daie, N., Elaad, E. & Ben-Shakhar, G. (1982). A method for evaluating the use of polygraph in a real-life situation. *Journal of Applied Psychology, 67,* 131-137.

Goodman, L. A., & Kruskal, W. H. (1954). Measures of association for cross-classification. *Journal of the American Statistical Association, 49,* 732-764.

Gustafson, L. A., & Orne, M. T. (1965). Effects of perceived role and role success on the detection of deception. *Journal of Applied Psychology, 49*, 412-417.

Hammond, D. L. (1980). *The responding of normals, alcoholics and psychopaths in a laboratory lie-detection experiment.* Unpublished doctoral dissertation, California School of Professional Psychology.

Heckel, R. V., Brokaw, J. R., Salzberg, H. C., & Wiggins, S. L. (1962). Polygraphic variations in reactivity between delusional, nondelusional, and control groups in a crime situation. *Journal of Criminal Law, Criminology and Police Science, 53*, 380-383.

Honts, C. R., & Hodes, R. L. (1982a). The effects of multiple physical countermeasures on the detection of deception. *Psychophysiology, 19*, 564-565.

Honts, C. R., & Hodes, R. L. (1982b). The effect of simple physical countermeasures on the detection of deception. *Psychophysiology, 19*, 564.

Honts, C. R., Raskin, D. C., & Kircher, J. C. (1983). Detection of deception: Effectiveness of physical countermeasures under high motivation conditions. *Psychophysiology, 20*, 446-447.

Horvath, F. S. (1977). The effect of selected variables on interpretation of polygraph records. *Journal of Applied Psychology, 62*, 127-136.

Horvath, F. S., & Reid, J. E. (1971). The reliability of polygraph examiner diagnosis of truth and deception. *The Journal of Criminal Law, Criminology and Police Science, 62*, 276-281.

Hunter, F. L., & Ash, P. (1973). The accuracy and consistency of polygraph examiners' diagnoses. *Journal of Police Science and Administration, 1*, 370-375.

Iacono, W. G., Boisvenu, G. A., & Fleming, J. A. (1983). *The effects of diazepam and methylphenidate on the electrodermal detection of guilty knowledge.* Unpublished manuscript, University of British Columbia, Vancouver, Canada.

Jones, E. E. & Sigall, H. (1971). The bogus pipeline: A new paradigm for measuring affect and attitude. *Psychological Bulletin, 76*, 349-364.

Kircher, J. C. (1983). *Computerized decision-making and patterns of activation in the detection of deception.* Unpublished doctoral dissertation, University of Utah, Salt Lake City.

Kircher, J. C., & Raskin, D. C. (1983). *Clinical versus statistical lie detection revisited: Through a lens sharply.* Unpublished manuscript, Department of Psychology, University of Utah, Salt Lake City.

Kleinmuntz, B., & Szucko, B. (1982). On the fallibility of lie detection. *Law and Society Review, 17*, 84-104.

Kleinmuntz, B., & Szucko, J. J. (1984). Lie detection in ancient and modern times: A call for contemporary scientific study. *American Psychologist, 39*, 766-776.

Kugelmass, S. (1976). *Reactions to stress* (Contract No. AF-61-[052]839). Washington, DC: U.S. Air Force Office of Scientific Research.

Kugelmass, S., & Lieblich, I. (1968). The relation between ethnic origin and GSR reactivity in psychophysiological detection. *Journal of Applied Psychology, 52*, 158-162.

Loftus, E. F. (1979).*Eyewitness testimony.* Cambridge, MA: Harvard University Press.

Lykken, D. T. (1974). Psychology and the lie detector industry. *American Psychologist, 29,* 725-739.

Lykken, D. T. (1979). The detection of deception. *Psychological Bulletin, 86,* 47-53.

Lykken, D. T. (1981). *A tremor in the blood: Uses and abuses of the lie detector.* New York: McGraw-Hill.

Marston, W. M. (1917). Systolic blood pressure changes in deception. *Journal of Experimental Psychology, 2,* 143-163.

Mullenix, P. A., & Reid, J. E. (1980). The pretest interview and its role in the detection of deception. *Polygraph, 9,* 74-85.

Orne, M. T. (1975). Implications of laboratory research for the detection of deception. In N. Ansley (Ed.), *Legal admissibility of the polygraph* (pp. 94-119). Springfield, IL: Charles C Thomas.

Orne, M. T., Thackray, R. I., & Paskewitz, D. A. (1972). On the detection of deception: A method for the study of the physiological effects of psychological stimuli. In N. Greenfield & R. Sternbach (Eds.), *Handbook of psychophysiology* (pp. 743-785). New York: Holt, Rinehart, & Winston.

Podlesny, J. A., & Raskin, D. C. (1978). Physiological measures and the detection of deception. *Psychological Bulletin, 84,* 782-799.

Quigley-Fernandez, B., & Tedeschi, J. T. (1978). The bogus pipeline as lie detector. Two validity studies. *Journal of Personality and Social Psychology, 36,* 247-256.

Raskin, D. C. (1976). *Reliability of chart interpretation and sources of errors in polygraph examinations* (Report No. 76-3, Contract No. 75-NI-99-0001). Washington, DC: National Institute of Law Enforcement and Criminal Justice, Law Enforcement Assistance Administration, U.S. Department of Justice.

Raskin, D. C. (1981). Science, competence and polygraph techniques. *Criminal Defense, 8,* 11-18.

Raskin, D. C. (1982). The scientific basis of polygraph techniques and their uses in the judicial process. In A. Trankell (Ed.), *Reconstructing the past: The role of psychologists in criminal trials* (pp. 317-371). Stockholm: Norstedt and Soners.

Raskin, D. C., & Hare, D. R. (1978). Psychopathy and detection of deception in a prison population. *Psychophysiology, 15,* 126-136.

Raskin, D. C., & Podlesny, J. A. (1979). Truth and deception: A reply to Lykken, *Psychological Bulletin, 86,* 54-58.

Reid, J. E., & Inbau, F. E. (1977). *Truth and deception, the polygraph technique* (2nd ed.). Baltimore: Williams and Wilkins Co.

Rovner, L. I., Raskin, D. C., & Kircher, J. (1978, September). *Effects of information and practice on detection of deception.* Paper presented at the meetings of the Society for Psychophysiological Research, Madison, WI.

Saxe, L. (1983). The perspective of social psychology: Toward a viable model for application. In R. F. Kidd & M. J. Saks (Eds.), *Advances in applied social psychology* (Vol. 2). Hillsdale, NJ: Erlbaum.

Saxe, L., & Dougherty, D. (in press). Technology assessment and congressional use of social psychology. In S. Oskamp (Ed.), *Applied social psychology annual* (Vol. 6). Newbury Park, CA: Sage.

Senese, L. (1976). Accuracy of the polygraph technique with and without card test stimulation. *Journal of Police Science and Administration, 4,* 274-276.

Sigall, H., & Page, R. (1972). Reducing attenuation in the expression of interpersonal affect via the bogus pipeline. *Sociometry, 35,* 629-642.

Slowik, S. M., & Buckley, J. P. (1975). Relative accuracy of polygraph examiner diagnosis of respiration, blood pressure and GSR recordings. *Journal of Police Science and Administration, 3,* 305-309.

Sternbach, R. A., & Tursky, B. (1965). Ethnic differences among housewives on psychophysical and skin potential responses to electric shock. *Psychophysiology, 1,* 241-246.

Stilwell, R. G. (1984). Statement before the Committee on Armed Services, United States Senate. In *Polygraphs for counterintelligence purposes in the Department of Defense* [(pp. 3-35) Hearings before the Committee on Armed Services, United States Senate, 98th Congress]. Washington, DC: U.S. Government Printing Office.

Szucko, J. J., & Kleinmuntz, B. (1981). Statistical versus clinical lie detection. *American Psychologist, 36,* 488-496.

Thackray, R. I., & Orne, M. T. (1968). Effects of the type of stimulus employed and the level of subject awareness on the detection of deception. *Journal of Applied Psychology, 52,* 234-239.

Timm, H. W. (1979). *The effect of placebos and feedback on the detection of deception.* Unpublished doctoral dissertation, College of Social Science, Michigan State University.

U.S. Central Intelligence Agency, Security Committee. (1980, May). *Investigative scope and adjudicative procedures among intelligence community agencies: Personnel security survey* (SE-COM-9-135). Langley, VA: Author.

U.S. Congress, Office of Technology Assessment. (1983). *Scientific validity of polygraph testing* (OTA-TM-H-15). Washington, DC: U.S. Government Printing Office.

U.S. Department of Defense. (1984). *The accuracy and utility of polygraph testing.* Washington, DC: Author.

Waid, W. M. (1976). Skin conductance response to both signaled and unsignaled noxious stimulation predicts level of socialization. *Journal of Personality and Social Psychology, 34,* 923-929.

Waid, W. M., & Orne, M. T. (1981). Cognitive, social, and personality processes in the physiological detection of deception. In L. Berkowitz (Ed.), *Advances in experimental social psychology* (pp. 61-106). New York: Academic Press.

Waid, W. M., & Orne, M. T. (1982). The physiological detection of deception. *American Scientist, 70,* 402-409.

Waid, W. M., Orne, E. C., Cook, M. R., & Orne, M. T. (1981). Meprobamate reduces accuracy of physiological detection of deception. *Science, 212,* 71-73.

Waid, W. M., Orne, M. T., & Wilson, S. K. (1979a). Effects of level of socialization on electrodermal detection of deception. *Psychophysiology, 16,* 15-22

Waid, W. M., Orne, M. T., & Wilson, S. K. (1979b). Socialization, awareness, and the electrodermal response to deception and self-disclosure. *Journal of Abnormal Psychology, 88,* 663-666.

Wicklander, D. E., & Hunter, F. L. (1975). The influence of auxiliary sources of information in polygraph diagnoses. *Journal of Police Science and Administration, 3,* 405-409.

Widacki, J., & Horvath, F. (1978). An experimental investigation of the relative validity and utility of the polygraph technique and three other common methods of criminal identification. *Journal of Forensic Science, 23,* 596-601.

2

THE DETECTION
OF DECEPTION

DAVID T. LYKKEN
University of Minnesota Medical School

The recent survey by Podlesny and Raskin (1977) conveys an impression that existing lie detector techniques are based on reasonable psycho-physiological theory and are supported by experimental findings of impressive validity. If current techniques already permit valid detection of deception in from 88% to 96% of subjects tested (Podlesny & Raskin, 1977, p. 787), even without the 9 or 10 new variables that the authors describe as "particularly promising" (p. 797), then the further research they call for might be expected to produce a virtually infallible lie detector. Who could then object to the growing trend toward lie detector screening of employees or the admission of lie test evidence in courts (Lykken, 1974)? If the polygraphist is correct 96% of the time

Author's Note. Requests for reprints should be sent to David T. Lykken, Department of Psychiatry, University of Minnesota Medical School, Box 392, Mayo Memorial Building, 420 Delaware Street, S.E., Minneapolis, Minnesota 55455.

even "on hardened criminals behind bars" (Raskin, quoted in Dunleavy, 1976), then allowing a fallible jury to deviate from the polygraphist's judgment—indeed, using a jury at all—can only diminish the accuracy of verdicts based solely on the lie test. In view of the claims that other exponents of the lie detector have been making over the years, it strikes one as curious that such implications of these claims seem never to be spelled out. If the lie test is 96% accurate, at least as Raskin performs it, and if Podlesny and Raskin are correct in suggesting that the few existing studies, most of which are defective in design, have as yet failed to exploit the potential of a host of "promising" additional test variables, it appears that we are dealing not only with the most valid psychological test ever devised but also with potentially the most important social problem ever to issue from the psychological laboratory.

THEORY OF THE LIE DETECTOR TEST

In an earlier treatment (Lykken, 1974), I attempted to show that the theory of the lie test is so naive and implausible that one should demand especially strong empirical evidence before accepting claims of extremely high validity. Podlesny and Raskin (1977) dismissed my analysis on the grounds that it "assumed that control questions are designed to be answered truthfully by the subject and that a lack of difference in magnitude of reactions to control and relevant questions constitutes the basis for a truthful result. Both of these assumptions are factually incorrect" (p. 787). The second of these alleged assumptions does not appear in my article (Lykken, 1974) which, on the contrary, correctly states that "the examiner is advised to classify tests that give intermediate [i.e., lack of difference] scores as 'inconclusive'" (p. 730). With respect to the first assumption, I stated accurately that "the control question is chosen with the intention that it will elicit an emotional response from the subject, preferably a response involving the attitude of guilt, for example, 'Can you remember ever stealing anything before you were 18 years old?'"; I added, "It is expected that the subject will answer it truthfully" (pp. 729-730). I should have also explained that many polygraphists claim that they can devise control questions, not concerned with the central issue of the interrogation, that the subject will answer deceptively and that will derive their guilty emotional impact from that attempted deception. Instead of somehow invalidating my analysis, this addendum reveals even more clearly the naiveté and implausibility of the theory of this control question lie test, as is illustrated below.

Let us consider an actual lie detector test administered by Raskin to a criminal defendant accused of homicide by stabbing (*Proceedings at Trial*, Note 1). The questions employed in that test are listed in Table 1. Questions 5, 7, and 10 are relevant questions pertaining to the incident; Questions 4, 6, and 0 are the control questions. The scoring procedure used by Raskin involves comparing the polygraph responses associated with each of the three adjacent pairs of relevant and control questions and assigning a numerical score to each pair, for example, –3 if the relevant question elicits a much larger response than the control, +3 if the control response is much the larger, and 0 if there is no difference. This is done for each of the three or four polygraph channels employed and for each of the two or three repetitions of the question list that may be used. If the sum of these scores is, say, +6 or higher, the subject is said to have been truthful; if the sum is –6 or lower, he is diagnosed as deceptive. In the 10% or so of cases in which the total score is near 0, the test is considered inconclusive.

It should be pointed out that a polygraph chart is very complex and the considerable subjectivity may influence the polygraphist's evaluation of the autonomic disturbance associated with a particular question. But let us assume that objective and consistent rules for evaluating polygraphic response amplitude were available and that some means were found to ensure that they were followed faithfully by polygraphists in practice. Then, referring to Table 1, if this defendant tended to give larger autonomic responses to the relevant questions (5, 7, and 10) than he did to the controls (4, 6, and 9), he would be classified *deceptive*. If his responses to the controls tended to be larger, he would be classified *truthful*. The question is whether it is reasonable to expect that such a test might have 96% validity.

Podlesny and Raskin (1977) explained, referring to the control questions, that "the subject is very likely to be deceptive to them or very concerned about them" (p. 786). I suspect that this defendant's *no* answers to Questions 4 and 9 were technically untrue because most people have "hurt someone" or have "lie[d] to get out of trouble" prior to the age of 20. But I do not know that these answers were false in this case and neither does Raskin. Indeed, it is quite possible that this defendant thought he was telling the truth in both instances, interpreting *hurt* to mean something serious like the mortal stab wound he was accused of inflicting and *trouble* to mean something serious like being charged with murder. In the case of the second control question (Question 6), I think it most likely that the subject's answer was entirely truthful. (I had never tried to "seriously hurt someone" prior to 1974!) A moment's reflection makes it plain that no polygraphist can reasonably claim to be able routinely to construct control questions that are somehow guaranteed to elicit deceptive

TABLE 2.1
List of Questions Used in Raskin's Lie Detector Test (Note 1)

1. Were you born in Hong Hong? (Yes)
2. Regarding the stabbing of Ken Chiu, do you intend to answer truthfully each question about that? (Yes)
3. Do you understand that I will ask only the questions we have discussed? (Yes)
4. During the first 18 years of your life, did you ever hurt someone? (No)[a]
5. Did you cut anyone with a knife on Dumfries St. on January 23, 1976? (No)[b]
6. Before 1974 did you ever try to seriously hurt someone? (No.)[a]
7. Did you stab Ken Chiu on January 23, 1976? (No)[b]
8. Is your first name William? (Yes)
9. Before age 19, did you ever lie to get out of trouble? (No)[a]
10. Did you actually see Ken Chiu get stabbed? (No)[b]

Note: Defendant's answers are in parentheses. If the autonomic disturbance associated with the relevant questions tends to be greater than that associated with the paired control questions, the subject is diagnosed as *deceptive.* Since it is assumed that an innocent subject is more concerned by the control than by the relevant questions, larger responses to the former are interpreted as evidence that the answers to the latter are *truthful.*
a. Control question.
b. Relevant question.

answers from the subject. If Podlesny and Raskin wish to claim that this is an essential feature of a properly administered lie test and that any analysis of the theory of the test must assume that the control responses are known lies, then further consideration of the lie test is pointless because no such test could possibly be devised except under extraordinary circumstances (viz., if the examiner happens to have proof of additional crimes committed by the subject but which the subject wishes to deny).

Clearly the purpose of the control question is that "it will elicit an emotional reaction from the subject" (Lykken, 1974, p. 730) or that the subject will be "very concerned" about the questions (Podlesny & Raskin, 1977). The emotional reaction occurs because the subject's answer is deceptive, because he is truthful but is ashamed to make that admission, or merely because the question touches on some painful or embarrassing issue. The issue to be decided, then, is whether a larger autonomic response to the relevant question (e.g., "Did you stab Ken Chiu on January 23, 1976?") than to the control question (e.g., "Before 1974 did you ever try to seriously hurt someone?") should plausibly be taken as strong evidence that the subject's answer to the relevant question is a lie.

To state it more generally, does the control question really function as a control in the usual scientific sense of that term, that is, does the autonomic response to the control question provide a reasonable estimate of what the subject's response to the relevant question ought to be if he is answering truthfully? Alternatively, one might ask whether the control response yields a reasonable estimate of what the relevant response should be if the answer to the relevant question is deceptive. This is the basic unavoidable assumption of the lie detector test, and it seems to me to be patently implausible. By what prescience did Raskin know how concerned the defendant was about Question 6? And yet he was obliged to titrate this concern with exquisite precision in advance of the test proper because his scoring assumes that the response to Question 6 will be greater than the response to Question 7 if the answer to Question 7 is truthful but that the response to Question 7 will be greater than the response to Question 6 if the relevant answer is a lie. One can imagine scenarios, all perfectly plausible, that might have led this defendant to be extremely, moderately, or negligibly concerned about the three control questions listed in Table 1. As a general rule, one would expect most subjects to be more concerned about the relevant questions than about the controls, whether they answer deceptively or truthfully, because it is the relevant questions that refer directly to the source of their immediate jeopardy. Thus one would expect most subjects to tend to "fail" lie detector tests in real-life situations, and this bias against the truthful subject is just what the data confirm, as is shown below.

On the other hand, no psychologist ought to rule out the possibility that some criminal defendants, even though guilty as charged, might develop habituation to, or psychodynamic defenses against, specific references to their crime and thus might be less responsive to the relevant than to the control questions so as to "pass" the lie test. A sophisticated criminal might know enough to augment his own reactions to the three control questions by flexing his toes, tensing his diaphragm, or biting his tongue at the appropriate moments. No good studies of the success of such countermeasures in real-life situations are available. Polygraphists claim that they could not easily be deceived in this way, whereas, on the contrary, I claim that I could train guilty suspects to successfully "beat" the control question lie test.

In the above case, Raskin testified that the defendant had in fact responded most strongly to the control questions and was truthful. The jury disagreed, finding the defendant to be guilty (*Proceedings at Trial*, Note 1). Did an innocent suspect in this instance behave in accordance with the assumptions of the lie detector or did a guilty suspect beat the test? One must turn to systematic validity studies to determine how the lie test, however implausible, actually works in practice.

ACCURACY OF THE LIE DETECTOR
IN THE FIELD

Although Podlesny and Raskin (1977) acknowledged that "there are many problems inherent in laboratory investigations of [psychophysiological detection of deception]" (p. 782), they stopped short of asserting that meaningful estimates of lie test accuracy in any field application must be obtained from appropriate field studies. Yet this clearly is the only reasonable conclusion. Giving lie tests to students who have enacted mock crimes or to prisoners who have competed for money prizes may be useful for other purposes but will not provide adequate predictions of what can be expected in real-life criminal investigation. Raskin's laboratory study using prison inmates (Raskin & Hare, 1978), for example, involved a deceptive context in which genuine and realistic fear of failure played no role whatever (surely the fear that one might fail to win a $20 prize is qualitatively different from a criminal suspect's fear that he may end up in prison). Thus when one looks for evidence concerning the accuracy of the lie test in its intended application, one must confine one's attention to real-life studies in the field.

Second, since interest lies in the contribution of the polygraph to the detection of deception rather than in the clinical judgment of the examiner, one must also exclude all studies in which the lie tests were scored globally, still a common practice among many polygraphists. With this method of scoring, all the examiner knows about the subject, the evidence against him, his demeanor during the examination, and the like is compounded in the mind of the examiner with the actual polygraph results by some unspecified subjective formula to produce the final judgment of deceptive or truthful. In the Bersh (1969) study, for example, the criterion of guilt or innocence was the majority verdict of four experienced prosecutors based on their reading of the completed files of 243 criminal suspects. These judges split 2:2 on 27 cases, leaving 216 that could be usefully compared to the polygraphist's previous diagnosis of deceptive or truthful. The polygraphists agreed with the criterion in nearly 88% of these cases. But because at the time of the examination the polygraphists knew what evidence was then available and were able to interview and observe the suspects at some length, one must suppose that their decisions about the suspects' guilt or innocence would have been substantially more accurate than chance expectancy (i.e., 50% agreement with the criterion) even if they had ignored the polygraph results entirely. In fact, one cannot be certain that the polygraph itself contributed at all to the accuracy rate that Bersh reported. Another part of the U.S. Army study from which Bersh's data came ("Use of Polygraphs," 1975) examined the agreement between the original polygraphist's decision and that of other polygraphists who read the same charts blindly. Agreement was low (kappa coefficients ranged from .15 to .51), indicating that the polygraph data could not have contributed much to the accuracy of the original examiner's judgments. Since field studies using blind scoring of polygraph charts do not show nearly so high an accuracy, Bersh's findings must be set aside as ambiguous and almost certainly are an overestimate of the validity of the polygraph test per se.

Clinical Versus Actuarial
Lie Detection

Polygraphists who endorse the use of global judgments stress that it is the examiner, not the polygraph, who functions as the lie detector. Trade journals such as *Polygraph* or *Journal of Polygraph Science* are full of unsubstantiated claims concerning interview behaviors said to be indicative of guilt or of innocence (Lykken, 1978). Is it fair, therefore, to insist on separate assessment of the contribution made by the polygraph charts themselves to the accuracy of the examiner's decisions?

The history of validity studies of projective techniques like the Rorschach Inkblot Test provides a limited but useful analogy. It appears that certain talented individuals, observing a subject responding to the Rorschach cards, are often capable of drawing clinical inferences of remarkable accuracy. But the majority of Rorschach test administrators are not nearly so accurate, and attempts to objectify the cues or reasoning employed by the skillful few have met with limited success. There undoubtedly are certain police detectives and polygraph examiners who are similarly skillful in determining by subjective evaluation of clinical observations, which suspect is lying and which is not. It is possible that more polygraphists might develop such skills if they were given formal training in psychology. But it is most doubtful that a trial judge would ever admit into evidence the clinical opinion of some self-styled "veracity expert," in the form, "I have observed this defendant, considered his story and the relevant evidence, and in my opinion he is (or is not) telling the truth," even if he were a fully accredited psychologist or psychiatrist. What business concern would employ someone who claims to be able to detect lying intuitively, through observing interview behavior, and would allow him to screen prospective employees for honesty or to determine which current employees are stealing from the company and should be fired?

Clearly, the mystique of the lie detector, the reason why the polygraph test is taken seriously by some courts, by business, and by the general public and why the lie detector industry is flourishing in this country, is wholly dependent on the technological or scientific aura of the polygraph itself. It is conceivable that some polygraph examiners are skillful clinical lie detectors, but this issue is of negligible scientific or social importance. What is important is whether, as Podlesny and Raskin contend, the polygraph test is an objective, teachable method of extraordinary validity.

The Evidence

Fortunately, subsequent to my 1974 review, two field studies appeared that provide estimates of lie test accuracy under real-life conditions, when the polygraph charts are scored blindly by someone other than the examiner who administers the test. Both authors were and are professional polygraphists and certainly were not hoping for unfavorable results. Horvath (1977) had 10 trained polygraphists independently score charts taken from the files of a large police department. There were 28 suspects who had subsequently been cleared by the confession of another person; 28 others had themselves confessed some time after the original testing. The 10 experienced polygraphists agreed with each other about 89% of the time, indicating presumably that they followed similar rules of chart interpretation. But the validity of their scoring was not nearly as impressive as their interjudge agreement; the 560 blind scorings were correct only 64% of the time. My analysis of the lie test suggested that it should discriminate against the truthful subject or at least against those subjects with sense enough to realize that the relevant questions are more important to their fates and more threatening than the (essentially irrelevant) control questions. This expectation was strongly confirmed by the Horvath study in which the known liars were correctly scored as deceptive about 77% of the time (against a chance expectancy of 50%), whereas the known truthful suspects were incorrectly scored as deceptive half of the time, giving a false positive rate of 39%.

The second recent study (Barland & Raskin, Note 2) employed Bersh's method of using a panel of lawyers or judges to determine, from all evidence excluding the lie test results, which suspects were guilty or innocent. Barland administered the test, and the charts were then scored independently by Raskin. A majority of the criterion judges agreed on 64 of the 92 cases tested, but 13 (20%) of these 64 tests were classified *inconclusive* by Raskin. On the remaining 51 tests, Raskin's scoring agreed with the criterion on 44 of them, a hit rate of about 86%, which the authors reported as their estimate of field accuracy. However, 39, or 78%, of these same cases were guilty by the criterion, which means that one might have achieved a hit rate of 78% on this sample just by calling everyone deceptive (Raskin in fact scored 88% as deceptive; see Table 2). Clearly, nonarbitrary accuracy estimates can only be obtained either by equalizing the numbers of guilty and innocent suspects and assuming Raskin would have been correct in the same proportion of 40 cases as he was in the actual 11 cases (see right-hand column of Table 2) or by considering the fate of the guilty and innocent subjects separately. Raskin scored 39 of the 47 guilty suspects as deceptive, 1 as truthful, and the remaining 7 as inconclusive. But only 5 of the 17 innocent suspects were correctly scored as truthful; 6 were called deceptive and 6 inconclusive. Had this study been designed like Horvath's (1977), with half the subjects guilty and half innocent, then—excluding inconclusives—one might expect about 71% hits overall and a false positive rate of 36%, very similar to the 39% false positives in the Horvath study. Although Raskin correctly diagnosed all but 1 of the guilty subjects as deceptive (not counting the 7 inconclusives), he did this at the expense of calling 55% of the innocent suspects deceptive also.

These two studies constitute the only evidence available concerning the accuracy of the control question lie test administered under real-life conditions and scored to exclude the influence of clinical judgment (or prejudice) and thus to provide some idea of the accuracy of the polygraph test itself. And the two studies agree quite well, showing an accuracy of from 64% to 71%, against a chance expectancy of 50%, and showing that of those who fail the test, 36% to 39% will be false positive, truthful subjects (assuming that half the subjects tested are innocent). Raskin failed a higher proportion of his subjects than Horvath's polygraphists did: 76% versus 63% if one again assumes that both studies used equal numbers of guilty and innocent subjects. Therefore, Raskin called a higher proportion of both the guilty and the innocent subjects deceptive. Podlesny and Raskin (1977) cited the Barland and Raskin (Note 2) study, but they did not mention the actual results; the Horvath (1977) study was not even cited. Instead, my arguments (Lykken, 1974) predicting that the lie test should show a high rate of false positives in real-life applications are supposedly refuted by a referral to the results of two mock crime laboratory studies by Raskin and his colleagues (Podlesny & Raskin, 1977, p. 787).

TABLE 2.2
Summary of Available Data on Accuracy of Control Question
Lie Test Using Blind Scoring

Item	Horvath (1977) Verified	Barland and Raskin (Note 2) Reported	Corrected[a]
Number guilty	28	40	40
Number innocent	28	11	40
Percent guilty	50%	78%	50%
Percent deceptive	63%	88%	76%
Percent correct (hit rate)	64%	86%	71%
False negative rate	31%	17%	5%
False positive rate	39%	13%	36%
Guilty called truthful	23%	3%	3%
Innocent called deceptive	49%	55%	55%

Note: Observe the high proportion of innocent suspects misclassified as deceptive and the associated high rate of false positive classification.
a. To provide meaningful estimates of accuracy and error rates, the data of Barland and Raskin had to be corrected for the high base rate (78%) of criterion-guilty subjects. This was done by assuming Raskin would have made the same proportion of errors (55%) if 40 innocent suspects had been tested as he made on the 11 innocent suspects who were tested, thus yielding a standardized base rate of 50% criterion-guilty subjects.

CONCLUSION

Thus one sees that the control question lie test is not 88%, 90%, or 96% accurate in real-life applications, but rather is in the neighborhood of 64% to 71% accurate when standardized for a chance expectancy of 50%. The actual false positive expectancy is not 8%, 4%, or 2%, but is more on the order of 36%-39%. A skillful examiner who is willing to call as many as three-fourths of all subjects deceptive can detect most liars (assuming the subjects are not equally skilled at beating the test), but he will at the same time call most of the truthful subjects deceptive also. An interesting research question not mentioned by Podlesny and Raskin is whether many deceptive subjects could be trained to beat the special form of lie test that they advocate. Any intelligent criminal could easily be taught to identify the three control questions and instructed to augment his autonomic reactions to these questions in a variety of covert ways. In fact, I venture another prediction; let me train guilty suspects in Barland and Raskin's next field study, and I predict their false negative rate may approach what their false positive rate is right now.

REFERENCE NOTES

1. *Proceedings at trial, Her Majesty the Queen v. William Wong.* Supreme Court of British Columbia, No. CC760628, Vancouver, Canada, October 1976.
2. Barland, G. H., & Raskin, D. C. *Validity and reliability of polygraph examinations of criminal suspects* (U.S. Department of Justice Report No. 76-1, Contract 75-NI—99-0001). Salt Lake City: University of Utah, Department of Psychology, March 1976.

REFERENCES

Bersh, P. J. A validation of polygraph examiner judgments. *Journal of Applied Psychology,* 1969, *53*, 399-403.

Dunleavy, S. Patty wasn't guilty. *The Star,* December 14, 1976, pp. 24-25.

Horvath, F. S. The effect of selected variables on interpretation of polygraph records. *Journal of Applied Psychology,* 1977, *62*, 127-136.

Lykken, D. T. Psychology and the lie detector industry. *American Psychologist,* 1974, *29*, 725-739.

Lykken, D. T. Uses and abuses of the polygraph. In H. L. Pick (Ed.), *Psychology: From research to practice.* New York: Plenum Press, 1978.

Podlesny, J. A., & Raskin, D. C. Physiological measures and the detection of deception. *Psychological Bulletin,* 1977 *84*, 782-799.

Raskin, D. C., & Hare, R. D. Psychopathy and detection of deception in a prison population. *Psychophysiology,* 1978, *15*, 126-136.

The use of polygraphs and similar devices by federal agencies: Hearings before the Foreign Operations and Government Information Subcommittee of the Committee on Governmental Operations, 93rd Congress, 2nd Session. Washington, DC.: U.S. Government Printing Office, 1975.

3

TRUTH AND DECEPTION
A Reply to Lykken

DAVID C. RASKIN
University of Utah
JOHN A. PODLESNY
Western Reserve Psychiatric Habilitation Center

In a critique of our recent article (Podlesny & Raskin, 1977), Lykken (1979) attempted to discredit our theoretical analyses and conclusions by using intuitive and speculative arguments and by selective and

Author's Note. Portions of the research reported in this article were supported by Grant FR-07092 from the National Institutes of Health, by Grant 75-NI-99-0001 from the National Institute of Law Enforcement and Criminal Justice, and by Grant 78-NI-AX-0030 from the Law Enforcement Assistance Administration, U.S. Department of Justice. Points of view or opinions stated in this article do not necessarily represent the official position or policies of the U.S. Department of Justice. Requests for reprints should be sent to David C. Raskin, Department of Psychology, University of Utah, Salt Lake City, Utah 84112.

misleading descriptions of the existing data and literature. Lykken also made bold claims about his ability to train people to "beat" the control question test, and he presented a misleading description of a polygraph test conducted by Raskin in a criminal case. This article attempts to correct those errors with a careful examination of the theory, the scientific data and literature, and the applications of control question tests for truth and deception.

THEORY OF CONTROL QUESTION TESTS

In spite of 5 years of contact with the literature and with concepts of control question tests (see Raskin, 1978), Lykken still does not understand the simple, basic theory. The theory holds that, following a detailed pretest interview, a guilty subject will show relatively stronger autonomic responses to the relevant questions and that an innocent subject will show relatively stronger responses to the control questions, which deal with acts of the same general nature as those covered by the relevant questions. The control question is a stronger stimulus for the innocent subject because he knows he is truthful to the relevant questions; he has been led to believe that the control questions are also very important in assessing his veracity; the manner of explaining the control questions to him and their wording have elicited a *no* answer; and he is either deceptive in his answers, very concerned about his answers, or unsure of his truthfulness because of the vagueness of the questions and problems in recalling the events. His concern about being diagnosed as deceptive produces autonomic reactions to the controls. There is no attempt to "titrate this concern with exquisite precision in advance of the test proper" (Lykken, 1979, p. 49). Control questions are emphasized to all subjects during the pretest interview and immediately following each chart (Podlesny & Raskin, 1978; Raskin & Hare, 1978).

Lykken was simply wrong when he stated that "the theory of the test must assume that the control responses are known lies" (p. 49) and that the purpose of the control question is to provide an estimate of the subject's autonomic response to a relevant question answered truthfully. We have never stated that the control question should "function as a control in the usual scientific sense of that term" (Lykken, 1979, p. 49). This statement describes the function of noncritical items in a guilty knowledge test, and it seems to indicate that Lykken does not understand the basic difference between guilty knowledge tests and control question tests. The actual purpose of the control question is to provide a stimulus that will produce a stronger autonomic reaction than the relevant question when the subject is innocent, thereby providing a positive identification of innocent subjects.

EMPIRICAL ISSUES

Our 1977 review (Podlesny & Raskin, 1977) dealt almost exclusively with laboratory research and made suggestions to maximize its generalizability to field applications, but Lykken arbitrarily dismissed the utility of laboratory experiments in estimating the accuracy of field detection of deception. This position betrays a profound lack of understanding of the scientific method and the value of controlled experimentation and diversity of evidence (Hempel, 1966). As we pointed out (Podlesny & Raskin, 1977), the best strategy "is to employ laboratory research that simulates field-deceptive contexts as closely as possible, along with field validation" (p. 784). We have used prisoners, criminal suspects, very realistic mock crimes (so realistic that some subjects decline to participate in the mock crime), substantial motivation, and potential loss of reward or punishment. In laboratory experiments with subjects recruited from the community by newspaper ads, with prison inmates, and with diagnosed psychopaths, we have consistently obtained accuracy rates above 90% (Podlesny & Raskin, 1978; Raskin & Hare, 1978; Rovner, Raskin, & Kircher, Note 1), and such findings are very useful in the scientific enterprise of estimating accuracy in real-life situations.

Lykken was correct in emphasizing the need for validation studies with criminal suspects using blind evaluation of polygraph charts. Unfortunately, he provided misleading interpretations of the two studies that he selected and he failed to mention five published studies that meet his criteria but provide strong evidence against his position. Lykken also failed to mention that in the Horvath (1977) study the original examiner was 100% correct and the cases were all verified by confessions. It has been pointed out (Raskin, 1978) that the unusually low level of accuracy attained by Horvath's blind evaluators was very likely due to their lack of formal training in systematic chart interpretation and their heavy emphasis on overt behavior symptoms rather than on systematic chart interpretation. Therefore, the Horvath study is of little value in assessing the accuracy of decisions based on systematic chart interpretation.

Lykken (1979) was incorrect when he stated that the Horvath (1977) and Barland and Raskin (Note 2) studies "constitute the only evidence available concerning the accuracy of the control question lie test administered under real-life conditions and scored to exclude the influence of clinical judgment (or prejudice) and thus to provide some idea of the accuracy of the polygraph test itself" (p. 52). There are five other published studies that meet Lykken's criteria of blind interpretation of confirmed polygraph charts from criminal suspects. The findings of these studies are presented in Table 1. The mean accuracy rates of 90% correct on guilty suspects and 89% correct on innocent suspects were based on a total of 1,204 independent decisions obtained by blind interpretation of polygraph charts by 55 different polygraph examiners. The data from Horvath and Reid (1971) show that experienced examiners are more accurate, and the Raskin (Note 3) data clearly demonstrate that the use of a relatively objective, systematic method of quantified chart interpretation yields significantly higher accuracy rates, which approach 100%.

The reliability of the numerical scoring system is extremely high. Using the numerical system with blind chart interpretation, we obtained a mean correlation of .86 for the 15 pairings of six independent evaluators (Barland & Raskin, 1975), a .91 correlation between numerical scores and 99% agreement with the examiner's original decisions on 102 criminal suspects (Barland & Raskin, Note 2), a .97 correlation between numerical scores and 100% agreement with the original examiner's decisions in a laboratory study (Podlesny & Raskin, 1978), and 95% accuracy and 100% agreement with decisions made 2 years before in a laboratory study of criminals and psychopaths (Raskin & Hare, 1978).

The extensive and consistent findings just described demonstrate the very high reliability and validity of blind chart interpretation when it is performed by competent examiners who have been adequately trained in chart interpretation and who do not make decisions based on the questionable procedure of observing behavior symptoms. The latter procedure has been shown to be ineffective in assessing truth and deception (Podlesny & Raskin, 1978; Raskin, Barland, & Podlesny, Note 4), and it is not surprising that examiners trained to rely on behavior symptoms instead of polygraph charts produce results hardly better than chance (Horvath, 1977).

In addition to the Horvath (1977) study, Lykken placed great weight on the high false positive rate in the Barland and Raskin (Note 2) study. In this study, as in field studies of lie detection generally, it was necessary to substitute criteria of guilt or innocence in place of factual knowledge. The two major criteria were decisions of a panel of legal experts based on case information (with all references to the polygraph tests deleted) and judicial outcomes. Those criteria failed to provide assessment of accuracy equivalent to that available in laboratory studies or confirmed criminal cases. Raskin (1978) has stated that the panel criterion is open to serious challenge because the information provided in the Barland and Raskin study was generally inadequate, agreement between the court decisions and the panel was less than

TABLE 3.1
Percentage of Correct Decisions in Five Studies with
Blind Interpretations of Polygraph Charts Obtained
from Verified Guilty and Innocent Subjects

Study	Guilty	Innocent
Horvath & Reid (1971)	75[a]	83[a]
	89[b]	94[b]
Hunter & Ash (1973)	88	86
Slowik & Buckley (1975)	85	93
Wicklander & Hunter (1975)	95	93
Raskin (Note 3)	93[c]	69[c]
	100[d]	95[d]
Combined results	90	89

a. Decisions were made by intern examiners.
b. Decisions were made by experienced examiners.
c. Evaluation was nonnumerical.
d. Evaluation was numerical.

perfect, and inherent bias may have existed toward judgments of innocence based on the tradition of the assumption of innocence in the absence of extremely strong evidence to the contrary. Furthermore, the number of criterion-innocent subjects was very small. As a result the 95% confidence interval for the false positives was 11%-59%, whereas the larger sample size for guilty subjects yielded a 95% confidence interval of 0%-16% for false negatives. Therefore we consider these data and those of Horvath (1977) to be of relatively low value in contrast to those presented in Table 1 and the other data described earlier that were ignored by Lykken.

ISSUES IN THE APPLICATION
OF CONTROL QUESTION TESTS

Lykken (1979) stated that a sophisticated criminal might be able to augment his reactions to the control questions and "pass" the test. The only published study with such procedures used the guilty knowledge test (Lykken, 1960), which is more susceptible to false negatives than the control question test (Podlesny & Raskin, 1977) because the guilty knowledge test employs only skin resistance measures, and a truthful outcome does not require larger responses to the noncritical items, as does the control question test. The subjects were medical students, staff psychiatrists, and psychologists who were given detailed instruction about the test structure, a strategy and methods to beat the test, and biofeedback training to control their skin resistance responses.

Even with minimal consequences for being detected, the accuracy was 100%. Lykken's (1960) failure to train sophisticated subjects with little at stake to be able to beat the simpler guilty knowledge test raises extreme doubt concerning Lykken's statement, "I claim that I could train guilty suspects to successfully 'beat' the control question lie test" (p. 50). Rovner et al. (Note 1) are presently engaged in an extensive laboratory study to assess the effects of detailed information and practice on the accuracy of control question tests.

Although we are opposed for a variety of scientific and ethical reasons to the use of polygraph tests in employment situations, Lykken's opposition to the use of polygraph evidence in court is based on his lack of understanding of the control question technique, his highly selective presentation of the scientific evidence, his misinterpretations of those data that he selected for discussion, and his gross misunderstanding of the criminal justice system. The issues surrounding court use of polygraph evidence involve the level of confidence that can be placed in a truthful or deceptive outcome, the way in which such outcomes are used in the criminal justice process, and the impact of such evidence on juries.

We agree that the data indicate that false positives are more likely than false negatives, even though the rates of both types of errors are low. Even if Lykken were correct concerning the rate of false positives, for practical purposes the confidence in a truthful outcome is higher than that in a deceptive outcome, since a truthful result is more likely to be correct than is a deceptive result. The use of such findings coincides with our judicial and moral standards for acquittal and conviction. Because criminal guilt must be demonstrated beyond a reasonable doubt, considerable evidence is required for conviction, and a deceptive polygraph result is far from sufficient. In the absence of other strong evidence of guilt, no competent or ethical prosecutor could or would try a case on the basis of a deceptive polygraph test. However, in the absence of overwhelming evidence to the contrary, the high degree of accuracy of a truthful polygraph result should be sufficient to cast the reasonable doubt required for dismissal or acquittal. It has become common practice for law enforcement agencies and prosecutors to dismiss charges in such situations. Given the very low accuracy of some types of evidence, such as eyewitness testimony, that are commonly used against defendants and the great weight accorded to this evidence by prosecutors and juries (Buckhout, 1974), it makes good sense to provide an opportunity for innocent suspects and defendants to clear themselves by means of a properly conducted polygraph test.

Lykken (1979) may have provided a misleading description of the William Wong case (*Proceedings at Trial*, Note 5) by failing to describe its outcome. Wong was accused of homicide on the basis of highly questionable eyewitness accounts. Wong was administered a polygraph test by Sergeant Smith of the Vancouver, British Columbia, police department and was retested prior to his trial by Raskin. He was found to be truthful by both examiners. Using standard techniques, Raskin employed typical control questions, including the question, "Before 1974 did you ever try to seriously hurt someone?" (Question 6). Lykken speculated that Wong was entirely truthful and unconcerned when he answered that question, and he implied that Wong showed a stronger autonomic response to the question, "Did you stab Ken Chiu on January 23, 1976?" (Question 7). On the contrary, Wong was more concerned about Question 6, and Figure 1 shows his substantially larger electrodermal and blood pressure responses to the control question (Question 6)! Wong obtained a clearly truthful score of +9, and these results were presented by Raskin to the jury as part of Wong's defense against the murder charge. It should also be mentioned that in the same court hearing, Lykken unsuccessfully opposed presenting to the jury the results of Raskin's and Sergeant Smith's polygraph tests in the defense of innocent homicide defendant William Wong. Lykken's position at the trial was in direct conflict to his previously published position that "judicious use of the polygraph in the criminal investigation context not only can improve the efficiency of police work but could also serve as a bulwark to protect the innocent from false prosecution" (Lykken, 1974, p. 738).

Lykken (1979) also claimed that the use of polygraph evidence in court would overwhelm the jury and might even be used to replace the jury system. His speculations are naive with regard to the judicial process and betray a lack of knowledge of the evidence concerning the impact of the testimony of polygraph experts on jury deliberations. As Tarlow (1975) pointed out, polygraph evidence is simply an aid to the jury in its complicated task of assessing the credibility of witnesses. As such, if the polygraph evidence has probative value, the jury is merely asked to consider it along with the other evidence in the case and to accord whatever weight the jury finds appropriate. We have not suggested that polygraph tests should replace the jury system. In fact, the available evidence (Tarlow, 1975) indicates that juries are very cautious and that they tend to be "underwhelmed" by polygraph testimony.

CONCLUSION

The results of many scientific studies in laboratory and field settings as well as our published report to the U.S. Department of Justice

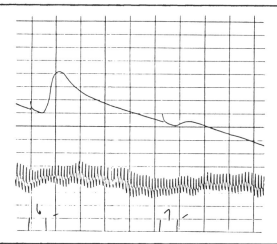

Figure 3.1 Skin resistance and blood pressure responses of homicide defendant William Wong to a control question (6) and a relevant question (7). The vertical marks indicate the beginning and end of the questions, and the minus sign indicates a *no* answer at the time.

(Raskin et al., Note 4) indicate that the accuracy and reliability of control question tests can be very high. On the basis of the present evidence, it is reasonable to conclude that the results of control question polygraph examinations conducted by competent and ethical examiners can have important and beneficial effects for the criminal justice process and for our society in general.

REFERENCE NOTES

1. Rovner, L. I., Raskin, D. C., & Kircher, J. C. *Effects of information and practice on detection of deception.* Paper presented at the meeting of the Society for Psychophysiological Research, Madison, WI, September 1978.

2. Barland, G. H., & Raskin, D. C. *Validity and reliability of polygraph examinations of criminal suspects* (U.S. Department of Justice Report No. 76-1, Contract 75-NI-99-0001). Salt Lake City: University of Utah, Department of Psychology, March 1976.

3. Raskin, D. C. *Reliability of chart interpretation and sources of errors in polygraph examinations* (U.S. Department of Justice Report No. 76-3, contract 75-NI-99-0001). Salt Lake City: University of Utah, Department of Psychology, June 1976.

4. Raskin, D. C., Barland, G. H., & Podlesny, J. A. *Validity and reliability of detection of deception* (U.S. Department of Justice Final Report, Contract 75-MI-99-0001). Salt Lake City: University of Utah, Department of Psychology, August 1967.

5. *Proceedings at trial, Her Majesty the Queen v. William Wong.* Supreme Court of British Columbia, No. CC760628, Vancouver, Canada, October 1976.

REFERENCES

Barland, G. H., & Raskin, D. C. An evaluation of field techniques in detection of deception. *Psychophysiology,* 1975, *12,* 321-330.

Buckhout, R. Eyewitness testimony. *Scientific American,* 1974, *231*(6), 23-31.

Hempel, C. G. *Philosophy of natural science.* Englewood Cliffs, NJ: Prentice-Hall, 1966.

Horvath, F. S. The effect of selected variables on interpretation of polygraph records. *Journal of Applied Psychology,* 1977, *62,* 127-136.

Horvath, F. S., & Reid, J. E. The reliability of polygraph examiner diagnosis of truth and deception. *Journal of Criminal Law, Criminology, and Police Science,* 1971, *62,* 276-281.

Hunter, F. L., & Ash, P. The accuracy and consistency of polygraph examiners' diagnoses. *Journal of Police Science & Administration,* 1973, *1,* 370-375.

Lykken, D. T. The validity of the guilty knowledge technique: The effects of faking. *Journal of Applied Psychology,* 1960, *44,* 258-262.

Lykken, D. T. Psychology and the lie detector industry. *American Psychologist,* 1974, *29,* 725-739.

Lykken, D. T. The detection of deception. *Psychological Bulletin,* 1979, *86,* 47-53.

Podlesny, J. A., & Raskin, D. C. Physiological measures and the detection of deception. *Psychological Bulletin,* 1977, *84,* 782-799.

Podlesny, J. A., & Raskin, D. C. Effectiveness of techniques and physiological measures in the detection of deception. *Psychophysiology,* 1978, *15,* 344-359.

Raskin, D. C. Scientific assessment of the accuracy of detection of deception: A reply to Lykken. *Psychophysiology,* 1978, *15,* 143-147.

Raskin, D. C., & Hare, R. D. Psychopathy and detection of deception in a prison population. *Psychophysiology,* 1978, *15,* 126-136.

Slowik, S. M., & Buckley, J. P. Relative accuracy of polygraph examiner diagnosis of respiration, blood pressure, and GSR recordings. *Journal of Police Science & Administration,* 1975, *3,* 305-309.

Tarlow, B. Admissibility of polygraph evidence in 1975: An aid in determining credibility in a perjury-plagued system. *Hastings Law Journal,* 1975, *26,* 917-974.

Wicklander, D. E., & Hunter, F. L. The influence of auxiliary sources of information in polygraph diagnoses. *Journal of Police Science & Administration,* 1975, *3,* 405-409.

SECTION I

SUMMARY

While it appears that all three chapters possess different and divergent interpretations of the veracity of the polygraph, they share a conclusion that the polygraph does have its limitations. Chapter 1 points out that the polygraph assumes that anxiety or arousal can reflect deceit; yet any feeling of emotion may lead to anxiety and hence autonomic responses to the polygraph questioning (Goleman, 1985). Another point by Saxe et al. in chapter 1 is that the use of the polygraph may have overreached its bounds in terms of known theoretical bases for such use. The polygraph, however, can be accurate above chance under certain conditions, and the conditions under which the test is administered may be the crucial element in its accuracy.

Lykken proposes that the accuracy rates claimed by adherents of the polygraph (88%, 90%, or 96%) should be decreased to 64% to 71%, reflecting some accuracy in polygraph testing. Yet does an accuracy rate between 64% and 71% merit the use of the polygraph to form binding conclusions or make firm decisions? Would you submit to a polygraph in the hypothetical employment situation mentioned in the introduction to this section with those accuracy rates? Perhaps, the most meaningful use of the polygraph would be to take advantage of the polygraph as a tool for investigatory purposes in criminal prosecution, in hopes of eliciting voluntary confessions.

Raskin and Podlesny, in chapter 3, point out another possible use for the polygraph. They suggest it be used as an aid for juries in determining credibility of witnesses. And in 20 states the results of the polygraph are admissible if both parties (defense and prosecution) agree. Further, two states (Massachusetts and New Mexico) allow its admissibility, even over objections of one of the parties. The crucial question then becomes does the polygraph evidence have a significant effect on juries. Cavoukian and Heslegrave (1980) addressed this question by providing mock jurors with three versions of a trial. The first contained major points of a case and the judge's instructions. The second contained the elements of the first version and added polygraph evidence showing the defendant was innocent. Finally, a third version contained all the prior elements plus an additional instruction by the judge that the polygraph had an accuracy rate of 80%, so jurors should be cautious in forming their verdicts. The results indicated acquittal rates of 48%, 72%, and 60%, respectively. Apparently, the caution that polygraph accuracy is limited has an effect on subsequent verdicts, but even without such instruction jurors didn't absolutely follow polygraph results. In a second study and with a different case, Cavoukian and Heslegrave (1980) found that the judge's instruction was more influential. The acquittal rate was reduced below that of the condition without polygraph evidence.

The jury, however, is charged to be the 'trier of fact' in any case, civil or criminal, and because of this charge admittance of polygraph evidence may infer to the jury that polygraph results are a reliable and valid measure of truthfulness. As triers of fact, the jury should be presented with factual evidence with which to weigh the credibility and circumstances surrounding any case. Until the polygraph can be described as an infallible truth finder, the use of the polygraph may, as Saxe et. al. point out, have overreached its bounds.

REFERENCES

Cavoukian, A., & Heslegrave, R. J. (1980). The admissibility of polygraph evidence in court. *Law and Human Behavior, 4,* 117-131.

Goleman, D. (1981, February). The 7,000 faces of Dr. Ekman. *Psychology Today,* pp. 43-49.

Jordan, N. (1984, June). Polygraph interviews: Blood, sweat, and fear. *Psychology Today,* p. 76.

Linehan, J. G. (1978). Lie detection pioneer profiles. *Polygraph, 7,* 95-100.

Lykken, D. T. (1979). The detection of deception. *Psychological Bulletin, 86,* 47-53.

Marston, W. M (1917). Systolic blood pressure changes in deception. *Journal of Experimental Physics, 2,* 117-163.

Raskin, D. C. (1981, May-June). Science, competence, and polygraph techniques. *Criminal Defense, 8,* pp. 11-18.

Raskin, D. C., & Podlesny, J. A. (1979). Truth and deception: A reply to Lykken. *Psychological Bulletin, 86,* 54-59.

Saxe, L., Dougherty, D., & Cross, T. (1985). The validity of polygraph testing. *American Psychologist, 40,* 355-366.

SECTION II
REFRESHING MEMORY THROUGH HYPNOSIS
Introduction

In a San Francisco case involving two young girls who were kidnapped and raped, the criminal was caught, apparently thanks to hypnosis. Traumatized by the incident, the victims seemed unable to recall anything about it. Then, under hypnosis, one of the girls remembered distinguishing rust spots on her abductor's car and the location of the service station where he stopped to have the car repaired. This story and others like it have made hypnosis a very popular device in criminal investigations that have an eyewitness who, for some reason, is unable to remember his or her observations.

This issue first confronted the legal system in *People v. Ebanks,* in 1897. In that case, the defendant sought to introduce as evidence the fact that he had made exculpatory statements while under hypnosis. The California Supreme Court wisely rejected that argument, noting that hypnosis is not a truth serum that renders an individual unable to lie in his own behalf. Today, the nation's courts are faced with another use of hypnosis—the question of whether it enables people to recall events they could otherwise not retrieve from memory. Judges vary on whether they allow witnesses who have been hypnotized to testify in front of a jury. Some courts look upon hypnosis as a scientifically valid memory-refreshing device. Others are more skeptical about the competence of a witness who has undergone hypnosis, and offer guidelines for when such testimony can be admitted. Still others maintain that hypnosis contaminates memory, and exclude entirely from the witness stand anyone whose testimony has been retrieved through such tampering.

Does it work? That is, can witnesses remember faces and situations under hypnosis that they could not otherwise recall in their normal waking lives? Is there danger that once hypnotized, witnesses become highly suggestible and, even worse, overconfident about the accuracy of their "new" recollections? This section addresses these lively and controversial issues.

The section opens with a chapter describing a real-life success in the use of hypnosis. Reiser (1974), its author, is a psychologist with the Los Angeles Police Department. At his Law Enforcement Hypnosis Institute, Reiser has trained more than 1,000 people, mostly police, to perform hypnosis. This chapter describes in detail a specific use of the technique with a witness who had previously been unable to identify her boyfriend's killer. Following this case study, as chapter 5, is Putnam's (1979) report of a controlled experiment designed to test the effectiveness of hypnosis as a memory aid. In this study, subjects watched a videotape of an accident and were then questioned about it either under hypnosis or in their normal waking state. The results of this study cast serious doubt about the effectiveness of hypnosis; they demonstrated that it might even have dangerous side effects.

The Reiser and Putnam chapters illustrate the marked discrepancy in the literature between actual case reports of hypnotic memory enhancement, on the one hand, and failures to verify that effect in the laboratory, on the other. Chapter 6 is an excellent review of this growing literature by Smith (1983). Smith considers several differences between the real-life and laboratory settings as possibly accounting for the discrepancy. Concluding that further research is needed, Smith describes certain nonhypnotic procedures that might be used instead. Consistent with Smith's recommendations, this section concludes with the recent report of an alternative technique that could be used to enhance eyewitness memory. In chapter 7, Geiselman, Fisher, MacKinnon, and Holland (1985) compare the effectiveness of the standard police interview, hypnosis, and what they call the "cognitive interview"—based on current memory theory. As we will see, their results add fuel to this important controversy.

4

HYPNOSIS AS AN AID
IN A HOMICIDE INVESTIGATION

MARTIN REISER
Los Angeles Police Department

In early January 1974, a detective assigned to the Wilshire Investigation Division phoned to ask about the feasibility of using hypnosis with a witness to a murder. Although not unique, having been done numerous times before in homicides, use of hypnosis in this case would be somewhat different because the witness had been drinking heavily and ingesting other drugs before and during the time the crime was committed. Because of the probable fuzziness of her original perceptions, there was considerable skepticism on the part of the psychologist as well as on the investigator's part as to the witness's ability to recall events with any accuracy. However, it was decided that nothing would be lost by giving hypnosis a try since the witness was very eager to do anything to help apprehend the killer of her male friend.

Routine interrogation by investigators had disclosed that on December 17 at approximately 1:30 a.m., the witness had been in the victim's apartment while the suspect was present for about 20 minutes. However, she was unable to remember any significant details about the individual although she did recall that five shots were fired on the front doorstep of the apartment and subsequently her friend's dead body was found outside the door. The investigators hoped that hypnosis would enable the witness to recall more details about the suspect and permit a police artist to draw an accurate composite picture which could be used in narrowing down the search.

On January 7, 1974, two investigators from Wilshire Division, a police artist,[1] and the witness arrived at the Department Psychologist's office to begin the hypnosis procedure. The investigators and the artist were present throughout the hypnosis session and toward the end actively participated in the dialogue with the witness. The session was tape recorded with the permission of all participants.

The witness was a mature adult female of middle age who was observably tense and anxious when ushered into the office. After being introduced, she was seated and asked about her feelings in regard to hypnosis. She indicated a lack of knowledge about hypnosis but reiterated her willingness to be hypnotized so she could be of assistance in the investigation. To aid in establishing rapport and to dispel any myths or misconceptions about hypnosis, a brief explanation was given to the effect that hypnosis is a state of concentrated attention which can be achieved by following suggestions, if the individual is intelligent and motivated to do so. It was mentioned that because of increased relaxation and greater awareness, there would be better recall of certain events. It was explained that the mind is like a video tape machine in that everything is recorded, perhaps at a subconscious level, and stored in the brain but available for recall under hypnosis.

She was told that there were only a couple of things to be learned in order to be able to go into hypnosis and these were simply to relax and to cooperate. She was asked to fix her eyes on the thumbtack which had been scotch taped to a metal blind in front of her about a foot and half below the ceiling. She was then told to tighten various muscle groups in order to experience the tension and to compare it with relaxation.

After tensing then relaxing muscles in the forehead, neck and shoulders, fist and arms, chest, stomach, feet and legs, she indicated some residual tension in her calf muscles. She was asked to retighten the muscles in her legs for five seconds after which she indicated that she no longer felt the tension there. It was then suggested she begin breathing deeply and slowly, as the second step in the process of learning how to relax, and that with each breath she would feel herself relaxing more and more. She was told that very shortly she would notice her eyes feeling very tired and heavy and under considerable strain, as do most people after looking at a fixed object for a long period of time. It was then explained that the psychologist would count slowly to 10 and that somewhere during the count her eyes would get very very heavy and close with no effort and that she would keep them closed until she was asked to open them. As the count proceeded, her eyes closed on the count of three after which suggestions were given that they close tighter and that she relax more deeply as the count continued. It was suggested that she could allow herself to relax even more deeply by visualizing the most pleasant, calm, peaceful scene she chose. Finger and arm levitation were achieved easily and suggestions were given of a fourfold increase in the state of relaxation and hypnosis with the descending of her arm from the vertical position.

She was then told that she would be asked some questions and that she could nod her head in response or answer verbally. When asked if she watched television, she nodded in the affirmative. To subsequent questions she verbalized that she usually sat in a favorite rocking chair, that her television was a color set and that it took a few minutes to warm up. She was asked to visualize herself sitting in her favorite rocking chair about to watch television and that she was going to see a very special program. This special program would be a TV movie which could slow down, stop and give close-ups on scenes or people thus enabling her to see more clearly certain things in this movie. However, whatever she viewed, she would remain relaxed and detached because she would know she was watching a television special produced by the network and therefore would be able to see things clearly and easily. She was then asked to visualize herself turning the TV set on and then returning to her rocking chair to wait for the set to light up. It was reiterated during this wait that this film was a documentary which would capture in detail everything that happened on the preceding December 17 from about midnight to about 2 a.m. It was suggested that the TV screen was now bright and she could see the movie clearly and to begin describing it.

Slowly, she began talking in a very low voice, saying they (meaning her friend and her) had been talking, dancing, and acting silly. However, their activities were not too clear to her. Then someone was at the door and a man came in. At this point, it was suggested to her that the film would stop and there would be a close-up giving sharp details of the man who had come in. She described him as tall and thin and in his early 20s. It was suggested that the camera would zoom in on his face for a more detailed close-up allowing her to see his features clearly. She described the shape of face, nose and nostrils, ethnic origin, hair style including sideburns, lips, size of head, mustache, beard, and clothing worn. At one point during the description, she commented that she couldn't see if the suspect had a mustache because she had had too much to drink. It was repeated that she could see him clearly because these details were automatically registered on her subconscious mind—more description followed.

It was suggested that the film would go into a slow-motion sequence beginning with the suspect's knocking at the door which would allow her to hear what had happened in detail at that point. She indicated that nothing was said after the knock, that the man was let in silently because her friend acted as if he knew the person although she had never seen him before. Then her friend came out of the kitchen with a gun in his back pocket and went outside on the steps with the visitor. She heard shots, felt scared and upset, turned the lights out and called the police.

At this point, with the witness's approval, the investigators and artist present were invited to ask questions. Another close-up of the suspect's face was suggested. She elaborated on facial features, hair style, whiskers and absence of glasses. The investigators felt that they now had exhausted the possible information, and it was decided to terminate the hypnotic interview. The witness was told that she was now turning off the television set, sitting back down in her rocking chair, feeling relaxed and comfortable. It was suggested she could or could not remember what she saw on the film as she chose, whatever was comfortable for her; she would awaken and become alert, feel very relaxed and rested and then any residual conflict over the traumatic event or the interview situation would gradually get resolved. A slow count to the letter E was initiated, interspersed with suggestions of feeling refreshed and relaxed upon awakening. It was also mentioned that she might recall something more later on, and if so, she would feel free to call the investigators with this information. She became alert on the count of the letter E, laughed and said that she felt very good. Additional conversation revealed a diminution in her original anxiety and upset. The psychologist mentioned that she would have the opportunity to talk further with him later about any phase of the incident or the hypnosis session, if she desired.

The police artist present during the interview indicated that he had gotten sufficient details to enable him to draw a composite picture of the suspect. Subsequently, it was learned that the suspect was identified in a police line-up and that he was "a dead ringer" for the composite drawing. It turned out that the suspect, although an accomplice, did not fire the actual shots in the homicide, there being two others involved in the case who were later identified. Apparently these three individuals had planned a robbery on the victim and the identified suspect tried to call it off at the last moment and flee the scene, but one of his accomplices had shot the victim anyway. This aspect had been complicated by the fact that although the witness was present during the incident, she did not observe the actual murder because it occurred outside on the front doorstep, with the door closed.

The investigators reported that the additional information obtained through the hypnosis interview was of considerable help in leading to the identification of the suspects and hopefully in gaining corroborating evidence which will ultimately clear the case.

This case suggests that, in spite of perceptions impaired by alcohol, other drugs, and traumatic shock incident to a murder, it is still possible that the use of hypnosis with a willing witness can contribute meaningfully to the investigation of the crime.

NOTE

1. Collaborators in this case were Investigators Philip L. Vannatter, Curtis F. Hussey and Police Artist Fernando G. Ponce.

5

HYPNOSIS AND DISTORTIONS IN EYEWITNESS MEMORY

WILLIAM H. PUTNAM
University of California, Santa Barbara

Many memory theorists view the retrieval of information from human memory as a constructive process (Bartlett, 1932; Bransford, Barclay, & Franks, 1972). This view of human memory suggests that information which occurs after an event is initially encoded can be integrated into the memory representation of that event. This perspective is contrasted with what can be called an "exact copy" theory of memory which posits that once information is encoded, it is represented veridically and is unaffected by subsequent inputs. These contrasting perspectives have practical implications which are nowhere more evident than in the questioning of eyewitnesses in criminal investigations.

One of the most important concerns of a criminal investigation is the need to obtain accurate information from witnesses. The smallest details are sometimes very important in apprehending criminals, and

Reprinted from the October 1979 *International Journal of Clinical and Experimental Hypnosis.* Copyrighted by the Society for Clinical and Experimental Hypnosis, October 1979.

police investigators are, therefore, grateful for any technique which can aid them in increasing witnesses' ability to recall the details of a crime. Recently, there has been an increasing interest in the use of hypnosis to improve the accuracy of eyewitness reports and the technique has proved useful in several investigations (Reiser, 1974, 1976; Schafer & Rubio, 1978; The Svengali Squad, 1976). The usual approach is to hypnotize witnesses and then have them mentally relive the original experience. Using this procedure, witnesses are reported to recall license plate numbers, facial descriptions, and other details that they were unable to recall prior to being hypnotized. The use of hypnosis has been so promising, in fact, that many police departments are now having investigators trained in its use.

As the use of hypnosis in criminal investigations increases, courts are faced with the problem of deciding if the evidence obtained under hypnosis is admissible. For instance, the court must consider whether or not recall under hypnosis is always more accurate or alternatively, if there are situations in which the hypnotized witness may distort details. There are surprisingly little data relating to this issue. While Arons (1967), a lay hypnotist, reported some demonstrations of the effectiveness of hypnosis in restoring memory, these were not controlled experiments and as such they have serious methodological flaws. From an experimental point of view, one problem with these demonstrations is that the witnesses were always questioned first in a waking state and then under hypnosis. In other words, hypnosis was introduced only after an already attempted recall. Erdelyi and his associates (Erdelyi & Becker, 1974; Erdelyi & Kleinbard, 1978) have shown that recall for pictures improves with repeated recall attempts, so that Arons's (1978) results need not be due to hypnosis at all. It is possible that if witnesses had first been questioned under hypnosis and then later in the waking state, recall would still have improved, even though the later attempt was in a waking state. On the other hand, there is such a large body of anecdotal evidence available that it is hard to believe that hypnosis does not improve eyewitness recall in at least some situations—particularly those in which the witness was emotionally upset by the witnessed event. In fact, Dorcus (1960) has argued that hypnosis aids recall in situations where it is used to overcome emotional blocking.

Whether or not hypnosis does improve memory is still an open question. There is the additional possibility, however, that under hypnosis an individual is more likely to supply inaccurate information. Stalnaker and Riddle (1932) found that whereas hypnotized Ss reported more information, this increase in the total amount recalled reflected not only an increase in the number of words recalled correctly, but a great deal of inaccurate information being recalled as well. Stalnaker and Riddle (as discussed in Hull, 1933) suggest that under hypnosis Ss may have been more suggestible and hence less critical of the information they recalled. Orne (1961) also discussed this possibility and concluded that "even those informants who believe they are telling the truth may in fact be offering a composite of delusion, fantasy, and reality [p. 195]."

Elizabeth Loftus and her coworkers (Loftus, 1975; Loftus & Zanni, 1975) have found that eyewitnesses questioned in a normal waking state often make errors if the interrogator asks questions in such a way that they suggest particular answers. Seemingly minor changes in the structure of the sentence have been shown to affect the accuracy of recall. For example, changing the question "Did you see a broken headlight?" to "Did you see the broken headlight?" increases the number of Ss who answer affirmatively, even when there was no broken headlight. Loftus (1977; Loftus, Miller, & Burns, 1978) has also shown that inaccurate information introduced in an earlier question can influence Ss' recall of a later question. The question addressed by the current research is whether hypnosis increases the witnesses' suggestibility and hence increases the likelihood that witnesses will make such errors.

While the present research was designed to address a fairly straightforward practical problem, it also addresses a more general issue which is potentially of greater practical importance. The growing use of hypnosis in criminal investigations reflects a particular view of how memory works. It is a view which is evident in the following quotation from a detective trained in the use of hypnosis.

> It is all there even if you are not aware of it. Everything that has ever happened to you, from birth to death, is recorded on your brain permanently. If that defense mechanism can be relaxed enough, it will enable the subject under hypnosis to describe what is written on the brain [White, 1977, p. 11].

This quotation reflects what can be termed an "implicit theory of memory." This detective has stated quite clearly how he believes human memory works and his behavior will be guided by this implicit theory. Statements such as this are not uncommon on television and in the popular press, and it is not surprising that this type of memory theory is held implicitly by many individuals—including police investigators. The detective has expressed an exact copy theory of memory which assumes that information is stored accurately and that forgetting is the result of an inability to retrieve the information. From this perspective, hypnosis is viewed as a method of eliminating retrieval difficulties and giving direct access to the stored information.

The Loftus (1975, 1977, Loftus & Zanni, 1975, Loftus et al., 1978) experiments, on the other hand, support a constructive theory of memory. Loftus argues that information presented after an event was witnessed is integrated into the memory representation of that event. In this way information acquired subsequent to the original event can cause a constructive addition or alteration of the information stored in memory. If individuals are more suggestible under hypnosis, they are more likely to alter their representations and should make more errors when asked leading questions than individuals who are not hypnotized.

The larger significance of the present experiment can be seen primarily in terms of the possible social implications of these two points of view. An individual (especially a policeman) who adheres to one of these positions will probably interview a witness differently from an individual who adheres to the other. For example, if an investigator's implicit theory of memory is an exact copy theory, he will not be concerned about the possible effects of suggesting answers to the witness. These suggestions will just be retrieval cues which can aid the witness in retrieving the needed information, which is either stored accurately or not stored at all. If the witness is confident of his or her response, the investigator will probably assume that the recall was accurate. A reconstructive theory, on the other hand, implies that suggestions by the investigator may be incorporated into the memory representation in such a way that the witness believes that they represent events which actually occurred.

In the experiment reported here, Ss viewed a video tape recording depicting a car-bicycle accident and were questioned about the details of the accident. Half of Ss were questioned under hypnosis and half of Ss were questioned in a normal waking state. Of primary interest was whether or not the hypnotized Ss would answer more of the leading questions inaccurately. In addition, the delay between seeing the video tape recording and the recall test was manipulated in order to determine whether hypnotic Ss would make more errors when answering leading questions as memory accuracy declined over time.

METHOD

Subjects

The Ss for the experiment were 16 undergraduate students from the University of California, Santa Barbara. The Ss had taken part in one previous hypnosis experiment, which consisted of being administered the Stanford Hypnotic Susceptibility Scale, Form A (SHSS:A) of Weitzenhoffer and Hilgard (1959). They were chosen for this experiment because their SHSS:A scores were available. The Ss were all paid $3.00 for their participation.

Materials

The stimulus material for the experiment was a video tape recording of a car-bicycle accident. In the video tape recording, a car is seen approaching an intersection, stopping at the intersection, and making a right-hand turn. As the car turns, it cuts in front of a bicycle which is passing it on the right, and the car and bicycle collide, knocking the bicycle and rider to the ground. The questions which were asked of Ss all pertained to details of the video tape recording.

There were 15 questions that were asked of all Ss; of these, 6 were leading questions. The leading questions were similar to those used by Loftus (1974, 1977, Loftus et al., 1978) and were designed to suggest a specific answer. Five of the questions were formed by using the article "the" instead of an "a" in a question such as "Did you see a stop sign?" These questions are listed in Table 1. The sixth question was based on a previous suggestion that a woman seen in the video tape recording had blond hair when in fact her hair was black. Just prior to beginning the question set, E asked S if she or he had recognized any of the people in the video tape recording, "For example the driver of the car, the blond woman who witnessed the accident, or the bicycle rider?" The sixth question asked S to describe the witness and to specify her hair color. (For ease of exposition, all 6 questions will be referred to as "leading," to contrast them with the objective questions.) The leading questions were randomly interpersed with the objective questions.

Procedure

The experiment was a 2×2 design with the independent variables state (hypnosis/no hypnosis) and delay (short/long). The 16 Ss were assigned randomly to one of the four conditions, with the constraint that SHSS:A scores for the four groups were approximately equal. The mean SHSS:A scores for the four groups out of 12 points possible were: hypnosis-short delay, 8.75; hypnosis-long delay, 8.25; no hypnosis-short delay, 8.50; and no hypnosis-long delay, 8.50.

When Ss arrived at the laboratory, they were informed that they were going to see a video tape recording that was taken on the

TABLE 5.1

Five of the Leading Questions Used in the Experiment[a]

1. Did you see the stop sign at the intersection?
2. Did you see the passenger in the car?
3. Did you see the license plate number of the car?
4. Did you see the broken glass from the bicycle light?
5. Did you see the bent wheel on the bike?

a. The sixth leading question is described in the text.

campus. They were instructed to watch the tape as if they were out walking around campus and saw the things which occurred. They were not instructed to memorize the events—only to pay attention to them. After watching the tape, Ss were instructed to imagine that they had just witnessed the accident that was depicted on the tape and knew that they were going to be questioned by the police about the details. They were told that keeping this in mind, they should try to remember the details as accurately as possible. At this point, Ss in the long delay condition were excused and reminded to return the next day; they were not informed as to whether they were in the hypnosis or no-hypnosis group. The Ss in the short delay group were asked to take part in a short cognitive task which was thought to correlate with visual memory. The task was a version of the Card Rotations Test (1962) and lasted approximately 15 minutes.

Following the short or long delay, Ss in the hypnosis condition were informed that they would be hypnotized in an attempt to improve their memory of the accident. They were told that under hypnosis it would be possible for them to see the entire accident again just as clearly as they had seen it the first time, only this time they would be able to slow it down or zoom in on details if they chose (Reiser, 1976). The Ss were asked to remove their shoes and to lie down on the couch and make themselves comfortable. The lights were dimmed and E administered the induction from SHSS:A. After the induction was completed, Ss were instructed to go back to the time when they were watching the video tape recording so that they could watch it again. They were told to listen to the questions that they were asked and to answer them by watching the video tape recording in their mind to determine the correct answer. On the questions that S had difficulty answering, these instructions were repeated with the additional instruction to form a clear image of the specific scene relevant to that question. When the image was clear, Ss were told to look at the image and pick out the information necessary to answer the question. After answering each question, Ss were asked to indicate how confident they were of their answer on a scale from 1 to 5, where 1 indicated a guess and 5 indicated absolute certainty. After answering all of the questions, Ss were returned to a normal waking state and were asked if they felt that they had been more accurate under hypnosis than if they had been questioned in a waking state. They were also asked whether they would prefer a normal or hypnotic interview if they actually witnessed an accident or crime.

The Ss in the no-hypnosis condition were treated identically to the hypnosis Ss, except that they were not given a hypnotic induction and were not questioned about the efficacy of hypnosis. After answering all of the questions, Ss in all four groups were shown the video tape recordings again so that they could check their own accuracy.

RESULTS

The dependent variable of primary interest is the number of errors Ss made answering the leading questions. A 2×2 analysis of variance was performed on these data with factors of hypnosis and delay. The main effect for hypnosis was significant ($F = 5.88$, d.f. = 1, 12; $p < .05$), indicating that more errors were made by Ss in the hypnosis condition. There were no other significant main effects or interactions. A 2×2 analysis of variance was also conducted on the confidence ratings for the leading questions with the same factors as the first analysis. There were no significant main effects or interactions in this analysis. The means for the number incorrect and the confidence ratings for the four groups are shown in Table 2.

The number of correct responses on the objective questions were also subjected to a 2×2 analysis of variance with main effects of hypnosis and delay. There were no significant main effects or interactions in this analysis, and there were also no significant main effects or interactions in an identical analysis which was done on the confidence ratings for these questions. The means for the number of correct and the confidence ratings for the four groups are given in Table 3.

The Ss made more errors when answering leading questions under hypnosis than in a normal waking state. This finding supports the hypothesis that Ss are more suggestible in the hypnotic state and are, therefore, more easily influenced by the leading questions. This result argues strongly that great caution should be exercised when using hypnosis to question eyewitnesses in criminal investigations. The need for caution is further emphasized by the analysis of the confidence ratings that were given by Ss for their responses. Even though the hypnotic Ss made more errors, they were just as confident as the normal Ss who made fewer errors. Moreover, when the hypnotic Ss

TABLE 5.2
Mean Incorrect and Confidence Ratings on Six Leading Questions

	Short Delay	Long Delay
Hypnosis:		
$\bar{X}$ incorrect	1.25	2.25
$\bar{X}$ confidence	4.18	4.06
No Hypnosis:		
$\bar{X}$ incorrect	1.00	0.75
$\bar{X}$ confidence	4.56	4.31

were asked if they felt that they were more accurate under hypnosis than if they had answered the questions in a waking state, they all felt that they had been more accurate under hypnosis. These Ss also stated that they would prefer to be questioned under hypnosis if they witnessed an actual accident or crime. All of these effects seem to indicate quite clearly that under hypnosis, Ss answer more leading questions incorrectly and they are unaware that their responses are inaccurate.

It is important to note that five of the leading questions consisted of merely changing the article "a" to "the," but this rather subtle change had substantial effects. For example, asking Ss if they saw "the license plate" when it was not visible at all, not only elicited positive responses from some of the hypnotic Ss, they also offered partial descriptions of the license plate number. One S said it was a California license plate which began with W or V. This constructed information was not obtained under any coercion. There is every reason to believe that the tendency to distort recall would be even greater in a real criminal investigation, where the witness may have a vested interest in recalling the information.

An even better example of the amount of distortion that can take place is found in the answers to the question regarding the color of the witness's hair. Her hair was a true black (she was oriental), but two Ss in the hypnosis condition (but none in the no-hypnosis condition) remembered it as being blond. An S who had been given extensive prior training in hypnosis and who was run in a pilot session to the present experiment gave the following description as she viewed the video tape recording at the end of the experiment:

It's really strange because I still have the blond girl's face in my mind and it doesn't correspond to her [pointing to the woman on the videotape] . . . I was so confident that I knew what she looked like, and when I saw her I just went wait—it was really weird.

TABLE 5.3
Mean Correct and Confidence Ratings on Nine Objective Questions

	Short Delay	Long Delay
Hypnosis:		
$\bar{X}$ correct	5.00	6.25
$\bar{X}$ confidence	4.22	4.33
No Hypnosis:		
$\bar{X}$ correct	6.75	5.25
$\bar{X}$ confidence	4.59	4.06

Her description makes it clear that she did not just guess at the hair color, she actually had a clear image of a woman with blond hair who witnessed the accident. She went on to say that the woman she remembered had hair that looked like her roommate's. It seems possible that she constructed the image from a combination of her memory of the accident, the suggestion of *E*, and her roommate's hair. The *S* who remembered the license plate as beginning with *W* or *V* also mentioned that she remembered it because a friend's license plate began with the same letters.

The comments of these *Ss* support the data from the experiment in suggesting that a reconstructive theory of memory provides a more accurate depiction of memory than an exact copy theory. Information acquired after witnessing the accident was apparently integrated into the representation of the accident, so that the hypnotic *Ss* could not distinguish between the things which actually occurred and those which had subsequently been suggested to have occurred. An exact copy theory cannot easily account for the increase in errors made by *Ss* when answering the leading questions, since hypnosis is purported to reduce retrieval difficulties and allow retrieval of a veridical memorial representation.

It is important to keep in mind that the exact copy theory is an implicit theory which is held by many police officers who have been trained in the use of hypnosis. It is not a formal theory of memory and this experiment was not designed to test formal theories. The exact copy theory as it has been described in the present paper is really a theory of memory combined with a theory of how hypnosis affects memory. This implicit theory was pointed out to suggest that the implications of this experiment go beyond just the use of hypnosis in questioning witnesses. If police officers understand the constructive aspects of human memory, it may influence the manner in which they question all witnesses. That is to say, theories of human memory can influence the behavior of members of the lay public by influencing their implicit theories of memory. Neisser (1976) has recently argued that it is important for cognitive psychology to address issues which will influence ordinary individuals and their conceptions of human nature; the suggestion of the present paper is that memory theorists are in a position to do just that.

On the objective questions, there was no difference between Ss questioned under hypnosis and those Ss questioned in a normal waking state. At first glance, this is a puzzling finding, since there are reports of increased recall from actual police investigations (Reiser, 1974, 1976; Schafer & Rubio, 1978, The Svengali Squad, 1976). In many of those cases, however, the witnesses were emotionally upset and their inability to recall important information may have been the direct result of their emotional state. In the present experiment, no attempt was made to upset Ss because of the obvious ethical considerations involved. The data indicate that hypnosis may not aid recall when there is little emotional involvement on the part of the witness; they do not indicate that hypnosis will never aid recall. It may be that hypnosis aids recall by reducing retrieval difficulties caused specifically by emotionally upsetting events. However, there is currently no evidence from rigorous empirical studies to support this notion. This topic is ripe for further investigation and the research is long overdue.

The Ss in the present study were university students who volunteered to take part in an experiment involving hypnosis, and who did not receive any special training beyond a single administration of SHSS:A. It seems reasonable to assume that these Ss are fairly typical of the type of college-age individuals who might volunteer to be hypnotized in an actual criminal investigation. Since no attempt was made to measure the depth of trance during the session when the questions were answered, Ss in the hypnosis group should be considered as a cooperative, interested group of individuals who responded to the induction to varying degrees. While there may be some differences between S populations and induction procedures used here and those used in actual criminal investigations, every effort was made to create a context analogous to that which occurs outside of the laboratory.

Taken as a whole, the data of the present experiment indicate that the decision to use hypnosis in a criminal investigation should not be taken lightly. There is a strong possibility that witnesses will recall inaccurate information under hypnosis that they would not have recalled if questioned in a normal waking state, and it is likely that witnesses questioned under hypnosis will believe that they have been quite accurate, when they have, in fact, made errors. Moreover, there is the possibility of no increase in recall on questions which do not lead the witness. These findings must be balanced against the previous reports of cases which were solved almost entirely on the basis of information recalled under hypnosis. The decisions which are made by police investigators and courts of law must weigh these factors appropriately for the particular situation at hand, but it is clear that these decisions should involve consideration of the pitfalls revealed by the present experiment.

REFERENCES

Arons, H. *Hypnosis in criminal investigations.* Springfield, Ill.: Charles C Thomas, 1967.

Bartlett, F. C. *Remembering: A study in experimental and social psychology.* Cambridge, Eng.: Cambridge Univer. Press, 1932.

Bransford, J. D., Barclay, J. R., & Frank, J. J. Sentence memory: A constructive versus interpretive approach. *Cognit. Psychol.,* 1972, *3*, 193-209.

Card Rotations Test, S-1. Princeton, N.J.: Educational Testing Service, 1962.

Dorcus, R. M. Recall under hypnosis of amnestic events. *Int. J. clin. exp. Hypnosis,* 1960, *8*, 57-60.

Erderlyi, M. H., & Becker, J. Hypermnesia for pictures: Incremental memory for pictures but not words in multiple recall trials. *Cognit. Psychol.,* 1974, *6*, 159-170

Erderlyi, M. H., & Kleinbard, J. Has Ebbinghaus decayed with time? The growth of recall (hypermnesia) over days. *J. exp. Psychol. hum. Learn. Mem.,* 1978, *4*, 275-289.

Hull, C. L. *Hypnosis and suggestibility: An experimental approach.* New York: Appleton-Century-Crofts, 1933.

Loftus, E. F. Reconstructing memory: The incredible eyewitness. *Psychol. Today,* Dec. 1974, *8*(7), 116-119.

Loftus, E. F. Leading questions and the eyewitness report. *Cognit. Psychol.,* 1975, *7*, 560-572.

Loftus, E. F. Shifting human color memory. *Memory & Cognition,* 1977, *5*, 696-699.

Loftus, E. F., Miller, D. G., & Burns, H. J. Semantic integration of verbal information into visual memory. *J. exp. Psychol. hum. Learn. Mem.,* 1978, *4*, 19-31.

Loftus, E. F., & Zanni, G. Eyewitness testimony: The influence of the wording of a question. *Bull. Psychonom. Soc.,* 1975, *5*, 86-88.

Neisser, U. *Cognition and reality: Principles and implications of cognitive psychology.* San Francisco: W. H. Freeman, 1976.

Orne, M. T. The potential uses of hypnosis in interrogation. In A. D. Biderman & H. Zimmer (Eds.), *The manipulation of human behavior.* New York: Wiley & Sons, 1961. Pp. 169-215.

Reiser, M. Hypnosis as an aid in a homicide investigation. *Amer. J. clin. Hypnosis,* 1974, *17*, 84-87.

Reiser, M. Hypnosis as a tool in criminal investigation. *The Police Chief,* 1976, *46*(5), 36; 39-40.

Schafer, D. W., & Rubio, R. Hypnosis to aid the recall of witnesses, *Int. J. clin. exp. Hypnosis*, 1978, *26*, 81-91.

Stalnaker, J. M., & Riddle, E. E. The effect of hypnosis on long-delayed recall. *J. gen. Psychol.*, 1932, *6*, 429-440.

The Svengali squad. *Time*, September 13, 1976, pp. 56-57.

Weitzenhoffer, A. M., & Hilgard, E. R. *Stanford Hypnotic Susceptibility Scale, Forms A and B.* Palo Alto, Calif.: Consulting Psychologists Press, 1959.

White, G. Hypnosis given key role in rape investigation. *Amarillo Globe-Times*, July 7, 1977, *338*, p. 1.

6

HYPNOTIC MEMORY ENHANCEMENT OF WITNESSES
Does It Work?

MARILYN CHAPNIK SMITH
Scarborough College, University of Toronto

Can memory be enhanced by hypnosis? In attempting to answer this question we are confronted with a paradox: Whereas hypnosis has frequently been reported to improve recall in real-life crime situations, there is a conspicuous absence of any improvement in the controlled environment of the laboratory. Because of its reported usefulness as an aid to recall in so many criminal cases (e.g., Arons, 1967; Bryan, 1962,

Author's Note. This research was supported by a grant to M. Smith from the National Science and Engineering Research Council of Canada and was written while the author was on sabbatical leave from the University of Toronto at Stanford University. I wish to thank the Psychology Department at Stanford University for facilities provided that year and Raymond W. Gibbs for his invaluable assistance. Requests for reprints may be sent to Marilyn C. Smith, Life Science Division, Scarborough College, University of Toronto, West Hill, Ontario M1C 1A4, Canada.

From *Psychological Bulletin*, 1983, 94(3), 387-407. Copyright 1983 by the American Psychological Association. Reprinted by permission of the publisher and author.

cited in Hayward & Ashworth, 1980; Reiser, 1976; Teitelbaum, 1969), there has developed among police and other investigative agencies an unshakable belief that through the appropriate use of hypnosis otherwise irretrievable memories may be recalled. Such a belief is evident in the statement by Federal Bureau of Investigation (FBI) agent Ault (1980) that "disagreements about the nature of hypnosis will continue, but whatever its nature or however it works, it does work with many people." This belief has resulted in the ever increasing use of hypnosis for "refreshing" memory, particularly since the recognition of hypnosis as a valid therapeutic technique to eliminate amnesia by both the American Medical Association and the American Psychological Association in the late 1950s (Hilgard, 1965, p. 4). The Los Angeles Police Department implemented a special program in hypnosis in 1975 through which nearly 300 people have been trained in the use of hypnosis and are regularly hypnotizing witnesses who claim lack of recall (Worthington, 1979). This trend toward the use of hypnosis to refresh memory is not limited to California—the New York City Police Department relies on two in-house hypnotists to aid in the interrogation of witnesses ("The Trials of Hypnosis," 1981), and the FBI has adopted a "team" approach whereby an FBI coordinator, a professional hypnotist, and an artist trained in drawing faces from verbal descriptions all work together during the hypnotic interrogation. The FBI considers hypnosis of such importance that it has established and published a set of guidelines outlining its proper use by this team (Ault, 1979). Similar trends appear outside the United States. The Israeli police make extensive use of hypnosis (Clifford & Bull, 1978), and in at least one Canadian case a defendant in British Columbia was hypnotized in front of a jury to help alleviate amnesia for events surrounding an alleged crime (Pitt, 1968, cited in Hayward & Ashworth, 1980).

The use of hypnotic memory enhancement by the police certainly appears justified in light of the hundreds of anecdotal case studies which indicate that otherwise unsolvable cases were miraculously solved through the elicitation of new information from hypnotized witnesses. Paradoxically, however, laboratory investigations of the effects of hypnosis on recall have generally been unable to demonstrate that memory is any better with hypnosis than without it (Buckhout, Eugenio, Licitra, Oliver, & Kramer, 1981). When proper control subjects are used and they attempt to recall the same material as the hypnotized subjects, with relevant variables held constant, performances for the two groups typically do not differ (as will be illustrated below). Further, hypnotic memory enhancement is based on the belief that human memory

is like a videotape machine that (1) faithfully records, as if on film, every perception experienced by the witness, (2) permanently stores such recorded perceptions in the brain at a subconscious level, and (3) accurately "replays" them in their original form when the witness is placed under hypnosis and asked to remember them. (Reiser, as quoted in *People v. Shirley*, 1982, p. 57)

However, recent research into the nature of human memory has been increasingly critical of the "videotape" concept of memory. Such research has emphasized the reconstructive nature of memory, whereby both externally provided information and the individual's own thoughts interact with and change the existing memory trace (e.g., Bartlett, 1932; Hintzman, 1978; Loftus, 1975; Loftus & Loftus, 1980). The very act of recalling under hypnosis may significantly change the witness's memory of an event, possibly resulting in the incorporation into memory of subtle cues or suggestions provided by the hypnotist—suggestions that become a part of and hence cannot be differentiated from the original memory (Diamond, 1980).

These conflicting viewpoints have led to considerable confusion in the courts on both the value and dangers of using hypnosis to enhance recall. Some indication of this confusion may be seen in the most recent judicial decision regarding the forensic use of hypnosis. In March of 1982 the California Supreme Court ruled that evidence acquired from a witness who has undergone hypnosis could not be admitted in court. Justice Stanley Mosk, writing for the six to one court majority (*People v. Shirley*, 1982) stated that "At the present time the use of hypnosis to restore the memory of a potential witness is not generally accepted as reliable by the relevant scientific community." The justices noted in their 60-page decision that at least five other state supreme courts—Michigan, Minnesota, Arizona, Maryland, and Pennsylvania—have already ruled similarly (see, for example, *Minnesota v. Mack*, 1980, and *Polk v. State*, 1981).

We have, thus, a strange situation: an ever increasing use of hypnosis by the police in the face of a growing disinclination by the courts to accept the testimony of witnesses who have undergone hypnosis. In light of this difficult situation, a closer examination of the issues is undoubtedly warranted. To provide some familiarity with the forensic use of hypnosis in the real world, I have arbitrarily selected two anecdotal reports of criminal cases in which hypnosis was "successfully" used for memory enchancement from a series of recent FBI cases published by Kroger and Douce (1979). These give credence to the enthusiasm with which hypnotic memory enhancement has been met by the police. I then present two laboratory studies similarly selected from the very large literature on the topic that provide an indication of the types of controls that can be incorporated in a laboratory study that are of course unlikely in the field: Given the very different results that the two types of studies yield concerning the value of hypnosis for memory improvement, several differences between the laboratory and real-life situations are reviewed that could conceivably account for the differential effects of hypnosis in the two situations. However, a review of several recent laboratory studies on hypnotic memory enhancement under more realistic conditions indicates that even the elimination of some of the obvious differences between laboratory and crime situations nonetheless fails to provide superior recall under hypnosis. Further, these studies point out a real danger inherent in the hypnosis situation: an increase in suggestibility. Because of the lack of any experimental support for hypnotic memory enhancement, together with this danger of increased suggestibility under hypnosis, suggestions for nonhypnotic methods of improving recall are provided through the isolation of several factors that may be operative in those cases where hypnosis appears to work. Finally, a brief historic review of the judicial attitude toward the forensic use of hypnosis is provided.

TWO ILLUSTRATIVE ANECDOTES

Perhaps the most frequently cited example of the successful use of hypnosis to refresh memory is the Chowchilla kidnapping case (*People v. Woods et al.,* 1977), In July 1976, 26 school children and their bus driver were abducted at gunpoint, herded into vans, and transferred to a remote rock quarry where they were sealed inside a rectangular-shaped tomb underneath the ground. After frantic efforts, the driver and two of the older boys succeeded in digging their way out and contacting the police. When the bus driver was questioned in the normal waking state[1] his recall was somewhat sketchy. He had seen and tried to memorize two of the van license plate numbers but had been too frightened to concentrate under the constant surveillance of the kidnappers. Under hypnosis, it was suggested to the driver that he imagine himself sitting in his favorite chair watching the events unfold as in a documentary film on a television screen. In the hypnotic state, he suddenly called out two license plate numbers. One of these numbers, with the exception of a single digit, proved to be the license plate number of the van driven by the kidnappers, information that expedited the solution of the case after one of the biggest manhunts in California history. The three kidnappers were convicted and sentenced to life imprisonment (Kroger & Douce, case 1, 1979, pp. 367-368).

A second case reported by Kroger and Douce involved the kidnapping and rape of two San Francisco area girls aged 7 and 15 who were abducted by a man describing himself as a member of the Symbionese Liberation Army (SLA). After terrifying the girls by telling them that the doors of his car were wired with an explosive device that he would trigger if stopped by police, he drove them to Mexico where the older girl was raped and sodomized in a motel room near the border. He released the girls a few days later with the warning that any disclosure of what had happened would mean certain death to their parents at the hands of the SLA. In interviews at the nonhypnotic level the girls had difficulty remembering the chronology of events, possibly due to the traumatic nature of their ordeal. The older girl did succeed in identifying the motel room where the suspect had registered under an assumed name, but nothing concrete could be found through investigation. At this stage, hypnosis was suggested for enhancing recall of the older girl. At the hypnotic level she was able to recall unique rust spots on the car body, as well as details about several articles inside the car such as the specific color and brand names of boxes of tissues and peanut butter cookies on the rear seat. She recollected that the gear shift knob of the car was held in place with a piece of tissue paper and that the right front passenger window made a noise when it was rolled up the last few inches. The only information that had been available at the nonhypnotic level was the color and general description of the car.

Of perhaps greatest value, under hypnosis the girl was able to recall a transaction at a San Diego gas station located on a hilltop where the suspect had had his car repaired. The hilltop location was instrumental in permitting the police to locate the gas station. Under hypnosis, the girl remembered conversations between the repairman and the suspect dealing with the nature of the repairs required, as well as the fact that the transaction was paid for by the use of a red, white, and blue credit card. Although she was totally unfamiliar with the type of repairs, she specifically remembered that the repairman had said to the suspect, "You need Freon." The FBI agents located the gas station and the repairman. The credit card transaction was quickly identified, and the suspect was arrested at his home in northern California. Examination of the car confirmed every single detail supplied by the girl while she was under hypnosis. In news releases made following the suspect's arrest, his photograph was recognized by other young girls who had been sexually assaulted. The suspect was convicted and is now serving an indefinite sentence in a state hospital for the criminally insane (Kroger & Douce, 1979, case 3, pp. 369-370).

PROBLEMS WITH ANECDOTAL REPORTS

Such anecdotal descriptions of criminal cases solved through the use of hypnosis are tremendously persuasive, and as more and more published reports appear it is not surprising that the forensic use of hypnosis to refresh memory is on the rise. Yet the use of hypnosis for this purpose is not without problems, some of which are indicated below.

No Objective Verification

Unfortunately, there is usually no way to objectively verify the accuracy of information reported under hypnosis. For example, although the recall of the license plate numbers in the Chowchilla kidnapping case was extremely helpful, many license plate numbers have been recalled under hypnosis for cars that investigation later showed could not possibly have been involved (Orne, 1979). An illustration of the problem of verifying hypnotic recall may be seen in the use of age regression, a procedure frequently used for memory enhancement that appears to enable individuals to relieve past events that occurred either many years ago or even relatively recently but are unavailable for recall, perhaps because of their traumatic nature. When a hypnotized individual is told, for example, that he is 6 years old and at his birthday party, he'll begin to act, talk, and to some degree think like a child. He may play like a child, address friends who apparently were there, describe in detail the room, the people who are there, the presents he's receiving, and so on. It all seems very compelling, natural, and beyond the skills of even a professional actor (Orne, 1979, p. 316). The problem is that the relived episodes frequently combine a great many fantasies with the actual events, as demonstrated in a laboratory investigation of age regression conducted by O'Connell, Shor, and Orne (1970). Whereas subjects did indeed recall more under hypnosis, they also tended to confabulate more. In checking descriptions the age-regression subjects made of their childhood classmates, the experimenters were shocked to find that some of the individuals so vividly described had not even been members of the subjects' class! If the hypnosis is being conducted for therapeutic purposes, the introduction of these confabulations is of little concern. If, however, we are concerned with the accuracy of the recalled material, the situation is quite different. As Orne (1979) has pointed out, imagine if Freud had acted on his patients' recollections and urged the authorities to imprison the fathers for incest! In addition to the problem of confabulation, a second significant factor emerged from this study: The actual number of factual events recalled, that is, the information of importance to the law, was no greater under hypnosis than it was under nonhypnotic recall. Thus although anecdotal reports may strongly suggest that hypnosis can enhance recall, they do not provide any way of determining first, the accuracy of the data being recalled and second, whether more information is being gleaned under hypnosis than could have been arrived at through nonhypnotic procedures.

No Control Group

If an individual is suddenly able, under hypnosis, to remember important details of a crime that were not reported earlier, the assumption is made that it was the hypnosis that was responsible for the improved recollection. However, in any situation other possible explanations exist. Perhaps the more relaxed atmosphere in which the recollection of the event took place contributed to the recall. Perhaps it was not the hypnosis per se, but the longer, more detailed questioning period and the reinstatement of context through the evocation of environmental and emotional cues that were of key importance. Since hypnosis can only be used with certain people—namely, those who are susceptible to hypnosis—it may be that such individuals differ from nonsusceptible subjects in other important ways, and that recall is due to these other factors rather than to the fact that they were hypnotized. In short, when new information is recalled under hypnosis in an extralaboratory situation, it is impossible to establish whether it was the hypnosis per se or some other factors in the testing situation that were responsible for the improved recall. To make this determination, an additional piece of information must be provided: how a nonhypnotized control group would have performed in an otherwise identical situation. Because anecdotal reports of criminal cases cannot by definition provide the requisite control group to allow a determination of whether factual recall is in fact improved under hypnosis, it is necessary to turn to laboratory studies that do include such controls. For this purpose two representative laboratory studies are presented that include somewhat different types of controls.

TWO ILLUSTRATIVE LABORATORY STUDIES

In 1975, Dhanens and Lundy conducted a study of hypnotic memory enhancement using both subjects with very low susceptibility to hypnosis and those with very high susceptibility. All subjects learned two types of materials in the waking state—a meaningful prose passage consisting of a short biography (184 words long) and a nonmeaningful list of 13 nonsense syllables. Approximately 1 week later all subjects attempted verbal recall of both kinds of materials, in the order in which they had learned them, and were then assigned to one of six treatment conditions. There were approximately 10 high-susceptible and 10 low-susceptible subjects in each condition. Four of the conditions involved no hypnosis: (a) The control group simply left the room for ½ hour, and on their return were asked to recall the material one more time. (b) The relaxation group left the room for 15 minutes and when they returned were given a 15-minute relaxation treatment with specific instructions not to become hypnotized. Following this treatment they attempted recall. (c) The regression group received regression instructions prior to recall that encouraged them to imagine the room in which they had heard the materials, to picture themselves back in time experiencing the room as if they were in it, and so on. (d) The motivation group left the room for 25 minutes and were told on their return to "make a real effort, to try as hard as you can to remember everything and not leave out anything." They were told that performance would improve if they concentrated and tried hard. Subjects in the remaining two conditions attempted to recall under hypnosis: (e) The regression group differed from the nonhypno-tized regression group only in that they were hypnotized before hearing the regression tape. (f) The motivation group resembled the nonhypnotized motivation group exactly except for the fact that they were hypnotized prior to receiving the motivating instructions and then proceeded to recall under hypnosis. For all conditions, half the subjects attempted recall with eyes closed, half with eyes open.

To measure recall performance, the prose passage was divided into 35 phrases or significant words, and one point was scored for each unit recalled. The performance measure used was the gain score between the first and second recall attempts during the second session. What did this carefully controlled laboratory study reveal about the effect of hypnosis on recall? Considering first recall of the nonsense syllables, the data are unambiguous. Recall did not differ significantly for any of the groups: Neither the main effect of hypnosis nor its interaction with such factors as motivation or susceptibility to hypnosis significantly affected recall of meaningless materials. The second clear result was that whether the eyes were kept open or closed was inconsequential in influencing recall. Interpretation of the effect of hypnosis on the recall of meaningful material, presented in Table 1, is somewhat more complex. The only subjects whose recall performance was significantly better than that of the control group were those who were both highly susceptible to hypnosis and had received hypnosis plus motivation instructions. Intuitively, this makes sense. Unless an individual is highly susceptible to hypnosis, it is not surprising that hypnosis has little effect. Further, the results suggest that it is not hypnosis per se,

TABLE 6.1
Mean Gain Scores in Recall Under Various Conditions:
Data from Dhanens and Lundy (1975)

| | Susceptibility to hypnosis | | |
| | High ($n = 61$) | Low ($n = 57$) | M |
Treatment			
No hypnosis			
Control	1.30	3.30	2.30
Relaxation instructions	.30	1.25	.78
Regression instructions	1.63	3.22	2.43
Motivation			
instructions	2.50	4.22	3.36
Hypnosis			
Regression instructions	2.00	1.50	1.75
Motivation			
instructions	4.33	1.89	3.11

but rather the inclusion of particular instructions under hypnosis that results in improved recall. Unfortunately, despite their intuitive appeal, careful examination of the data indicates that even these conclusions are far from clear. Although failing to reach significance, the improvement in memory for the low-susceptible subjects who received motivation instructions without hypnosis was very similar to that of the group who did show a significant effect. As may be seen in Table 1 this improvement did not differ significantly from that of the control group because of the surprisingly large and unexplained improvement the low-susceptibility subjects displayed in the control situation. Hence even where hypnosis has an effect, it is difficult to interpret.

Yet another problem in interpreting the outcome of this study comes to light when we turn to a second laboratory study conducted to evaluate the effect of hypnosis on recall, a study by Cooper and London (1973). In place of the between-groups design used by Dhanens and Lundy, an important feature of this experiment was the fact that each subject served as his or her own control, recalling in both the hypnotic and waking states. Subjects were initially classified as showing either high susceptibility or low susceptibility to hypnosis by means of both group and individual testing over three sessions. They were then asked to read a short, factual article dealing with the properties of a rare chemical. Two weeks later, recall was tested by asking subjects 33 short-answer questions. As previously mentioned, recall was tested twice—once under hypnosis and once when awake, with order of recall counterbalanced. The data, shown in Table 2, were striking in their failure to provide any support for the contention that hypnosis can improve memory. The only effect found to be significant was that recall was better on the second test. This observation is important to keep in mind, for hypnosis is typically administered after an initial recall attempt, and any improvement in memory is usually considered to be the result of the hypnosis rather than the fact that it is the subject's second recall trial. Thus, for example, Sears (1954) reported that recall of an array of items displayed on a table was significantly better in the hypnotic state than it had been on a prior nonhypnotic test. In light of the Cooper and London study such data are now suspect, as the improvement could have been the result of always testing hypnotic recall second. In fact, had such a procedure been used by Cooper and London, with all subjects tested first awake and then under hypnosis, it would indeed have appeared as though hypnosis caused a large memory improvement for high-susceptible subjects (from 8.6 to 10.0) and a small improvement for low-susceptible subjects (from 8.64 to 9.09). It is only when the effect of order is controlled that it becomes clear that any improvement is not the result of hypnosis. In this regard previous studies purporting to demonstrate hypnotic enhancement must be carefully reexamined. The phenomenon of hypermnesia found with repeated testing will be discussed in some detail later on.

It is also of interest in this study to consider how the data might have been interpreted had a between-subjects design been employed. If Cooper and London had used four separate groups—two groups of high-susceptible subjects and two groups of low-susceptible subjects—with one group of each tested either awake or under hypnosis, it would have looked as though the high- and low-susceptible groups were similar in the waking state (8.60 and 8.64, respectively), but that hypnosis enhanced memory for high-susceptible subjects (9.20) and diminished it for low-susceptible subjects (7.64). Similarly, if they had looked at their data without controlling for the effect of order, and if they had not tested subjects under both hypnotic and waking conditions, it would have looked as though hypnosis did indeed have some beneficial effect on memory. "Had the group of high susceptible subjects been measured only once, in the hypnotized condition, and the group of low susceptible subjects been measured only once, in the waking condition, the former would have yielded a mean memory score of 9.20 and the latter a mean memory score of 8.64" (Cooper & London, 1973, p. 320), thereby making it appear as if hypnosis did have an effect. It is only in the presence of the appropriate controls that the absence of any hypnotic memory enhancement becomes clear.

TABLE 6.2
Means of Memory Scores: Data from Cooper and London (1973)

		Condition	
Order	n	Hypnotized	Waking
High-susceptible group			
Hypnosis first	15	9.20	9.80
Waking first	15	10.00	8.60
Low-susceptible group			
Hypnosis first	11	7.64	7.91
Waking first	11	9.09	8.64
M		8.98	8.76

DIFFERENCES BETWEEN LABORATORY STUDIES AND THE CRIME SITUATION

The failure of these two laboratory studies to demonstrate a clear advantage for hypnotic recall is representative of the majority of laboratory studies that have investigated hypnotic hypermnesia (see, for example, reviews in Barber & Calverley, 1966; DePiano & Salzberg, 1981; Dhanens & Lundy, 1975), a failure that is in marked contrast to the apparently beneficial effects of hypnosis reported so frequently in real-life case studies. What is the basis for this discrepancy? Undoubtedly laboratory studies differ from crime situations in a variety of ways (DePiano & Salzberg, 1981), and it may be because of these differences that beneficial hypnotic effects do not appear in the laboratory.

Type of Material Being Recalled

One of the most important differences between the laboratory and real-life studies is in the type of materials subjects are required to recall. In the crime situation an individual experiences a meaningful event or series of events in an everyday setting, complete with a rich array of visual cues, both pictorial and verbal. Further, these stimuli are typically dynamic, certainly not presented statically in serial order at a fixed presentation rate. In contrast, most laboratory studies, as illustrated by the two discussed above, have concentrated on verbal stimuli such as lists of words, lists of nonsense syllables, or short prose passages containing factual information. Where nonverbal stimuli have been used they tend to be such abstract stimuli as symbols or color patterns. Compared with the real world, these stimuli are far less vivid and certainly less meaningful. Hence, failure to find any effect of hypnosis in the laboratory may be related to this vast difference in the kinds of materials being tested.

Level of Arousal

A second difference between the two situations relates to the typical level of arousal. Most crime situations have strong emotional overtones that for both practical and ethical reasons are usually absent in the lab. Another possibility, then, to account for the failure of lab studies to indicate any effect of hypnosis on memory is that hypnosis may improve memory only when the initial learning situation is traumatic, perhaps leading to repression or motivated forgetting.

Intentional Versus Incidental Learning

In crime situations the witness is not specifically asked to pay attention to or to try to memorize anything; any learning that takes place is of an incidental nature. Once again, this differs from the laboratory where most learning studies use an intentional learning paradigm. Could it be the case that hypnosis is only effective in improving the recall of incidentally learned material?

Consequences of Recall

"Witnesses" in a laboratory study know that neither they nor the "offender" will experience the consequences of either a correct or an incorrect judgment. In contrast, a human life could very well depend on the material recalled in a courtroom. This vast difference in the consequences of recall may result in the operation of different basic underlying memory mechanisms, such that hypnosis may have little impact in the benign laboratory setting and yet be of considerable value in the police station.

LABORATORY STUDIES IN MORE REALISTIC SETTINGS

During the past 3 years there have been at least five studies reported that have addressed these very issues and have examined hypnotic hypermnesia under more forensically relevant conditions either by having subjects view a film depicting a crime or an accident or by exposing subjects to a mock crime. Although no one study included all the factors that are typically present in a crime situation but absent from the laboratory situation, across the set of five it is possible to determine the relevancy of these factors for hypnotic memory enhancement.

Nature of the Stimuli Used

In an attempt to use more ecologically valid stimuli, Putnam (1979) had a group of subjects who were highly susceptible to hypnosis view a video tape recording of a car-bicycle accident and then answer a series of questions about the events in the film. Half the subjects were questioned in the waking state and half under hypnosis. Although the stimuli portrayed in the film resembled a real-life situation far more closely than the word lists typically used in laboratory experiments, the subjects in the hypnosis condition showed no better recall than the waking subjects. Similar results are reported in a study by Buckhout and his associates (Buckhout, Eugenio, Licitra, Oliver, & Kramer, Note 1), in which 75 undergraduate students were exposed to a simulated crime within their classroom. Recall for the perpetrator of the crime was tested after a 1-week retention interval either under hypnosis or in the waking state. As in Putnam's study, there was no significant hypnosis effect.

Similar trends appear in a forensically relevant study conducted by McEwan and Yuille (Note 2). The critical event observed by student volunteers, all of whom had previously been diagnosed as having high hypnotic susceptibility, was a 90-sec videotape of a simulated bank robbery. This film was produced by the Vancouver Police Department in conjunction with the Royal Bank of Canada, and is in fact used by the bank to train new tellers. The simulated robbery depicted two men entering a fairly crowded bank, with one pushing his way past the waiting customers to the teller's wicket while the other, armed with a sawed-off shotgun, guarded the entrance. The principal bank robber aimed a revolver at the teller and passed her a note demanding money. After receiving the cash, both men fled. Subjects were interviewed 1 week later, half of them under hypnosis, and were asked a series of questions patterned after a form used by the Vancouver Police Department to obtain suspect descriptions from eyewitnesses. As in the previous studies, recall did not differ in the hypnotic and nonhypnotic conditions. Although it is unrelated to the issue of hypnosis, it is of interest to note that subjects in this study were generally quite accurate (approximately 70%). McEwan and Yuille attribute this good performance to the fact that they used questioning techniques developed by professional interviewers (i.e., the police) rather than the more artificial interviewing methods research psychologists may use.

Such results suggest that it is not merely the use of verbal or nonnatural stimuli that has prevented the emergence of any hypnotic enhancement effect in the laboratory setting. Even with dynamic, relatively lifelike stimulus events, there is no evidence of hypnotic hypermnesia.

Emotional Arousal

Although the inclusion of meaningful, naturalistic stimuli may be a necessary condition for the elicitation of hypnotic hypermnesia, it may not be a sufficient condition. Perhaps hypnosis improves recall only when the meaningful stimuli were originally viewed under stressful conditions. There is some recent evidence that memory for details of an event can be interfered with by the subsequent viewing of a traumatic incident, such as the witnessing of someone being shot (Loftus & Burns, 1982). Perhaps it is in precisely such situations of impaired memory due to trauma that hypnosis may be most beneficial for memory enhancement. To investigate this hypothesis, Zelig and Beidleman (1981) have recently replicated the Putnam study, replacing the film portraying a car-bicycle accident with an 8-minute stress-provoking film. In this film, viewers saw several shocking shop accidents, including a worker having a finger amputated and, in another incident, a piece of wood being ejected from a circular saw and impaling and killing a worker. After seeing the film, half the subjects were hypnotized (all had indicated high hypnotic susceptibility in a pretest 1 week earlier) and then all subjects were asked a series of multiple-choice questions based on the film, the experimental setting, and the physical description of the experimenter who ran the projector. An example of the questions used is, "The victim who was killed by the board was engaged in what activity just prior to the accident? (a) carrying a large piece of plywood; (b) carrying tools; (c) sweeping the floor."

Despite the highly emotional content of the films, creating a level of stress that might be considered comparable to that which a witness experiences in viewing a crime, hypnosis did not enhance recall of factual information. Of the 15 questions asked, subjects were accurate on almost nine questions in both groups, with the two groups displaying comparable confidence levels as well. It might perhaps be argued that hypnosis failed to improve recall because the 20-minute interval between seeing the film and being questioned was simply too short, and that hypnosis is of benefit only when there has been fading of the memory trace. However, in both the Buckhout et al. (Note 1) and the McEwan and Yuille (Note 2) studies described previously, no beneficial effect of hypnosis on recall was found even after a 1-week retention interval, suggesting that the short retention interval alone cannot account for the absence of any effect of hypnosis in this study.

The role of emotional arousal was tested more systematically in a study by DePiano and Salzberg (1981). Using films again, three levels of arousal were induced. A traumatic arousal level considered comparable to that produced in a crime situation was attained through the viewing of a surgical procedure in which surgeons performed a transorbital lobotomy. To determine whether physiological arousal in general or traumatic arousal in particular was the key factor, sexual arousal was created in another group of subjects by showing them a romantic sequence that ended with sexual intercourse. Finally, a low-arousal group watched a film depicting either horses gently running in a field or people socializing, two sequences that had a generally calming effect. Physiological indices of stress such as skin conductance, heart rate, and pulse rate were monitored during the viewing of the films, and provided evidence that the films did indeed cause differential arousal. Subjects attempted recall either under hypnosis or awake. The results with regard to arousal level were clear: Level of arousal did not differentially affect memory, nor did it interact with any hypnosis effect. (The effect of hypnosis per se on recall in this study is discussed below.) Hence, the hypothesis that hypnosis is more likely to benefit memory for stressful events has thus far failed to gain experimental support. Although the possibility exists that it is not memory for stressful events per se that benefits from hypnosis but only memory for those stressful events resulting in repression, this is still an open question, and one that would be extremely difficult to investigate experimentally.

Incidental Versus Intentional Recall

Another suggestion to account for the typical absence of hypnotic hypermnesia in the laboratory in contrast to the apparently beneficial effect of hypnosis in the real world is that events being tested in the real world are learned incidentally; that is, witnesses of a crime rarely attempt memorization intentionally, as they do in the laboratory. The study by DePiano and Salzberg (1981) mentioned previously with regard to level of arousal was addressed to this very issue. Recall was tested not for events portrayed in the film itself, but for various events incidental to the showing of the film. In the rooms in which the subjects viewed the films three posters were hung conspicuously on the walls, and recall of information contained in these posters was one aspect of the incidental information that was later tested. Second, all subjects wore headphones, over which they heard a recorded message about the physiological recording equipment being used to measure arousal level. This message provided the second piece of incidental information to be tested. Finally, before the film was shown there was a supposed audio problem, and subjects listened to a "radio broadcast" while the audio equipment was being repaired. Information from this radio broadcast provided the final incidental material for testing. After viewing the film, all subjects were brought into a second room, randomly assigned to either a hypnosis or no-hypnosis condition, and tested for recall of the three incidental pieces of information. Unlike the results of the previous experiments, in this study the hypnotic recall group displayed better memory for the incidental material than did the nonhypnotized group, even though the latter group received identical task-motivating instructions. Unfortunately, the experimenters did not test for recall of the film itself, so it cannot be determined whether it was the incidental nature of the recalled material that contributed to the improved recall under hypnosis in this study, as the authors argue, or whether some other unknown aspect of the paradigm was responsible for the improvement under hypnosis.

Perceived Consequences of Recall

Despite the use of realistic and even arousal-producing stimuli in the "real-life" studies described above, subjects nonetheless were aware at all times that they were participants in an experiment. In attempting to recognize or describe the "offender" or the "crime" they had no reason to fear either the incrimination of an innocent person or the retribution of an angry suspect. Thus it could very well be that failure to find any benefit of hypnosis in the lab is the result of qualitatively different recall behavior by those subjects relative to witnesses involved in a criminal investigation. Malpass and Devine (1980) have stated the problem as follows: "Without knowledge of whether (or in what ways) awareness of the possible consequences of their actions affect witness's [lineup] decisions, and the ways in which the behavior of experimental 'witnesses' differs from realistic witnesses as a result of these consequences, we cannot evaluate the external validity of eyewitness identification studies" (p. 352). Ideally, then, hypnotic recall should be assessed under situations that subjects believe to have serious consequences. There are as yet no studies of this kind. There are, however, three recent studies that examined the eyewitness behavior of subjects who believed both that they had witnessed a real crime and that their recollections would have serious consequences. The question of interest is whether either the qualitative or the quantitative nature of recall differs in these circumstances from that found in typical laboratory studies. If it does not, there is little reason to believe that hypnosis would differentially affect recall in the laboratory and in the field.

Sanders and Warnick (1981) have compared eyewitness behavior under two different settings, one explicitly experimental with no real-life consequences and the other perceived to be real and to have serious consequences for the witness (loss of time; potential embarrassment), for the offender (his reputation), and for the university (the validity of a scholarship competition). Subjects were led to believe they had accidentally witnessed someone cheating in an important scholarship competition. They were then told either that they were in a psychology experiment (no consequence group) or that someone was actually suspected of cheating (consequence group). All subjects were asked to attempt recognition of the cheater from among a group of semifinalists. To provide more impact, participants in the consequence group were told that if they made an identification they and the experimenter would go to the proctor of the scholarship competition with the information and would then confront the suspected cheater. Analysis of the distribution of correct responses, false identifications, and refusals to make any positive identification showed no significant differences between the consequence and no-consequence conditions. Subjects were just as willing to offer information when it could affect someone's academic standing and the validity of a scholarship competition as they were when it had no consequences at all; there was no difference in the accuracy of their responses in the two cases.

In perhaps the most realistic field study of eyewitness identification, Brigham, Maass, Snyder, and Spaulding (1982) studied a population that is a frequent target of crimes: clerks working in convenience stores in Tallahassee, Florida. This group more closely approximates the typical eyewitness than does the university student population most frequently studied. Two casually dressed male confederates, one black and one white, each visited a total of 63 stores posing as customers. The visits to a given store occurred 5 minutes apart. The visits were 3 to 4 minutes in duration and were designed to be somewhat unusual without being improbable. One customer asked for a pack of cigarettes and then paid entirely with pennies. The second customer carried a product to the counter, discovered he didn't have enough money, fumbled in his pocket for more change, started to the door, found enough change, and came back to the counter to complete the transaction. In addition, each customer asked directions to a fairly distant locale, thereby requiring that the clerk maintain eye contact in order to determine that the instructions were understood. Two hours later two males dressed in suits entered the store, identified themselves to the clerk as law interns with a local law firm, and stated that "We have reason to believe one or both of two people we are interested in may have been in your store within the last 24 hours." They then asked the clerk to attempt an identification from each of two sets of six photographs, one portraying whites, and the other blacks. These photographic lineups were constructed by the personnel at the Tallahassee Police Department who construct such lineups for actual criminal cases. If an identification was made, the clerks were asked whether they were sufficiently certain of their choice to testify in court.

Eyewitness identification in the laboratory has generally been quite poor (see Clifford & Bull, 1978; Loftus, 1979; and Yarmey, 1979 for reviews). Despite both the naturalistic field setting and the assumed serious consequences of identification, the results of this study did not differ significantly from more traditional laboratory studies: overall, the clerks were accurate only 34% of the time, with chance in this situation being 1/6 or 16.7%. In fact, Brigham et al. (1982) reported that whereas original plans for the study had included a group who were to be tested after 24 hours, pilot work at 15 additional stores indicated that at that retention interval the rate of correct identification was at chance. The similarity between eyewitness identification performance in this situation and that found in many laboratory studies suggests that lack of perceived consequences is not a primary determinant of the generally poor performance. Hence, there is little reason to believe that different processing mechanisms that may be more amenable to hypnosis come into play if the consequences of recall are not trivial. One interesting way in which the results of this study did differ from the findings of most laboratory studies is in the relation between confidence and accuracy. In a review of the relevant literature, Deffenbacher (1980) found a significant relationship to exist only under ideal viewing conditions, such as awareness that a future memory test would be given, low stress, ample opportunity to view the target, high familiarity with the target, brief retention interval, and so forth—conditions not typically present in a naturalistic eyewitness situation. Under less optimal conditions that more closely resemble forensically relevant situations, Deffenbacher found no correlation between confidence and accuracy. In contrast to these results, clerks in the Brigham et al. study who felt certain enough of their accuracy to testify in court were accurate 85% of the time, those who were merely "pretty sure" were accurate 55% of the time, and those who "thought" they had the right person were accurate only 28% of the time, leading to a correlation coefficient of .5.

In a third study, specifically designed by Malpass and Devine (1980) to examine the effects of perceived consequences, 200 students attended a lecture on biofeedback techniques and witnessed the following:

> During the lecture a disagreement occurred between one of the investigators and a student volunteer (actually a confederate of the investigators). The disagreement ended in the student pushing over an expensive-appearing rack of electronics equipment and escaping through a rear door. Following the act of vandalism the lecture was discontinued. The witnesses were not informed that the vandalism had been staged and thus they left the lecture believing they had witnessed an actual crime. On the next two days police officers appeared on the campus and held [5-person corporeal] eyewitness identification lineups in a room in the student center. Two uniformed and armed police officers attended the lineups. (p. 352)

In addition to the realism attempted in this study, the severity of the consequences to the offender was directly manipulated by arranging for the witness to overhear a brief conversation between one of the investigators and the police officer in charge of the lineup. In the trivial consequences condition the officer suggested that the student would probably "just get a good talking to from the Dean," whereas in the severe consequences condition it was suggested that "The College will press charges and he'll probably have to pay for the equipment. And prosecution could mean a felony conviction and possibly some time in jail."

The major finding of interest in this study was the differential effect of expected punishment on rate of choosing someone from the lineup: 83% of those in the severe punishment condition made a lineup choice, whereas only 26% of those in the trivial punishment condition made a choice. Apparently in this study the positive value of "getting the guy" overshadowed the negative value of making an identification error. The overall error rate depended on whether the offender was present or absent from the lineup. When the vandal was absent any choice represented an error, so that the error rate was considerably higher in the serious consequence condition. However, when the vandal was present, the severe punishment manipulation led to a decrease in errors because some of the more numerous identifications made were correct. Averaging across the present and absent conditions, the error rate of 48% did not differ for the two seriousness manipulations and was well within the range of errors found in most laboratory studies.

The results of these three studies do not support the hypothesis that processes underlying recall differ when there are perceived serious consequences associated with that recall. Overall accuracy was not quantitatively different from that found in more traditional laboratory studies, and no consistent differences emerged in willingness to choose the offender. (A discussion of changing decision criteria under hypnosis follows below.) Consequently, at this time there is no reason to believe that failure to find hypnotic memory enhancement in the laboratory results from an absence of perceived serious consequences.

In conclusion, of the various possibilities suggested to account for the apparently differential effect of hypnosis in crime and laboratory situations, it appears that it is not simply the failure to use more dynamic, meaningful stimuli to elicit arousal during the viewing of these stimuli or to incorporate perceived serious consequences of recall that can account for the absence of improved recall under hypnosis in the laboratory. The only hypothesis to receive even modest support is the possibility that hypnosis improves memory only for incidentally learned material, and investigation of this effect should certainly be pursued. All in all, however, one is struck by the absence of any strong experimental support for the improvement of memory through hypnosis. Coupled with this failure to find clear beneficial effects of hypnosis for recall is the indication of an important negative effect of hypnosis: increased suggestibility.

Increased Suggestibility Under Hypnosis

Of the five recent real-life studies described above that have used hypnosis, three have examined another issue of great importance to the forensic use of hypnosis to improve memory, namely, the question of whether hypnotized subjects show greater suggestibility than waking subjects. The studies of Putnam (1979), Zelig and Beidleman (1981), and McEwan and Yuille (Note 2), in questioning subjects about the film they had seen, included two types of questions: leading and nonleading. Leading questions were defined as ones that suggested to the subject the occurrence of a particular item or event that had in fact not been present. In the Putnam study, five leading questions were randomly interspersed among the objective questions, and were of the form: "Did you see the stop sign at the intersection?" The correct answer to these questions was always "no." Loftus and Zanni (1975) had previously demonstrated that the inclusion of the definite article "the" in the question frequently misled subjects to assume that the item had in fact been present, and often resulted in their "recalling" that item at a later time. The Loftus and Zanni study had been conducted with nonhypnotized witnesses, and the question of interest was whether hypnosis would serve to further accentuate this suggestibility. In addition to these five leading questions, subjects were given a piece of misinformation in the form of a question that asked whether they had recognized any of the people in the film, such as "the driver of the car, the *blonde* woman who witnessed the accident, or the bicycle rider." The actual hair color of the woman in the film was not blonde. A sixth leading question asked subjects to describe the witness and to specify her hair color. Again, Loftus, Miller, and Burns (1978) had previously demonstrated in nonhypnotized witnesses the incorporation of information from the questions into their memory for the actual event, even when this information was incorrect. After answering each question, subjects indicated their confidence in their answers on a scale of 1 to 5. As mentioned above, in this study hypnotized subjects did no better than waking subjects on the objective, nonleading questions.

For performance on the six leading questions, it was found that hypnotized subjects made more errors; that is, they displayed a greater tendency to say "yes" to the suggestions put forward in the leading questions than did nonhypnotized subjects. Furthermore, although they made more errors, their confidence level was just as high as that of the waking subjects. Similar results were reported by Zelig and Beidleman (1981), who, following the 15 nonleading questions, asked their subjects five leading questions, all of the yes/no format, such as "Did you see the man wearing safety goggles at the beginning of the film?" Again, the correct answer to all these questions was "no." Once more, hypnotized subjects showed greater suggestibility by incorrectly saying "yes" to the leading questions significantly more often than the waking group, while demonstrating a confidence level that was just as high as the nonhypnotized group. Because the confidence displayed by a witness is an important determinant of that witness's credibility (Wells, Lindsay, & Ferguson, 1979), this high confidence for erroneous materials is especially dangerous. Finally, McEwan and Yuille (Note 2) included five leading questions within the total set of 42 questions that subjects were asked concerning the robbery they had witnessed. For example, a question relating to the principal bank robber asked: "Did you notice if his gloves were leather?" when, in fact, he was not wearing gloves. The other four questions were similarly constructed to presuppose either the presence of an article of clothing or the color of an object. As in the other two studies, it was found that hypnotized witnesses were more likely to be affected by the misleading information and to answer these questions incorrectly.

The interpretation of these results should be made with caution, for the studies contain several possible experimental confounds. For example, to be accurate, the leading questions always required a "no" response. Would subjects still have shown significant suggestibility if the correct answer required was "yes?" In other words, are hypnotized subjects more suggestible in general or do they simply have a greater tendency to say "yes"? In the Zelig and Beidleman (1981) study, leading questions were of a different form—the former were in a yes/no format, the latter in a multiple-choice format. Since an effect of hypnosis, albeit a negative one, was found only for the leading questions, it was not possible to determine whether it was the nature of the questions—leading or nonleading—or their format that accounted for the differential results of hypnosis. Finally, no measures of recall performance were taken when the subjects were returned to the waking state. Although they demonstrated greater suggestibility under hypnosis, it is not known to what extent this would have carried over to the waking state. That is, did the hypnotized group have a greater tendency to incorporate misinformation into their memories when they awoke than the control subjects who answered the leading questions in the waking state? Although the demonstration of increased suggestibility under hypnosis is of great interest, a key issue in the courts is whether memory is permanently and irrevocably interfered with because of such suggestibility under hypnosis. The inclusion of an additional recall test following hypnosis would have gone far in answering this question. Nonetheless, this significant trend toward greater suggestibility is an important one for the implications it contains of possible bias in any statements made by a hypnotized witness.

FACTORS IN HYPNOSIS THAT MAY IMPROVE RECALL

Given the lack of any clear experimental support for the enhancement of memory through hypnosis, together with the very real problems of suggestibility and confabulation under hypnosis, it would appear that the courts' reluctance in accepting hypnotically induced evidence is warranted. Yet it is difficult to disregard totally the wealth of anecdotal reports extolling the virtues of hypnotic memory enhancement. Perhaps one way of solving this dilemma is by searching out and isolating those factors in the hypnotic situation that are responsible for improved recall where it seems to occur. If such factors were successfully isolated, they could perhaps be applied under nonhypnotic conditions to enhance the memory of witnesses. Several factors that present themselves as possible candidates are discussed below.

Criterion Change

According to signal-detection theory, perception of an event does not occur passively, but rather involves an active process of decision making on the part of the observer. So, for example, a vital component in the process of detecting a stimulus is deciding whether a given internal level of activation resulted from the occurrence of a true signal or random firing in the neural network (Green & Swets, 1966). Because random firing provides a background of noise against which all signals are received, observers must adopt a cut-off point or criterion level for their decisions, deciding that any level of activity beyond that point will be responded to as a true event in the world, and that any level of activity below that point will be considered noise not to be acted on. Activation of memory traces may receive similar analysis, with weak memories providing signals whose level of strength or activation differs very little from that of the background (Wickelgren, 1979). In applying the concepts of signal detection theory to an eyewitness identification context, Malpass and Devine (1980) have pointed out that there is a sharp distinction between an observer's actual ability to identify the person previously seen (the strength of vividness of the memory) and the observer's identification *decision criterion*, which they define as "the strength or vividness of recollection an observer requires before being willing to report that a given person is the person who was previously seen performing an offense." The theory of signal detection suggests that the particular criterion an observer adopts depends on the payoff—both rewards and punishments—associated with each of the four possible outcomes: a "hit" or correct identification, a "false alarm" or false identification, a "miss' or false rejection, and a correct rejection. Malpass and Devine have suggested some of the positive and negative factors that could enter into such a payoff matrix, a copy of which is reproduced in Table 3. The value of making an identification is found by summing the values of a hit and a false identification, and the value of not making an identification is found by summing the values of a correct rejection and a false rejection.

TABLE 6.3

Payoff Matrix Associated with Choosing an Offender from
a Lineup (from Malpass and Devine, 1980, p. 354)

Witness's response	States of the world	
	The best candidate in the lineup is the offender	The best candidate in the lineup is not the offender
Choose the best candidate in the lineup	Correct identification Consequences: catch a criminal (+); look good to authorities (+); spend time in court (−); face the criminal and family (−); fear retribution (−); get even for offense (+).	False identification Consequences: look stupid (−); cause wrongful imprisonment (−); have to face innocent person (−); be on losing side in court (−); guilty person running free (−).
Do not choose the best candidate in the lineup	False rejection Consequences appear uncooperative (−); offender goes unpunished (−); offender may commit other crime (−); look stupid if he's guilty (−); get out of further involvement (+); investigation continues wrongly (−).	Correct rejection Consequences: search for guilty continues (+); not implicating innocent persons (+); avoid unnecessary legal proceeding (+); looking good to authorities (+); disagree with police ideas about who's guilty (−); appear uncooperative (−).

Note: + = positive aspect associated with choice; − = negative aspect associated with choice. From "Realism and Eyewitness Identification Research," by R. S. Malpass and P. G. Devine, *Law and Human Behavior*, 1980, 4, 347-357. Copyright 1980 by Plenum Publishing Corporation. Reprinted by permission.

Consider now the situation in which recall of a witnessed crime is very poor; that is, the type of situation in which police are most likely to suggest hypnosis. Applying a signal detection theory analysis, false alarms or confabulations occur when the subjects erroneously select a message from the background noise, mistaking it for a signal, that is, for the memory of the actual event. To avoid such errors the typical strategy of normal recall is to adopt a cut-off point of criterion level that is sufficiently stringent to assure that false alarms are minimized. Unless the strength of a trace is well beyond that of the background, it is not reported. Weak signals, because they could well be merely background noise, are disregarded.

Although such a mode of operating ensures that there will be few confabulations or false alarms, it also means that the recaller will reject weak signals that may in fact represent true memories, thereby leading to more misses and hence to the generation of less potentially useful information in a criminal investigation. Several theorists (e.g., Orne, 1979; DePiano & Salzberg, 1981) have suggested that when hypnosis produces an increase in recall it does so by encouraging subjects to lower the criterion level, thereby allowing previously unacceptable weak memories to be reported. Following the payoff matrix suggested by Malpass and Devine, under hypnosis there may be a relative reweighting of rewards and punishments, making the positive value associated with a correct identification of even greater value while reducing the negative value associated with a false identification, thereby giving a relatively greater total value to attempting a recall. Further, the strong interpersonal relationship established with the hypnotist may make the present social situation of greater salience than possible future consequences for both the witness and the suspect. Some evidence for this greater willingness to hazard a guess under hypnosis is provided by Buckhout et al. (1981), who found that although not a single witness was able to correctly recall the shirt number of the perpetrator of a mock crime, 90% of the hypnotized witnesses were motivated to try to recall the number, compared with only 20% in the control group. The authors interpreted this finding to mean "that hypnotized witnesses felt that they had a sanction to guess, even if they had no memory of certain critical details" (p. 69).

If hypnosis increases the amount of material recalled by causing subjects to lower the criterion, it may be possible to elicit the greater recall frequently reported under hypnosis simply by instructing subjects to adopt a very lax or lenient criterion. In a variety of laboratory studies using both detection and memory paradigms, subjects have shown themselves capable of adjusting their criterion levels (see Murdock, 1974, for a general review). There is some evidence that this can also be accomplished by witnesses attempting to remember incidents from a crime situation by encouraging them to "guess" (Hastie, Landsman, & Loftus, 1978). However, such a procedure is not without dangers of its own. To study the impact of guessing, Hastie et al. (1978) urged some of the students who had previously viewed a series of slides depicting a street crime to guess about information contained in those slides on questions where they were uncertain. For example, they were asked to guess an answer to the question "What color was the station wagon that passed the accident?" (In fact, there had not been a station wagon present.) This may be considered comparable to what subjects are doing under hypnosis when they are encouraged to make overt any guesses at all which they may have relating to the crime. Relative to control subjects, those who guessed were more likely to commit false alarms on a later test; that is, to report that there *had* been a station wagon present. Hastie et al. suggested that the very process of guessing actually causes a change in the memorial representation of "filling in" gaps in memory, with the result that the material guessed at is incorporated into memory, thereby becoming indistinguishable from events that actually occurred. Further, although the initial guess was typically made with low confidence, confidence level was found to rise on the later recall test.

Thus even without the use of hypnosis, simply encouraging witnesses to lower their criterion level and hazard a guess brings about at least one of the problems associated with hypnosis: increased false alarms or confabulations. Perhaps the only advantage to encouraging witnesses to lower their criterion is that one of the benefits of hypnosis, the generating of leads in a situation where there is otherwise no information available, could be achieved without the accompanying biasing effect of increased suggestibility inherent in the hypnotic situation, and without endangering the future eligibility of the witness to take the stand in court.

Reinstatement of Context

Several recent studies suggest that providing information about the context in which an event initially appeared can improve recollection of that event, information such as physical location, room size, objects and persons present, odors, sounds, temperature, lighting and so on (Smith, 1979). In one group of studies, this contextual information was provided by reinstating the original environment in which the material was learned. Thus, for example, Gooden and Baddeley (1975) compared the recall of scuba divers on dry land and underwater for word lists originally learned in either the same or the alternative environment. Recall was significantly improved when learning and test environments were the same. Similarly, if subjects studied two lists of words in two different rooms and were later tested in one of these two environments, words were remembered best when tested in the room in which the list had originally been studied (Smith, Glenberg, & Bjork, 1978; Smith, 1979). Of perhaps greater forensic interest, reinstatement of context has been shown to aid recognition of faces as well. Watkins, Ho, and Tulving (1976) manipulated context by testing the recognition of a face either in the presence of the face or descriptive phrase with which it had been paired during study (same context) or with a different face or phrase (different context), and found clear evidence of memory enhancement in the same context condition. Results similar to those of Watkins et al. have been reported in a situation where pairs of faces were studied as male-female couples (Winograd & Rivers-Bulkeley, 1977): Changing context from study to test either by deletion or substitution of context significantly impaired face recognition.[2]

In the studies described above, memory for critical stimuli was tested with the actual study context present. Must context be physically present for enhancement to occur? Some suggestion that it need not be is provided in the ancient mnemonic method of loci, in which an individual imagined that various items to be learned were located in different physical locations or loci. Recall was accomplished by visualizing each location and thereby discovering the object

(Norman, 1976, chapter 7). Experimental attempts to improve memory by having subjects imagine the original viewing situation have yielded mixed results. As described earlier in discussion on the Dhanens and Lundy (1975) study, nonhypnotized subjects who received regression instructions to picture themselves back in time experiencing the situation as if they were once more in it did no better in recalling than did the control subjects. However, more promising findings have been reported in several recent studies. Smith (1979) found that when subjects were tested in an environment different from their study environment, instructions to remember the study environment facilitated recall just as effectively as returning them to that environment. Whereas this study used traditional laboratory stimuli (lists of words), which limits its forensic relevance, similar results have been reported by Malpass and Devine (1981) in a real-life crime situation. A staged act of vandalism was viewed by 72 witnesses who attempted, 5 months later, to select the perpetrator of the crime from photographic lineups. Prior to making the selection, half the witnesses were reminded of the events of the evening of the vandalism in a detailed guided memory interview in which their feelings, their memory both of details in the room and of the vandal, and their immediate reactions to the events were all explored. Context reinstatement through this guided memory procedure increased the rate of accuracy from 40% to 60%, a substantial improvement in recognition accuracy after a 5-month delay. Further, the guided memory procedure appeared to have no biasing effects, in that it had no effect on either the rate of choosing or the type of errors subjects made in making their selection. A critical component of contextual enhancement may be the reinstatement of the original mood of the observer in the learning situation. In a variety of studies (e.g., Bower, 1981), Bower and his colleagues have demonstrated that recall is better when the mood subjects experienced during learning is reinstated during recall. Interestingly, this mood reinstatement is frequently accomplished through hypnosis, though other means have also been used.

If one of the important elements of improved recall under hypnosis is the reinstatement of context that is frequently used, particularly in age regression, use of contextual reinstatement without hypnosis may be sufficient to enhance memory, thereby eliminating the problems of hypnotic bias.

Experimental Hypermnesia

When a subject who has attempted to recall everything he or she can about an event is asked after some period of time to attempt yet another recall, it is frequently observed that more information is indeed retrieved, particularly when pictorial stimuli are used (Erdelyi & Klienbard, 1978). This phenomenon of improved recall with repeated testing is called "hypermnesia," and it may well be that part of the improved recall attributed to hypnosis may simply result from the fact that subjects are attempting a second or third recall of previously inaccessible information, a situation that leads to hypermnesia even in the absence of hypnosis. Of theoretical interest is the observation that the improved recall of hypermnesia is not due to the mere passage of time, but is directly related to the act of recalling. With retention interval held constant, recall increases directly with the number of recall tests administered, perhaps because repeated testing leads to the more efficient organization and retrieval of recalled material (Roediger & Payne, 1982). Erdelyi and Kleinbard (1978) suggest that hypermnesia is most effective when meaningful, imagistic stimuli are used, and therefore argue that hypermnesia would be most likely to operate when dealing with "complex, real-life stimuli, which inevitably are imagistic" (p. 277). These are, of course, the very type of stimuli that subjects are attempting to recall under hypnosis in the crime situation. An important component of hypermnesia appears to be the evocation of imagery in subjects attempting recall, again, an instruction frequently included in hypnosis instruction.

It may be that the use of repeated testing sessions together with an emphasis on imagery may produce most of the memory enhancement attributed to hypnosis. At any rate, the occurrence of hypermnesia has direct implications for questioning of witnesses: Repeated interrogation sessions should be used, thereby increasing the possibility that previously inaccessible information will become available for recall. A word of caution is needed, however. A recent study by Eugenio, Buckhout, Kostes, and Ellison (1982), in which subjects were questioned repeatedly, indicated an increase in confabulation resulting from the strong pressure to keep producing more information. Clifford and Bull (1978) have described the witness response to interrogation as follows:

> under interrogative report he will be asked questions to which he has no relevant memory, but because he is being asked by an authority figure an answer is likely to be given; also, by the very fact of being asked a question the implication is that he ought to know the answer, and is considered capable of giving it. When an answer has been given, however uncertainly and haltingly, it becomes a "fact" and the witness leaves all doubt behind and accepts his output as the outcome of genuine recall, and this is especially the case if the interrogator seems pleased with the answer and goes on to ask further, consecutive, or follow-up questions. (p. 156)

If the interrogation is aimed primarily at the generation of possible leads, no matter how remote, the occurrence of such confabulation may be relatively unimportant. If the witness is to testify in court, however, this confabulation represents a serious problem. A second problem of repeated testing is related to the subjects' subjective feelings of certainty. When a witness recalls an event repeatedly, there occurs a ritualization or formalization of responses (Bartlett, 1932), accompanied by an increase in confidence concerning the accuracy of the recollection. Of greatest importance, this increase in confidence occurs regardless of whether or not the recollection is in fact accurate (Hastie et al., 1978). Given the powerful correlation between confidence and credibility, this increase in confidence is a grave danger. Finally, whether a witness is questioned repeatedly or only once, the effect of interrogation per se can influence what it is the witness will recall at a later time. Hilgard and Loftus (1979), discussing the influence question format can have on both the quality and quantity of information a witness reports, suggested that free recall—the report which a witness gives when asked simply to report whatever he or she can remember about an event—results in the highest accuracy but lowest quality of recall. As increasingly specific questions are asked, amount recalled goes up, but at the cost of overall accuracy. An additional problem arises when specific questions are asked: an increase in suggestibility, defined as the inclusion of information transmitted by the interrogator into the witness's recall. Associated with the impact of interrogation per se is the effect of briefing on memory. In a study by Wells, Ferguson, and Lindsay (1981), eyewitnesses to a staged crime were briefed by a "prosecutor" who suggested they rehearse answers to potential questions that would be asked under cross-examination. Not only did briefed witnesses rate themselves as more confident that they had identified the thief than did nonbriefed witnesses, but they were also more successful in convincing subject-jurors of the guilt of the thief. This was true regardless of whether the witnesses were right or wrong in their identification! Clearly, the entire question of the effect both of questioning and of briefing is an important one, and worthy of extensive research.

JUDICIAL ACCEPTANCE OF HYPNOTIC MEMORY ENHANCEMENT

Historically, forensic interest was related primarily to whether an individual could be compelled to carry out antisocial behavior under hypnosis, with the consequent question of legal responsibility (Orne, 1979). More recently, there has been an upsurge of legal cases in which hypnosis has been used in at least four different ways (Bryan, 1962, cited in Hayward & Ashworth, 1980). The first of these is in voir dire of jury challenge, whereby the hypnotic screening of potential jurors may be used in an attempt to detect prejudices or other personality characteristics that could have some relevance to jury deliberations. A second use is related to mens rea and the possible role of hypnosis in investigating either the mental state of an accused individual at the time of the alleged crime or his or her possible motive. A third recent use of hypnosis has been in the preparation of nervous witnesses for cross-examination. Apparently the posthypnotic suggestion to relax permits a witness to withstand the stress of cross-examination and to give evidence with maximum effectiveness. It is the fourth capacity, improving the process of remembering, in which hypnosis has had its greatest impact and that has generated the greatest judicial controversy (Diamond, 1980).

Within the judicial system, the question of the admissibility of evidence induced by hypnosis has arisen primarily in two contexts. The first relates to the truth of a statement made under hypnosis, most typically by a defendant. Thus, for example, in one of the earliest cases involving hypnosis (*People v. Ebanks*, 1897), the defense attempted to introduce as testimony a statement made by the defendant while under hypnosis in which he denied any guilt in the murder of which he was accused. The decision of the court at that time was that "The law of the United States does not recognize hypnotism" (p. 1053), and based on the most recent judicial statement on hypnosis, made in March 1982 by the California Supreme Court (*People v. Shirley*, 1982), this is still the case: "It appears to be the rule in all jurisdictions in which the matter has been considered that statements made under hypnosis may not be introduced to prove the truth of the matter asserted because the reliability of such statements is questionable" (p. 33). It is thus generally accepted by the courts that hypnotism does not act as a truth serum, and that individuals are capable of lying or distorting the truth for their own good purposes even under hypnosis. In contrast, the law with respect to the use of hypnosis for memory enhancement is still in a state of flux. The seminal case in this regard was that of *Harding v. State* (1968), in which the court held that the fact that evidence was obtained under hypnosis went to the weight but not the admissibility of the evidence, with the result that cross-examination was considered an adequate test of the witness's credibility. Throughout the next decade, however, there was growing judicial awareness of the danger of suggestibility inherent in using hypnosis, a danger that could not necessarily be overcome through cross-examination because the witness believed totally that the suggested event did indeed happen. To forestall these dangers, an increasingly elaborate set of procedural "safeguards" developed, as outlined in State v. Hurd (1981). These safeguards required, for example, that the trial court evaluate both the specific hypnotic techniques used, as well as the degree of hypnotic susceptibility of the witness, since people capable of entering deeper trances may be more suggestible. Further, it was the burden of the party offering the testimony to prove compliance with six procedural requirements suggested by Dr. Martin Orne (State v. Hurd, 1981).

The increasing complexity of these safeguards has led the California Supreme Court to argue that their use, by adding considerably to both the time and expense of trial, has made "the game not worth the candle" (People v. Shirley, 1982, p. 40). Instead, they fall back on the Frye rule (Frye v. United States, 1923), which states that for a scientific procedure to be admissible, it must be generally acceptable as reliable in the relevant scientific community. Considering the review of recent experimental studies of hypnotic memory enhancement presented here, it is obvious that such a state of acceptability simply does not exist at present. If hypnosis is to be used forensically to improve memory, it must be established beyond a doubt that (a) hypnosis can improve memory, and (b) it is possible in some way to differentiate between valid memories and confabulations. Clearly, further research is required before hypnosis can safely be used to enhance the memories of witnesses.

SUMMARY

Despite the publication of a large number of case studies in which hypnosis has apparently been invaluable in the solving of a crime, experimental attempts to demonstrate improved memory under hypnosis have thus far not been successful. It has been suggested that the failure of laboratory studies to demonstrate hypnotic memory enhancement may result from the absence of certain essential features present in the crime situation, such as meaningful, dynamic stimulus materials, high emotional arousal, and the realization that a human life may depend on what is recalled. Furthermore, the study of stimulus events in the crime situation is rarely done intentionally, as it is in the laboratory. However, several recent laboratory studies that have attempted to include these very characteristics nonetheless persist in failing to demonstrate hypnotic memory enhancement. One exception worth pursuing is the suggestion of improved recall under hypnosis for incidentally learned materials. What these studies do demonstrate quite clearly, however, is that when witnesses are interrogated under hypnosis they are more suggestible, showing a greater tendency to agree with the interrogator. Because of this problem, and an apparent trend for the courts to reject the testimony of witnesses who have undergone hypnosis, a search for nonhypnotic procedures of memory enhancement appears warranted. Three factors that may be responsible for the improved memory under hypnosis reported in so many anecdotes were suggested: (a) encouraging witnesses to lower their criterion level during memory retrieval; (b) contextual reinstatement via a guided memory procedure; and (c) repeated testing sessions that allow for the occurrence of experimental hypermnesia. If witnesses to a crime may be helped to remember the details of the crime through the application of these procedures without hypnosis, the benefits of memory enhancement could be achieved without the problematic effects of bias inherent in hypnosis. Further research to investigate these factors is required.

NOTES

1. *Waking state* in this paper is used merely to indicate the normal nonhypnotic state. It is not meant to imply the necessary existence of a sleep-like or trance state in hypnosis.
2. Although Bower and Karlin (1974) failed to demonstrate a statistically significant effect of context on the recognition of faces, Watkins et al. (1976) suggested that this failure might have resulted from the inclusion of too few observations per condition in the study.

REFERENCE NOTES

1. Buckhout, R., Eugenio, P., Licitra, T., Oliver, L., & Kramer, T. H. *Hypnosis and eyewitness memory: The effects of unintentional bias.* Paper presented at the annual meeting of the American Psychological Association, Washington, DC, August 1982.
2. McEwan, N. H., & Yuille, J. C. *The effect of hypnosis as an interview technique on eyewitness memory.* Paper presented at the annual meeting of the Canadian Psychological Association, Montreal, Quebec, June 1982.

REFERENCES

Arons, H. *Hypnosis in criminal investigations.* Springfield, Ill.: Charles C Thomas, 1967.

Ault, R. L. F.B.I. guidelines for the use of hypnosis. *International Journal of Clinical and Experimental Hypnosis,* 1979, *27,* 499-451.

Ault, R. L. Hypnosis: The F.B.I.'s team approach. *F.B.I. Law Enforcement Bulletin,* January, 1980.

Barber, T. X., & Calverley, D. S. Effects on recall of hypnotic induction, motivational suggestions and suggested regression: A methodological and experimental analysis. *Journal of Abnormal Psychology,* 1966, *71,* 169-180.

Bartlett, F. C. *Remembering: A study in experimental and social psychology.* London: Cambridge University Press, 1932.

Bower, G. H. Mood and memory. *American Psychologist,* 1981, *36*(2), 129-148.

Bower, G. H., & Karlin, M. B. Depth of processing pictures of faces and recognition memory. *Journal of Experimental Psychology,* 1974, *103,* 751-757.

Brigham, J. C., Maass, A., Snyder, L. D., & Spaulding, K. Accuracy of eyewitness identifications in a field setting. *Journal of Personality and Social Psychology,* 1982, *42,* 673-681.

Buckhout, R., Eugenio, P., Licitra, T., Oliver, L., & Kramer, T. H. Memory, hypnosis and evidence: Research on eyewitnesses. *Social Action and the Law,* 1981, *7*(5 & 6), 67-72.

Clifford, B. R., & Bull, R. *The psychology of person identification.* London: Routledge & Kegan Paul, 1978.

Cooper, L. M., & London, P. Reactivation of memory by hypnosis and suggestion. *International Journal of Clinical and Experimental Hypnosis,* 1073, *21,* 312-323.

Deffenbacher, K. Eyewitness accuracy and confidence: Can we infer anything about their relationship? *Law and Human Behavior,* 1980, *4,* 243-260.

DePiano, F. & Salzberg, H. C. Hypnosis as an aid to recall of meaningful information presented under three types of arousal. *International Journal of Clinical and Experimental Hypnosis,* 1981, *29,* 383-400.

Dhanens, T. P., & Lundy, R. M. Hypnotic and waking suggestions and recall. *International Journal of Clinical and Experimental Hypnosis,* 1975, *23,* 68-79.

Diamond, B. L. Inherent problems in the use of pretrial hypnosis on a prospective witness. *California Law Review,* 1980, *68,* 313-349.

Eugenio, P., Buckhout, R., Kostes, S., & Ellison, K. W. Hypermnesia in the eyewitness to a crime. *Bulletin of the Psychonomic Society,* 1982, *19,* 83-86.

Erdelyi, M. H., & Kleinbard, J. Has Ebbinghaus decayed with time? The growth of recall (hypermnesia) over days. *Journal of Experimental Psychology: Human Learning and Memory,* 1978, *4,* 275-289.

Frye v. United States, 293 F. 1013 (D.C. Cir. 1923).

Godden, D. R., & Braddeley, A. D. Context-dependent memory in two natural environments: On land and underwater. *British Journal of Psychology,* 1975, *66,* 325-331.

Green, D. M., & Swets, J. A. *Signal detection theory and psychophysics.* New York: Wiley, 1966.

Harding v. State, 5 Md. App. 230 [246 A.2d 302] (1968).

Hastie, R., Landsman, R., & Loftus, E. F. Eyewitness testimony: The dangers of guessing. *Jurimetrics Journal,* 1978, *19,* 1-8.

Hayward, L., & Ashworth, A. Some problems of evidence obtained by hypnosis. *Criminal Law Review*, 1980, 469-485.

Hilgard, E. R. *Hypnotic susceptibility.* New York: Harcourt, Brace & World, 1965.

Hilgard, E. R., & Loftus, E. Effective interrogation of the eyewitness. *International Journal of Clinical and Experimental Hypnosis*, 1979, *27*, 342-357.

Hintzman, D. L. *The psychology of learning and memory.* San Francisco: W. H. Freeman, 1978.

Kroger, W. S., & Douce, R. G. Hypnosis in criminal investigation. *International Journal of Clinical and Experimental Hypnosis*, 1979, *27*, 358-374.

Loftus, E. F. Leading questions and the eyewitness report. *Cognitive Psychology*, 1975, *7*, 560-572.

Loftus, E. F. *Eyewitness testimony.* Cambridge, Mass.: Harvard University Press, 1979.

Loftus, E. F., & Burns, T. E. Mental shock can produce retrograde amnesia. *Memory and Cognition*, 1982, *10*, 318-323.

Loftus, E. F., & Loftus, G. R. On the permanence of stored information in the human brain. *American Psychologist*, 1980, *35*, 409-420.

Loftus, E. F., Miller, D. G., & Burns, H. J. Semantic integration of verbal information into a visual memory. *Journal of Experimental Psychology: Human Learning and Memory*, 1978, *4*, (1), 19-31.

Loftus, E. F., & Zanni, G. Eyewitness testimony: The influence of the wording of a question. *Bulletin of the Psychonomic Society*, 1975, *5*, 86-88.

Malpass, R. S., & Devine, P. G. Realism and eyewitness identification research. *Law and Human Behavior*, 1980, *4*, 347-357.

Malpass, R. S., & Devine, P. G. Guided memory in eyewitness identification. *Journal of Applied Psychology*, 1980, *66*, 343-350.

Minnesota v. Mack, Minn, 292 N.W.2d 764 (1980).

Murdock, B. B. *Human memory: Theory and data.* Potomac, Md: Erlbaum, 1974.

Norman, D. A. *Memory and attention* (2nd ed.). New York: Wiley, 1976.

O'Connell, D. N., Shor, R. E., & Orne, M. T. Hypnotic age regression: An empirical and methodological analysis. *Journal of Abnormal Psychology Monograph*, 1970, *76*(3, Pt. 2).

Orne, M. T. The use and misuse of hypnosis in court. *International Journal of Clinical and Experimental Hypnosis*, 1979, *27*, 311-374.

People v. Ebanks, 117 Cal. 652. 40 P. 1049 (1897).

People v. Shirley, Crim. No. 21775, Mar. 11, 1982; 31 Cal. 3d 18.

People v. Woods et al., No. 63187ABNC (Alameda Co., Cal., December, 15, 1977).

Polk v. State Md. Appl., 427 A.2d 1041 (1981).

Putnam, W. H. Hypnosis and distortions in eyewitness memory. *International Journal of Clinical and Experimental Hypnosis*, 1979, *27*, 437-448.

Reiser, M. Hypnosis as a tool in criminal investigation. *The Police Chief*, 1976, *43*(11), 39-40.

Roediger, H. L., & Payne, D. G. Hypermnesia: The role of repeated testing. *Journal of Experimental Psychology: Learning, Memory, and Cognition*, 1982, *8*, 66-72.

Sanders, G. S., & Warnick, D. H. Truth and consequences: The effects of responsibility on eyewitness behavior. *Basic and Applied Social Psychology,* 1981, *2,* 67-79.

Sears, A. B. A comparison of hypnotic and waking recall. *International Journal of Clinical and Experimental Hypnosis,* 1954, *2,* 296-304.

Smith, S. M. Remembering in and out of context. *Journal of Experimental Psychology: Human Learning and Memory,* 1979, *5,* 460-471.

Smith, S. M., Glenberg, A., & Bjork, R. A. Environmental context and human memory. *Memory and Cognition,* 1978, *6,* 342-353.

State v. Hurd, 86 N.J. 525 [432 A.2d 86] (1981).

Teitelbaum, M. *Hypnosis induction techniques.* Springfield, Ill.: Charles C Thomas, 1969.

The trials of hypnosis. *Newsweek,* October 19, 1981, p. 96.

Watkins, M. J., Ho, E., & Tulving, E. Context effects in recognition memory for faces. *Journal of Verbal Learning and Verbal Behavior,* 1976, *15,* 505-517.

Wells, G. L., Ferguson, T. J., & Lindsay, R. C. L. The tractability of eyewitness confidence and its implications for triers of fact. *Journal of Applied Psychology,* 1981, *66,* 688-696.

Wells, G. L., Lindsay, R. C. L., & Ferguson, T. J. Accuracy, confidence and juror perceptions in eyewitness identification. *Journal of Applied Psychology,* 1979, *64,* 440-448.

Wickelgren, W. A. *Cognitive psychology.* Englewood Cliffs, N.J.: Prentice-Hall, 1979.

Winograd, E., & Rivers-Bulkeley, N. T. Effects of changing context on remembering faces. *Journal of Experimental Psychology: Human Learning and Memory,* 1977, *3,* 397-405.

Worthington, T. S. The use in court of hypnotically enhanced testimony. *International Journal of Clinical and Experimental Hypnosis,* 1979, *27,* 402-416.

Yarmey, A. D. *The psychology of eyewitness testimony.* New York: Free Press, 1979.

Zelig, M., & Beidleman, W. B. The investigative use of hypnosis: A word of caution. *The International Journal of Clinical and Experimental Hypnosis,* 1981, *29*(4), 401-412.

7

EYEWITNESS MEMORY ENHANCEMENT IN THE POLICE INTERVIEW
Cognitive Retrieval Mnemonics Versus Hypnosis

R. EDWARD GEISELMAN
University of California, Los Angeles
RONALD P. FISHER
Florida International University
DAVID P. MacKINNON
HEIDI L. HOLLAND
University of California, Los Angeles

The Rand Corporation (1975), in a comprehensive study of criminal-investigation processes, reported that the principal determinant of whether or not a case is solved is the completeness and accuracy of the

Author's Note. This research was supported by a grant from the National Institute of Justice (USDJ-83-IJ-CX-0025). We thank the 17 law-enforcement volunteers who served as the interviewers and Lisa Hutton, Diane Sindel, Kim O'Reilly, Robin Cohen, and Phil Garnier, who played integral roles in the conduct and analysis of the experiment. We

eyewitness account. Nevertheless, eyewitness reports are known to be incomplete, unreliable, partially constructed (confabulated), and malleable during the questioning procedure (Clifford & Hollin, 1983; Loftus, 1975, 1979; Loftus, Miller, & Burns, 1978; Wells, Ferguson, & Lindsay, 1981). The purpose of the present study, therefore, was to suggest methods to enhance the accuracy of eyewitness reports and to test these methods empirically in a controlled, yet ecologically valid, laboratory setting.

Research on eyewitness memory retrieval has produced few positive suggestions for law-enforcement personnel. Two notable exceptions involve the ordering of the questions to be asked during the interview and the phrasing of the questions. First, witnesses should be asked to report the incident in their own words before being asked any specific questions (Geiselman et al., 1984; Hilgard & Loftus, 1979; Timm, 1983). This procedure reduces the possibility of the interviewer leading the witness, and the information given by a witness during a free report has been found to be more accurate, although more incomplete, than information given in response to specific questions. Second, to further avoid leading the witness, the specific questions should be phrased using indefinite articles rather than definite articles (Loftus & Zanni, 1975). A third, guided-memory technique was shown to facilitate eyewitness recognition performance in lineup procedures (Malpass & Devine, 1981); but with the exception of Geiselman et al. (1984), little has been done to follow up on such memory-enhancement techniques.

Otherwise, as noted by Clifford and Lloyd-Bostock (1983), "The work in the eyewitness field [has been] essentially negativistic. . . . In short, the witness [has been] shown to be a somewhat pathetic figure in the face of extramemorial factors occurring at encoding, during storage or at retrieval" (p. 286). Yuille (1980) has proposed that considerable effort now be focused on how we can improve eyewitness performance. Wells (1978) made a similar argument with his distinction between variables that can be manipulated to reduce eyewitness fallibility (system variables) and those that cannot be controlled in actual crime cases (estimator variables). He concluded that system-variable research has greater potential for positive contributions to criminal justice.

also express our appreciation to the Los Angeles Police Department and the Inglewood Police Department for their cooperation in this project. Requests for reprints should be sent to R. Edward Geiselman, Department of Psychology, University of California, Los Angeles, California 90024.

From *Journal of Applied Psychology*, 1985, 70(2), 401-412. Copyright 1985 by the American Psychological Association. Reprinted by permission of the publisher and authors.

One dramatic technique for eyewitness memory enhancement is the hypnosis interview. Hypnosis has been reported to be useful in criminal cases (Reiser, 1974, 1976; Resier & Nielsen, 1980; Schafer & Rubio, 1978; Stratton, 1977), especially when trauma to the witness is involved. Enhanced memory under hypnosis also obtains in some controlled laboratory experiments (DePiano & Salzberg, 1981; Griffin, 1980; Stager & Lundy, 1985). On the whole, though, the evidence about memory under hypnosis is mixed. Many studies find no memory enhancement with hypnosis (see M. Smith, 1983, for a review). Of greater practical consequence, hypnosis may distort the memory process. It has been suggested that hypnotized subjects (a) introduce fabrication into their reports and exhibit increased error rates (Diamond, 1980; Dywan & Bowers, 1984; Orne, 1979), (b) are more susceptible to leading questions (Putnam, 1979; Sanders & Simmons, 1983), and (c) are more likely to view distorted memories as being accurate (Orne, 1961; Sheehan & Tilden, 1983). In addition, the accuracy of information generated under hypnosis appears to be unrelated to the witnesses' confidence in the information (Zelig & Beidleman, 1981). The case against hypnosis also is equivocal, as some researchers have found hypnosis to improve memory without showing increased confabulation or greater susceptibility to misleading questions (Griffin, 1980; Stager & Lundy, 1985). Furthermore, even nonhypnotized witnesses are highly subject to memory alterations (Loftus, 1979; Timm, 1981, 1983; Wells et al., 1981), and nonhypnotized witnesses are often inaccurate about the quality of their reports (Deffenbacher, 1980; Wells & Lindsay, 1983). Nevertheless, as a general safeguard against the potential problems encountered with memory under hypnosis, several United States states have placed some restrictions on the admissibility of hypnosis recall in a court of law.

In light of the legal problems and the tenuous empirical support for the hypnosis interview, we set out to develop nonhypnotic mnemonics to assist police in interviewing eyewitnesses. Over the course of the last 2,000 years, persons interested in memory enhancement have developed a variety of mnemonics, ranging from the Greeks' use of imagery (method of loci) to the more modern notions of depth of processing and organization. And, whereas these mnemonics have proven effective in many learning tasks, they are inappropriate for police investigation because they must be employed at the encoding or acquisition stage. In the typical crime scenario, the events unfold rapidly under emotionally charged conditions. Eyewitness attention is most likely narrow in focus, and eyewitness memory is incidental. Therefore, effective memory search procedures are required. Our focus, then, was to develop mnemonics that could be used to facilitate the retrieval stage.

The theoretical underpinnings that guided our thinking are based on two generally accepted principles of memory. First, the memory trace is composed of several features (Bower, 1967; Underwood, 1969; Wickens, 1970), and the effectiveness of a retrieval cue is related to the amount of feature overlap with the encoded event (Flexser & Tulving, 1978). Second, there may be several retrieval paths to the encoded event, so that information not accessible with one retrieval cue may be accessible with a different cue (Tulving, 1974). Based on this theoretical framework, Geiselman et al. (1984) developed a memory-retrieval procedure for eyewitnesses called the cognitive interview that consists of four retrieval mnemonics. Of these, two attempt to increase the feature overlap between encoding and retrieval contexts: (a) mentally reinstating the environmental and personal context that existed at the time of the crime (Bower, Gilligan, & Monteiro, 1981; Malpass & Devine, 1981; S. Smith, 1979) and (b) reporting everything, even partial information, regardless of the perceived importance of the information (M. Smith, 1983). The other two mnemonics encourage using many retrieval paths: (c) recounting the events in a variety of orders (Burns, 1981; Whitten & Leonard, 1981), and (d) reporting the events from a variety of perspectives (Anderson & Pichert, 1978; Firstenberg, 1983).

The cognitive interview was evaluated positively in a preliminary experiment conducted by Geiselman et al. (1984). In that research, actors disrupted a classroom situation and the students were interviewed subsequently as eyewitnesses via a questionnaire. Students who were instructed in the four memory retrieval mnemonics at the time of test recalled more correct information about the incident than did subjects who were told simply to keep trying to remember more information. Furthermore, the cognitive interview showed none of the drawbacks sometimes found with hypnosis: It did not lead to more incorrect information being generated, nor did it lead to greater eyewitness confidence in the incorrect information. Based on these preliminary results, the cognitive interview represents a promising alternative to the hypnosis interview.

Although the results from Geiselman et al. (1984) are encouraging, one major limitation in that study was that the conditions of the experiment were somewhat dissimilar to those found in a real crime. The "crime" itself was a low-arousal innocuous event, and the "interview" was an impersonal, standardized, written questionnaire. The present study was designed to maximize the ecological validity of the results: The stimulus materials were emotionally arousing films of simulated crimes; the eyewitness recall protocols were collected using interactive interviews rather than fixed questionnaires; and the interviews were conducted by experienced law enforcement personnel. The present study also extended the earlier work of Geiselman et al. by comparing the cognitive interview to the hypnosis interview and to the standard (control) police interview. Each of these procedures is described in detail in the Method section below. The three types of interview were compared on (a) the number of correct items of information elicited, (b) the number of incorrect items of information elicited, and (c) the number of confabulated items of information generated.

METHOD

Subjects

The subjects were 89 undergraduate students, 55 males and 34 females, recruited from three introductory psychology classes and one psychology of learning class at the University of California, Los Angeles. Before agreeing to participate in the study, all subjects were informed that (a) they would be viewing a film depicting a violent crime, (b) they would be interviewed about the contents of the film by an experienced law enforcement professional, and (c) approximately one-third of them would be interviewed while under hypnosis.

Subjects from the introductory psychology classes were offered 2 hr of credit toward completion of their experiment participation requirement. Subjects from the learning course were offered no inducement.

Interviewers

The interviewers were recruited principally through an announcement placed in the *International Journal of Investigative and Forensic Hypnosis*. Additional participants were obtained from various police departments in Southern California. The final group of interviewers, 16 men and 1 woman, represented a variety of professions within the law enforcement domain: police detectives, Central Intelligence Agency investigators, polygraph specialists, and private detectives. To ensure homogeneity among the interviewers, each interviewer had completed a 40-hr course on forensic hypnosis and had subsequent field experience on hundreds of cases. Each interviewer was offered a $70.00 honorarium for participation.

Each interviewer was randomly assigned to one of the three interview conditions (cognitive = 6, hypnosis = 7, and standard = 4). The results of the interviews suggested that the interviewer population was homogeneous given that the effect of interviewer within interview conditions was not significant (see the Results and Discussion section).

Three of the 17 interviewers had seen one or two of the films described below, but over two years had passed since that exposure. The five interviews that might have been affected by this prior exposure produced data consistent with the other interviews in those interview conditions.

Materials and Apparatus

Films. The four films used in this experiment were borrowed from the training academy of the Los Angeles Police Department (LAPD). The academy uses these films as part of a computerized training process in which police officers are exposed to simulated, life-threatening situations (Decision Evaluation Firearms Trainer). Each film presents an audiovisual scenario of a violent crime or crime situation that lasts approximately 4 min. The scenarios of the four films include a bank robbery, a liquor store holdup, a family dispute, and a search through a warehouse. In each film, at least one individual is shot and killed. The scenarios are realistic in that monitored physiological reactions of officers in training have been found to be comparable to reactions that would be expected in similar street situations (LAPD). The films are rich in quantifiable information including person descriptions, mannerisms, weapons, and sequences of events.

The films were projected onto a 9 ft-by-9 ft (2.7 m $\times$ 2.7m) mm projector equipped with 4-track nonoptical sound. All films were shown in the same large lecture hall.

Interview environment. The interviews were conducted at the Center for Computer-Based Behavioral Studies (CCBS) in the Department of Psychology at the University of California, Los Angeles. Among the facilities at CCBS are separate cubicles (approximately 6 ft-by-6 ft; 1.8 m $\times$ 1,8 m) such that several interviews can be carried out simultaneously in an undisturbed fashion.

All interviews were audio recorded on standard cassette player/recorders, and the subjects wore lapel microphones. In addition to the audio recordings, subjects in the hypnosis condition were monitored using video cameras that were mounted in every room, regardless of the interview condition. A graduate student trained in hypnosis from the clinical psychology program at UCLA observed the ongoing hypnosis sessions on monitors in a control room.

Interview Conditions

Three weeks prior to the interviews, each interviewer received instructions for one, and only one, of the following three interview procedures:

Standard interview. These interviewers were told to use the questioning procedures that they normally would use without a hypnotic induction procedure. The only restriction was that each "witness" was to be asked first to describe in his or her own words what he or she remembered (open-ended report). Then, and only then, were the interviewers to ask any specific questions about the film based on the witnesses's account. The practice of asking for an open-ended report first is commonly followed by most investigators that we have interviewed, and it is supported in basic research reported by Geiselman et al. (1984), Hilgard and Loftus (1979), and Timm (1983). That is, information given during the open-ended report typically is more accurate.

Hypnosis interview. In accordance with the guidelines of Orne, Soskis, Dinges, and Orne (1984) for conducting a hypnosis interview, the subjects in this condition first were to be asked to describe the film in their own words prior to any hypnosis induction. The interviewer then was to perform a hypnosis induction, and subsequently ask the witness to restate what he or she remembered from the film, followed in turn by any specific question about the film based on the witnesses's report. Only verbal responses were to be permitted; that is, no finger-movement responses were allowed.

To preserve ecological validity, the interviewers were free to use whatever techniques they wanted to perform the hypnosis induction.

Cognitive interview. In this condition, the interviewers were to describe four general memory-retrieval techniques to the subject before the questioning began. A four-item list of the techniques was placed in full view of the witness during the entire interview as a reference guide. Otherwise, the format of this interview was the same as that for the standard interview. The following descriptions of the techniques were read by the interviewer to the subject verbatim at the beginning of the interview:

(a) Reinstate the Context: Try to reinstate in your mind the context surrounding the incident. Think about what the surrounding environment looked like at the scene, such as rooms, the weather, any nearby people or objects. Also think about how you were feeling at the time and think about your reactions to the incident.

(b) Report Everything: Some people hold back information because they are not quite sure that the information is important. Please do not edit anything out of your report, even things you think may not be important.

(c) Recall the Events in Different Orders: It is natural to go through the incident from beginning to end. However, you also should try to go through the events in reverse order. Or, try starting with the thing that impressed you the most in the incident and then go from there, working both forward in time and backward.

(d) Change Perspectives: Try to recall the incident from different perspectives that you may have had, or adopt the perspectives of others that were present during the incident. For example, try to place yourself in the role of a prominent character in the incident and think about what he or she must have seen.

All interviewers were informed that it was preferable to err in the direction of terminating an interview prematurely if that should become necessary. In particular, the interviewers were asked to terminate an interview if the subject appeared to become more anxious about the interview as the session progressed. None of the interviews was terminated prematurely.

Procedure

Each subject participated in two sessions. During the first session, groups of 8 to 10 subjects each saw one of the four films. The subjects were asked to refrain from discussing the film among themselves. After the film, a graduate student trained in hypnosis from the Department of Psychology at UCLA informed all subjects about misconceptions concerning hypnosis and answered any questions. This presentation was based on our observations of presentations made by hypno-investigators in the field and on suggestions made by Reiser (1980) in his handbook on investigative hypnosis.

Approximately 48 hr after viewing the film, the subjects were interviewed by the law-enforcement personnel. Upon arrival at this second session, the subjects were assigned randomly to one of the three interview conditions (cognitive = 33, hypnosis = 30, and standard = 26). The subjects were given the eye-roll test for hypnotic susceptibility (Spiegel, 1972), and the subjects were interviewed individually in separate rooms. Each interviewer questioned approximately five subjects during the course of the day, and each interviewer interviewed at least one witness of each crime. Before each interview, the interviewer was told only the title of the crime scenario that had been witnessed by the subject (e.g., bank robbery).

Analysis of Protocols

Each tape-recorded interview was transcribed by two of four different research assistants trained by the authors. The second listener filled in any information missed in the original transcription. The transcriptions of the tapes then were given to another member of the research team who categorized the information into three exhaustive lists for each film: persons, objects, and events. The persons category included physical appearance, clothing, mannerisms, and speech characteristics. The objects category included guns, knives, cars, and carried articles. The events category included movements, number of shots, interperson contacts, conversations, and general sequencing. These exhaustive lists were compiled and matched against the information contained in the four films for accuracy. Opinionated responses, such as "the suspect was nervous," were not scored and were deleted from the lists.

This catalogue of information then was used to score each subject's transcribed report for (a) the number of correct bits of information recalled, (b) the number of incorrect bits of information generated (e.g., the wrong hair color of a suspect), and (c) the number of confabulated bits of information generated (e.g., a description of a suspect's face when the face was not shown in the film). In the few cases where a subject changed a response during the interview, only the final response was scored. This scoring was carried out by five members of the research team. Each person worked independently and was randomly assigned at least one transcription from each interview condition and each film. To evaluate the reliability of this process across the interview conditions, a two-way analysis of variance (ANOVA) was performed on each of the three memory-performance variables with interview condition and scorer as the factors. Although the main effect of scorer was significant for both the number of correct items $F(4, 74) = 4.59$, $p < .003$, and the number of incorrect items $F(4, 74) = 2.48$, $p < .05$, the Scorer $\times$ Interview Condition interaction was not significant in any of the three analyses (all Fs < 1.21, $p > .30$). Thus although some scorers may have been more liberal in counting a response as correct or incorrect, these differences did not appear differentially for any one of the three interview conditions.

Design and Statistical Analysis

A 3 (interview condition) by 4 (type of crime/film) by 2 (hypnotic susceptibility: low = 1-6, high = 7-11) between-subjects ANOVA design was used. There were three memory-performance dependent variables (number of items correct, number incorrect, and number confabulated). In addition to the three memory variables, further measures of interest were questioning time (total interview time excluding casual conversation, the hypnosis inductions, and the retrieval methods training) and the number of questions asked. Subject gender differences in performance also were examined.

RESULTS AND DISCUSSION

Memory-Performance Measures

Table 1 presents five performance measures as a function of the type of interview procedure. Prior to the substantive statistical analyses of the memory-performance data, three nested, random-effects ANOVAs were conducted on the number of correct, number incorrect, and number confabulated dependent variables to determine whether the scores differed reliably between interviewers within the interview conditions. The univariate F with 14 to 72 degrees of freedom was computed to be 1.55 ($p > .12$) for number correct, 1.51 ($p > .13$) for number incorrect, and 1.23 ($p > .27$) for number confabulated. Thus the pooled error terms (the variance between subjects across interviewers within each interview condition) were used in the between-interview comparisons (Winer, 1962, p. 207) to maximize the potential power of the tests.

The main effect for the number of correct items generated was significant, $F(2,77) = 5.27, p < .008$. A Tukey's posttest showed that both the cognitive and hypnosis interviews elicited a greater number of correct items of information than the control interview ($ps < .05$) but that the cognitive and hypnosis interviews did not differ. The main effect for the number of incorrect items of information generated was not significant, $F(2,77) = 1.99, p > .14$. This result is unlikely to be a floor effect because the average error rate was 16%. Furthermore, as will be described shortly, the incorrect information data are sensitive enough to show some reliable differences—between males and females. In sum then, the enhanced recall with the cognitive and hypnosis interviews reflects more effective memory retrieval and cannot be interpreted as a shift in response criterion (Dywan & Bowers, 1983).[1] The main effect for the number of confabulated items also was not significant $F(2,77) = 2.48, p > .09$. As can be seen in Table 1, given our definition of a confabulated item of information, few subjects confabulated in any of the interview conditions.

The results for the cognitive interview closely replicate those obtained by Geiselman et al. (1984), in which subjects were interviewed about a classroom intrusion using a structured questionnaire. In both experiments a greater number of correct items of information were generated with the cognitive interview than with the control interview,

TABLE 7.1
Performance Measures for the Three Interview Procedures

Variable	Cognitive	Hypnosis	Standard
No. correct (C)	41.15	38.00	29.40
No. incorrect	7.30	5.90	6.10
No. confabulated	0.70	1.00	0.40
Question time (QT): min	39.70	28.20	32.10
C: QT (covariate)	39.46	38.77	29.56
No. questions asked	54.90	34.82	68.90

and without an increase in the number of incorrect items. Thus the cognitive interview has been shown to be useful for the enhancement of eyewitness memory performance both under conditions of experimental control and under conditions of high ecological validity.

Whereas the present study showed enhanced memory with the hypnosis interview, this is not the most frequently reported outcome of laboratory experiments designed to evaluate the effects of hypnosis on memory performance. In studies where emphasis has been placed on experimental control, hypnosis procedures most often have been shown either to not affect memory performance or they have been found to lead to more incorrect information (Orne et al., 1984). There are many differences between the present design and those of previous studies, and further research is required to specify the factors responsible for the differences in outcome. We believe the principal candidate factor to be: the nature of the materials, the interactive nature of the interviews, and the population of interviewers. The present equality of performance observed with the cognitive and hypnosis procedures is consistent with Timm's (1983) speculation that any memory-enhancement effects of the hypnosis interview lie in its memory-guidance components.

Examination of the interview recordings produced no new insight on the issue of whether witnesses are more susceptible to leading questions under hypnosis. This is because virtually no leading questions (questions containing "given" information that was not provided by the witness) were asked by the present interviewers in any of the conditions. Even though most interviewers questioned more than one witness from at least one of the crime scenarios, only one question in the 89 interviews was identified as clearly leading the witness. Given that, to our knowledge, the present study is the first to record and analyze the interviews of experienced law-enforcement investigators, this outcome itself is an important normative result. In contrast, Yuille (1984) reported the results of a survey in which a significant percentage of Canadian police personnel agreed that "direct (often leading) questions must be asked so that the witness is reminded of relevant facts" (p. 20). It is possible, therefore, that the present population of interviewers exhibited exceptional interviewing skills and/or that the college subjects who served as the eyewitnesses showed atypical memory performance. In either case, leading questions would not have been necessary to generate reasonably complete reports. There is some indication from a recent replication experiment in our laboratory (Geiselman, Fisher, MacKinnon, & Holland, 1985) that a greater number of leading questions are asked when nonstudents serve as the witnesses (20 leading questions in 53 interviews). Nevertheless, even this incidence can be considered to be infrequent. A final possibility is that the interviewers were exceedingly careful in conducting the interviews because they were aware of being observed. Although this possibility would be difficult to test empirically, it does not appeal to the authors because such conservatism would have suppressed differences between the interview conditions. There were no obvious indications that the interviews were stilted.

Questioning Time

Table 1 also presents the average total time that the interviewers spent questioning the witnesses. As noted in the Method section, these times exclude any intervals spent in casual conversation or in the hypnosis inductions or cognitive retrieval methods training. The main effect for questioning time was significant, $F(2, 77) = 5.49$, $p < .006$. A Tukey's posttest showed that the interviewers who used the cognitive procedure spent more time asking questions than did interviewers who used either the hypnosis or standard procedures, which did not differ. Perhaps the superior recall in the cognitive over the standard interview occurred because of the greater time spent in questioning the witness. Because of this possibility, the number-correct data were reanalyzed with questioning time as a covariate. The adjusted means from this analysis are presented in the bottom row of Table 1. As before, the main effect was significant, $F(2,76) = 4.65$, $p < .02$; and a Tukey's posttest showed that both the cognitive and hypnosis interviews led to more correct information than the standard interview (ps $< .05$).

Number of Questions Asked

The average number of questions asked in each interview condition is presented in the bottom row of Table 1. The main effect for type of interview was significant, $F(2,77) = 5.87$, $p < .006$, with significantly fewer questions asked in both the cognitive and hypnosis conditions than in the standard condition ($p < .05$ and $< .01$, respectively). Thus the memory enhancement achieved with the cognitive and hypnosis procedures cannot be explained in terms of the interviewers asking more questions. To the contrary, the cognitive and hypnosis techniques were more efficient (0.75 and 1.09 items correct per question, respectively, versus 0.42 items correct per question in the standard condition).

Type of Crime Scenario

The three memory-performance measures are presented in Table 2 as a function of the type of interview and crime scenario (film). The crime scenario interacted with the type of interview only for the number of correct items of information generated, $F(3, 77) = 8.80$, $p < .001$. As can be seen in Table 2, the superiority of the cognitive and hypnosis interviews is most evident with the bank robbery and liquor store holdup scenarios. This result was not due to a ceiling effect on the number of correct items possible in the other two films because, with each film, the highest subject score was at least three standard errors above the mean for either the cognitive or hypnosis conditions.

The authors had no a priori hypotheses regarding this interaction. However, an after-the-fact examination of the four films revealed one striking difference between the two crime scenarios that showed a significant effect of interview method and the two that did not. In both the bank robbery and liquor store holdup, several actions occurred simultaneously, and the number of events per unit time was high. In contrast, in both the family dispute and warehouse search scenarios, the events took place in a sequential fashion at a relatively slower pace. Perhaps the guided memory-search procedures common to both the cognitive and hypnosis interviews were more beneficial when processing of the to-be-remembered information was restricted at encoding by the density of events.

Hypnotic Susceptibility

Table 3 presents the three memory-performance measures as a function of the type of interview and level of hypnotic susceptibility (as indexed by the Spiegel eye-roll score). Neither the main effect of hypnotic susceptibility nor the interaction between type of interview and hypnotic susceptibility was significant for any of the three memory-performance measures (all $Fs < 1$). The lack of significant

TABLE 7.2
Performance Measures for the Three Interview Procedures
as a Function of Crime Scenario

	Bank robbery			Family dispute			Liquor store			Warehouse		
Variable	C	H	S	C	H	S	C	H	S	C	H	S
No. correct	40.4	35.4	28.7	40.6	35.5	33.3	57.3	50.8	29.9	24.3	28.9	21.7
No. incorrect	7.8	5.9	7.0	6.8	5.9	6.8	8.0	8.6	3.1	5.5	3.4	5.5
No. confabulated	0.7	0.4	0.7	0.6	0.8	0.2	0.6	1.6	0.7	0.9	1.0	0.0

Note: C = cognitive, H = hypnosis, S = standard.

differences, especially for the hypnosis interview, was surprising but does not affect the above interpretation of the results. In fact, this outcome is consistent with the hypothesis that the facilitative effects of the hypnosis interview lie in the memory-guidance procedures (Timm, 1983) and not in the induction.[2]

Gender of Eyewitness

The gender of the eyewitness was found to be unrelated to: (a) the number of correct items generated, $F(1, 65) < 1$; (b) the number of confabulated items generated, $F(1, 65) < 1$; and (c) questioning time, $F(1, 47) = 1.64, p > .20$. The only significant difference was found in the number of incorrect items generated $F(1, 65) = 8.50, p < .005$: Males generated a greater number of incorrect items than females (7.12 versus 4.92). Given that this result was not accompanied by an increase in correct information, the conclusion is that the females exhibited superior memory performance. This difference did not interact with other factors in the experiment, and therefore, the conclusions drawn here about interview methods hold for both male and female eyewitnesses.

Recall of Critical Facts

The preceding analyses of the memory performance data were carried out irrespective of the relative importance of the information that was generated across the interview conditions. Therefore, 20 facts from both the bank robbery and liquor-store holdup films, where differences in overall memory performance were observed, were chosen for selective scoring as the most important items of information from those crime scenarios. The lists of critical facts were generated independently by five members of the research staff, and these lists

TABLE 7.3
Performance Measures for the Three Interview Procedures
as a Function of Eye-Roll Score

Variable	Cognitive		Hypnosis		Standard	
	Low	High	Low	High	Low	High
No. correct	39.9	39.3	37.2	37.6	28.3	28.2
No. incorrect	7.1	6.8	5.6	6.4	6.2	5.4
No. confabulated	0.7	0.8	0.8	1.1	0.3	0.4

Note: Low—eye roll = 1-6; high—eye roll = 7-11 (eye-roll scores were not recorded for 3 subjects).

were discussed and merged in a subsequent meeting of the entire group. Then, the protocols from the 46 subjects who witnessed either of the two target films were scored for the 20 critical facts. Each protocol was scored by one member of the staff. Neither the main effect of scorer nor the Scorer $\times$ Interview Procedure interaction was significant for either the number correct or number incorrect memory variables ($Fs < 1.03$).

The average memory-performance scores are presented in Table 4. The main effect for interview condition was significant only for the number of correct items of information generated, $F(2, 40) = 3.64, p < .04$. As in the overall analysis, both the cognitive and hypnosis procedures led to the recall of more correct items than did the standard interview ($ps < .05$). Thus the cognitive and hypnosis interviews were successful in the enhancement of eyewitness memory for the most critical facts, not simply for ancillary facts. These effects did not depend on the crime scenario, the gender of the witness, or the level of eye-roll score (all $Fs < 1$).

CONCLUSIONS

The major finding of this study is that both cognitive-retrieval mnemonics and techniques inherent in the forensic use of hypnosis are effective for the enhancement of eyewitness memory retrieval in the police interview. This was observed to be true especially for crime scenarios in which the density of events was high. We believe these effects to lie in the guided memory-search components of the cognitive and hypnosis interviews. Both of these procedures encourage the eyewitness to mentally reinstate the contextual elements that were present at the time of the crime. In addition, the hypnosis procedure frequently draws upon a videotape replay analogy with "fixed-frame" and "zoom-in" capabilities (Reiser, 1980). It is plausible that this

TABLE 7.4
Performance Measures for Twenty Critical Facts

| | Bank robbery | | | Liquor store | | |
Variable	C	H	S	C	H	S
No. correct	11.2	11.9	8.5	12.7	12.8	9.9
No. incorrect	1.3	1.5	1.8	0.9	2.0	1.0

Note: C = cognitive, H = hypnosis, S = standard.

technique, in effect, simulates components of the no-edit and varied retrieval perspectives mnemonics from the cognitive interview. In contrast, the standard interview as observed here consists mainly of repeated attempts to recall the target information, each time in the same way without supplemental memory-retrieval guidance.

Further research will delineate which of the retrieval mnemonics are most effective for the recovery of specific kinds of information. At present, it is instructive to note that the cognitive interview can be learned and applied with little training. The interviewers who carried out the cognitive interviews in the present research, for example, studied a two-page description of the cognitive methods and participated in a 15-min discussion prior to conducting the interviews. In addition to the savings in training time, the present study showed that less time is required on average to instruct a witness in the general cognitive mnemonics (6.7 min) than to perform a hypnosis induction (27.1 min). One further advantage of the cognitive interview is that it circumvents the present legal problems that surround the forensic use of hypnosis. However, the effectiveness of the cognitive interview relative to the hypnosis interview in cases of severe trauma to a victim or witness remains to be evaluated.

The present study evaluated the cognitive interview in a more ecologically valid setting than that employed by Geiselman et al. (1984). The stimulus materials were selected and presented to enhance the arousal of the witness; an interactive questioning format was followed; and the interviews were carried out by experienced law-enforcement personnel. The importance of validating laboratory data on eyewitness phenomena under more natural conditions has been stressed by other authors (Malpass & Devine, 1980; Monahan & Loftus, 1982; Reiser, 1980). The discrepancy between the memory-enhancement qualities of forensic hypnosis observed here and results typically obtained under more artificial conditions underscores the importance of this validation. There still are major differences between the present laboratory setting and a real-world crime. For example, the element of personal involvement can never be achieved completely in studies of this type. However, it is interesting to note that the majority of the present subjects responded to the questions using personal pronouns, in a role-playing manner, as if they had actually experienced the crime. Another potentially important factor is the element of surprise (Murray & Wells, 1982). The present subjects knew that they eventually would be questioned about what they saw in the films. Nevertheless, the results that were obtained here with the cognitive interview are consistent with those reported by Geiselman et al. (1984) in which the subjects' memories were incidental.

Finally, the present results are not consistent with an interpretation that would attribute the enhancement of memory performance to heightened subject or interviewer motivation. First, with such an interpretation, performance in the hypnosis condition logically should have exceeded that with the cognitive interview because all subjects volunteered for the experiment only after being informed of the possibility that they would be hypnotized. Immediately before the interviews, the subjects in the cognitive condition, as well as the subjects in the standard condition, were told that they would not be hypnotized. Average performance in the hypnosis condition was not limited by a ceiling effect on the number of correct items possible. Second, it was our impression that the subjects in all conditions were well motivated in the experiment. The majority of the subjects in all conditions role played in answering the questions. Third, the interviewers were given a description of the interview condition in which they were to participate. Furthermore, the questioning time was shortest of all for the hypnosis interview where memory performance was relatively good, and the average number of questions asked was smaller in both the cognitive and hypnosis conditions than in the standard condition. These results would appear to contradict any interpretation where the quality of the interviews is hypothesized to have been inadvertently manipulated by the interviewers. Fourth, the superiority of the cognitive and hypnosis interviews was observed for only two of the four crime scenarios, those with rapidly and simultaneously occurring events. If subjects were simply more motivated in the cognitive and hypnosis groups, we could reasonably expect the superiority to extend across all four scenarios. Fifth, there is no evidence that memory retrieval performance is improved with greater motivation in any case (Weiner, 1966). Sixth, and most important, the effects of the cognitive and hypnosis interviews were specific to the generation of correct items of information. That is, the results cannot be couched in terms of a simple shift in response criterion resulting in greater overall productivity or a willingness to please the interviewer with embellished reports in reaction to demand characteristics.

NOTES

1. The reader may note the percentage of correct responses (number correct/number correct + number incorrect + number confabulated) is approximately equal across the interview conditions: .84 for cognitive, .85 for hypnosis, .82 for standard). This equivalence does not imply that memory is equally good because the three groups differed in terms of the total number of responses: The cognitive (49.5) and the hypnosis (44.9) groups made more responses than did the standard (35.9) group. It has been shown in other recall studies (Roediger, 1973) that there is a tradeoff between accuracy and number of responses made: As the subject makes more responses, the percentage of incorrect responses (intrusions) increases. Thus one must take into account both accuracy and extent of recall to measure memory properly. In the present study, the cognitive and hypnosis interviews elicited more responses without a drop in accuracy rate, testifying to their superiority over the standard interview. Without taking into account both measures (accuracy and number of responses), one might be led to the conclusion that an interview that elicited only one, but correct, response (100% accuracy) is as effective as one that elicits one hundred, all correct, responses (100% accuracy). The problem is similar to the speed-accuracy tradeoff: One must examine both speed and accuracy simultaneously. Equivalent accuracy rates reflect equal performance only if speed is constant across conditions.

2. It is interesting to note that some of the interviewers stated in an informal debriefing session that they disagreed with the belief that only a small percentage of individuals are highly susceptible to hypnosis. If one induction method fails with a given person, another method might prove effective. Perhaps with their approach, any single index of susceptibility will not reflect the level of hypnosis ultimately achieved.

REFERENCES

Anderson, R. C., & Pichert, J. W. (1978). Recall of previously unrecallable information following a shift in perspective. *Journal of Verbal Learning and Verbal Behavior, 17,* 1-12.

Bower, G. (1967). A multicomponent theory of the memory trace. In K. W. Spencer & J. T. Spence (Eds.), *The psychology of learning and motivation* (Vol. 1, pp. 230-325). New York: Academic Press.

Bower, G. H., Gilligan, S. C., & Monteiro, K. P. (1981). Selectivity of learning caused by affective states. *Journal of Experimental Psychology: General, 110,* 451-472.

Burns, M. J. (1981). The mental retracing of prior activities: Evidence for reminiscence in order retrieval. (Doctoral dissertation, University of California, Los Angeles, 1981). *Dissertation Abstracts International, 42,* 2108B.

Clifford, B. R., & Hollin, C. R. (1983). The effects of discussion on recall accuracy and agreement. *Journal of Applied Social Psychology, 13,* 234-244.

Clifford, B. R., & Lloyd-Bostock, S. M. A. (1983). Witness evidence: Conclusion and prospect. In S. M. A. Lloyd-Bostock & B. R. Clifford (Eds.), *Evaluating witness evidence* (pp. 285-290). New York: Wiley.

Deffenbacher, K. A. (1980). Eyewitness accuracy and confidence: Can we infer anything about their relationship? *Law and Human Behavior, 4,* 243-260.

DePiano, F. A., & Salzberg, H. C. (1981). Hypnosis as an aid to recall of meaningful information presented under three types of arousal. *International Journal of Clinical and Experimental Hypnosis, 29,* 383-400.

Diamond, B. L. (1980). Inherent problems in the use of pretrial hypnosis in a prospective witness. *California Law Review, 68,* 313-349.

Dywan, J., & Bowers, K. S. (1983). The use of hypnosis to enhance recall. *Science, 222,* 184-185.

Firstenberg, I. (1983). The role of retrieval variability in the interrogation of human memory. (Doctoral dissertation, University of California, Los Angeles, 1983). *Dissertation Abstracts International, 44,* 1623B.

Flexser, A., & Tulving, E. (1978). Retrieval independence in recognition and recall. *Psychological Review, 85,* 153-171.

Geiselman, R. E., Fisher, R. P., Firstenberg, I., Hutton, L. A., Sullivan, S., Avetissian, I., & Prosk, A. (1984). Enhancement of eyewitness memory: An empirical evaluation of the cognitive interview. *Journal of Police Science and Administration, 12,* 74-80.

Geiselman, R. E., Fisher, R. P., MacKinnon, D. P., & Holland, H. L. (1985). *Eyewitness memory enhancement with the cognitive interview.* Manuscript submitted for publication.

Griffin, G. R. (1980). Hypnosis: Towards a logical approach in using hypnosis in law enforcement agencies. *Journal of Police Science and Administration, 8,* 385-389.

Hilgard, E. R., & Loftus, E. F. (1979). Effective interrogation of the eyewitness. *International Journal of Clinical & Experimental Hypnosis, 27,* 342-357.

Loftus, E. F. (1975). Leading questions and eyewitness report. *Cognitive Psychology, 7,* 560-572.

Loftus, E. F. (1979). *Eyewitness testimony.* Cambridge, MA: Harvard University Press.

Loftus, E. F., Miller, D. G., & Burns, H. G. (1978). Semantic integration of verbal information into visual memory. *Journal of Experimental Psychology: Human Learning and Memory, 4,* 19-31.

Loftus, E. F., & Zanni, G. (1975). Eyewitness testimony: The influence of the wording of a question. *Bulletin of the Psychonomic Society, 5,* 86-88.

Malpass, R. S., & Devine, P. G. (1980). Realism and eyewitness identification research. *Law and Human Behavior, 4,* 347-358.

Malpass, R. S., & Devine, P. G. (1981). Guided memory in eyewitness identification. *Journal of Applied Psychology, 66,* 343-350.

Monahan, J., & Loftus, E. F. (1982). The psychology of law. *Annual Review of Psychology, 33,* 441-475.

Murray, D. M., & Wells, G. L. (1982). Does knowledge that a crime was staged affect eyewitness performance. *Journal of Applied Social Psychology, 12,* 42-53.

Orne, M. T. (1961). The potential uses of hypnosis in interrogation. In A. D. Biderman & H. Zimmer (Eds.), *The manipulation of human behavior* (pp. 169-215). New York: Wiley.

Orne, M. T. (1979). The use and misuse of hypnosis in court. *The International Journal of Clinical and Experimental Hypnosis, 27,* 311-341.

Orne, M. T., Soskis, D. A., Dinges, D. F., & Orne, E. C. (1984). Hypnotically induced testimony. In G. L. Wells & E. F. Loftus (Eds.), *Eyewitness testimony: Psychological perspectives* (pp. 171-213). Cambridge University Press.

Putnam, W. H. (1979). Hypnosis and distortions in eyewitness memory. *International Journal of Clinical and Experimental Hypnosis, 27,* 437-448.

Rand, Corporation, (1975, October). *The criminal investigation process* (Vol. 1-3). Rand Corporation Technical Report R-1776-DOJ, R-1777-DOJ, Santa Monica, CA.

Reiser, M. (1974). Hypnosis as an aid in homicide investigation. *American Journal of Clinical Hypnosis, 17,* 84-87.

Reiser, M. (1976). Hypnosis as a tool in criminal investigation. *The Police Chief, 46,* 39-40.

Reiser, M. (1980). *Handbook of investigative hypnosis.* Los Angeles: LEHI.

Reiser, M., & Neilsen, M. (1980). Investigative hypnosis: A developing specialty. *American Journal of Clinical Hypnosis, 23,* 75-84.

Roediger, H. L. (1973). Inhibition in recall from cuing with recall targets. *Journal of Verbal Learning and Verbal Behavior, 12,* 644-657.

Sanders, G. S., & Simmons, W. L. (1983). Use of hypnosis to enhance eyewitness accuracy: Does it work? *Journal of Applied Psychology, 68,* 70-77.

Schafer, D. W., & Rubio, R. (1978). Hypnosis to aid the recall of witnesses. *International Journal of Clinical and Experimental Hypnosis, 26,* 81-91.

Sheehan, P. W., & Tilden, J. (1983). Effects of suggestibility and hypnosis on accurate and distorted retrieval from memory. *Journal of Experimental Psychology: Learning, Memory, & Cognition, 9,* 283-293.

Smith, M. (1983). Hypnotic memory enhancement of witnesses: Does it work? *Psychological Bulletin, 94,* 387-407.

Smith, S. (1979). Remembering in and out of context. *Journal of Experimental Psychology: Human Learning and Memory, 5,* 460-471.

Spiegel, H. (1972). An eye-roll test for hypnotizability. *The American Journal of Clinical Hypnosis, 15,* 25-28.

Stager, G. L., & Lundy, R. M. (1985). Hypnosis and the learning and recall of visually presented material. *International Journal of Clinical and Experimental Hypnosis, 33,* 27-39.

Stratton, J. G. (1977). The use of hypnosis in law enforcement criminal investigations: A pilot program. *Journal of Police Science and Administration,* April, 399-406.

Timm, H. W. (1981). The effects of forensic hypnosis techniques on eyewitness recall and recognition. *Journal of Police Science and Administration, 9,* 188-194.

Timm, H. W. (1983). The factors theoretically affecting the impact of forensic hypnosis techniques on eyewitness recall. *Journal of Police Science and Administration, 11,* 442-450.

Tulving, E. (1974). Cue-dependent forgetting. *American Scientist, 62,* 74-82.

Underwood, B. J. (1969). Attributes of memory. *Psychological Review, 76,* 559-573.

Weiner, B. (1966). The effects of motivation on the availability and retrieval of memory traces. *Psychological Bulletin, 65,* 24-37.

Wells, G. L. (1978). Applied eyewitness testimony research: System variables and estimator variables. *Journal of Personality and Social Psychology, 36,* 1546-1557.

Wells, G. L., Ferguson, T. J., & Lindsay, R. C. L. (1981). The tractability of eyewitness confidence and its implications for triers of fact. *Journal of Applied Psychology, 66,* 688-696.

Wells, G. L., & Lindsay, R. C. L. (1983). How do people infer accuracy? In S. M. A. Lloyd-Bostock & B. R. Clifford (Eds.), *Evaluating witness memory* (pp. 41-56). New York: Wiley.

Whitten, W., & Leonard, J. (1981). Directed search through autobiographical memory. *Memory & Cognition, 9,* 566-579.

Wickens, D. (1970). Encoding categories of words: An empirical approach to meaning. *Psychological Review, 77,* 1-15.

Winer, B. J. (1962). *Statistical principles in experimental design.* New York: McGraw-Hill.

Yuille, J. C. (1980). A critical examination of the psychological and practical implications of eyewitness research. *Law and Human Behavior, 4* 335-345.

Yuille, J. C. (1984). Research and teaching with police: A Canadian example. *International Review of Applied Psychology, 33,* 5-23.

Zelig, M., & Beidleman, W. B. (1981). The investigative use of hypnosis: A word of caution. *International Journal of Clinical and Experimental Hypnosis, 29,* 401-412.

SECTION II

SUMMARY

What is hypnosis, and what effect does it have on human memory? Psychologists continue to argue over whether or not hypnosis is an altered state of consciousness. The methods for inducing hypnosis may vary, but they all share certain features in common; typical is Reiser's (1974) technique, as it encourages subjects to relax, visualize the critical event, and report—without self-censorship—whatever comes to mind. But what about Reiser's treatment of the memory system as a video tape recorder with subjects pausing, focusing, zooming in, and replaying events in slow motion? Doesn't that procedure lead people to believe that they must have something to remember, even if they do not? And does that expectation lead people to report something even if they have to invent it? In section III, we see that the human memory is malleable, that it should not be viewed within the metaphor of a videotape recorder.

Putnam's (1979) experiment is an excellent test of the effects of hypnosis on eyewitness testimony. After watching a videotape of a car-bicycle accident, subjects were questioned about their observations. Subjects who "testified" under hypnosis were no more accurate overall than those who were questioned in a normal waking state. Yet they made errors when asked leading questions (or should we say, misleading) questions. That latter finding is consistent with prevailing theories which view hypnosis, by definition, as a state of heightened suggestibility.

As Smith's (1983) review indicates, Putnam's results have been replicated by other researchers. On the other hand, so is Reiser's case merely one of several that appear to attest to the positive effects of hypnosis. What are we to conclude from this consistent discrepancy between in-the-field case studies and controlled laboratory experiments? Smith analyzed these literatures, looking for differences between the two types of situations. She considered such factors as the amount of stress between real- and subject-witnesses, the kinds of events they are asked to recall, and the consequences of their testimony. In the end, Smith concluded that it would be worth searching for procedures that incorporated only elements of Reiser's technique (i.e., encouraging witnesses to report whatever comes to mind, contextual reinstatement through guided memory, and repeated testing). What, then, is *hypnosis? And when does a mnemonic aid cross the line from being* nonhypnotic to hypnotic?

That question becomes even more difficult to answer in the shadow of the recent work by Geiselman et al. (1985). In their study, three procedures were used to elicit eyewitness reports—the standard police interview, hypnosis, and the "cognitive interview" based on retrieval mnemonics identified by memory psychologists. These investigators found that both hypnosis and the cognitive interview increased subjects' ability to recall the contents of a crime, especially in high-action situations. What, then, is the difference between these two techniques? Regardless of the answer to that question, it is clear that the cognitive interview could offer an ideal, easily learned method of obtaining information from witnesses without the dangers associated with hypnotic induction. Indeed, a follow-up study conducted by Geiselman, Cohen, and Surtes (1986), shows that this technique might actually decrease suggestibility to leading questions.

As our collection of articles indicates, the jury is still out on the questions of whether hypnosis (a) enhances memory and (b) increases suggestibility. It is beginning to look as if there are elements of the hypnotic interview that, consistent with current theories of memory, could very well act as an effective mnemonic device. But under what circumstances might this technique work, and what about the ever-present danger of suggestibility and confabulation? Are there procedural safeguards that would increase their potential for effectiveness and, at the same time, minimize their inherent biases? As with many genuinely controversial topics, we can only conclude by saying that more research is needed. In the meantime, until there is a consensus of opinion among the experts, the courts should proceed cautiously and with their eyes open to the possible dangers.

REFERENCES

Geiselman, R. E., Cohen, G., & Surtes, L. (1986). *Eyewitness responses to leading and misleading questions under the cognitive interview.* Unpublished Manuscript, University of California at Los Angeles.

SECTION III

EYEWITNESS ACCURACY
Introduction

In July 1983, Richard Williams was arrested for rape. After being in jail for two weeks he was released, because another man confessed to the crime. How did an innocent man land in jail? He was identified by a 5-year-old eyewitness. In August 1983, Wayne D. Bruce was arrested for rape and aggravated sodomy. After spending one-and-one-half months in jail he was released when another man confessed to the crime. Why was Bruce arrested? He had been identified by the victim as the assailant from over 200 photographs, after being identified in a courtroom, and identified during the preliminary hearing. What these two events have in common is that they were both cases of inaccurate eyewitness identification, and both men were charged by the same prosecuting attorney in a two-month period (Fischer, 1983). The prosecuting attorney claimed that eyewitness identification is very important and oftentimes the only evidence available; "what else are we supposed to rely on?" she asked. However, the County Public Defender countered that law enforcement should be certain it has corroborating evidence before arresting a suspect who has been identified by an eyewitness; "eyewitness identification is not enough" (Fischer, 1983).

Inaccurate eyewitness identifications have been a serious problem in criminal and civil investigations for a long time. And efforts by social scientists to investigate parameters of accuracy on eyewitness identifications have a long history as well. The first effort in the United States came from Hugo Munsterberg in 1908 with his book, *On the Witness*

Stand (1908/1976). In the last decade, the field has rapidly expanded, and it has been estimated that 85% of eyewitness research has been published after 1978 (Wells & Loftus, 1984). Thus the purpose of this section is to examine some of the basic issues relevant to the controversy over the general level of accuracy of eyewitnesses.

Chapter 8, by Gary L. Wells, explores the types of variables that are assessed in eyewitness research and estimator-variable research. System variables are (or can be) under the direct control of and manipulated by the criminal justice system. Examples would be the procedures used in lineups, show-ups, and photo-array viewing. Estimator variables, on the other hand, are characteristics of the witnesses themselves (i.e., ability to remember faces or to make cross-racial identifications). This chapter draws conclusions about why distinguishing between these two types of variables is important.

Chapters 9 and 10 are examples of system and estimator variables research. Chapter 9, by Elizabeth Loftus, David Miller, and Helen Burns, focuses on how information supplied after an event may affect memory for the event. This type of research would be considered system-variable research, because it has the potential to be generalized to procedures used in the questioning of eyewitnesses at the time of identification.

Chapter 10, by Roy S. Malpass and Jerome Kravitz, can be considered an example of estimator-variable research. Oftentimes, witnesses are called on to make cross-racial identifications, and this chapter examines how accurate eyewitnesses are when making an identification when a member of one race tries to identify a member of another. Research of this kind addresses characteristics of witnesses that provide information on how accurate one might anticipate witnesses to be, given the circumstances surrounding an encounter.

REFERENCES

Fischer, J. (1983, October 6). Eyewitness identifications called unreliable. *Topeka Capital Journal*, p. 1.

Munsterberg, H. (1976). *On the witness stand*. New York: AMS Press. (Originally published 1908)

Wells, G. L., & Loftus, E. F. (1984). Eyewitness research: Then and now. In G. L. Wells & E. F. Loftus (Eds.), *Eyewitness testimony: Psychological perspectives*. New York: Cambridge University Press.

8

APPLIED EYEWITNESS-TESTIMONY RESEARCH
System Variables and Estimator Variables

GARY L. WELLS
University of Alberta

Clearly, some eyewitness-testimony research can be thought of as concerning basic, theoretical issues in perception, learning, and memory (see Loftus & Palmer, 1974, for a possible example). However, most research that is *specifically* directed at eyewitness testimony either explicitly states its concern as "applications to criminal justice" or implies such a concern by operationalizing variables in a "real-

Author's Note. The author would like to thank Anthony N. Doob, Tamara Ferguson, Anthony G. Greenwald, R. C. L. Lindsay, and E. F. Loftus for comments throughout the preparation of this article. Requests for reprints should be sent to Gary L. Wells, Department of Psychology, University of Alberta, Edmonton, Alberta, Canada T6G 2E9.

From *Journal of Personality and Social Psychology*, 1978, *36*(12), 1546-1557. Copyright 1978 by the American Psychological Association. Reprinted by permission of the publisher and author.

world" fashion. The concern in the current article is with this latter type—applied eyewitness-testimony research.

Despite evidence of psychological interest in applied eyewitness-testimony research that dates back to the early part of the 20th century (e.g., Whipple, 1909), the goal of such research has not been well defined. Generally, researchers allude to a concern with or application to criminal justice. However, in reviewing the eyewitness literature, one finds no statement regarding what is meant by such phrases as "applications to criminal justice," "concerns with the concept of criminal justice," and so on. In order to have a working definition, this article will assume that the goal of applied eyewitness-testimony research is to generate scientific knowledge that will maximize the chances that a guilty defendant will be justly convicted while minimizing the chances that an innocent defendant will be mistakenly convicted.[1] In addition, the term *criminal justice system* will refer to any governmental policy or practice that potentially affects criminal justice as defined above.

To the extent that eyewitness-testimony research has been directed toward applications to criminal justice, the research has not had a great impact (Buckhout, Note 1; Hastie, Loftus, Penrod, & Winkler, Note 2).[2] Buckhout (Note 1) accounts for this weakness by characterizing the criminal justice system as reactionary and closed minded. Yet, the reactions of the criminal justice system may be quite understandable. For example, in an oft-cited *Scientific American* article, Buckhout (1974) operates on the explicitly stated supposition that "eyewitness testimony is unreliable" (p. 23). Such blanket discountings of eyewitness testimony, even if they are correct, are bound to be greeted with negative reaction by the criminal justice system. Clearly, the criminal justice system will never eliminate eyewitness testimony altogether. It can be noted that (a) the initial report from a victim that a crime has occurred is in itself a testimony; (b) police officials' statements that they received a report of the crime is a testimony; and (c) to discount all eyewitness testimony is to discount any possibility of the defendant's having an alibi, thereby placing innocent defendants in a precarious situation.

Thus this article begins with the position that the total *elimination* of eyewitness testimony is neither a desirable nor a feasible approach to improving criminal justice. In addition, it will later be argued that such a position is not necessarily a scientifically sound conclusion to be drawn from the eyewitness literature.

Hastie, Loftus, Penrod, and Winkler (Note 2) suggest that court reluctance to utilize scientific psychology in the courtroom may stem from the lack of an adequate published summary of relevant laboratory and field research. In line with this idea, the current author notes that there has not been a complete review (either applied or theoretical) of the eyewitness-testimony literature in an American Psychological

Association journal since Whipple's *Psychological Bulletin* article in 1918. But the field of applied eyewitness-testimony research needs more than a review; it needs criticism and a collimated line of focus. Researchers of basic theory have maintained direction and focus by precisely demonstrating how their operations apply to a *theory*. Applied eyewitness-testimony researchers, however, have generally been somewhat unclear as to how their operations apply to criminal justice. Although it is the responsibility of individual researchers to make this link, it might prove fruitful to have a general category system that relates eyewitness variables to criminal justice concepts.

Investigators concerned with theoretical analyses of memory processes use a tripartite system that includes acquisition, retention, and retrieval phases. While it is possible to adopt this categorization scheme in summarizing eyewitness research (see Hastie et al., Note 2, for an excellent example), it is not a categorization system that is inherently related to *criminal justice applications*. For purposes of criminal justice applications, a categorization of eyewitness research should relate eyewitness-research variables to their domain of utility for criminal justice. In the next section, a two-category system is proposed that might help eyewitness researchers define the applications of their research. In addition, a sampling of relevant research in each category as it relates to criminal justice is provided.

The reader is cautioned against assuming that the placement of a given piece of research into one category or the other category is, in itself, a comment on the *general* utility of that research. This article focuses only on *applied* utility, and the categorization system is designed with that in mind. There is no intention to "pigeonhole" research or discredit studies because they lack applied utility for criminal justice. Indeed, some of the research was not designed or billed by the investigators as applied eyewitness research. The purpose is to introduce a categorization system that may prove useful to researchers in designing their research operations so as to increase the applied utility of their results if, in fact, they are interested in applications to criminal justice. Specific research examples from the literature are included primarily as an exemplary aid for the categorization system. The next section briefly introduces the categorization system.

ESTIMATOR AND SYSTEM VARIABLES IN EYEWITNESS RESEARCH

Fallible eyewitness testimony threatens the concept of criminal justice, and there are two types of research directed at this issue. The first type investigates variables that affect eyewitness accuracy but are not under the control of the criminal justice system. That is, although these variables may be manipulable in research, they cannot be controlled in actual criminal cases. Such variables will be termed *estimator variables* because, in actual crimes, one can at best only *estimate* the role of such factors. Independent control over estimator variables is, for all practical purposes, impossible for actual crimes. For example, moderately severe crimes may produce greater witness accuracy than very severe crimes (Johnson & Scott, Note 3), but the criminal justice system cannot directly control the severity of crimes so as to produce less fallible eyewitness accounts. The criminal justice system could, however, use such knowledge to *estimate*, post hoc, the likely accuracy of a witness.

The second type of eyewitness research investigates variables that are (or potentially can be) under the direct control of the criminal justice system. These variables will be termed *system variables* because of their relevance for application to change in the criminal justice system. An example of a system variable is the length of time between the initial criminal event and subsequent testimony. Evidence that this variable affects eyewitness-testimony performance (Shepard, 1967) might be directly used to advocate changes in the scheduling of police interrogations.

A CLOSER EXAMINATION OF THE ESTIMATOR-VARIABLE LITERATURE

There are several ways in which estimator-variable research might contribute to aiding criminal justice. One possibility is to assess experimentally the conditions that influence accuracy, "plug in" these conditions for an actual criminal case, and make a professional estimate regarding how likely it is that the witness(es) could give accurate or inaccurate testimony under such conditions. Another possibility is for the psychologist to appear in court as an expert witness and draw upon estimator-variable research to caution jurors and judges against the acceptance of certain types of testimony. There are other approaches, such as the *general* statement approach, to wit: "eyewitness testimony is unreliable." But, whatever the approach, estimator-variable research has a natural restriction in its application to criminal justice: Estimator-variable research cannot alter the accuracy of a given witness's account of a real crime; it can only reduce or increase the court's reliance on the witness's testimony. In itself, this may appear to be a small restriction; after all, it provides the court with an empirically derived set of decision rules. However, before that point is addressed, a review of the estimator-variable literature is in order.

Characteristics of the Criminal Event

Crime seriousness. Leippe, Wells, and Ostrom (1978) speculated that a trivial criminal event would produce a lower base rate of accuracy than a criminal event of moderate seriousness. Staging a crime in which a stolen object was believed by subjects to be worth about $50 versus $1.50, Leippe et al. found subjects better able to pick the "criminal" from a six-person photo spread in the case of the high-value object (56% correct identifications) than in the case of the low-value object (19% correct identifications). In addition, Leippe et al. included two cells in which the subject-witnesses did not know the value of the stolen object until 60 sec after the "criminal" had vanished. Under these conditions, crime seriousness had no reliable effect. This led Leippe et al. to suggest that crime-seriousness effects are limited to cases wherein the witness(es) knows how serious the crime is *at the time of witnessing.*

Leippe et al. (1978) also suggested that the relationship between crime seriousness and eyewitness accuracy may actually be curvilinear. At some point, a crime may be so serious that it produces a high level of arousal that interferes with information processing or enhances a motivation to not get involved, thereby decreasing eyewitness accuracy. However, Johnson and Scott (Note 3) staged an event in which subject-witnesses overheard a hostile interaction complete with the sound of breaking bottles and crashing chairs. Subsequently, subject-witnesses viewed a criminal-confederate bolt into their room with a bloodied letter opener and blood on his hand then quickly exit. In another condition, a confederate who was *not* overheard in a hostile interaction entered the subject-witnesses' room with a pen in hand and grease on his arms and then quickly exited. The general conclusion from their data is that "high arousal *facilitated* the retrieval of information" (Johnson & Scott, Note 3, p. 27). Assuming, as do Johnson and Scott, that subjects believed this horror, it may be beyond the ethical and practical limits of social psychologists to demonstrate the kind of crime severity necessary to adequately test Leippe et al.'s curvilinear hypothesis. Alternatively, perhaps the curvilinear hypothesis is incorrect.

Exposure time. Another characteristic of the criminal event that varies from case to case is the amount of time that the witness is exposed to the relevant stimuli. The research of Loftus (1972) and

Hintzman (1976) shows that picture recognition is a monotonically increasing function of functional exposure time. Of course, this monotonic function is not linear, since there are threshold-type effects and ceiling effects. Interestingly, even above threshold, the data appear more like a psychophysical function than a learning curve. This may be related to Schaffer and Schiffrin's (1972) observation that picture recognition does not resemble verbal learning in that providing a rest or rehearsal period following picture exposure does not increase performance.

Complexity. Research by Loftus (1972) and Wells (1972) suggests that the complexity of an event can increase later recognizability. Franken and Davis (1975) corroborated this suggestion with photographs that varied in the complexity of the image. However, as Hastie et al. (Note 2) point out, "While complexity quite plausibly improves recognition (perhaps by increasing the chances that a subject will observe distinctive features), exactly the reverse effect seems to occur in recall situations." For example, Schiffman and Bobko (1974) found that increasing the complexity of an event resulted in greater overestimations of the duration of that event. Temporal overestimation effects have also been reported in staged crimes (e.g., Buckhout, 1974; Marshall, 1969; Johnson & Scott, Note 3).

Familiarity. Familiarity with the physical surroundings that form the context of the criminal event may also affect recall accuracy. Lack of familiarity with the size and/or distance of surrounding objects can produce large distortions in estimates of the size, distance, and acceleration of the perceptual target (Grether & Baker, 1972).

Hastie et al.'s (Note 2) point regarding the distinction between recall and recognition brings up a more general issue. It may be that some factors that enhance facial recognition actually inhibit recognition or recall of other characteristics. For example, Leippe et al. (1978) found no significant effect for the crime-seriousness manipulation on recall for various physical characteristics of the criminal. In fact, the low-seriousness conditions produced nonsignificantly greater recall accuracy than the high-seriousness conditions. It seems only reasonable that direct attention to the facial characteristics of a criminal serves to reduce the amount of time that a witness is attending to the multitude of other characteristics of the event. Consistent with this, Johnson and Scott's (Note 3) data indicate an average within-cell correlation of −.21 between their subjects' accuracy of facial identification and errors of commission in recalling the event (errors of omission were not analyzed). This finding becomes especially interesting to the extent that a cross-examination of a witness results in a discounting of that witness's testimony via showing that the witness gave a fallible account of some lesser characteristic of the event.

Characteristics of the Defendant

Race. Perhaps the most researched characteristic of the defendant is race. Malpass and Kravitz (1969) found that photographs of black faces were more difficult to recognize than those of white faces regardless of the witness's race. Since blacks show less variation in hair color and eye color than their white counterparts, this result may have a basis in stimulus characteristics. However, most cross-racial identification research shows an interaction between race of defendant and race of witness, thereby giving rise to attitudinal and familiarity explanations. In general, white witnesses show a much higher recognition accuracy for white faces than for black faces, whereas black witnesses only show a slight difference or no difference in their ability to recognize whites versus blacks (Cross, Cross, & Daly, 1971; Elliot, Wills, & Goldstein, 1973; Luce, 1974). Adding Orientals as witnesses and defendants increases the complexity of the pattern (see Cross et al., 1971; Luce, 1974), but a general rule that accounts for a large percentage of the data is that within-race identifications are better than cross-racial identifications.

Attractiveness. The social psychological literature shows a number of biases regarding a target person's physical attractiveness (Berscheid & Walster, 1974), and the eyewitness literature is no exception. Cross et al. (1971) reported that recognition memory for facial photographs that subjects perceived as attractive was higher than for the average facial photograph. However, we should note that Cross et al.'s procedure may have helped induce an attractive effect. Specifically, Cross et al. told their subjects that they were studying beauty, and the subject's task was to indicate which faces (from a set of photographs) he or she thought were pretty. If the study has been described as being interested in "ugliness" and the subjects had been asked to sort out the *unattractive* pictures, perhaps the results would have been reversed.

Sex. Early work by Howells (1938) suggested that sex of the target person has little effect on identifiability. Cross et al.'s (1971) research, however, suggests that while sex of the target person has no effect on male subjects, female subjects are better at recognizing female faces than they are at recognizing male faces.

Age. Another characteristic of the defendant that might influence accuracy is the defendant's age. Unfortunately, only one study has included the target person's age as a factor (Cross et al., 1971), and for reasons unknown to the current author, the published version of that study did not report a statistical breakdown of that factor.

Characteristics of the Witness

As with characteristics of the defendant, the witness variable that has probably received the most attention is the witness's race. However, because the witness's race generally interacts with the race of the defendant, these results were discussed in the previous section. Sex of the witness was also discussed in the previous section because of its interaction with sex of the defendant.

Perceptual set. The perceptual set of a witness may influence eyewitness accuracy. Borrowing from Craik and Lockhart's (1972) levels-of-processing concept, Bower and Karlin (1974) found that memory for a face is better if, upon initial exposure to the face, individuals are asked to make judgments that require more thought about or analysis of the face (for example, making judgments of honesty as opposed to judgments of sex).

A Critical Evaluation of
Estimator-Variable Research

Can we make specific estimates of accuracy? How can estimator-variable research be applied to criminal justice? There are several ways to apply this research, but they entail untested (and sometimes untestable) suppositions. Earlier it was suggested that one might assess the merits of a given witness by "plugging in" the relevant factors. For example, one may have a checklist such as "What is the victim's race? What is the defendant's race? How attractive was the defendant? What is the witness's sex? How old is the defendant? How severe was the crime? What was the witness's perceptual set? visual context? exposure time?" and so on. But surely any psychologist must realize the futility of such an approach. Can it be assumed that these factors only combine as main effects? Of course not. A defendant's sex would surely not maintain its effect over long exposure times. Using only the research reviewed thus far, one would have to look at a 19th-order interaction! If new research is added showing that the defendant's facial expression affects accuracy (thereby making it a 20th-order interaction), we have learned more and, therefore, can we apply more? Some may answer "yes" to this question, apparently believing it possible to execute such projects in which all levels of the 20 estimator variables (in a few years will it perhaps be 40 variables?) are factorially combined and their interactions and main effects assessed. But, if one only used two levels of each of the 20 variables and created a factorial design to assess all possible interactions there would be 2^{20}, or 1,048,576, cells in the design.

Can we make general statements? Instead of making specific estimates of eyewitness accuracy, perhaps estimator-variable research can yield *general* statements of use to the courts. For example, one might conclude that because the experimental literature shows such poor accuracy rates in general, jurors and judges must be informed of this fact by psychologists. Yet, even this trivial contribution to criminal justice involves risky suppositions. For example, it assumes that judges and jurors currently believe that witnesses are less fallible than they are. Yet *there is no empirical evidence to support the assumption that jurors and judges are overbelieving of witnesses.* Thus where is the empirical justification for this courtroom intervention? How can we be assured that psychologists' expert testimony will not create jurors and judges who are *less* believing of witnesses than they should be? Perhaps even more problematic is the fact that to make a statement about the fallibility of eyewitness testimony on the basis of estimator-variable research, the expert would supposedly rely on an *average* level of accuracy, a *typical* accuracy rate, or an average accuracy rate of a "typical study." If the expert is able to do so (which is questionable) he or she is also assuming that the literature is unbiased. Yet it can be proposed that the literature is replete with potential biases. For one thing, only one eyewitness study used the concept of "volunteerism" (i.e., only those witnesses who overtly indicate that they could possibly make a positive identification are allowed to see pictures or a lineup). Thus a study that shows 30% of the witnesses correct and 70% incorrect might find a very high accurate/inaccurate ratio if it selected witnesses as police often do (i.e., testing only witnesses who *freely* indicate that they saw the criminal, freely indicate that they had a sufficient view, and freely volunteer their services).

Another factor that might make the accuracy rates of eyewitness research somewhat unrepresentative is that subject-witnesses almost always know that the "crime" was staged by the time they are given a recall or recognition task. This knowledge could increase the tendency of those who have limited information to go ahead and identify someone. If it were a real crime, however, a false identification would have important implications, and this possibility could reduce the percentage of witnesses who simply guess.

In addition, no research exists in which the subject-witness is also the victim, yet such situations apply to virtually all rape, robbery, and assault cases. It may be that accuracy is extremely high under these conditions, as opposed to the relatively uninvolved, passive-role conditions typical of staged crimes.

There are other reasons why accuracy rates in estimator-variable research may be misleading. The current author suspects that in general, low accuracy rates may be *preferred* among researchers. Specifically, researchers may perceive it as infinitely more interesting, more publishable, and more socially important to show low eyewitness accuracy in eyewitness research than to show high accuracy. A high accuracy rate is an implicit null hypothesis that is to be rejected, and the stronger the rejection, the better. Not surprisingly, eyewitness researchers sometimes feel a greater need to dismiss high accuracy, but not low accuracy, as a research fluke. For example, Buckhout (1974), in reporting the results of a staged crime, noted that subject-witnesses were quite accurate in estimating the "criminal's" height and concluded, "This may be because the suspect was of average height" (Buckhout, 1974). Buckhout's observation may be correct, but it introduces the possibility that researchers do not want high accuracy or that high-accuracy data warrant discounting, whereas low-accuracy data speak for themselves.

There is yet another possible reason to question the representativeness of staged "crimes." Personal communications between the author of the current article and other eyewitness researchers suggest that criminal-confederates may be chosen by researchers on an unrepresentative basis. Eyewitness researchers often go to great lengths to insure that their criminal-confederates do not have outstanding features. It is not clear how this concern for "no outstanding features" becomes operationalized in the selection of a criminal-confederate. However, it is possible that the chosen criminal-confederates have physical features that go a long way toward being unrepresentative, and therefore, perhaps criminal-confederates are more difficult to recognize than most criminals.

It may be possible to use estimator-variable research in a way that does not depend upon *direct* generalizations from data. As Schlenker and Bonoma (Note 4) have pointed out, generalizations are made on the basis of corroborated theories, not data alone. Thus in principle, estimator-variable research has the potential for application to criminal justice through the theoretical development of eyewitness processes. However, in practice, there is little evidence of the kind of theoretical developments that would yield such applicability. Estimator-variable research tells us that the eye is not like a camera, but this concept of perception has been known for centuries, and continued documentation of the fact is probably unnecessary. In the next section, another type of eyewitness research (system-variable research) is described. Instead of simply documenting that the human eye is not like a camera, system-variable research investigates variables that might be useful for *reducing* the discrepancy between the eye and the camera.

A CLOSER EXAMINATION OF THE
SYSTEM-VARIABLE LITERATURE

As noted earlier, system-variable research differs from estimator-variable research in that the former investigates variables that are manipulable by the criminal justice system, whereas the latter investigates variables whose influence can be estimated (but not controlled) by the criminal justice system. The distinction between estimator- and system-variable research may be important for the eventual establishment of a useful, nonreactionary, applied criminal justice literature. However, before the potential merits and drawbacks of system-variable research are addressed, a review of that literature is in order.

Retention Interval

Time. Apparently, the belief that recall and recognition memory performace decays with the passage of time is so well accepted that no one has bothered to test it with a live, staged crime. Recently, however, Lipton (1977) exposed subjects to a filmed, simulated murder and tested subjects either immediately or after a 1-week delay. As expected, subjects' recall accuracy was poorer (4.3% less) with the delay than when they were immediately tested.

Suggestive interrogation. Eyewitness researchers' primary interest in the retention interval, however, is not time per se, but rather the intervening material. Foremost in this area is the research of Loftus and her colleagues. This research is exemplified by Loftus and Palmer (1974), who showed subjects a film of a traffic accident and varied the format of an intervening interrogation. When asking subjects about the speed of the cars, Loftus and Palmer either used the question "About how fast were the cars going when they *hit* each other?" or substituted the phrase "smashed into" for "hit." One week later, subjects who were earlier asked the question with the phrase "smashed into" were more likely to indicate that they saw broken glass than were subjects who were earlier asked the question with the verb "hit" in the sentence. Loftus, Altman, and Geballe (1975), and Loftus, Miller, and Burns (1978) have shown similar distortions in recall as a function of other types of intervening interrogation procedures.

Composite drawings. Recognition-memory performance may be hindered not only by disguised suggestions on the part of an interrogator but also by an open task that is largely structured by the witness. Hall and Ostrom (Note 5) presented subjects with a facial photograph, and subjects were later required to try to identify the person from a corporal lineup. However, during the time interval between the initial exposure to the face and the subsequent lineup identification some subjects worked with an artist to create a composite drawing of the to-be-recognized person's face. The results indicated that irrespective of whether the person to be recognized was present in the lineup, the subjects in the composite-drawing conditions made more errors (average = 50% errors) than did subjects in the no-composite-drawing conditions (average = 31% errors).

Mug shots. In addition to composite drawings, it may be that the process of examining mug shots can lead to subsequent misidentifications in a lineup. Brown, Deffenbacher, and Sturgill (1977) exposed subjects to five strangers, with instructions to the subject that they would later be required to identify the strangers from a lineup. Before the lineup tasks, however, subjects viewed a set of mug shots that included some of the original strangers and some new faces. In the subsequent lineup test, the percentage of "incidental" members (i.e., faces that were seen only in the mug shots) who were falsely identified was more than double the percentage of false identifications of completely new faces (i.e., seen in neither the original set nor the mug shots). This result suggests that exposure to mug shots themselves may debilitate subsequent recognition-memory performance.

Testing

Question structure. Perhaps the most frequently researched of the system variables, testing structure, can have powerful effects on the witnesses' performance. Lipton's (1977) research in which subjects were shown a filmed murder indicated that completely unstructured testimony (i.e., free elaboration without the use of any questioning) produced greater accuracy (91%) than any other type of questioning. Open-ended questions yielded somewhat greater accuracy (83%) than either leading questions (72%) or multiple-choice questions (56%). Each of these question types was significantly different from the others. The quality of the testimony, however, tended toward the reverse patterning (21%, 32%, 79%, and 75% for each of the preceding question types, respectively). Similar results showing that accuracy declines with question structure and specificity have been reported by Borst (cited in Whipple, 1909), Snee and Lush (1941), Marquis, Marshall, and Oskamp (1972), and Marshall (1969). Yet, Lipton's (1977) research also shows that because specific questions can be either negatively biased (i.e., suggesting an incorrect response) or positively biased (i.e., suggesting a correct response), the degree of difference in accuracy between specific and nonspecific questions is attenuated by question bias.

Lineup instructions. Lineups, a multiple-choice type of interrogation, are a particularly appealing focus of research because of the
obvious ability of police investigators to control characteristics of a
lineup and the pervasive utilization of such evidence in court. Hall and
Ostrom (Note 5) found that the instructions delivered to a witness
prior to a lineup task can influence false identifications. Specifically,
Hall and Ostrom found that telling the witness that the suspect "is in
the lineup" led to more false identifications than did telling the
witness that the suspect "may or may not" be in the lineup.

Lineup structure. Characteristics of the lineup itself can also
influence accuracy. Wells et al. (Note 6) have outlined an empirical
technique for helping to ensure the fairness of a lineup. They point out
that witnesses are often motivated to pick "someone" out of a lineup
because of witnesses' frequent belief that the police have a good set of
reasons for organizing the lineup and that the police have amassed
evidence against one of the lineup members. If the witness can detect
which lineup member is suspected by the police, it may increase the
chances of the witness choosing that person. One can imagine an
extreme example of such a bias wherein the witness observed a tall,
black man commit a crime. If the subsequent lineup is composed of
one tall, black man and five others who are either Caucasian, female,
or short, the witness can clearly discern whom the police suspect.
Although this is an extreme example. Wells et al. point out that any
lineup has both a "functional size" (i.e., the number of *feasible* lineup
members) and a nominal size (number of persons in lineup). The
functional size can be calculated using a simple role-playing paradigm.
The role-playing paradigm utilizes "mock witnesses" who are given a
general description of the suspect as described by (a majority of) the
witness(es). Usually this would include race, height, weight, sex, and
age. The mock witnesses are then given a picture of the corporal
lineup (which must be provided by the prosecution for the defense
counsel) with instructions to "choose the person whom you believe
the police suspect." Functional size is then calculated at N/X, where X
is the number of mock witnesses choosing the defendant and N is the
total number of mock witnesses who make a choice. Thus a lineup in
which half of the mock witnesses choose the defendant has a
functional size of two, irrespective of the lineup's nominal size. Similar
arguments regarding biases in police lineups have been offered by
Doob and Kirshenbaum (1973).

While Wells et al.'s (Note 6) technique for assessing functional size
can account for some types of lineup bias, other types of lineup bias do
not enter into this analysis. For example, intentional or unintentional
cuing by the official(s) in charge of conducting the lineup may
influence witness responding. The influence of nonverbal cuing in
lineup situations has been demonstrated in a study by Fanselow and

Buckhout (Note 7). Fanselow and Buckhout showed subjects a 21-sec, silent color film of a staged mugging and shooting incident. Subsequently, subjects were individually shown six photographs in which one photograph (target picture) was associated with a "positive treatment" (investigator establishes eye contact with subject-witness, leans forward and smiles), a negative treatment (investigator looks away from subject-witness, frowns, leans backward), or a neutral treatment (no unusual treatment of picture). Each picture was associated with each treatment an equal number of times. After going through all six pictures individually, the subject-witness was requested to go back and look at them again and choose the "mugger." The results revealed that both the positive and negative treatments resulted in more choices of the target picture (23% and 16%, respectively) than did neutral treatment (5%). Note, however, that these percentages suggest that the effect may be primarily due to an inhibition-of-choice effect for the neutral treatment condition in this study, leaving the precise interpretation unclear.

An Evaluation of
System-Variable Research

How can system-variable research be applied to the betterment of criminal justice? One possibility is to use it in the courtroom as an estimator variable. For example, an expert could suggest to the court that the conditions of the lineup, courtroom procedures, or length of time between the original event and subsequent testing is so great that the witness is quite likely to be wrong. However, any such courtroom statement, no matter how it is phrased, would imply a likelihood of accuracy with regard to the case at hand. Suppose, for example, that the expert observed a biased lineup. Can he or she say that it is likely that the witness was incorrect because past research shows strong effects for biased lineups? No. If all of the measurable and unmeasurable influencing factors for that specific case were known (lighting, exposure time, etc.) it may be that the probability of accuracy would be .95 without a biased lineup and .92 with a biased lineup. Biased lineups may have consistently debilitating effects, but likelihood of accuracy depends on too many factors in a given case of any semblance of reasonable estimation. In other words, *this* use of system-variable research entails the same problems of applications as did the estimator-variable research. As discussed earlier, discounting eyewitness testimony is a practice that is based upon questionable derivations from the eyewitness literature (overinduction) and fails to provide an alternative source of evidence.

The alternative use of system-variable research is to manipulate the relevant variables so as to *reduce the inaccuracies of witnesses*. For example, system-variable research can be used to advocate short witness-testing intervals, fairer lineups, reduced use of composite drawings, and so forth. This gives the criminal justice system empirically derived tools with which to better the criminal justice process. It provides an alternative to current practices without advocating the elimination of eyewitness testimony as a rule of evidence. Using system-variable research in this manner can contribute to criminal justice without the practice of post hoc discounting of an eyewitness.

There is one problem that afflicted the application of estimator-variable research that may also apply to the application of system-variable research, namely, the issue regarding statistical interactions. However, this may be less problematic for system-variable applications than it is for estimator-variable applications. In applying estimator variables to a specific case, *all* types of interactions are important. For example, the effect of high versus low crime severity on eyewitness accuracy could be enhanced, moderated, or reversed by another variable. Any of these three types of interaction would be important in determining the likely accuracy of a witness for courtroom presentation. However, in applying system variables, the enhancement and moderation-type interactions present no special problems. For example, the effect of a short versus long incident-test interval may be moderated or enhanced by another variable, but a problem exists only if the directional influence is *reversed* (i.e., a long interval facilitates memory more than a short interval) by the presence of another variable.

CONCLUSION

It would be bad advice to suggest a halt to estimator-variable research. However, in understanding an *applied* project, it is incumbent on a researcher to demonstrate the applied utility of an eyewitness study. In this regard, estimator-variable research may not be highly fruitful. This statement does not speak to any specific study reviewed in the estimator-variable section. Some of those studies were not intended to be applied, and some of those studies may have more applied utility than their membership in that category suggests. Yet, the overall conclusion is maintained: System-variable research in eyewitness identification may, as a general rule, have greater applied utility for criminal justice than does estimator-variable research.

On the other hand, there may be certain types of estimator-variable research than can circumvent the application problems that have been listed. For example, instead of focusing on the *situation* as the unit of postdictive analysis, efforts could be made to use the *individual* as a unit of analysis. Specifically, self-report information (e.g., various measures of the witness's confidence in his or her identification) may be diagnostic of accuracy. This cognitive approach assumes that situational factors prior to and during the crime (estimator variables) affect some measurable response (e.g., confidence) in a manner that is statistically related to the accuracy factor. Unfortunately, only three studies have measured any such cognitive storage (see Brown et al., 1977; Leippe et al., 1978; Wells, Lindsay, & Ferguson, in press), and the postdictive utility of the cognitive measure (confidence) has been unproductive.

NOTES

1. This article will assume that convicting an innocent defendant (false alarm) is no more of an injustice than is releasing a guilty defendant (miss). While this may seem to contradict the views of many social-action groups concerned with criminal justice, any differential weighing of these two types of error might restrict researchers' focus on the broader issues and/or inappropriately affect how researchers operationalize eyewitness variables. On the other hand, differential weighing might be defended by the often-overlooked fact that for "false alarms," the falsely accused suffers *and* the true criminal is still at large, whereas for "misses," only the latter factor is operative. In addition, a "miss" is not considered a vindication of the criminal suspect.

2. This is not to say that the psychological literature on eyewitness testimony has been ignored by law journals or lawmakers. Levine and Tapp's (1973) article in the *Pennsylvania Law Review* outlines the psychological literature's relevance for the criminal identification process. This was recently updated by Woocher (1977) in the *Stanford Law Review*. A recent government-solicited report (Devlin, 1976) has also shown sensitivity to the apparent inadequacy of eyewitness identifications.

REFERENCE NOTES

1. Buckhout, R. *Nobody likes a smartass: Expert testimony by psychologists.* Paper presented at the annual convention of the American Psychological Association, Washington, DC, September 1976.

2. Hastie, R., Loftus, E. F., Penrod, S., & Winkler, J. D. *Eyewitness testimony: Review of the psychological literature.* Unpublished manuscript, Harvard University, 1977.

3. Johnson, C. S., & Scott, B. *Eyewitness testimony and suspect identification as a function of arousal, sex of witness, and scheduling of interrogation.* Paper presented at the annual convention of the American Psychological Association, Washington, DC, September 1976.

4. Schlenker, B. R., & Bonoma, T. V. *Fun and games: The validity of games for the study of conflict.* Unpublished manuscript, University of Florida, 1976.

5. Hall, D. F., & Ostrom, T. M. *Accuracy of eyewitness identification after biased or unbiased instructions.* Unpublished manuscript, Ohio State University, 1975.

6. Wells, G. L. et al. *Guidelines for empirically assessing the fairness of a lineup.* Manuscript submitted for publication, 1978.

7. Fanselow, M. S., & Buckhout, R. *Nonverbal cueing as a source of biasing information in eyewitness identification testing.* Unpublished manuscript, Brooklyn College, 1976.

REFERENCES

Berscheid, E., & Walster, E. Physical attractiveness. In L. Berkowitz (Ed.), *Advances in experimental social psychology* (Vol 11). New York: Academic Press, 1974.

Bower, G. H., & Karlin, M. B. Depth of processing pictures of faces and recognition memory. *Journal of Experimental Psychology,* 1974, *103,* 751-757.

Brown, E., Deffenbacher, K., & Sturgill, W. Memory for faces and the circumstances of the encounter. *Journal of Applied Psychology,* 1977, *62,* 311-318.

Buckhout, R. Eyewitness testimony. *Scientific American,* 1974, *321,* 23-31.

Craik, T. I. M., & Lockhart, R. S. Levels of processing: A framework for memory research. *Journal of Verbal Learning and Verbal Behavior,* 1972, *11,* 671-684.

Cross, J. F., Cross, J., & Daly, J. Sex, race, age and beauty as factors in recognition of faces. *Perception & Psychophysics,* 1971, *10,* 393-396.

Devlin, Rt. Hon. Lord Patrick. *Report to the Secretary of State for the House Department on Evidence of Identification in Criminal Cases.* House of Commons, April 26, 1976. London: Her Majesty's Stationery Office.

Dobb, A. N., & Kirshenbaum, H. M. Bias in police lineups—Partial remembering. *Journal of Police Science and Administration,* 1973, *1,* 287-293.

Elliot, E. S., Willis, E. J., & Goldstein, A. G. The effects of discrimination training on the recognition of white and oriental faces. *Bulletin of the Psychonomic Society,* 1973, *2,* 71-73.

Franken, R. E., & Davis, J. Predicting memory for faces from rankings of interestingness, pleasingness, complexity, figure-ground and clarity. *Perceptual and Motor Skills,* 1975, *41,* 243-247.

Grether, W. F., & Baker, C. A. Visual presentations of information. In H. P. van Cott & R. G. Kinkade (Eds.), *Human engineering guide to equipment design.* Washington, DC: U.S. Government Printing Office, 1972.

Hintzman, D. L. Repetition and memory. In G. L. Bower (Ed.), *The psychology of learning and motivation* (Vol. 10). New York: Academic Press, 1976.

Howells, T. H. A study of ability to recognize faces. *Journal of Abnormal and Social Psychology,* 1938, *33,* 124-127.

Leippe, M., Wells, G. L., & Ostrom, T. Crime seriousness as a determinant of accuracy in eyewitness identification. *Journal of Applied Psychology,* 1978, *3,* 345-351.

Levine, F. J., & Tapp, J. The psychology of criminal identification: The gap from Wade to Kirby. *University of Pennsylvania Law Review,* 1973, *121,* 1079-1131.

Lipton, J. P. On the psychology of eyewitness testimony. *Journal of Applied Psychology*, 1977, *62*, 90-95.

Loftus, E. F., Altman, D., & Geballe, R. Effects of questioning upon a witness's later recollections. *Journal of Police Science and Administration*, 1975, *3*, 1-2; 165.

Loftus, E. F., Miller, D. G., & Burns, H. J. Semantic integration of verbal information into a visual memory. *Journal of Experimental Psychology: Human Learning and Memory*, 1978, *4*, 19-31.

Loftus, E. F., & Palmer, J. P. Reconstruction of automobile destruction: An example of the interaction between language and memory. *Journal of Verbal Learning and Verbal Behavior*, 1974, *13*, 585-589.

Loftus, G. R. Eye fixations and recognition memory. *Cognitive Psychology*, 1972, *3*, 525-557.

Luce, T. S. Blacks, whites and yellows: They all look alike to me. *Psychology Today*, November 1974, 105-108.

Malpass, R. S., & Kravitz, J. Recognition for faces of own and other race. *Journal of Personality and Social Psychology*, 1969, *13*, 330-334.

Marshall, J. *Law and psychology in conflict*. New York: Doubleday-Anchor, 1969.

Marquis, K. H., Marshall, J., & Oskamp, S. Testimony validity as a function of question form, atmosphere and item difficulty. *Journal of Applied Psychology*, 1972, *56*, 167-186.

Schaffer, W. O., & Schriffin, R. M. Rehearsal and storage of visual information. *Journal of Experimental Psychology*, 1972, *92*, 292-296.

Schiffman, H. R., & Bobko, D. J. Effects of stimulus complexity on the perception of brief temporal intervals. *Journal of Experimental Psychology*, 1974, *103*, 156-159.

Shepard, R. N. Recognition memory for words, sentences and pictures. *Journal of Verbal Learning and Verbal Behavior*, 1967, *6*, 156-163.

Snee, T. S., & Lush, D. E. Interaction of narrative and interrogatory methods of obtaining testimony. *Journal of Psychology*, 1941, *11*, 229-236.

Wells, G. L., Lindsay, R. C. L., & Ferguson, T. J. Accuracy, confidence, and juror perception in eyewitness identification. *Journal of Applied Psychology*, in press.

Wells, J. E. Encoding and memory for verbal and pictorial stimuli. *Quarterly Journal of Experimental Psychology*, 1972, *24*, 242-252.

Whipple, G. M. The observer as reporter: A survey of the "psychology of testimony." *Psychological Bulletin*, 1909, *6*, 153-170.

Whipple, G. M. The obtaining of information: Psychology of observation and report. *Psychological Bulletin*, 1918, *15*, 217-248.

Woocher, F. D. Did your eyes deceive you? Expert psychological testimony on the unreliability of eyewitness identification. *Stanford Law Review*, 1977, *29*, 969-1030.

9

SEMANTIC INTEGRATION OF VERBAL INFORMATION INTO A VISUAL MEMORY

ELIZABETH F. LOFTUS
University of Washington
DAVID G. MILLER
University of Houston
HELEN J. BURNS
University of Washington

Almost two centuries ago, Immanuel Kant (1781/1887) spoke to the human tendency to merge different experiences to form new concepts and ideas. That tendency has crucial implications for one's ability to

Author's Note. This research was supported by grants to the first author from the Urban Mass Transportation Administration and from the National Institute of Mental Health. Special thanks are due to R. Abelson, W. Cole, C. MacLeod, G. Loftus, T. Nelson, E. Tulving, and S. Woods for reading and commenting on an earlier draft of this article. R. Shiffrin suggested Experiment 2. Requests for reprints should be sent to Elizabeth F. Loftus, Department of Psychology, University of Washington, Seattle, Washington 98195.

report his or her experiences accurately. When one has witnessed an important event, such as a crime or an accident, one is occasionally exposed to subsequent information that can influence the memory of that event. This occurs even when the initial event is largely visual and the additional information is verbal in nature (Loftus, 1975; Pezdek, 1977). For instance, in a previous study, subjects saw films of complex fast-moving events such as automobile accidents or classroom disruptions (Loftus, 1975). Immediately afterward, the subjects were asked a series of questions, some of which were designed to present accurate, consistent information (e.g., suggesting the existence of an object that did exist in the scene), while others presented misleading information (e.g., suggesting the existence of an object that did not exist in the original scene). Thus a subject might have been asked, "How fast was the car going when it ran the stop sign?" when a stop sign actually did exist (Experiment 1). Or the subject might have been asked, "How fast was the white sports car going when it passed the barn while traveling along the country road?" when no barn existed (Experiment 3). These subjects were subsequently asked whether they had seen the presupposed objects. It was found that such questions increased the likelihood that subjects would later report having seen these objects. It was argued that the questions were effective because they contained information—sometimes consistent, sometime misleading—which was integrated into the memorial representation of the event, thereby causing a reconstruction or alteration of the actual information stored in memory.

In these earlier experiments, the original event was presented visually, the subsequent information was introduced verbally via questionnaires, and the final test was also verbal in nature. In the present experiments, a recognition procedure was used; it involved showing a series of slides depicting a complex event and afterward exposing subjects to verbal information about the event. This study phase was followed by a recognition test in which the subjects were presented with target pictures identical to ones seen before and distractor pictures altered in some way. The first reason for this change was that if one subscribes to the view that verbal and visual information are stored separately, one could argue that Loftus's (1975) final test, being verbal in nature, helped subjects access the subsequent verbal information, thereby resulting in an incorrect response.

The second reason for using a recognition test procedure was that if recognition is assumed to be a relatively passive and simple process of

From *Journal of Experimental Psychology: Human Learning and Memory*, 1978, 4(1), 19-31. Copyright 1978 by the American Psychological Association. Reprinted by permission of the publisher and authors.

matching stimuli to specific locations in a content-addressable storage system, one would expect a representation of the actual (or true) scene to result in a match, whereas an alteration would fail to match. In other words, if the original visual scene is stored in memory, presenting the subject with the original stimulus might result in a match between the memory representation and the stimulus. If the original scene had been transformed so that an altered version was stored in memory, presenting the subject with the original stimulus would not result in a match between the memorial representation and the stimulus.

These considerations motivated the present series of studies. Before turning to them, we describe a pilot study in some detail, since the materials and procedures were similar to those used in the remaining experiments.

PILOT EXPERIMENT

In a pilot experiment (Loftus, Salzberg, Burns, & Sanders, Note 1), a series of 30 color slides, depicting successive stages in an auto-pedestrian accident, was shown to 129 subjects. The auto was a red Datsun seen traveling along a side street toward an intersection having a stop sign for half of the subjects and a yield sign for the remaining subjects. These two critical slides are shown in Figure 1. The remaining slides show the Datsun turning right and knocking down a pedestrian who is crossing at the crosswalk. Immediately after viewing the slides, the subjects answered a series of 20 questions. For half of the subjects, Question 17 was, "Did another car pass the red Datsun while it was stopped at the stop sign?" The remaining subjects were asked the same question with the words "stop sign" replaced by "yield sign." The assignment of subjects to conditions produced a factorial design in which half of the subjects received consistent or correct information, whereas the other half received misleading or incorrect information. All subjects then participated in a 20-min filler activity, which required them to read an unrelated short story and answer some questions about it. Finally, a yes-no recognition test was administered either immediately or 1 week later. The two critical slides (i.e., those containing the stop and yield signs) were randomly placed in the recognition series in different positions for different groups of subjects.

The results indicated that relative to the case in which consistent information was received, misleading information resulted in significantly fewer hits (correct recognitions of the slide actually seen)

Figure 9.1 Critical slides used in the acquisition series.

and slightly more false alarms (false recognitions of the slide not actually seen). With misleading information, the percentage of hits was 71 and the percentage of false alarms was 70, indicating that subjects had zero ability to discriminate the sign they actually saw from the sign they did not see.

Some aspects of the data from this study preclude a clear interpretation of the results and beg for a variation in design. Most of the subjects responded "yes" to the slide shown first in the recognition series, even though the opposite sign had been seen and mentioned in the questionnaire. This indicates that the two critical slides are so similar that subjects failed to make any distinction between them. Perhaps when the second slide appeared, some subjects responded "yes" again, thinking it was the same slide, while others felt obliged to respond "no," having already responded "yes" to the earlier slide. For these reasons, a forced-choice recognition test seemed necessary, since it eliminates the problem of successive recognition tests and forces the subjects to discriminate between the two critical slides.

OVERVIEW OF THE EXPERIMENTS

In Experiment 1, subjects were presented with the acquisition series of slides, an intervening questionnaire, and a final forced-choice recognition test. It is shown that misleading information results in substantially less accurate responding than does consistent information. Next, we consider the possibility that subjects are simply agreeing with the information in their questionnaires, fully remembering what they actually saw. Experiment 2 was actually a demonstration designed to show that the results thus far cannot be explained simply by the demand characteristics of the procedure. In Experiment 3, we asked whether information presented verbally has a different effect depending on whether it is introduced immediately after the initial event (i.e., at the beginning of the retention interval) or just prior to the final test (i.e., at the end of the retention interval). It was found that misleading information has a greater impact when presented just prior to a recognition test rather than just after the initial event. Finally, we addressed the question of whether the verbally presented information actually results in a transformation of an existing representation or whether it is simply a supplementation phenomenon. To answer this issue one needs to know whether the original sign entered memory in the first place. If not, then the subsequent verbal information may simply introduce a sign where none existed, supplementing the existing memorial representation. If the sign originally did get into memory, the subsequent information has caused either an alteration in the original representation (i.e., one sign replaced the other in memory) or the creation of a new, stronger representation that successfully competes with the original one, rendering the latter so dramatically suppressed as to be, for all intents and purposes, gone. Experiment 4, in conjunction with Experiment 3, indicates that the traffic sign is encoded by most subjects when they view the series of slides. Experiment 5 demonstrates the generality of the findings with other materials.

EXPERIMENT 1

Method

Subjects were 195 students from the University of Washington who participated in groups of various sizes. With a few exceptions, the procedure was similar to that used in the pilot experiment. The subjects saw the same series of 30 color slides, seeing each slide for approximately 3 sec. Approximately half of the subjects saw a slide depicting a small red Datsun stopped at a stop sign, whereas the remaining subjects saw the car stopped at a yield sign. Immediately after viewing the acquisition slides, the subjects filled out a questionnaire of 20 questions. For half of the subjects, Question 17 was, "Did another car pass the red Datsun while it was stopped at the stop sign?" For the other half, the same question was asked with the words "stop sign" replaced with "yield sign." Thus, for 95 subjects, the sign mentioned in the question was the sign that had actually been seen; in other words, the question contained consistent information. For the remaining 100 subjects, the question contained misleading information.

After completing the questionnaire, the subjects participated in a 20-min filler activity that required them to read an unrelated short story and answer some questions about it. Finally, a forced-choice recognition test was administered. Using two slide projectors, 15 pairs of slides were presented, each pair of slides being projected for approximately 8 sec. One member of each pair was old and the other was new. For each pair, the subjects were asked to select the slide that they had seen earlier. The critical pair was a slide depicting the red Datsun stopped at a stop sign and a nearly identical slide depicting the Datsun at a yield sign. The slides that the subjects actually saw varied in the left and right positions.

Results

The percentage of times a subject correctly selected the slide he or she had seen before was 75 and 41, respectively, when the intervening question contained consistent versus misleading information, $Z = 4.72$, $p < .001$. If 50% correct selection is taken to represent chance guessing behavior, subjects given consistent information performed significantly better than chance, $Z = 5.10$, $p < .001$, whereas those given misleading information performed significantly worse than chance, $Z = 1.80$, $p < .05$ (one-tailed test).

EXPERIMENT 2

Some time ago, Orne (1962) proposed that certain aspects of any psychological experiment may provide clues, or *demand characteristics*, that permit observant subjects to discern the experimental hypothesis. Obliging subjects may then try to confirm that hypothesis. In the context of the present paradigm, it is possible that some or all the subjects not only remembered what traffic sign they observed but also remembered what sign was presupposed on their questionnaire and then "went along" with what they believed to be the experimental hypothesis and chose the sign from their questionnaire. A slightly different version of this position would argue that at the time of the final test, subjects said to themselves, "I think I saw a stop sign, but my questionnaire said 'yield sign,' so I guess it must have been a yield sign." Experiment 2 was designed to investigate this possibility.

Method

The method was similar to that of Experiment 1 with a few exceptions. Ninety subjects saw the slide series. Half of them saw a stop sign, and half a yield sign. Immediately after slides, the subjects filled out the questionnaire. For 30 subjects, the critical question was, "Did another car pass the red Datsun while it was stopped at the intersection?" In other words, it did not mention a sign. For 30 other subjects, the critical question mentioned a stop sign, and for the remaining 30 it mentioned a yield sign. Thus for one-third of the subjects, the key question contained a true presupposition; for one-third, the presupposition was false; and for the remaining one-third, the question made no reference to a sign at all. A 20-min filler activity occurred followed by a forced-choice recognition test.

Finally, the subject was given a "debriefing questionnaire." It stated,

The study in which you have just been involved was designed to determine the effects of subsequent information on eye-witness testimony. In the beginning, you saw a series of slides which depicted an accident. One of the slides contained either a stop sign or a yield sign. Later you were given a questionnaire. One of the questions on this questionnaire was worded to assume that you had seen either a stop sign or a yield sign or else it contained no information about what kind of sign you saw.

Please indicate which sign you think you saw and what was assumed on your questionnaire.

I Saw	My Questionaire Mentioned
A stop sign	A stop sign
A yield sign	A yield sign
	No sign

This final debriefing questionnaire permitted a subject to claim, for example, that he or she had seen a stop sign but that the questionnaire had mentioned a yield sign. In other words, it gave the subjects the opportunity to be completely "insightful" about their condition in the experiment.

Results

Of the 90 subjects who took the forced-choice recognition test, 53 chose the correct sign; 37 chose the incorrect sign. As in the previous experiment, accuracy depended on whether the subject had been given consistent, misleading, or no information on the intervening questionnaire. This relationship can be seen in Table 1.

The subjects who chose the correct sign during the forced-choice test were more than three times as likely as incorrect subjects to be completely correct on the debriefing questionnaire. Overall, 43% of the subjects choosing the correct sign accurately responded to the debriefing questionnaire, whereas only 14% of the incorrect subjects were completely accurate, $Z = 2.96$, $p < .01$. Again, whether the subjects responded accurately to the debriefing questionnaire depended on whether they had been given consistent, misleading, or no information on their intervening questionnaires.

Of central concern was the performance of subjects who had been given misleading information and who had subsequently chosen incorrectly on their forced-choice test. For example, they saw a stop sign, read that it was a yield sign, and subsequently chose the yield sign on the forced-choice test. These subjects were the ones who may have been acting the way the experimenter wanted them to act. They may have been deliberately choosing the sign mentioned on their questionnaire although fully remembering what they saw. Yet, when given the debriefing questionnaire that afforded them the opportunity to say. "I think I saw the stop sign, but my questionnaire said yield," only 12% did so.

TABLE 9.1
Data from Experiment 2

Information given	Incorrect subjects on forced-choice test		Correct subjects on forced-choice test	
	n	% correct on debriefing questionnaire	n	% correct on debriefing questionnaire
Consistent	9	22	21	52
Misleading	17	12	13	31
None	11	9	19	42
Weighted M		14		43

EXPERIMENT 3

The issue that motivated Experiment 3 was whether the information introduced subsequent to an event has a different impact when it is introduced immediately after the event than when it is introduced just prior to the final test. To determine this, we varied the time interval between the initial slides and the final forced-choice test. The intervening questionnaire was presented either immediately after the acquisition slides or it was delayed until just prior to the final test.

Method

Subjects were 648 students from the University of Washington who either participated for course credit or were paid for their participation. They participated in groups of various sizes.

The procedure was nearly identical to that used in Experiments 1 and 2, with the major variations being the retention interval and the time of the intervening questionnaire. Subjects saw each acquisition slide for approximately 3 sec. Half saw the key slide that contained a stop sign, and half saw a yield sign. A questionnaire was administered, followed by a forced-choice recognition test. The forced-choice test occurred after a retention interval of either 20 min, 1 day, 2 days, or 1 week, with 144 subjects tested at each interval. Half of the subjects at each retention interval answered the questionnaire immediately after viewing the acquisition slides (immediate questionnaire), and the other half answered it just before the final forced-choice test (delayed questionnaire). In addition, 72 subjects saw the slides, received the questionnaire immediately afterward, and immediately after that were given the forced-choice test. For purposes of analysis, we consider this group to have been tested at a retention interval of zero.[1]

Except at the zero retention interval, all subjects read a short, unrelated "filler" story for 20 min and then answered some questions about it. Subjects who were given the immediate questionnaire completed the filler activity after answering the questionnaire. Subjects who were given the delayed questionnaire completed the filler activity after viewing the acquisition slides.

Question 17 on the questionnaire was the critical question. It mentioned a stop sign, a yield sign, or no sign at all. Equal numbers of subjects received each version. Thus one-third of the subjects were given consistent information, one-third were given misleading information, and one-third were given no information at all relevant to a traffic sign.

In the final forced-choice recognition test, subjects were asked to choose the slide they had seen before and give a confidence rating from 1 to 3, where 1 indicated the subject was sure of the answer and 3 indicated a guess.

Results and Discussion

Proportions of correct responses as a function of retention interval are displayed separately for subjects in different conditions in Figure 2. The data for subjects tested at a retention interval of zero appear twice in Figure 2, once under immediate questionnaire and once under delayed questionnaire, because the questionnaire occurred, by definition, both immediately after the slides and just prior to the final test. In a sense, it was both an immediate and a delayed questionnaire.

Before presenting statistical analyses, we shall point out some major observations. First, for both the immediate and delayed questionnaire, longer retention intervals led to worse performance. Type of information given also had an effect: Relative to a control in which subjects were given no information, consistent information improved their performance and misleading information hindered it. The functions obtained when no relevant information was given show the usual forgetting over time. By 2 days, subjects were performing at chance level. Immediately after viewing the slides, however, there was relatively good memory for them (up to 87% correct).

The first analysis considered only the immediate-questionnaire data. A 5 (retention intervals) $\times$ 3 (types of information) analysis of variance of the arc sine transformed proportions was conducted (Mosteller & Tukey, 1949, p. 189). All F tests reported here are with MS_e = .01 and $p < .01$, unless otherwise indicated. The analysis showed that longer retention intervals led to less accurate performance, $F(4, \infty)$ = 5.67. Further, the type of information to which a subject was exposed affected accuracy, $F(2, \infty)$ = 50.19, and there was an interaction

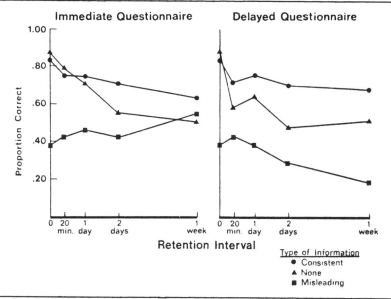

Figure 9.2   Proportion of correct responses as a function of retention interval displayed separately for subjects given an immediate questionnaire and subjects given a delayed questionnaire in Experiment 3. (The curve parameter is type of information the subject received during the retention interval.)

between these factors, $F(8,\infty) = 5.19$. A test for monotonic trend for the subjects who were given consistent information yielded a significant trend, $F(1, \infty) = 10.38$. Similarly, the trend was significant for subjects given inconsistent and no information, $F(1,\infty) = 4.43$ and $F(1,\infty) = 43.13$, respectively.

The second analysis considered the data from subjects who received a delayed questionnaire. A 5×3 analysis of variance of the arc sine transformed proportions indicated that longer retention intervals led to less accurate performance, $F(4,\infty) = 13.37$. Type of information and the interaction were also significant, $F(2, \infty) = 90.91$, and $F(8,\infty) = 2.98$, respectively. Again, the monotonic trends for each of the three types of information also reached significance: $F(1, \infty) = 5.92$ for subjects given consistent information, 14.05 for inconsistent information, and 35.85 for no information (all $ps < .05$).

Consistent information. Not surprisingly, when a subject is exposed to information that essentially repeats information previously encoded, recognition performance is enhanced. With an immediate questionnaire, the visual and verbal repetitions are massed, whereas with a delayed questionnaire, they are spaced. Whereas in most memory tasks, successive repetitions affect memory less than do repetitions that are spaced apart in time (Hintzman, 1976), this outcome was not obtained in the present experiment. A popular explanation for the spacing effect is in terms of voluntary attention. The subject chooses to pay less attention to the second occurrence of an item when it closely follows the first occurrence than he does when the interval between the two is longer. In the present case, it appears as if the subject may have paid more attention to the second occurrence when it closely followed the first, resulting in memory enhancement that was able to survive longer retention intervals.

Misleading information. When misleading information occurs immediately after an event, it has a different effect than when it is delayed until just prior to the test. The immediate procedure results in a nearly monotonically increasing function, whereas the delayed procedure leads to a monotonically decreasing function. This result makes intuitive sense. When false information is introduced immediately after an event, it has its greatest impact soon. Therefore, when the test was immediate, such subjects performed well below chance. But after an interval of, say, 1 week, both the event and the misleading information apparently had faded such that the subject performed near chance levels. On the other hand, when the misleading information was delayed, it was able to influence the subjects' choice more effectively as the delay increased. Presumably, the weaker the original trance, the easier it is to alter.

To see more clearly the effects of an immediate versus a delayed questionnaire, we excluded the data for subjects tested at a retention interval of zero and collapsed the data over the four remaining retention intervals. The results of these computations are shown in Figure 3. The proportion correct is presented as a function of the type of information given, with the immediate versus delayed questionnaire data shown separately. It is again evident that the delayed questionnaire had a larger impact than the immediate one when the subjects were given misleading information: When misleading information was introduced immediately after the incident, 46% of the subjects were correct; however, when it was delayed until just prior to the final test, that percentage dropped to 31.5%, $Z = 2.06$, $p < .05$.

We should mention here that Dooling and Christiaansen (1977) have found a different effect of misleading information. They found that such information had a greater effect on memory distortion when it occurred before the retention interval rather than afterward. As these investigators rightfully point out, there are so many differences between their experimental paradigm and ours that it is difficult to essay a resolution of the difference in results. Our subsequent manipulation focuses on one particular detail of the material to be remembered, and a peripheral detail at that. In Dooling and Christiaansen's task, the subsequent information consists of the name of a

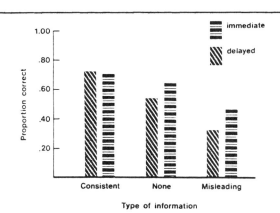

Figure 9.3 Proportion of correct responses for subjects given different type of information in Experiment 3. (Data for subjects given an immediate questionnaire
are shown separately from data for those given a delayed questionnaire.)

famous person about whom subjects already have a great deal of
knowledge stored in memory. Unfortunately, neither they nor we
have been able to come up with an appealing hypothesis for why these
paradigmatic differences should lead to different results.

Surprisingly, it appears that even when the questionnaire contained
no information relevant to the traffic sign, performance on this key
item was somewhat better when subjects were interrogated immediately after the event rather than later. Although this difference failed
to reach significance by a Z test involving all four retention intervals, Z
= 1.41, $.10 < p < .20$, it held up for those retention intervals that,
showed some memory performance above chance. For the 20-min
and 1-day intervals, the immediate questionnaire had about a 15%
advantage over the delayed. Perhaps the early questionnaire permitted
the subjects to review the incident in order to answer questions about
it, and in the course of this review, some of them refreshed their
memory for the traffic sign even though they were not specifically
queried on this detail.

Confidence ratings. Recall that subjects indicated how confident
they were in their responses, circling "1" if they felt certain and "3" if
they were guessing. The rating "2" was used for intermediate levels of
confidence. Figure 4 illustrates how these ratings varied as a function
of the type of information a subject was exposed to, the timing of that
information, and whether the response was correct or incorrect.

A $3 \times 2 \times 2$ unweighted-means analysis of variance (Winer, 1962, p.
241) was performed on all but the zero retention-interval data. This
analysis included the 576 subjects who were unambiguously given
either an immediate or a delayed questionnaire. The error for all F tests

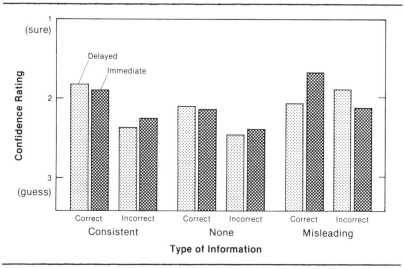

Figure 9.4   Mean confidence ratings as a function of type of information given, immediate versus delayed questionnaire, and correct versus incorrect responses in Experiment 3.

is .493, and $p < .01$ unless otherwise indicated.

Type of information affected confidence, $F(2, 564) = 9.15$, as did whether the subject responded correctly or incorrectly $F(1, 564) = 23.64$; in other words, subjects were more confident if correct than if incorrect (1.92 vs. 2.18). The main effect of timing (whether the questionnaire was answered immediately or whether it was delayed) was not significant ($F < 1$). The Response Accuracy × Type of Information interaction was marginally significant, $F(2, 564) = 2.71$, $.05 < p < .10$, while the other two-way interactions were not ($Fs < 1$). Finally, the triple interaction reached significance, $F(2, 564) = 5.01$. It is evident from Figure 4 that a subject's confidence is boosted by being told anything, whether it is true or not. Further, delaying misleading information raises confidence in incorrect responses above the corresponding value associated with correct responses.

To summarize the major results, there appear to be two discernible consequences of exposing a subject to misleading information. First, the likelihood is lowered that a subject will correctly recognize the object previously seen. This is particularly true if the information is introduced just prior to the final test. Second, the misleading information affects a subject's confidence rating. Generally subjects are more confident of their correct responses than their incorrect ones. However, when exposed to delayed misleading information, they are less confident of their correct responses.

EXPERIMENT 4

Loftus (1975) argued that the information contained in a questionnaire influences subsequent choices because that information is integrated into an existing memorial representation and thereby causes an alteration of that representation. This view assumes that when a person sees the initial event, the items of interest are actually encoded at the time of viewing. In the context of present stimuli, this position would hold that when a person sees a stop sign, for example, the sign gets into memory (i.e., is encoded). If a subsequent questionnaire reports that the sign was a yield sign, that information might, according to this view, enter the memory system and cause an alteration of the original representation. The subject can now be assumed to have a yield sign incorporated into his or her memorial representation of the event.

A question arises as to whether the stop sign actually got into memory in the first place. If it did not, then the subsequent verbal information may simply be introducing a sign where none existed. In other words, the existing memorial representation of the accident is simply supplemented. On the other hand, if the sign was encoded into memory, then the subsequent information may have caused what is functionally a transformation of the original representation. Thus it is theoretically important to determine whether subjects attend to and/or encode the sign. A portion of the data from Experiment 3 suggests that people do. Notice in Figure 2 that when no information is contained in the questionnaire, subjects show some ability to discriminate the sign they saw from the one they did not, up to and including a retention interval of 1 day. For these subjects, the sign must have been encoded, otherwise performance would have been at chance level. Experiment 4 was designed to provide a further test of whether subjects encoded the sign they saw in the acquisition series.

Method

Ninety subjects were shown the same series of slides described above, each slide for approximately 3 sec. Following the series, they were given a sheet of paper with a diagram on it similar to that shown in either Figure 5a or 5b. Forty-five subjects received Diagram 5a, and 45 received 5b. The instructions were to fill in as many details as could be remembered.

The reason for using two versions of the diagram stems from an observation made during a pilot study. Recall that the slides depict a

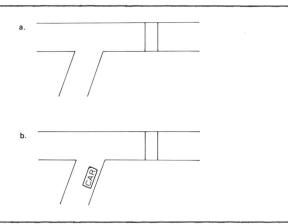

Figure 9.5   Diagrams used in Experiment 4.

red Datsun traveling along a side street toward an intersection. From there the car turns right and knocks over a pedestrian in the crosswalk. If the diagram contains no sketch of the car (5a), the subjects tend to concentrate their attention on details at the crosswalk, which is where the accident took place. They may have seen the sign at the corner, but do not draw it, since it does not seem important to the accident. What is needed is a way to focus their attention on the intersection, and the placing of a car near the intersection as in Figure 5b appeared to be a way of accomplishing this. The experiment lasted less than 10 min.

Results

For purposes of analysis, we counted as correct the drawing made by any subject who either drew the sign he had seen or wrote its name. Overall, 45% of the subjects indicated the correct sign. Of those subjects given the outline without a car (Figure 5a), 35% correctly drew the stop sign, while 32% correctly drew the yield sign. Of those subjects given the outline with a car (Figure 5b), 60% correctly drew the stop sign, while 52% correctly drew the yield sign. An analysis of variance of the arc sine transformed proportions indicated that more subjects depicted a sign when a car was used to direct their attention to the intersection (Figure 5b) than when the diagram contained no car (5a), $F(1, \infty) = 19.94$, $MS_e = .01$. Whether the subject had actually seen a stop sign or a yield sign did not significantly affect the likelihood of drawing the correct sign, $F(1, \infty) = 1.51$, $MS_e = .01$, $p < .20$. The interaction also failed to reach significance ($F < 1$). Three of the 50 subjects who saw a yield sign incorrectly drew a stop sign in their diagram; none of the "stop sign" subjects drew a yield sign.

The results indicate that when subjects view the particular series of slides used throughout these experiments, at least half of them (and perhaps more) do encode the correct sign. The data from subjects given Diagram 5b (with a car to focus their attention on the intersection) indicate that over half have encoded the sign to the point of including it in their diagrams. Others may also have encoded it, but this was not revealed by the present procedure.

EXPERIMENT 5

The purpose of Experiment 5 was to demonstrate the generality of our studies beyond the single-stimulus pair used in the previous studies.

Method

A new series of 20 color slides depicting an auto-pedestrian accident was shown to 80 subjects. A male pedestrian is seen carrying some items in one hand and munching on an apple held with the other. He leaves a building and strolls toward a parking lot. In the lot, a maroon Triumph backs out of a parking space and hits the pedestrian.

Four of the 20 slides were critical. One version of each critical slide contained a particular object (such as a pair of skis leaning against a tree), while the other version contained the identical slide with a changed detail (a shovel leaning against a tree). Each subject saw only one version of the critical slides, and each critical slide was seen equally often across subjects.

Following the slides, which had been seen at a 3-sec rate, subjects completed a 10-min unrelated filler activity. Then they read a three-paragraph description of the slide series supposedly written by another individual who had been given much more time to view the slides. The description contained four critical sentences that either did or did not mention the incorrect critical object. For example, if the subject had seen skis leaning against a tree, his statement might include a sentence that mentioned "the shovel leaning against the tree." The statements were designed so that the mention or nonmention of a critical incorrect detail was counterbalanced over subjects for the four critical items.

After an interval of 10 min, subjects were given a forced-choice recognition test. Using two slide projectors, 10 pairs of slides were presented. The 4 critical pairs were randomly intermixed with the remaining filler pairs. One member of each pair had been seen before, whereas the other had not. The slides that the subject had actually seen varied in the left and right positions.

Results

The percentage of times a correct selection occurred was 55.3 when the intervening statement contained misleading information and 70.8 when it contained no information. For purposes of analysis, two portions were calculated for each of the 4 critical slide pairs. One was the proportion of correct selections when misleading information had intervened, and the other, when no information had intervened. A t test for related measures indicated that the mean percentages (given above) were statistically different from each other, $t(3) = 9.34$, $SE_{diff} = 1.66$.

Discussion

The analysis of Experiment 5 permits us to generalize our findings beyond the single stop-sign/yield-sign stimulus pair. In the present experiment, subjects who saw a slide containing a particular detail, A, but who were given the information that the slide contained Detail B, were subsequently more likely than control subjects to select on a forced-choice recognition test a slide containing B rather than a slide with A.

Note that even with misleading information, subjects were correct about 55% of the time, a figure that is much higher than the approximately 42% figure obtained with the stop-yield stimuli in Experiment 2 after a comparable retention interval. There is probably good reason for this. Any particular object, such as a shovel, can assume many forms. The particular shovel that any subject imagines while reading the story may not agree with the version shown during the recognition test. A subject can then successfully reject the slide containing the shovel, not because he or she recognizes the other slide (containing the skis) but because of not having seen the particular shovel presented during the recognition test.

With common traffic signs, this would not tend to happen. If a subject imagines a stop sign while answering a question that mentions a stop sign, the imagined sign will certainly match the stop sign that would be presented during the recognition test.

GENERAL DISCUSSION

When a person witnesses an important event, he or she is often exposed to related information some time afterward. The purpose of the present experiments was to investigate how the subsequent information influences memory for the original event.

In the pilot experiment, subjects saw a series of slides depicting an accident, and afterward they were exposed to a questionnaire that contained either consistent or misleading information about a particular aspect of the accident. The misleading information caused less accurate responding on a subsequent yes-no recognition test. Similarly, in Experiment 1, misleading information resulted in poorer performance on a forced-choice recognition test. For example, in one condition, subjects saw a stop sign but a subsequent question suggested it was actually a yield sign. Some time later they were given a forced-choice test and asked to choose the sign they thought they had seen. Over half of these subjects incorrectly chose the yield sign.

It has been suggested that the reason this happens is that when the misleading information is presented, it is introduced into the memorial representation for the accident and causes an alteration of that representation. Another interpretation is that subjects are simply agreeing with the information contained in their questionnaires, even though they actually remember what they saw. This is a demand-characteristics explanation. Experiment 2 showed that when subjects were told that they might have been exposed to misleading information and were asked to state whether they thought they had, most of them persisted in claiming that they had seen the incorrect item.

A second interpretation of the forced-choice results is that the original sign information may not have been encoded in the first place. If it had not been encoded, then the subsequent question may have introduced a sign where none existed. In other words, the phenomenon may be one of supplementation. On the other hand, if the sign got into the original memory (i.e., was encoded), then the subsequent information caused either an alteration in the original representation or the creation of a new, stronger representation that competed with the original representation. Experiment 4 showed that a least half of the subjects encoded the initial sign to the point where it was included in a drawing they made of the incident.

The paradigm used throughout this research involves two critical time intervals: the time between the initial event and the presentation of subsequent information and the final test for recollection of the event. In Experiment 3, these intervals were examined. Subjects received their final test after a retention interval of 0 min, 20 min, 1 day,

2 days, or 1 week. The subsequent information was introduced either immediately after the initial event or just prior to the final test. The usual retention-interval results were observed: poorer performance after long intervals than after short ones. Of major interest was the finding that misleading information had a larger impact if presented just prior to a recognition test rather than just after the initial event.

We have noted two interpretations for our results—namely, that either the subsequent information alters the original memory or both the original and the new information reside in memory, and the new competes with the old. Unfortunately, this extremely important issue cannot be resolved with the present data. Those who wish to maintain that the new information produces an alteration cannot prove that the earlier information will not one day spontaneously reappear. Those who wish to hold that new and old information both exist in memory will argue that a person who responds on the basis of new information alone does so because the proper retrieval cue or the right technique has not been used. The value of the present data lies in the fact that they clear up a number of alternative explanations for previously published phenomena. Furthermore, they indicate something about the conditions under which new information is more or less likely to affect accuracy.

The present work bears some resemblance to earlier work on the influence of verbal labels on memory for visually presented form stimuli. Much of the earlier work was designed to test the Gestalt hypothesis that progressive memory changes in the direction of a "better" figure occur autonomously. Riley (1962), in an excellent review of that earlier literature, concluded that the hypothesis of autonomous change is probably not testable. Despite this drawback, the work on verbal labels was useful in revealing that reproductions and recognition memory (Carmichael, Hogan, & Walter, 1932; Daniel, 1972) of simple forms were affected by the labels applied to those forms. The present work represents a much needed extension in that it reveals that these effects occur not only with artificial forms but also with highly naturalistic scenes under conditions that have a high degree of ecological validity. Further, the present work convincingly demonstrates both the integration of information from more than one source into memory and the use of that information to reconstruct a "memory" that was never actually experienced.

NOTE

1. A better design would have orthogonally varied the two critical intervals, namely, the interval between the slides and the questionnaire and the interval between the

questionnaire and the recognition test. However, such a design would have required nearly three times as many subjects to obtain reasonably stable proportions in each cell, and the authors' colleagues were already becoming distressed at the rapidity with which these experiments were depleting the psychology department's subject pool. We doubt that any conclusions would be changed as a result of the fuller design.

REFERENCE NOTE

1. Lofuts, E. F., Salzberg, P. M., Burns, H. J., & Sanders, R. K. *Destruction of a visual memory by verbal information.* Paper presented at the annual meeting of the Psychonomic Society, Denver, November 1975.

REFERENCES

Carmichael, L., Hogan, H. P., & Walter, A. A. An experimental study of the effects of language on the reproduction of visually perceived form. *Journal of Experimental Psychology*, 1932, *15*, 73-86.

Daniel, T. C. Nature of the effect of verbal labels on recognition memory for form. *Journal of Experimental Psychology*, 1972, *96*, 152-157.

Dooling, D. J., & Christiaansen, R. E. Episodic and semantic aspects of memory for prose. *Journal of Experimental Psychology: Human Learning and Memory*, 1977, *3*, 428-436.

Hintzman, D. L. Repetition and memory. In G. H. Bower (Ed.), *The psychology of learning and motivation* (Vol. 10). New York: Academic Press, 1976.

Kant, I. [*Critique of pure reason*] (Translated by J. M. D. Meiklejohn). London: George Bell, 1887. (Originally published, 1781)

Loftus, E. F. Leading questions and the eyewitness report. *Cognitive Psychology*, 1975, *7*, 560-572.

Mosteller, F., & Tukey, J. W. The uses and usefulness of binomial probability paper. *Journal of the American Statistical Association*, 1949, *44*, 174-212.

Orne, M. T. On the social psychology of the psychological experiment: With particular reference to demand characteristics and their implications. *American Psychologist*, 1962, *17*, 776-783.

Pezdek, K. Cross-modality semantic integration of sentence and picture memory. *Journal of Experimental Psychology: Human Learning and Memory*, 1977, *3*, 515-524.

Riley, D. A. Memory for form. In L. Postman (Ed.), *Psychology in the making*. New York: Knopf, 1962.

Winer, B. J. *Statistical principles in experimental design*. New York: McGraw-Hill, 1962.

10

RECOGNITION FOR FACES
OF OWN AND OTHER RACE[1]

ROY S. MALPASS[2]
University of Illinois
JEROME KRAVITZ
Howard University

The traveler's observation that "all those Orientals [Blacks, Arabs] look alike" has support in anecdote and presumption, but little in empirical research. Many studies have been done concerning perception of minority group membership or recognition of facial expression. Some of the latter have included recognition of facial expression in persons of race different from the perceiver. But few studies have centered on interethnic differences in mutual recognition (Howells, 1938; Seeleman, 1940).

A relative inability to recognize persons of another race, should it exist, would have obvious social implications including identification

Reprinted from the *Journal of Personality and Social Psychology*, 1969, 13(4), 330-334. Copyright 1969 by the American Psychological Association. Reprinted by permission of the publisher and authors.

of persons and related legal questions. Among correlates of differential ability that would bear investigation are the distribution of experience with physiognomies of different types and its relation to physiognomic perception and recognition. Questions concerning cue utilization habits and their acquisition would become relevant and would lead to investigation of physiognomic experience as a determinant of recognition, the amount of experience required for the ability to reach asymptote, and the ecology of physiognomic experience related to recognition ability. "Race" as used in this connection is merely a shorthand way of referring to differences in physiognomy that correlate with and are cues to the race of the stimulus person. The present study is an attempt to demonstrate differential recognition ability for faces of own and other race. A 2×2 (Race of Subject $\times$ Race of Stimulus Person) factorial design was used, with race of stimulus person a repeated measure. Differential recognition ability would appear as the interaction effect.

METHOD

Subjects

Subjects were 26 students from introductory psychology courses at the University of Illinois (13 black, 13 white), and 14 first year graduate students at Howard University (7 black, 7 white). Subjects were paid for their participation.

Stimulus Photographs

Forty black and 40 white males of college age were photographed, and the photographs were used as stimuli. All photographs were taken with an Asahi Pentax Hv 35-millimeter camera with a lens of 210-millimeter effective focal length. Photographs were taken on Kodacolor-X negative film from a distance of 7 feet. Stimulus persons were instructed to look directly into the camera lens and assume a "neutral" expression. To reduce nonphysiognomic cues, stimulus persons wore a plain white T shirt and were photographed full face, facing the camera. The background in all photographs was a neutral surface of 90% reflectance. Illumination was provided by a Honeywell Strobonar Model 600. Exposure was determined by calculation. Black stimulus persons were given twice the exposure calculated for white stimulus persons. Color transparencies were made and served as the stimuli in the experiment.

Procedure

Subjects were seated in a room approximately 20 × 30 × 15 feet high. Illumination was provided so that subjects could see the response sheet and perform the response task. Ten minutes adaptation was given in the experimental room. Subjects then heard the following instructions presented by tape recording.

> The experiment you are participating in concerns the ability to recognize faces. You will be shown 20 close-up slides, 1 each, of 20 college age men. Each of the 20 slides will be on the screen for about 2 seconds. After you have seen the 20 slides we will mix them in with 60 more and then see if you can recognize the ones you saw before. All 80 will be shown one at a time.
>
> You have in your hand a marking pen and a sheet of paper on which to mark your responses to each of the 80 pictures in the second series. If you recognize a picture, circle the word "yes" opposite its number. If you do not recognize a picture circle the word "no." Be sure to circle either "yes" or "no" for each picture before the next picture goes on the screen. Only circle "yes" if you are fairly sure you saw the picture before, in the first series.
>
> The experiment is being conducted with pictures of different racial groups: black, white, and oriental. The pictures you will see today will be of young men of two of these racial groups.
>
> Now we will show you the first series of pictures. They will appear on the screen rather rapidly, so be ready. Pay keen attention.

Following this the stimulus sequence was projected by a Kodak Carousel projector. Image size was approximately 32 × 48 inches. Subjects were seated at distances varying from 10 to 20 feet from the screen, in no case being displaced from the axis perpendicular to the image by more than 10 feet. Transparencies were projected for approximately 1½ seconds, with an interstimulus interval of approximately ½ second. The 20 stimulus transparencies were chosen randomly (10 from a pool of 40 white photos, 10 from a pool of 40 black photos) and sequenced randomly with the restriction that no more than three stimuli of given race could appear in sequence.

When the stimulus sequence had been shown, the following instructions were presented by means of the tape recorder:

Now we will show you the second series. There are 80 pictures in the series: the 20 you just saw and 60 others you have never seen before. Your task is to recognize the pictures you just saw. If you recognize a picture, circle the word "yes" opposite its number. Be sure that you mark "yes" or "no" for each picture. If you do not make a mark for each picture, you will not be able to tell what number the pictures you recognize are, and will lose your place on the answer sheet. It is important that you keep up with the pace at which the pictures are shown, and mark one of the two responses for each and every picture. Circle "yes" if you are fairly sure you saw the picture before in the first series. Be careful.

The interval between the stimulus sequence and the beginning of the recognition sequence was 1 minute. The 40 black and 40 white stimulus photographs of the recognition sequence were randomly ordered with the restriction on succession noted above. Exposure duration during the recognition sequence was 4 seconds with a ½-second interstimulus interval. Following the recognition sequence, a questionnaire was administered to collect data concerning experience with the "other race." The experimenter at Illinois was white, and at Howard, black.

RESULTS AND DISCUSSION

Two measures of recognition were obtained: the number of correct identifications and the number of false identifications. These two measures are used to find the index d'. This index was derived in the context of signal detection theory (Swets, Tanner, & Birdsall, 1964) and discussed in the context of studies of short-term recognition memory by Bernback (1967). It is taken as a measure of either discriminability of a stimulus or the acuity of the perceiver, the two being confounded. d' is a measure indicating the superiority of performance over chance expectation where performance is a joint function of the probability of a correct response and the probability of a positive response in the absence of the stimulus (the guess rate). Values of d' for each subject were obtained from tables given by Elliot (1964).[3] Analyses reported here use the square root of the d' measure obtained for each subject. This is done because of the nonlinearity of the d' scale, which is bounded at the lower end, but not at the upper end. The transformation does not effect the ordering of the group means, but does make the analysis more sensitive than would be true in the case of the nontransformed d' scale. All differences between the Illinois and

Howard samples are richly confounded, so their data will be reported and analyzed separately.

Means and standard deviations for the three measures are presented in Table 1. A 2 × 2 analysis of variance (fixed-effects model) with repeated measures (race of stimulus) was performed. The analysis of variance for the two samples is summarized separately in Table 2. A main effect for race of stimulus is observed in the data for both samples, white stimuli being recognized more than black stimuli. This finding may reflect differences in distinctiveness of the stimuli and should lead to investigation of the dimensionality of faces of the two races, along with the variation on these dimensions normally seen. The findings may also reflect brightness differences in the stimulus photographs. A hypothesis that black faces are more homogeneous than white faces is consistent with the present data, if it could be shown that the stimulus samples are not differentially biased samples of their respective physiognomic populations. Independent specification of physiognomic homogeneity is required as a test of this hypothesis. Also consistent with this finding is the hypothesis that the distribution of social experience is such that both black persons and white persons will have had more exposure to white faces than black faces in public media and also will have had more contact with white persons where discriminative ability has positive motivational value.

The Race of Subject × Race of Stimulus interaction, such that subjects recognize faces of own race better than faces of other race, appears in the Illinois data at a conventionally acceptable significance level, and at a marginal level in the Howard data. The authors interpret the findings as indicating a Subject × Stimulus interaction, the marginal level of the findings attributed to sample size. The findings in the Howard sample of superiority of black subjects with white faces is unexpected. This finding disappears, however, if one white subject with distinctly deviant scores is eliminated from the analysis. The order of d' means then becomes: white subjects, white stimuli, 1.44; black subjects, white stimuli, 1.41; black subjects, black stimuli, 1.39; white subjects, black stimuli, 1.07—the same order as in the Illinois sample. A parallel analysis based on d' scores fails to show any significant effects in the Howard data, while showing both the stimulus main effect ($p <$ .05) and the Race of Subject × Race of Stimulus interaction ($p < .025$) in the Illinois data.

In order to provide a check on the possibility that the results were specific to the particular stimulus photographs used, data was collected from three additional groups of subjects, each group being exposed to a set of stimulus pictures different from each other and from those used in the first experiment. The recognition pool remained the same but was reordered. Procedures were identical to those described for

TABLE 10.1
Means and Standard Deviations of Correct Response,
False Identifications, and $\sqrt{d'}$ Measures

University	Ss	Stimuli					
		Black			White		
		Correct responses	False identifications	$\sqrt{d'}$	Correct responses	False identifications	$\sqrt{d'}$
Illinois	Black	7.38[a]	5.69	1.314[c]	6.77	3.61	1.345
	(n = 13)	1.39[b]	3.75	.325	1.88	2.56	.272
	White	6.08	4.85	1.085	7.92	3.46	1.463
	(n = 13)	1.91	3.00	.383	1.19	2.07	.297
Howard	Black	6.14	2.43	1.391	7.14	3.00	1.416
	(n = 7)	2.61	2.37	.406	1.77	2.31	.325
	White	5.57	5.86	.990	6.14	2.14	1.303
	(n = 7)	1.81	2.12	.256	1.77	1.86	.499

a. Means.
b. Standard deviations.
c. Mean $\sqrt{d'}$ scores were obtained by first calculating the square root of individual subjects' d' score and then calculating group means on these roots.

the first experiment. Because of availability, the present experiment was restricted to white subjects at the University of Illinois. Subjects participated in the study as part of a course requirement. The analysis of variance is summarized in Table 3.

The superiority of white subjects with white faces as compared with black faces is strongly borne out with all stimulus sets. While this finding is expected on the basis of both the interaction and main effect found in the first experiment, no effect due to stimulus set and no interaction with stimulus set were found.

A third experiment was carried out to investigate the generality of the findings to similar experimental tasks. Specifically, the question was whether intermixing of black and white stimuli for white subjects in the first experiment would yield results comparable to those obtained when white subjects were given either black or white stimuli only. Procedures were identical to those in the previous experiments with the exception that there were 20 stimuli of one race only and the recognition pool contained 40 stimuli of the same race. Subjects were from the same population as subjects in the second experiment. Three different stimulus sets and orders were used. An analysis of variance (Race of Stimulus × Stimulus Set) was performed and is presented in Table 4. Again, the effect of race of stimulus is clear with no effect of stimulus set or Stimulus Set × Race of Stimulus interaction.

The findings are consistent with a hypothesis of differential experience with persons of other race and differential acquisition of cue utilization habits. If physiognomic discriminations among persons of other race are frequently made, within-group discriminative cue utilization habits will be formed. If contrasts of persons of other race

TABLE 10.2

Analysis of $\sqrt{d}'$ Measure for Black and White Subjects Exposed
to Black and White Stimuli at Black and White Institutions

Source	df	MS	F
Illinois Ss			
Between Ss	25		
Race of S (A)	1	.0393	.2905
Ss within groups	24	.1353	
Within Ss	26		
Race of stimulus (B)	1	.9727	13.435**
A × B	1	.3912	5.403*
B × Ss within groups	24	.0724	
Howard Ss			
Between Ss	13		
Race of S (A)	1	.3566	2.525
Ss within groups	12	.1412	
Within Ss	14		
Race of stimulus (B)	1	.2880	5.323*
A × B	1	.2161	3.994
B × Ss within groups	12	.0541	

$*p < .05; **p < .01.$

TABLE 10.3

Analysis of Variance of $\sqrt{d}'$ Measure for White Subjects
at a White Institution Exposed to One of Three Sets
of Black and White Faces

Source	df	MS	F
Race of stimuli (A)	1	1.5333	13.73*
Stimulus set (B)	2	.3332	2.98
A × B	2	.1056	
Within cell	114	.1117	

$*p < .001.$

from own race are predominant, between-group (contrasting) cue
utilization habits will be formed. The latter may operate to decrease
use or acquisition of the former. One form of the differential
experience hypothesis is that experience (in general) with persons of
other race is related to physiognomic recognition ability, until
experience is sufficient to bring recognition ability to asymptote.
Another form suggests differences in the importance of various types
of physiognomic experience, such that experience occurring when

TABLE 10.4

Analysis of Variance of $\sqrt{d'}$ Measure for White Subjects
at a White Institution Exposed to One of Three Sets
of Black or White Faces

Source	df	MS	F
Race of stimulus (A)	1	1.5767	20.719*
Stimulus set (B)	2	.0761	1.000
A × B	2	.0219	
Within cell	113	.0761	

*$p < .001$.

physiognomic discriminations are of instrumental value are more important than other forms, such as "mere" exposure.

Questionnaire data collected in the present study bears on the first form of the differential experience hypothesis. A positive relation should exist between a measure of experience with other race and recognition for other-race faces. The questionnaire asked about the number of other-race persons of various roles and occupational categories encountered in the course of an average week's time. This number and the number identified as persons known by first name (reciprocally) was added to a score obtained by inquiring about the number of other-race persons in various capacities in the subject's school classes from elementary to secondary school.

While Illinois black subjects reported more experience with persons of other race than did white subjects (median test, $X^2 = 5.538, p < .02$, using Yates correction), the Howard data did not show this difference. Further, median tests showed no relation between the experience index or any of its components and recognition for either group of subjects at both universities. These are weak tests of the differential experience hypothesis, however, and the number of cases is small. Hypotheses that factors other than experience mediate the acuity findings should be entertained.

NOTES

1. The research reported here was supported in part by the National Science Foundation supported Undergraduate Research Participation Program (Grant NSF GY 2850) of the Department of Psychology, University of Illinois, and the University Research Board of the University of Illinois. The authors are indebted to Hector Myers for his assistance during the research and to Harold Hake for his comments on an earlier version of the manuscript.

2. Requests for reprints should be sent to Roy S. Malpass, Department of Psychology, University of Illinois, Urbana, Illinois 61801.

3. Another procedure of obtaining d' scores which yields more information than the "yes/no" procedure used here is described by Green and Moses (1966). Essentially their procedure allows gradations within the "yes" and "no" categories and thus can take account of information concerning the decision criterion used by subjects.

REFERENCES

Bernbach, H. A. Decision processes in memory. *Psychological Review*, 1976, *74*, 462-480.

Elliot, P. B. Tables of d'. In J. A. Swets (Ed.), *Signal detection and recognition in human observers.* New York: Wiley, 1964.

Green, D. M., & Moses, F. L. On the equivalence of two recognition measures of short-term memory. *Psychological Bulletin*, 1966, *66*, 228-234.

Howells, T. H. A study of ability to recognize faces. *Journal of Abnormal and Social Psychology*, 1938, *33*, 124-127.

Seeleman, V. The influence of attitude upon the remembering of pictorial material. *Archives of Psychology*, 1940, *36*, 258.

Swets, J. A, Tanner, W. P., & Birdsall, T. G. Decision processes in perception. In J. A. Swets (Ed.), *Signal detection and recognition in human observers.* New York: Wiley, 1964.

SECTION III

SUMMARY

In making a contribution to understanding how eyewitnesses may err in seeking accuracy, Loftus, Miller, and Burns in chapter 9 found that information presented after an event does indeed alter the memory for the events. Moreover, the longer the delay between experiencing the event and final testing for recognition, the more recognition suffered. This decrement in memory due to time was established as early as 1879-1880 with the work of Ebbinghaus (1855/1964). But Loftus, Miller, and Burns have expanded this finding to determine the periods when presentation of additional information is crucial. Their research found that presenting the information just prior to the final recognition test produced a larger decrement in accuracy than if the information was presented after the event.

These findings are important for two reasons. One is the potential for improving both criminal justice and civil procedures so that any information presented subsequent to the event will not infringe on a witness's recall. Another potential use of this type of memory and information-processing research is the degree to which assessments can be made of the accuracy of potential witnesses. A case in point is that of *Gilbert v. California* (1967), where upward of 100 witnesses from several robberies were allowed to converse together both before and after their participation in a lineup identification. The potential for information to be provided which would change a witness's memory can only be imagined, but the research in chapter 9 allows the criminal justice system to be more sensitive to prejudiced proceedings.

The research reported in chapter 10 (Malpass & Kravitz, 1969) found that cross-racial eyewitness identifications are especially subject to error. In fact, their study indicated that persons are able to recognize members of their own race with more accuracy than members of another race. It was also apparent that whites were more easily recognizable than blacks; the theory being that whites were more often seen in the media, and their features were, therefore, more easily discernible. Luce (1974) extended this finding by including orientals. As expected, findings indicated subjects identified members of their own race more easily than others. In contrast to Malpass and Kravitz, Luce found exposure to another race did not increase identification accuracy. In particular, blacks were not as accurate in identifying whites, as they were other blacks. Whites were almost as accurate in identifying orientals, as they were other whites. Surprisingly, orientals could distinguish between each other (Japanese versus Chinese), but had difficulty in identifying blacks and even more difficulty with whites. This latter finding appears inconsistent with Luce's contention that exposure to members of another race does not increase accuracy in recognition. Schema and cognitive systems theory would contend that exposure to members of another race would improve recognition accuracy (Rumelhart, 1984; Sherman & Corty, 1984). Specifically, the process of creating new schemata with which to compare new incoming stimuli involves what Rumelhart and Norman (1978) term *patterned generation*. Here the creation of a new schema is achieved by copying the old one and adding a few modifications. Thus the more members of another race an observer sees, the greater the likelihood that the observer will achieve accurate recognition, because the observer has created schemata to account for variations of features.

Malpass and Kravitz's (1969) greatest contribution lies in assessing cross-racial identifications, one of the characteristics of eyewitnesses that may influence accuracy. Other related characteristics of eyewitnesses that may influence accuracy are the sex and age of the witness. Yarmey and Kent (1981) found females inferior to males in verbal accounts of a violent event, but no significant differences were apparent for nonviolent situations. However, females were more accurate than males in recognition of bystanders at a crime scenario, which was seen as a female ability to recognize faces more accurately than males can. It has also been found that elderly persons, as compared to young adults, were less accurate in verbal descriptions of an incident, especially when the elderly were questioned with suggestive clues (Yarmey & Kent, 1981).

The chapter by Gary Wells evaluates the utility of research like that contained in chapters 9 and 10. Specifically, for estimator-variable research he mentions the characteristics of both the event and the witness that may influence accurate suspect identifications. Such aspects include the seriousness of the criminal event, the witnesses' exposure time to the defendant, demographic characteristics of the defendant, the defendant's attractiveness, and the witness's familiarity with the surroundings where the criminal event occurs.

System variables that are examined include the time between the event and recall or recognition (usually termed the *retention interval*) of the event, suggestive interrogations, composite drawings, mug shots, question and lineup structuring, and lineup instructions. The research by Loftus, Miller, and Burns is relevant here, because they demonstrated that information provided during any of the above proceedings may alter a witness's memory for the event or criminal.

Wells suggests that the criminal justice system take advantage of the research done on system variables and use such findings to improve the processes involved in eliciting an identification from a witness. Although estimator variables are not under the control of the criminal justice system, their utility may lie in assessments of witnesses' potential accuracy. Here, however, Wells argues that both system and estimator variables are limited in that neither can determine the accuracy of an individual witness, and expert testimony can relate general findings on limitations to accuracy, but cannot make predictions as to the accuracy of any single witness. The conclusion of Wells, then, is to provide the criminal justice system with alternatives to expert testimony, namely, that findings of research be applied to criminal justice practices in order to facilitate eyewitness accuracy.

REFERENCES

Ebbinghaus, H. E. (1964). *Memory: A contribution to experimental psychology.* New York: Dover. (Originally published 1885; translated, 1913)
Fischer, J. (1983, October 6). Eyewitness identifications called unreliable. *Topeka Capital Journal*, p. 1.
Gilbert v. California, 388 U.S. 263 (1967).
Loftus, E. F., Miller, D. G., & Burns, H. J. (1978). Semantic integration of verbal information into a visual memory. *Journal of Experimental Psychology: Human Learning and Memory, 4*, 19-31.
Luce, T. S. (November, 1984). They all look alike to me. *Psychology Today*, pp. 103-108.
Malpass, R. S., & Kravitz, J. (1969). Recognition for faces of own and other race. *Journal of Personality and Social Psychology, 13*, 330-334.
Munsterberg, H. (1976). *On the witness stand.* New York: AMS Press. (Originally published 1908)
Rumelhart, D. E. (1984). Schemata and the cognitive system. In R. S. Wyer & T. K. Srull (Eds.), *Handbook of social cognition*, Vol. 1. Hillsdale, NJ: Lawrence Erlbaum.

Rumelhart, D. E., & Norman, D. A. (1978). Analogical processes in learning. In J. R. Anderson (Ed.), *Cognitive skills and their acquisition.* Hillsdale, NJ: Lawrence Erlbaum.

Sherman, S. J., & Corty, E. (1984). Cognitive heuristics. In R. S. Wyer & T. K. Srull (Eds.), *Handbook of social cognition,* Vol. 1. Hillsdale, NJ: Lawrence Erlbaum.

Wells, G. L. (1978). Applied eyewitness testimony research: System variables and estimator variables. *Journal of Personality and Social Psychology, 36,* 1546-1557.

Wells, G. L., & Loftus, E. F. (1984). Eyewitness research: Then and now. In G. L. Wells & E. F. Loftus (Eds.), *Eyewitness testimony: Psychological perspectives.* New York: Cambridge University Press.

Yarmey, A. D., & Kent, J. (1981). Eyewitness identification by elderly and young adults. *Law and Human Behavior, 4,* 359-371.

SECTION IV
EXPERT WITNESS TESTIMONY
Introduction

Section III examined the numerous variables that are involved in eyewitness identifications and the research that has been conducted on eyewitness accuracy. Section III also examined the place for such research in the improvement of the criminal justice system. Section IV expands on these concepts to examine the role of expert psychological testimony in court proceedings where eyewitness identifications are used as evidence. The issue is whether or not psychologists should testify before juries and inform them of research on the parameters of eyewitnesses' accuracy (in their job as triers of fact) or are instructions to the jury sufficient to enunciate the unreliability of eyewitness testimony? The judge can provide cautionary instructions to alert the jury to consider whether the eyewitness's identification was accurate.

Psychologists have long been aware of the vagaries in eyewitness testimony and have long espoused the need for making jurors more knowledgeable of the areas in which eyewitness identifications may possibly be inaccurate. Sigmund Freud (1906/1979) cautioned lawyers to use psychology to ascertain truth in courts, as early as 1906. Two years later, Hugo Munsterberg (1908/1976) furthered the plea by specifically recommending that psychologists be used to testify and elucidate psychological research on memory and recall in courts of law. Prior to his arrival in the United States, William Stern (1939) acted as an expert witness in the German courts. His evaluation of the trustworthiness of eyewitness testimony led to reform in German law on its admissibility, and he felt the United States should include consultation of psychologists on the accuracy of testimony, as normal procedure. However, collaboration between the courts and expert psychologists on assessing eyewitness testimony has changed little, since Stern's last lecture in 1937.

Legal publications addressed the inaccuracy of eyewitness testimony over 40 years ago, but eyewitness accounts continue to be used widely in the criminal justice system (Addison, 1978). Spear (1982) reports that calls for instructions to juries (if not expert psychologists' testimony) on eyewitness identifications' unreliability have come from legal publications, since 1942. However, the legal system has been reluctant to adopt findings of eyewitness research and apply them to reforming long-standing procedures.

Chapter 11, by Michael McCloskey and Howard Egeth, examined the rationales that have been advanced for why jurors need assistance in determining eyewitness reliability. The two main assumptions are that (1) jurors cannot determine which eyewitnesses are accurate and which are not, and (2) jurors are overbelieving of eyewitnesses. Chapter 11's analysis then centers on whether the benefits of expert psychological testimony outweigh the costs that might accrue, both to the jury and to the psychological profession as a whole. McCloskey and Egeth have serious doubts that expert testimony can fulfill its intended role; although they do concede that if a psychologist testifies concerning eyewitnesses, where it is clear that witnesses could not have seen what they have reported, then such testimony is relevant.

A rejoinder to the McCloskey and Egeth stance is offered in chapter 12 by Elizabeth Loftus. The argument in chapter 12 is that jurors need to be educated concerning the unreliability of eyewitness research, and without the testimony of expert psychologists, jurors' decision making (as triers of fact) will not be based on sound evidence and factual knowledge.

Loftus reiterates the arguments set forth by McCloskey and Egeth, refutes their conclusions, argues that the legal system often seeks input from psychology (rather than the other way around), and examines relevant court cases where legal experts can be seen to differ in their opinions on expert eyewitness testimony. Finally, chapter 12 proposes that scientific knowledge, whether perfected or not, should be used and that particularly research on eyewitness accuracy should be used by the courts.

Chapter 13, by Maass, Brigham, and West, directly addresses the controversy surrounding chapters 11 and 12 by examining the persuasiveness of expert testimony on eyewitness accuracy. Specifically, the research investigates the persuasiveness of expert testimony using two court cases and six different information conditions. The cases include a burglary or a convenience store robbery, while the information conditions consist of a case description, a case description plus eyewitness testimony, sample-based versus person-based information (information related to people on the average or related directly to the witness), and whether or not the information was causal or noncausal (why the witness was or was not accurate). Thus the research explores if expert eyewitness testimony would be persuasive and what forms of such testimony would appeal to a jury. Chapter 13, then, examines what effect—if any—expert testimony would have on jurors' perceptions of the credibility of eyewitness testimony.

REFERENCES

Addison, B. M. (1978). Expert testimony on eyewitness perception. *Dickinson Law Review, 83,* 465-485.

Freud, S. (1979). Psycho-analysis and the ascertaining of truth in courts of law. *Collected Papers, 2,* 13-24. (Originally published 1906; translated 1924)

Munsterberg, H. (1976). *On the witness stand.* New York: AMS Press. (Originally published 1908).

Spear, J. B. (1982). Evidence: does the eyewitness really see. *Washburn Law Review, 21,* 698-706.

Stern, W. (1939). The psychology of testimony. *Journal of Abnormal and Social Psychology, 34,* 3-20.

11

EYEWITNESS IDENTIFICATION
What Can a Psychologist
Tell a Jury?

MICHAEL McCLOSKEY
HOWARD E. EGETH
Johns Hopkins University

Imagine the following scene. An experimental psychologist is sitting in his or her office, lost in thought, when the phone rings. An attorney is calling.

Psychologist: Hello.

Attorney: Hello, Dr. Smith, this is Joe Doaks; I'm an attorney. I've been retained by a man who has been charged with armed robbery. The prosecution's case does not look very impressive to me except for one point—at a lineup my client was positively identified by an eyewitness to the crime.

Author's Note. During the preparation of this article, the authors were supported in part by National Science Foundation Grant BNS 80-22670. We would like to thank John Jonides, Judith McKenna, Allyson Washburn, Elizabeth Webb, Stephen Grossman, Rod Lindsay, Elizabeth Loftus, and Gary Wells for their helpful comments. Requests for reprints should be sent to Michael McCloskey, Department of Psychology, Johns Hopkins University, Baltimore, Maryland 21218.

What I'm calling about is to ask if you'd be willing to serve as an expert witness for the defense to explain to the jury the problems with eyewitness testimony.

Psychologist: Well, I don't know. I don't think I'd be comfortable going into a courtroom and impugning the testimony of a witness.

Attorney: No, no, of course not. I would not want you to try to tell the jury whether or not the eyewitness is right. The judge would never allow such testimony anyway. All I would like to do is talk in fairly general terms about the problems in perception and memory that can occur when a person observes a crime. I mean, the whole thing took place very quickly, the witness was very frightened, and the lineup didn't take place until 10 days after the crime. And on top of that, my client is black and the witness is white. These factors all can affect the accuracy of an eyewitness identification.

Psychologist: You seem to be quite knowledgeable about eyewitness testimony yourself; what do you need me for?

Attorney: Basically, I can only ask questions. I'm not permitted to lecture the jury about psychology. But you can. You would not be the first psychologist to give expert testimony about problems with eyewitnesses. Many of your colleagues have testified as experts in cases involving eyewitnesses, and many more probably will in the near future. Judges sometimes don't allow this sort of expert psychological testimony, but in many cases they do admit it.

Psychologist: This sounds very interesting, but I don't want to rush into it. Let me think about it for a few days and do some reading.

Attorney: Very good. I'll get back to you in a few days. Goodbye.

Psychologist: Goodbye.

What should the psychologist do? What considerations should inform the decision to testify or not to testify? In the following pages, we discuss several basic questions that we think the psychologist should consider in the process of reaching his or her decision. It should be made clear at the outset that this article has been written by and (largely) for experimental psychologists. The content is psychological. We have made no effort to consider legal aspects of the problem, such as laws affecting the admissibility of psychological testimony in various jurisdictions (such discussions are provided by Ellison & Buckhout, 1981; Gass, 1979; Loftus & Monahan, 1980; Woocher, 1977). A basic premise of our discussion is that intervention in the workings of the justice system should not be undertaken lightly. In particular, we take the position that expert psychological testimony

From *American Psychologist*, (May, 1983), pp. 550-563. Copyright 1983 by the American Psychological Association. Reprinted by permission of the publisher and authors.

about perception and memory in eyewitnesses[1] should be offered only if there is clear evidence that such testimony has salutary effects. As we discuss in greater detail below, the use of expert psychological testimony in the absence of clear evidence of its utility would carry substantial risks both for the system of justice and for the psychological profession. Consequently, in the following evaluation of arguments that have been offered in favor of the use of expert psychological testimony, we ask not, Does this claim seem plausible? or Might this assumption be valid? but rather, What does the available evidence say about this argument?

The final decision about whether to testify is up to the individual psychologist. However, we suggest that contrary to the claims of several psychologists and lawyers (e.g., Addison, 1978; Ellison & Buckhout, 1981; Loftus, 1979; Loftus & Monahan, 1980; Lower, 1978; Starkman, 1979; Woocher, 1977), the available evidence fails to demonstrate the general utility of expert psychological testimony and in fact does not even rule out the possibility that such testimony may have detrimental effects.

RATIONALES FOR THE USE OF EXPERT PSYCHOLOGICAL TESTIMONY

Two major rationales have been offered for the use of expert psychological testimony. First, the *discrimination* rationale asserts that jurors cannot discriminate adequately between accurate and inaccurate eyewitnesses (Lindsay, Wells, & Rumpel, 1981; Loftus, 1979; Loftus & Monahan, 1980; Wells, Lindsay, & Ferguson, 1979; Wells, Lindsay, & Tousignant, 1980). Consequently, the argument continues, jurors often disbelieve accurate witnesses and believe inaccurate witnesses. According to this view, expert psychological testimony could improve juror discrimination by informing jurors about factors known to influence witness accuracy and by cautioning against reliance on irrelevant factors.

The second rationale for the use of expert psychological testimony asserts that jurors are in general too willing to believe eyewitness testimony (Ellison & Buckhout, 1981; Lindsay et al., 1981; Loftus, 1974, 1979; Loftus & Monahan, 1980; Wall, 1965; Wells et al., 1980). According to this *overbelief* rationale, an expert witness could increase juror skepticism to a more appropriate level by discussing research demonstrating the unreliability of eyewitness testimony and by pointing out aspects of the case at hand (e.g., stress experienced by the witness) that might have led to witness inaccuracy. Loftus (1979) provides a strong statement of the overbelief claim: "Since jurors rarely regard eyewitness testimony with any skepticism, the expert testimony will increase the likelihood of this happening. This is its value" (p. 197).

Both the discrimination and the overbelief rationales make two fundamental claims: (a) Jurors need help in evaluating eyewitness testimony and (b) expert psychological testimony can provide this help. In the following sections we examine these claims.

Do Jurors Need Help?

Overbelief. Consider first the claim that jurors are too willing to believe eyewitnesses. Several arguments have been advanced in support of this claim. One argument that is frequently implicit in discussions of juror evaluation of eyewitness testimony (e.g., Ellison & Buckhout, 1981; Loftus, 1979; Woocher, 1977) is that the conclusion of juror overbelief follows from research showing that eyewitness testimony is often unreliable. An important but unstated assumption here is that jurors are not aware of the unreliability of eyewitnesses and consequently are too willing to believe eyewitness testimony. However, there is virtually no empirical evidence that people are unaware of the problems with eyewitness testimony. Further, there appears to be no reason to assume a priori that people are not cognizant of these problems. Cases of mistaken identification are often widely publicized and wrongful conviction on the basis of mistaken or perjured eyewitness testimony is a rather common theme in fiction. In addition, there is no consensus within the legal community that jurors are unaware of the unreliability of eyewitnesses and consequently give too much credence to eyewitness testimony. For example, in ruling against the admission of expert psychological testimony, the trial judge in the case of *People v. Guzman*[2] stated: "It is something that everyone knows about, the problems of identification. The jurors here were well questioned regarding their experience . . . with having mistakenly identified people. Everyone knows these things happen." Thus in the absence of evidence that jurors are unaware of the unreliability of eyewitness testimony, the conclusion that jurors are too willing to believe eyewitnesses cannot legitimately be drawn from research demonstrating that eyewitnesses are often inaccurate.

A second argument asserts that juror overbelief is demonstrated by the existence of documented cases in which defendants were wrongfully convicted on the basis of eyewitness testimony later shown to be mistaken. The implicit assumption here seems to be that if jurors were appropriately skeptical, wrongful convictions based upon erroneous identifications would never occur. But this is not a tenable position. It must be borne in mind that the degree of skepticism jurors exhibit toward eyewitnesses will affect not only the likelihood that an innocent defendant will be convicted but also the likelihood that a guilty defendant will be convicted. Thus an increase in juror skepticism toward eyewitness testimony would decrease convictions of the guilty as well as convictions of the innocent, and a degree of skepticism that eliminated wrongful conviction on the basis of eyewitness testimony would also eliminate any role of eyewitnesses in the conviction of the guilty. In signal-detection terms, it is unfortunate but true that except in situations involving very high signal-to-noise ratios, one cannot eliminate false alarms without eliminating hits merely by shifting one's decision criterion. Consequently, some wrongful convictions must be accepted as the unavoidable price for convicting guilty defendants. As Rembar (1980) puts it, "A system of justice that has no miscarriages of justice is not a workable system of justice" (p. 95).

To demonstrate juror overbelief in eyewitnesses, one must show not merely that erroneous convictions based on eyewitness testimony sometimes occur but that the ratio of conviction of the innocent to conviction of the guilty is unacceptably high. However, documented cases of wrongful conviction resulting from mistaken eyewitness testimony obviously represent only a small fraction of 1% of the cases in which defendants were convicted at least in part on the basis of eyewitness testimony. Thus although we cannot say what should be considered an acceptable ratio of conviction of the innocent to conviction of the guilty, it would seem to be difficult to argue that documented cases of wrongful conviction establish that the ratio is unacceptably high. Consequently, the known cases of erroneous convictions fail to demonstrate that jurors are too willing to believe eyewitness testimony (Pachella, 1981).

Our point here is not that the frequency of wrongful conviction is acceptably low but merely that known cases of erroneous conviction fail to establish that the frequency is unacceptably high. Thus our argument is not affected by the possibility that documented cases of wrongful conviction represent only the tip of the iceberg. In the absence of a means of estimating the number of undocumented cases of wrongful conviction, these undocumented cases cannot be used as evidence that erroneous conviction on the basis of eyewitness testimony occurs too often.

A third argument offered in favor of the overbelief claim is based on an experiment by Loftus (1974, 1979; see also Cavoukian, Note 1). In this experiment, university students read a very brief summary of evidence presented at a robbery-murder trial and voted individually for conviction or acquittal. In the no-eyewitness condition, the trial description mentioned only physical evidence against the defendant (e.g., money found in the defendant's room). Only 18% of the subjects in this condition voted for conviction. In the eyewitness condition, the trial description mentioned the physical evidence and also indicated that an eyewitness had identified the defendant as the robber. In this condition, 72% of the students voted to convict. Finally, in the discredited-eyewitness condition, subjects were told about the physical evidence and the eyewitness identification. However, they were also informed that the defense attorney "claimed the witness had not been wearing his glasses the day of the robbery, and since he had vision poorer than 20/400, he could not possibly have seen the face of the robber from where he stood" (Loftus, 1979, p. 117). In this condition, 68% of the students voted to convict. The high percentage of subjects voting for conviction in the eyewitness condition and the lack of difference between the eyewitness and discredited-eyewitness conditions, it is argued, indicate that people give too much credence to eyewitness testimony.

Several recent studies, however, cast doubt on this conclusion. First, an experiment was recently conducted in our laboratory in which subjects read detailed summaries (4,000-6,500 words) of a fictitious bank robbery trial and voted individually for conviction or acquittal (McKenna, Mellott, & Webb, Note 2). The bank teller who was robbed chose the defendant from a lineup two days after the robbery and positively identified him during the trial. In addition, the prosecution demonstrated that an amount of money closely matching that stolen from the bank was found in the defendant's possession.

The defense consisted of the testimony of the defendant's mother. She stated that the money found in the defendant's possession was a loan from her so that the defendant could buy a car and that the defendant had followed his normal routine the day of the robbery, coming home from his night job in the morning, going to sleep, and getting up at 5 p.m. On cross-examination, the defendant's mother admitted that she could not be sure that the defendant was at home at the time of the robbery, as his door was closed.

Part of our original purpose in conducting this study was to examine the impact of expert psychological testimony. Hence, the experiment included a no-expert-testimony condition, in which only the testimony described above was presented, and an expert-testimony condition, in which the trial summary included testimony of an experimental psychologist concerning factors (e.g., stress) that may lead to inaccurate eyewitness identification.

In spite of the teller's positive identification of the defendant, guilty verdicts were obtained from only 2 of the 24 subjects (8%) in the no-expert-testimony condition and 3 of the 48 subjects (6%) in the condition involving expert testimony. Examination of the subjects' explanations for their verdicts revealed that many, including those in the no-expert-testimony condition, felt that although the defendant may well have been guilty, it was possible that the teller had made an erroneous identification. Consequently, they were not certain enough of the defendant's guilt to vote for conviction. In subsequent experiments, we have replicated these results using adults from the Baltimore community as subjects and with a trial scenario in which the defense case in a robbery-murder trial consisted solely of the defendant's testimony that he was at home alone at the time of the crime.

Similar findings have been obtained by Hosch, Beck, and McIntyre (1980). In their study, subjects serving in eight six-person juries viewed a trial in which an eyewitness positively identified the defendant. Four of the juries heard expert psychological testimony; the other four juries did not. After deliberating, all eight juries voted unanimously for acquittal. These results are somewhat difficult to reconcile with Loftus's claim that "jurors rarely regard eyewitness testimony with any skepticism."

Other studies have examined the claim that jurors will believe even a discredited eyewitness. In an experiment in which subjects made individual guilty/not guilty decisions after reading a detailed summary of a robbery-murder trial, we found that the subjects disregarded a prosecution eyewitness who was convincingly discredited (Mc-Closkey, Egeth, Webb, Washburn, & McKenna, Note 3). Hatvany and Strack (1980) and Weinberg and Baron (1982) have obtained similar results.

Thus studies using methodologies similar to that of the Loftus (1974, 1979) experiment have shown that (a) a high percentage of subjects do not routinely vote guilty when an eyewitness has positively identified the defendant and (b) when a witness is convincingly discredited, his or her testimony is disregarded. Although definite conclusions about the behavior of jurors in actual trials cannot readily be drawn from these studies, the results clearly suggest that the Loftus study should not be taken as strong support of the juror overbelief argument.[3]

A final argument in favor of the claim that jurors overbelieve eyewitnesses stems from a recent series of experiments by Wells, Lindsay, and their colleagues (Lindsay et al., 1981; Wells et al., 1980). In these experiments, subjects serving as witnesses viewed a staged crime and then attempted to identify the criminal from an array of photographs. Witnesses who made accurate identifications as well as witnesses who identified the wrong person were then videotaped as they answered questions about the viewing conditions, the appearance of the criminal, and so forth. Additional subjects serving as jurors watched videotapes of witnesses and judged for each whether the witness had made an accurate identification. Under some witnessing conditions, the percentage of jurors believing a witness was higher than the percentage of witnesses who made accurate identifications. For example, in one situation 50% of the witnesses made an accurate identification. However, jurors viewing videotapes believed witnesses from that condition 66% of the time. Lindsay et al. (1981) and Wells et al. (1980) argue on the basis of these results that jurors are too willing to believe eyewitness testimony.

Although the Wells and Lindsay argument seems plausible, it is not entirely valid. The logic of the argument appears to be as follows: The findings that juror belief rates exceed witness accuracy rates implies that jurors overestimate the probability that an eyewitness is accurate, and this in turn implies that jurors are too willing to believe eyewitnesses.

There are some difficulties with the first step in this argument, because the finding that the percentage of jurors believing a witness was higher than the percentage of witnesses who were accurate does not necessarily imply that the jurors overestimated the probability that the witness was accurate.[4] However, even if we ignore this problem and assume that in some situations jurors overestimate the probability that an eyewitness is accurate, the conclusion that jurors are too willing to believe eyewitnesses does not follow. As we discussed earlier, to say that jurors are too willing to believe eyewitnesses means that jurors are too willing to *convict* on the basis of eyewitness testimony (or, more technically, that the weight given by jurors to eyewitness testimony results in an unacceptably high ratio of number of innocent defendants convicted to number of guilty defendants convicted).

Although we would expect the likelihood of conviction to increase monotonically with jurors' degree of belief in a prosecution eyewitness, data suggesting that jurors overestimate the probability that eyewitnesses are accurate do not necessarily imply that jurors are overly willing to convict on the basis of eyewitness testimony. The reasonable doubt criterion, among other things, intervenes between judging the likelihood that a witness is accurate and voting to convict or to acquit. In our research, we have frequently seen subjects, who read trial summaries and arrived at verdicts, vote not guilty in spite of a stated belief that an eyewitness who identified the defendant was probably correct. These subjects generally say that although they believe the defendant is probably guilty, they are not certain beyond a reasonable doubt. Thus if the criterion for convict decisions is sufficiently stringent, juror overestimates of witness accuracy need not result in an overwillingness to convict on the basis of eyewitness testimony. More generally, our point here is that in the absence of data concerning jurors' criteria for convict/acquit decisions, we cannot determine from juror estimates of witness accuracy (or, more specifically, from the belief/disbelief judgments collected by Wells et al. and Lindsay et al.) whether jurors are insufficiently likely, just likely enough, or too likely to convict on the basis of eyewitness testimony.

One other point should be made regarding the Wells et al. and Lindsay et al. results. In considering whether jurors overbelieve eyewitnesses, we have focused on the question of whether juror evaluation of eyewitness testimony results in an acceptable ratio of number of innocent defendants convicted to number of guilty defendants convicted. However, one may also ask whether jurors give eyewitness testimony appropriate weight relative to other sorts of evidence (e.g., the defendant's fingerprints found at the scene of the crime, money found in the defendant's possession, alibi evidence). If it could be determined that jurors give eyewitness testimony too much weight relative to some other types of evidence, it might be argued that at least in some sense jurors overbelieve eyewitness testimony. (Of course, if in this situation juror evaluation of eyewitnesses produced appropriate conviction rates, it might more reasonably be concluded that the other evidence was underbelieved.)

Unfortunately, the question of whether jurors give eyewitness testimony too much weight relative to other sorts of evidence is difficult to answer, for at least two reasons. First, there are few studies comparing the weight given to eyewitness testimony with that accorded other types of evidence. Second, and most important, it is difficult to determine how much weight various sorts of evidence should be given relative to each other. Thus we have little to say about juror evaluation of eyewitnesses relative to other types of evidence. However, we should point out that the Wells et al. and Lindsay et al. findings suggesting that subject-jurors may sometimes overestimate the probability that an eyewitness identification was accurate do not imply that jurors overvalue eyewitness testimony relative to other sorts of evidence. It is certainly conceivable that studies using the Wells-Lindsay paradigm, with other kinds of evidence substituted for eyewitness testimony, might show that jurors "overbelieve" (in the Wells-Lindsay sense) those other kinds of evidence as well. (Although, as mentioned earlier, this sort of overbelief would not necessarily imply an overwillingness to convict.) Thus the Wells et al. and Lindsay et al. findings demonstrate neither that jurors are overly willing to convict on the basis of eyewitness testimony nor that eyewitness testimony is overvalued relative to other sorts of evidence.

Finally, in discussing juror overbelief we should mention two recent studies of actual trial outcomes that cast doubt on the claim that jurors rarely regard eyewitness testimony with any skepticism. Chen (1981) tabulated the outcomes of all criminal cases in the Los Angeles County system from July 1977 through December 1978. Other factors partialed out, the ratio of convictions in cases with at least one eyewitness identification of the defendant to convictions in cases without identification was 1.1 to 1. Similarly, Myers (1979) examined the 201 criminal cases tried by jury in Marion County, Indiana, between January 1974 and June 1976. She found that convictions were no more likely in cases involving identification of the defendant by a victim or other eyewitness(es) than in cases where there was no eyewitness identification. These sorts of results are, of course, not definitive. For example, the prosecution may have brought otherwise weaker cases to trial when an eyewitness was available than when there was no eyewitness. Nevertheless, the Chen and Myers findings cast doubt on the claim that jurors rarely regard eyewitness testimony with any skepticism. A dramatic illustration of this point is provided by the case of a man who was arrested 13 times and tried 5 times in an 18-month period for a series of crimes that were later confessed to by another man. What is noteworthy about this case is that he was acquitted in all five trials, even though one or more eyewitnesses testified against him in each (Shoemaker, 1980).

In summary, the available evidence fails to show that jurors are overly willing to believe eyewitness testimony. This does not mean that jurors exhibit an appropriate degree of skepticism toward eyewitness testimony. Our point is simply that contrary to the claims of many psychologists and lawyers (e.g., Ellison & Buckhout, 1981; Lindsay et al., 1981; Loftus, 1974, 1979; Loftus & Monahan, 1980; Wells et al., 1980; Woocher, 1977), juror overbelief in eyewitnesses has not been demonstrated. Consequently, it is by no means clear that there is a need for expert psychological testimony to make jurors more skeptical.

Discrimination. The discrimination rationale asserts that regardless of whether jurors are generally skeptical or generally credulous of eyewitness testimony, they cannot distinguish well between accurate and inaccurate eyewitnesses. According to this view, expert psychological testimony could improve juror discrimination.

The claim that jurors cannot readily discriminate accurate from inaccurate eyewitnesses appears to be well founded. Cases of wrongful conviction based on mistaken eyewitness testimony demonstrate that juror discrimination is not perfect, and the recent studies of Wells, Lindsay, and their colleagues suggest that jurors' ability to distinguish accurate and inaccurate eyewitnesses may indeed be quite poor. As we mentioned above, these researchers conducted a series of studies in which subjects serving as jurors judged whether witnesses to staged crimes made an accurate or inaccurate identification of the perpetrator. They found that within a given crime situation, jurors were as likely to believe inaccurate witnesses as they were to believe accurate witnesses (Lindsay et al., 1981; Wells et al., 1979, 1980).

Although these results are clearly very disturbing, the situation is perhaps not as bleak as it first appears. In the Lindsay et al. (1981) study, the witnesses viewed a staged crime under either good, moderate, or poor viewing conditions (in the *poor* condition, for example, the criminal was visible for only 12 seconds and wore a hat that completely covered his hair, whereas in the *good* condition the criminal's head was uncovered and he was visible for 20 seconds). Accurate identification of the criminal was made by 33%, 50%, and 74% of the witnesses in the poor, moderate, and good viewing conditions, respectively. Jurors in the study (see also Wells et al., 1980) were just as likely to believe inaccurate as accurate witnesses *within a given viewing condition.* (For example, inaccurate witnesses from the good viewing condition were believed as often as accurate witnesses from the same condition.) However, jurors were less likely to believe witnesses, the less favorable the viewing conditions. Specifically, juror belief rates were 77%, 66%, and 62%, for witnesses in the good, moderate, and poor viewing conditions, respectively. These results suggest that jurors weighing eyewitness testimony are able to take into account at least some factors that influence witness accuracy. Nevertheless, it seems clear that jurors' ability to discriminate accurate from inaccurate witnesses is far from perfect.

Can Psychologists Provide
the Needed Help?

Our conclusions above are that (a) it is by no means clear that jurors need expert testimony to make them appropriately skeptical but that (b) there is room for improvement in the ability of jurors to discriminate accurate from inaccurate witnesses. In this section, we consider the possible effects of expert psychological testimony on jurors.

Three recent studies suggest that expert psychological testimony may serve to make jurors more skeptical of eyewitness testimony (Hosch et al., 1980; Loftus, 1980; Wells et al., 1980). For example, Wells et al. found that expert psychological testimony reduced the likelihood that a subject would believe that an eyewitness to a staged crime made an accurate identification, and Loftus reported that subjects who read brief trial summaries were less likely to vote guilty when the summaries included expert psychological testimony than when no such testimony was included. It is not a straightforward matter to extrapolate the results of these studies to the verdicts of real juries. However, even if we accept the findings at face value, we are left with the following question: Given the absence of clear evidence that jurors overbelieve eyewitnesses, is it really appropriate for psychologists to offer expert testimony that serves to reduce jurors' overall level of belief in eyewitnesses?

If we turn now to the possible effects of expert psychological testimony on jurors' ability to discriminate accurate from inaccurate eyewitnesses, we find only one relevant study (Wells et al., 1980). This study employed the basic Wells-Lindsay paradigm described above, in which subjects serving as jurors judged whether or not witnesses to a staged crime accurately identified the perpetrator. In the Wells et al. (1980) study, half of the "jurors" received expert psychological advice before judging the credibility of witnesses, and the remaining "jurors" received no expert advice. The expert testimony emphasized two general points. The first was that eyewitness identification in criminal cases is quite different from recognizing one's friends and associates, in that research using staged crimes has shown that, depending on conditions, 15% to 85% of eyewitnesses may choose the wrong person from a lineup. The second major point was that there is considerable evidence to show that witness confidence may have little or no relationship to witness accuracy. The psychologist also mentioned that jurors should pay attention to situational factors that might affect witness accuracy.

"Jurors" in the expert-advice and no-expert-advice conditions viewed videotapes of witnesses and made belief/disbelief judgments. The videotapes were taken from the Lindsay et al. (1981) study in which witnesses observed a staged crime under poor, moderate, and good viewing conditions (resulting in 33%, 50%, and 74% accurate identifications, respectively).

As mentioned above, the expert psychological testimony reduced the jurors' overall willingness to believe eyewitnesses. However, the expert testimony had absolutely no effect on jurors' ability to discriminate accurate from inaccurate witnesses.

In summary, the available evidence suggests that there may be a rather ironic mismatch between the type of help needed by jurors and the possible effects of expert psychological testimony. Specifically, jurors clearly need help in discriminating accurate from inaccurate eyewitnesses but may not need to be made more skeptical overall. Expert testimony, on the other hand, may serve to increase juror skepticism but not to improve juror discrimination.

Of course, firm conclusions at this point would be premature. This is especially true with regard to the effects of expert psychological testimony on juror discrimination. As we have seen, only one study relevant to this issue has been conducted (Wells et al., 1980). Furthermore, the expert testimony used in that study may not have been optimal for improving juror discrimination. Aside from the negative advice to ignore witness confidence, jurors were told only to examine "situational factors." It is certainly conceivable that expert testimony that provided a detailed discussion of specific factors that affect witness accuracy would result in better juror discrimination. Nevertheless, we must conclude that at present there is no evidence that expert psychological advice improves juror evaluation of eyewitness testimony.

EXPERT PSYCHOLOGICAL TESTIMONY
AND THE FACTORS
AFFECTING WITNESS ACCURACY

At this point, an advocate of the use of expert psychological testimony might argue as follows: "Although the Wells et al. (1980) study failed to show an improvement in juror discrimination of accurate and inaccurate witnesses as a result of expert advice, this failure probably reflects, as mentioned above, the vagueness of the expert's remarks. There is every reason to believe that more specific expert testimony would improve juror discrimination. Empirical research has identified many variables that affect witness accuracy in ways that are not obvious to the lay juror. Expert testimony that discusses these factors in detail would, and in practice does, increase jurors' ability to distinguish accurate from inaccurate eyewitnesses."

The validity of this argument can be assessed only through additional research. We suggest, however, that there is less reason than might be supposed for optimism about the effects of expert psychological testimony on juror discrimination. The claim that detailed expert testimony would improve juror discrimination rests on the assumption that there are many variables for which both the following are true: (a) The relationship between the variable and eyewitness accuracy is known to psychologists as the result of empirical research, and (b) jurors do not understand how the variable is related to witness accuracy. However, it turns out to be surprisingly difficult to find variables of this sort. In other words, for many (if not most) variables that have been listed as suitable topics for expert testimony, either the effects of the variable on witness accuracy are not well documented, or these effects are probably obvious to the juror. A few examples will illustrate this point.

For a variable such as exposure duration, the well-documented effects are probably obvious to jurors. It is difficult to imagine that jurors are not aware of the fact that longer exposures lead to increased witness accuracy.

For retention interval, the situation is slightly more complex. Since the time of Ebbinghaus (1885/1913), the verbal-learning literature has quite consistently shown that retention declines as a function of the delay between the learning experience and the subsequent test. For face recognition, there are fewer studies, and the available data are not entirely consistent. Many studies show run-of-the-mill retention losses. For example, Shepherd and Ellis (1973) measured recognition performance a few minutes, 6 days, or 35 days after exposure. Performance declined from 87% correct to 71% over that period. However, others have failed to find performance declining over time. For example, Goldstein and Chance (1971) found accuracy to be unaffected by delay over the range 0-48 hours. Similarly, Laughery, Fesser, Lenorovitz, and Yoblick (1974) found no difference in recognition performance among the six retention intervals they studied (4 minutes, 30 minutes, 1 hour, 4 hours, 1 day, and 1 week). Finally, it is worth noting that Carr, Deffenbacher, and Leu (Note 4; see also Deffenbacher, Carr, & Leu, 1981) actually found a reminiscence effect—recognition of faces was slightly better 2 weeks after original viewing than 2 minutes after. This pattern of results did not obtain for the other classes of stimuli that were tested (concrete nouns, pictures of common objects, and pictures of landscapes).

There are two ways in which this situation can be assessed. First, one could conclude that at present the effects of retention interval on face recognition are not sufficiently well understood to be discussed in expert testimony. Alternatively, one could argue that the available evidence on memory in general overwhelmingly supports the generalization that retention declines with delay between acquisition and test. According to this view, the face recognition studies showing no effect of retention interval, or reminiscence, would be said to fail to reflect the true state of affairs. If this latter position is taken, however, it follows that the true effects of retention interval on face recognition probably match jurors' beliefs about these effects and consequently that expert testimony about retention interval may be unnecessary.

Consider now the cross-racial identification effect. Several studies have shown that cross-racial identification (e.g., white witness-black defendant) is more difficult than within-racial identification (e.g., black witness-black defendant; Malpass & Kravitz, 1969). This result is often discussed (e.g., Loftus, 1979) as if it were not obvious to the lay juror. However, the claim that jurors are unaware of the difficulty of cross-racial identification is questionable at best. For example, the cliche "they all look alike to me" used in reference to members of another race suggests that there may be a general awareness of the difficulty of cross-racial identification. In fact, the Devlin (1976) report describes studies of cross-racial identification as "support for what is widely accepted on the basis of common intuition" (p. 73).

Loftus (1979; see also Deffenbacher & Loftus, 1982; Yarmey & Jones, 1983), in a study of beliefs about factors affecting witness accuracy, found that only 55% of the subjects correctly answered a four-alternative multiple-choice question concerning cross-racial identification. However, this result probably should not be taken too seriously as evidence that people do not understand the difficulty of cross-racial identification, because Loftus's question was extremely complex and difficult to understand:

> Two women are walking to school one morning, one of them an Asian and the other white. Suddenly, two men, one black and one white, jump into their path and attempt to grab their purses. Later, the women are shown photographs of known purse snatchers in the area. Which statement best describes your view of the women's ability to identify the purse snatchers?
> (a) Both the Asian and the white woman will find the white man harder to identify than the black man.
> (b) The white woman will find the black man more difficult to identify than the white man.
> (c) The Asian woman will have an easier time than the white woman making an accurate identification of both men.
> (d) The white woman will find the black man easier to identify than the white man. (p. 172)

In a similar study, Deffenbacher and Loftus (1982) asked subjects their opinion of the cliche "they all look alike to me." The answer Deffenbacher and Loftus deemed correct, "it is true," was chosen by only about 20% of the subjects. However, this result should not be taken to indicate that people are unaware of the difficulty of cross-racial identification because "they all look alike to me" is obviously a gross overstatement. Thus many people may judge this statement to be technically false even though they feel that there is a kernel of truth in it.

At present, then, it is by no means clear that jurors are unaware of the difficulty of cross-racial identification.

Finally, for several variables that purportedly have nonobvious effects on accuracy and consequently are cited as appropriate topics for expert testimony, there is in fact little empirical evidence about how (or even if) these variables affect eyewitness performance. Consider, for example, weapon focus, which is the alleged tendency of a person threatened with a weapon to focus on the weapon and consequently pay little attention to the appearance of his or her assailant. Although weapon focus is frequently cited as an important factor in assessing eyewitness accuracy and has been discussed in expert testimony (see Loftus, 1979, pp. 223-224), there is virtually no evidence that the phenomenon actually occurs. The single unpublished experiment cited as a demonstration of weapon focus (Johnson & Scott, Note 5) is "suggestive . . . but it is far from conclusive" (Loftus, 1979, p. 36). As another example, it is widely claimed (e.g., Loftus, 1979; Woocher, 1977) that stress or arousal experienced by a witness during an event has detrimental effects on the accuracy of the witness's testimony, and this claim is frequently a prominent feature of expert testimony. Unfortunately, there is little basis for this claim. Deffenbacher (1982), in a review of research concerning the effects of arousal on the reliability of eyewitness testimony, lists 19 relevant studies. He reports that 10 of these studies found decreases in eyewitness accuracy with increased arousal, whereas the remaining 9 found that increases in arousal improved eyewitness performance or had no effect.

Deffenbacher claims that these seemingly disparate results conform to the Yerkes-Dodson law, which states that the function relating stress or arousal to performance is an inverted U, such that performance is poorer at very high or very low levels of arousal than at intermediate levels. This claim is unwarranted, however, because Deffenbacher fits the data to the Yerkes-Dodson function simply by assuming that studies showing that performance increased with arousal involved levels of arousal below the optimal arousal level, whereas studies showing impairment of performance with increasing arousal involved arousal levels above the optimal level. Deffenbacher also claims that actual crime situations usually involve arousal levels higher than the optimal level and so concludes that eyewitness performance in these situations is adversely affected. Again, however, the claim that stress in crime situations is above the optimal level is merely an assumption. Deffenbacher's claims about arousal and eyewitness performance may well be correct, but at present there is little empirical basis for these claims.

There may be variables that have well-documented effects that are not obvious to jurors. Biases in identification procedures provide one possible example. However, it is by no means the case that there are a large number of variables with well-documented nonobvious effects. Thus the argument that expert psychological testimony could almost certainly improve juror discrimination does not appear to be well founded. Testimony that asserts as fact effects that have not been demonstrated (e.g., effects of stress or weapon focus) is clearly inappropriate (and in any event there is no reason to believe that the introduction of undocumented assertions would improve juror performance); testimony limited to documented phenomena, however, may tell jurors little that they don't already know.[5]

It might be argued that expert testimony about obvious variables such as exposure duration, lighting retention interval, and so forth could be beneficial even if jurors understand the effects of these variables, because jurors might not spontaneously think about such variables when evaluating a witness's testimony. However, this argument ignores the fact that the defense attorney in a case involving an eyewitness identification will (in opening and closing statements and in the examination of witnesses) certainly call to the jury's attention any factors (e.g., poor lighting) suggesting that the identification may be inaccurate. Similarly, the prosecutor will point out factors (e.g., long exposure duration) suggesting that the identification is accurate. Thus expert psychological testimony does not appear to be needed to call the jury's attention to obvious variables.

THE RISKS OF PREMATURE INTERVENTION

We have argued that the available evidence fails to demonstrate that expert psychological testimony will routinely improve jurors' ability to evaluate eyewitness testimony. However, neither do the data rule out the possibility that expert testimony could have beneficial effects.

Clearly, what is needed is additional research concerning eyewitness testimony, juror evaluation of eyewitness testimony, and the effects on jurors of various sorts of expert psychological testimony.[6] If this research establishes that jurors are willing to convict on the basis of eyewitness testimony or that jurors give disproportionate weight to eyewitnesses relative to other sorts of evidence, then expert psychological testimony should be considered as one of several possible methods of improving juror performance. Similarly, if research demonstrates that expert testimony can improve jurors' ability to discriminate accurate from inaccurate witnesses without producing undesirable side effects, such testimony clearly should be employed in the courtroom.

In the meantime, however, what should a psychologist do when asked to testify? When we have discussed our misgivings about expert psychological testimony with our colleagues, the reaction has often been something like this: "Well, maybe your're right when you say that it hasn't been demonstrated that expert psychological testimony helps the jury. However, it might help, and at least it can't hurt, so why not use it?"

We strongly disagree with this argument for several reasons. First, contrary to the claim that "at least it can't hurt," the possibility that psychological testimony has detrimental effects cannot be ruled out. For example, if jurors are already appropriately skeptical about eyewitness testimony, expert psychological testimony might make jurors too skeptical.[7] In addition, in discussing phenomena that are incompletely understood, an expert might give groundless information to the jury (see, e.g., discussion of stress and weapon focus above). Thus it is even conceivable that expert testimony could decrease the ability of jurors to discriminate accurate from inaccurate witnesses.

A second difficulty with the argument that expert psychological testimony should be used because it might help is that a trial judge would not admit expert testimony on this basis. For expert testimony to be admitted, stronger arguments in its favor would have to be offered. Thus a psychologist who decided to testify on the basis of the "it might help-at least it can't hurt" argument would in some sense have to misrepresent his or her testimony to the court.

Finally, the use of expert psychological testimony in the absence of clear evidence that it benefits the jury carries risks to the psychological profession as a whole. Because the effects of expert testimony are currently unclear, it is inevitable that psychologists will disagree with one another about its use. This disagreement is likely to lead ultimately to a "battle of experts" in at least some cases where attempts are made to introduce expert psychological testimony. The battle of experts could take several different forms. For example, when the defense attempted to introduce expert psychological testimony, the prosecution could use its own expert to argue that the defense psychologist should not be allowed to testify in front of the jury. The prosecution expert could state that many of the assertions that would be made by the defense expert (e.g., about effects of stress or weapon focus) are not firmly established by psychological research and that the expert testimony could conceivably have detrimental effects on the jurors' evaluation of eyewitness testimony. If the judge nevertheless decided to admit the testimony of the defense expert, the prosecution psychologist could also testify in front of the jury, arguing that support was lacking for many of the defense psychologist's claims. The prosecution expert might also attempt to counter the defense expert's arguments about the unreliability of eyewitness testimony by pointing out factors in the case at hand that would facilitate eyewitness performance (e.g., long exposure duration, good lighting).

A battle of experts could also take more subtle forms. For example, a psychologist could simply serve as an advisor to the prosecutor, helping him or her to prepare an effective cross-examination of the defense expert. In any event, regardless of the form taken by a battle of experts, courtroom confrontation between defense and prosecution psychologists would almost certainly work to the detriment of the psychological profession, creating (or sustaining) the impression of psychology as a subjective, unscientific discipline and of the psychologist as a "gun for hire." The current situation with regard to psychiatric and psychological expert testimony concerning insanity, dangerousness, and the like should serve as food for thought to experimental psychologists.

It may have occurred to the reader that courtroom battles involving members of other professions (e.g., chemists, engineers, physicians) occur quite frequently but that these professions do not seem to have suffered serious loss of credibility. Perhaps, then, there is little reason to be concerned about the consequences of battles involving experimental psychologists.

Unfortunately, the comparison to professions such as medicine, chemistry, and the like may be misleading. We strongly suspect that courtroom battles in which opposing experts positively assert contradictory propositions do decrease public respect for a profession. Nevertheless, professions such as medicine and physics may escape serious loss of credibility because of clear records of past accomplishments and frequent reports of new achievements. Unfortunately, psychology probably does not have the sort of strong public reputation needed to endure battles of experts without significant damage. This may be especially true of the reputation of psychology among members of the legal profession. Consider, for example, the following excerpt from an appeals court decision[8] in which it was ruled that a trial judge had not erred in excluding expert psychological testimony about eyewitnesses:

> How far should the trial judge go in allowing *so-called scientific testimony, such as that of polygraph operators, hypnotists, "truth drug" administrants, as well as purveyors of general psychological theories,* to substitute for the common sense of the jury? Surely the answer is "not in all cases, or even in the ordinary or unusual case."

Apart from the possible effects of a battle of experts on the reputation of the field, there is also a question of what the effects of such a battle might be on the outcome of a trial. A battle of experts could conceivably improve juror decision making. On the other hand, both experts might end up being ignored. As with many of the other issues discussed in this article, this one probably should be decided empirically rather than by guesswork.

To illustrate our points about the possible consequences of a battle of experts, we conclude with an example of one of the milder forms that such a battle might take. Specifically, we present a hypothetical cross-examination of a defense psychologist by a prosecutor who has been thoroughly briefed by his or her own expert. We ask the reader to consider whether this sort of occurrence would benefit either the psychological profession or the justice system.

Prosecutor: Are you suggesting that it is impossible for an eyewitness to accurately identify a criminal?

Psychologist: No, but accurate identification is quite difficult.

Prosecutor: In the studies conducted by yourself and your colleagues, do any of the participants do very well at identifying people?

Psychologist: Yes, some subjects do quite well, but others do very poorly.

Prosecutor: Dr. Smith, are you aware of studies showing that subjects made accurate identifications over 90% of the time?

Psychologist: Yes, there are such studies. Usually, however, the performance of witnesses is worse than that.

Prosecutor: Isn't it true that the accuracy rates in identification studies depend heavily on the conditions of the experiment, such as how many faces each subject sees, how long each face is seen, and so forth?

Psychologist: Yes, that is obviously true of any experiment.

Prosecutor: Isn't it also the case that conditions in most experiments are deliberately arranged so that accuracy is low?

Psychologist: Well, yes, in a way that's true. If none of the subjects makes any errors we don't learn anything from an experiment. For example, if we wanted to see whether poor lighting makes identification harder, we would do an experiment where subjects see people under good and poor lighting conditions. We would then look to see whether accuracy was lower with poor lighting. If the task were too easy, most or all of the subjects might make accurate identifications and we wouldn't learn anything about the effects of lighting. To find out whether lighting is important we have to have a situation in which subjects make some errors. So to ensure that errors occur, we might let the subjects view people for only a short period of time, from some distance away, and so forth.

Prosecutor: Isn't it true, Dr. Smith, that even in tests giving low overall accuracy, some witnesses identify the right person?

Psychologist: Yes.

Prosecutor: Is there any way you can tell beforehand which witnesses will make an accurate identification and which witnesses will be inaccurate?

Psychologist: No, at the present time, we have no good way of telling in a particular situation which witnesses will be accurate and which ones will be inaccurate. All we can say is that certain conditions yield lower accuracy than others.

Prosecutor: You have testified, Dr. Smith, that in your psychological tests, the accuracy of witnesses varies widely according to the conditions of the test. You have also stated that in conducting tests, psychologists deliberately create situations that produce low accuracy. Finally, you have said that there is no way you can tell whether a particular individual will make an accurate or inaccurate identification in a particular situation. How, then, can your tests be applied to the present case, in which a bank teller looked at a single bank robber for a much longer time than in most research studies? How can the results of experiments be used to suggest that the witness is inaccurate in his identification?

Psychologist: I cannot comment on the accuracy of any particular witness. All I can do is explain what sorts of conditions lead to a good or poor eyewitness performance.

Prosecutor: I am very interested in what you have called "weapon focus," Dr. Smith. Can you tell us about some of the experiments that demonstrate this effect?

Psychologist: Well, there is one experiment that gives some support for the weapon focus idea, but it isn't really conclusive. Actually . . .

Prosecutor: I am very surprised, Dr. Smith, that you are willing to testify about a theory for which there is no experimental evidence.

Psychologist: Well, the idea of weapon focus was developed not so much from experiments but because people threatened with weapons often report having seen the weapon very clearly and often can describe it in great detail.

Prosecutor: That's very interesting. Are you saying that people who are able to give a clear description of, say, a gun, and who claim to have seen it clearly, would be said to have focused on the gun?

Psychologist: Yes.

Prosecutor: Mr. Robinson, the eyewitness in this case, has testified that he saw the robber's face clearly, and he gave a clear description of the robber. Would you say, then, Dr. Smith, that Mr. Robinson must have focused on the robber's face?

Psychologist: Well . . .

Prosecutor: I would like to ask you about your testimony concerning cross-racial identification. Are you saying that a white person could *never* identify a black person?

Psychologist: No. I merely said that it is more difficult for a white person to identify a black person than a white person.

Prosecutor: Are you suggesting that *most* cross-racial identifications are wrong?

Psychologist: No, I did not say that.

Prosecutor: Well, then, are cross-racial identifications *often* incorrect?

Psychologist: I cannot say exactly how often cross-racial identifications are erroneous, only that cross-racial identifications are less likely to be correct than within-racial identifications.

Prosecutor: How much less likely?

Psychologist: It is difficult for me to answer that question without having the studies in front of me. However, I can say that several studies have found that cross-racial identifications were significantly less likely to be correct than within-racial identifications.

Prosecutor: Does that mean that there might be a difference of about 80% in the accuracy of within- versus cross-racial identifications?

Psychologist: No, the difference in accuracy is not that large.

Prosecutor: Would 50% be a more reasonable figure?

Psychologist: No, the difference is somewhat smaller than that.

Prosecutor: Well, Dr. Smith, can you estimate for the jury just how much less likely a cross-racial identification is to be correct than a within-racial identification?

Psychologist: I can't be sure of the exact figures, but I believe that most studies show about a 10% difference in accuracy between within- and cross-racial identifications.

Prosecutor: That's very interesting. I'm surprised that such a small difference could be considered significant. Would every subject show this effect? In other words, would everyone be very slightly less likely to correctly identify a person of another race?

Psychologist: Not necessarily. In most studies, the results are not exactly the same for every subject. The 10% difference between within- and cross-racial identifications would represent the average performance of a group of subjects.

Prosecutor: So it is probably the case that some people in these studies did just as well at cross-racial identification as within-racial identification?

Psychologist: That's possible.

Prosecutor: So you can't say for any individual that you haven't tested whether that individual is less likely to be correct in a cross-racial or a within-racial identification?

Psychologist: All I can say is that, in general, cross-racial identifications are more difficult than within-racial identifications.

Prosecutor: I would like to ask you a few questions about your testimony on the effects of stress on performance. You testified, I believe, that people under a moderate amount of stress are better at remembering and perceiving than people under very high or very low stress.

Psychologist: That's right. As I said before, the relationship between stress and performance is expressed by what is called the Yerkes-Dodson law, which is a well-known principle of psychology.

Prosecutor: How much stress, Dr. Smith, is moderate stress? That is, what level of stress must a person be under before his or her performance deteriorates?

Psychologist: That depends on the type of task involved. Some tasks can be performed well under a fair amount of stress, and in other tasks the same amount of stress would impair performance. In general, the more complex the task, the lower the level of stress that gives the best performance.

Prosecutor: I assume that since you have testified about the effects of stress on eyewitness identification, psychologists must have studied this issue extensively.

Psychologist: Yes, there have been a number of studies on stress and identification.

Prosecutor: Do all of these studies show that people do poorly when they are under stress?

Psychologist: Well, many of the studies show a detrimental effect of stress.

Prosecutor: Are there also studies in which people under stress did as well as or even better than people who were not under stress?

Psychologist: Yes, there are such studies, but they generally used rather low levels of stress. The studies showing improved performance under stress probably involved stress levels below the point of optimum stress, whereas studies finding impaired performance probably involved stress above the optimal level. So all of the studies fit the Yerkes-Dodson law I described earlier.

Prosecutor: I see. So I guess you are saying that there is some method psychologists use to measure the stress people experience in an experiment, and these measurements show that stress levels were lower in studies where stress helped than in studies where it hurt.

Psychologist: Well, no, not exactly. No single measure of stress was used in all of the studies. But if we look at the procedures that were used, it appears that studies showing improved performance under stress involved lower stress levels than studies showing impairment.

Prosecutor: Are you aware of a study by Clifford and Hollin [Note 6] in which people who were stressed by loud noise did more poorly at identifying faces than people who were not exposed to noise?

Psychologist: Yes, I know of that study.

Prosecutor: So according to what you have said, this study probably involved levels of stress above the optimal level. Is that right?

Psychologist: Yes, that is correct.

Prosecutor: Are you aware of a study by Majcher [1974] in which people exposed to loud noise did better at recognizing faces than people who were not stressed?

Psychologist: Yes.

Prosecutor: So you would say that this study involved stress below the optimal level. Is that right?

Psychologist: Well, yes, I guess so.

Prosecutor: I must admit I am confused, Dr. Smith. Isn't it true that the stress-inducing noise was actually louder in the Majcher study, which you said involved below-optimal stress levels, than in the Clifford and Hollin study, which you said involved above-optimal stress?

Psychologist: Well, yes, I believe that's right.

Prosecutor: Do you know some other details of these studies that lead you to believe that induced stress was higher in the Clifford and Hollin study even though the noise was louder in the Majcher experiment, or are you simply making whatever assumptions are needed to make these studies fit your Yerkes-Dodson law?

Psychologist: I do not know enough of the details of these particular studies to comment on them further.

Prosecutor: Are you aware of a study by Johnson and Scott [Note 5] in which people sitting in a waiting room heard a violent altercation in a nearby room and then saw a person carrying a bloody letter opener come out of that room into the waiting room?

Psychologist: Yes.

Prosecutor: How would you compare the stress experienced by someone facing an apparently violent person who has a bloody letter opener with the stress induced by loud noise?

Psychologist: Well, it's hard to say exactly, but the stress would probably be greater in the situation involving the person with the letter opener.

Prosecutor: So you would say that the stress in this situation was probably above the optimal level?

Psychologist: Again, it's hard to say for sure, but I would say that is likely.

Prosecutor: Isn't it true that men who experienced this stressful situation in the Johnson and Scott experiment did better on several memory tests, including an identification test, than men who were exposed to a nonstressful situation?

Psychologist: Well . . . yes, I believe that is correct. However, I believe that for female subjects in that study, the stressful situation led to worse performance on some tests, including the identification test.

Prosecutor: Wouldn't you agree, Dr. Smith, that the picture emerging from psychological studies of the effects of stress on eyewitness identification is somewhat less than crystal clear?

Psychologist: In any set of studies there are bound to be a few inconsistencies. In general, however, the research shows that high stress impairs eyewitness identification.

Prosecutor: Let me ask you one other thing about stress, Dr. Smith. Would the effects of stress in a task be the same for everyone? In other words, would the level of stress at which performance begins to be impaired be the same for all individuals?

Psychologist: Not necessarily. It is quite possible that a level of stress that impaired performance for one person might have little effect on another.

Prosecutor: According to your testimony, the level of stress at which performance begins to be impaired is different for different situations and for different people. Would you agree, then, that for a particular person in a particular situation, it would be impossible to tell how much stress would be necessary to impair perception and memory without testing that person directly in that situation?

Psychologist: Yes, but as I have said, in general high stress impairs performance.

Prosecutor: How much time have you spent testing Mr. Robinson, the eyewitness in this case?

Psychologist: I have not tested him at all. I have never even met him.

Prosecutor: Then how can you testify about the effects of stress on his ability to identify the person who robbed him?

Psychologist: I cannot make any judgment about whether Mr. Robinson as an individual is an accurate or inaccurate witness. I can only describe the principles concerning eyewitness identifications that have been discovered through psychological research.

Prosecutor: How can these vague principles be of help to the jury, Dr. Smith, when you, with all your knowledge and experience, cannot use them to tell whether a witness was accurate or not?

Psychologist: It is not my function to decide that.[9]

NOTES

1. We will henceforth use the phrase "expert psychological testimony" as a convenient shorthand for the more cumbersome "expert psychological testimony about perception and memory in eyewitnesses." It should be understood that we are referring only to expert testimony about eyewitnesses and not to other sorts of expert psychological testimony.

2. People v. Guzman, 47 Cal. App. 3rd 380, 121 Cal. Rptr. 69 (1975).

3. One question of interest at this point is, What are the reasons for the differences in results between the Loftus experiment and later studies? Results we have obtained (McCloskey et al., Note 3) suggest that Loftus obtained high percentages of guilty

verdicts whereas subjects in our study and in that of Hosch et al. (1980) rarely voted guilty because subjects in the latter two studies, but not in the Loftus experiment, received judges' instructions on the *beyond a reasonable doubt* criterion for voting guilty. However, the reasons for the discrepancies between the Loftus study and other experiments in regard to the effects of discrediting manipulations are not clear (see Weinberg & Baron, 1982).

4. A simple example serves to make this point. Consider a situation in which 90% of witnesses make an accurate identification. If jurors accurately estimate the probability that a witness was accurate at .9, all jurors will probably make *believe* decisions, and the juror belief rate (100%) will exceed the witness accuracy rate (90%).

5. It is worth pointing out here that even if there were a large number of variables with well-documented nonobvious effects, expert psychological testimony concerning these variables would not necessarily improve juror evaluation of eyewitness testimony. The information provided by the psychologist would be probabilistic in nature (Loftus & Monahan, 1980; Pachella, 1981) and would not provide the jury with a basis for deciding that an eyewitness was definitely accurate or definitely inaccurate. Furthermore, the expert testimony generally would not give the jury any basis for deciding how large an effect a particular factor would have in the situation at hand. Thus the expert psychological testimony might be of little benefit to the jurors and could even have detrimental effects if, for example, jurors grossly overestimated the importance of one or more of the factors discussed by the psychologist.

6. It is beyond the scope of this article to discuss what form future research should take. However, we note that due to a lack of external validity, many of the studies we have discussed may be limited in the extent to which their results can be generalized to actual situations. We have chosen not to dwell on problems of external validity in our discussion of previous research, but the external validity issue should be given careful consideration in future work (see, e.g., Konecni & Ebbesen, 1979).

7. It is worth mentioning here that the expert testimony in the Wells et al. (1980) study apparently caused subject-jurors in at least some conditions to underestimate the probability that an eyewitness had made an accurate identification. In a condition yielding 50% witness accuracy, subject-jurors who heard expert testimony believed witnesses only about 32% of the time. Similarly, in a condition producing 74% witness accuracy, the juror belief rate was only about 53%. If we assume that jurors make *believe* decisions when they estimate the probability of witness accuracy to be greater than .5, these results suggest substantial underestimation of the probability that a witness was accurate. Of course, such underestimation does not necessarily imply underwillingness to convict. Nevertheless, as the Wells et al. results suggest, the possibility that expert psychological testimony may make jurors too skeptical deserves careful consideration.

8. People v. Guzman, *supra*, p. 72, emphasis added.

9. It is worth reiterating here that the points we have made in this article are meant to apply only to expert testimony. We do not intend to imply that experimental psychologists have no useful role to play in the judicial system. On the contrary, there are probably many useful functions experimental psychologists could serve (e.g., assisting a defense attorney in determining whether there are possible sources of bias in a lineup identification of a defendant). In fact, there may even be special circumstances in which expert psychological testimony would be justified. In particular, expert testimony might be warranted in situations where the psychologist could assert positively that a witness could not have seen what he or she claimed to have seen. Suppose, for example, that a crucial element in a case was whether or not an eyewitness could have noted the color of a sweater worn by a defendant on a clear, moonless night (in the absence of any artificial source of illumination). Given that measurements indicated that the illumination was far below the threshold of photopic vision, a

psychologist could testify that the witness simply could not have correctly identified the color of the sweater.

REFERENCE NOTES

1. Cavoukian, A. *Eyewitness testimony: The ineffectiveness of discrediting information.* Paper presented at the meeting of the American Psychological Association, Montreal, August 1980.
2. McKenna, J., Mellot, A., & Webb, E. *Juror evaluation of eyewitness testimony.* Paper presented at the meeting of the Eastern Psychological Association, New York, April 1981.
3. McCloskey, M., Egeth, H., Webb, E., Washburn, A., & McKenna, J. *Eyewitness jurors and the issue of overbelief.* Unpublished manuscript, Johns Hopkins University, 1981.
4. Carr, T. H. Deffenbacher, K. A., & Leu, J. R. *Is there less interference in memory for faces?* Paper presented at the meeting of the Psychonomic Society, Phoenix, November 1979.
5. Johnson, C., & Scott, B. *Eyewitness testimony and suspect identification as a function of arousal, sex of witness and scheduling of interrogation.* Paper presented at the meeting of the American Psychological Association, Washington, D.C., September 1976.
6. Clifford, B. R., & Hollin, C. R. *Experimentally manipulated arousal and eyewitness testimony.* Unpublished manuscript, North East London Polytechnic, 1978.

REFERENCES

Addison, B. M. Expert testimony on eyewitness perception. *Dickinson Law Review,* 1978, *82,* 464-485.
Chen, H. T. *Disposition of felony arrests: A sequential analysis of the judicial decision making process.* Unpublished doctoral dissertation, University of Massachusetts, 1981.
Deffenbacher, K. A. The influence of arousal on reliability of testimony. In B. R. Clifford & S. Lloyd-Bostock (Eds.), *Evaluating witness evidence: Recent psychological research and new perspectives.* Chichester, England: Wiley, 1983.
Deffenbacher, K. A., Carr, T. H., & Leu, J. R. Memory for words, pictures and faces: Retroactive interference, forgetting and reminiscence. *Journal of Experimental Psychology: Human Learning and Memory,* 1981, *7,* 299-305.
Deffenbacher, K. A., & Loftus, E. F. Do jurors share a common understanding concerning eyewitness behavior? *Law and Human Behavior,* 1982, *6,* 15-30.
Devlin, Hon. Lord P. (Chair). *Report to the secretary of state for the home department of the departmental committee on evidence of identification in criminal cases.* London: Her Majesty's Stationery Office, 1976.

Ebbinghaus, H. [*Memory: A contribution to experimental psychology*] (H. A. Ruger & C. E.Bussenues, trans.). New York: Teacher's College, Columbia University, 1913. (Originally published 1885)

Ellison, K. W., & Buckhout, R. *Psychology and criminal justice*. New York: Harper & Row, 1981.

Gass, R. S. The psychologist as expert witness: Science in the courtroom. *Maryland Law Review*, 1979, *38*, 539-621.

Goldstein, A. G., & Chance, J. Visual recognition memory for complex configurations. *Perception and Psychophysics*, 1971, *9*, 237-241.

Hatvany, N., & Strack, F. The impact of a discredited key witness. *Journal of Applied Social Psychology*, 1980, *10*, 490-509.

Hosch, H. M., Beck, E. L., & McIntyre, P. Influence of expert testimony regarding eyewitness accuracy on jury decisions. *Law and Human Behavior*, 1980, *4*, 287-296.

Konecni, V. J., & Ebbesen, E. B. External validity of research in legal psychology. *Law and Human Behavior*, 1979, *3*, 39-70.

Laughery, K. R., Fessler, P. K., Lenorovitz, D. R., & Yoblick, D. A. Time delay and similarity effects in facial recognition. *Journal of Applied Psychology*, 1974, *59*, 490-496.

Lindsay, R. C. L., Wells, G. L., & Rumpel, C. M. Can people detect eyewitness-identification accuracy within and across situations? *Journal of Applied Psychology*, 1981, *66*, 79-89.

Loftus, E. F. Reconstructing memory: The incredible eyewitness. *Psychology Today*, 1974, *8*, 116-119.

Loftus, E. F. *Eyewitness testimony*. Cambridge, Mass.: Harvard University Press, 1979.

Loftus, E. F. Impact of expert psychological testimony on the unreliability of eyewitness identification. *Journal of Applied Psychology*, 1980, *65*, 9-15.

Loftus, E. F., & Monahan, J. Trial by data: Psychological research as legal evidence. *American Psychologist*, 1980, *35*, 270-283.

Lower, J. S. Psychologists as expert witnesses. *Law and Psychology Review*, 1978, *4*, 127-139.

Majcher, L. L. *Facial recognition as a function of arousal level, exposure duration and delay interval*. Unpublished master's thesis, University of Missouri, 1974.

Malpass, R. S., & Kravitz, J. Recognition for faces of own and other race. *Journal of Personality and Social Psychology*, 1969, *13*, 330-334.

Myers, M. A. Rule departures and making law: Juries and their verdicts. *Law and Society*, 1979, *13*, 781-797.

Pachella, R. G. The truth and nothing but the truth (Review of *Eyewitness testimony* by E. F. Loftus and *The psychology of eyewitness testimony* by A. D. Yarmey). *Contemporary Psychology*, 1981, *26*, 85-87.

Rembar, C. *The law of the land: The evolution of our legal system*. New York: Simon & Schuster, 1980.

Shepherd, J. W., & Ellis, H. O. The effect of attractiveness on recognition memory for faces. *American Journal of Psychology*, 1973, *86*, 627-634.

Shoemaker, J. 18 months of hell for rapist's lookalike. *Chicago Tribune,* December 28, 1980.

Starkman, D. The use of eyewitness identification evidence in criminal trials. *Criminal Law Quarterly,* 1979, *21,* 361-386.

Wall, P. M. *Eyewitness identification in criminal cases.* Springfield, Ill.: Charles C Thomas, 1965.

Weinberg, H. I., & Baron, R. S. The discredible eyewitness. *Personality and Social Psychology Bulletin,* 1982, *8,* 60-67.

Wells, G. L., Lindsay, R. C. L., & Ferguson, T. J. Accuracy, confidence and juror perceptions in eyewitness testimony. *Journal of Applied Psychology,* 1979, *64,* 440-448.

Wells, G. L., Lindsay, R. C. L., & Tousignant, J. P. Effects of expert psychological advice testimony. *Law and Human Behavior,* 1980, *4,* 275-285.

Woocher, F. D. Did your eyes deceive you? Expert psychological testimony on the unreliability of eyewitness identification. *Stanford Law Review,* 1977, *29,* 960-1030.

Yarmey, A. D., & Jones, H. P. T. Is the psychology of eyewitness identification a matter of common sense? In B. R. Clifford & S. Lloyd-Bostock (Eds.), *Evaluating witness evidence: Recent psychological research and new perspectives.* Chichester, England: Wiley, 1983.

12

SILENCE IS NOT GOLDEN

ELIZABETH F. LOFTUS
University of Washington

Recently, Paul Henderson, a reporter for the Seattle *Times*, won a 1982 Pulitzer Prize for a series of stories that revealed the innocence of a man who had been convicted of rape. The innocent man, 31-year-old Steve Titus, had been convicted in February 1981 of raping a 17-year-old woman on a secluded road just south of Seattle-Tacoma International Airport. The victim positively identified Titus, breaking into tears as she made her identification. While awaiting sentencing, Titus battled to clear his name and eventually, with the help of Henderson, was able to achieve the exceedingly rare victory of having his conviction overturned.

Author's Note. I am grateful to the National Science Foundation, which has supported my research both on human memory and on jury behavior. Many colleagues gave their time to discuss the issues raised here with me in some detail. I am especially grateful to Ken Deffenbacher, Roy Malpass, Seth Greenberg, Geoff Loftus, and many students. Requests for reprints should be sent to Elizabeth F. Loftus, Department of Psychology, University of Washington, Seattle, Washington 98195.

From *American Psychologist*, May 1983, pp. 564-572. Copyright 1983 by the American Psychological Association. Reprinted by permission of the publisher and author.

How common are such wrongful convictions? No one really knows. Our evidence here is purely anecdotal. Even the "sad, pathetic cases" to come before Erle Stanley Gardner's Court of Last Resort provide us with nothing more than a list of anecdotes. Gardner, the creator of Perry Mason, took cases of persons who were serving life sentences for murders they claimed they had not committed and reopened the cases that seemed meritorious. By far the greatest cause of conviction of innocent defendants, in 2,000 cases out of over 20,000 appeals for help, was mistaken identification (Houts, 1981, p. 2).

What is known for certain is that the Titus case is one of many documented cases of mistaken eyewitness testimony that have had tragic consequences. Other instances can be found in recent books on eyewitness testimony (e.g., Loftus, 1979; Wells & Loftus, 1983; Yarmey, 1979), in the report of an investigation conducted in Great Britain (Devlin, 1976), and in a scan of recent newspaper stories. My friends and colleagues often send me clippings from their hometown papers, and I have now amassed a rather substantial pile. An article in the New York *Post* (December 30, 1980) begins "An innocent South Carolina man, charged with the murder of [a police officer] expressed a sigh of relief yesterday when told he was cleared." Three eyewitnesses searching police mug shot files picked out this man, but he was eventually able to prove that he had been at work that day. The *Washington Post* (November 17, 1981) reported that "a Southwest Washington teenager was arrested, tried, and convicted for the street robbery of an elderly woman. Two days after his conviction, city prosecutors discovered that another individual had previously confessed to the crime." The Seattle *Times* (November 15, 1980) ran a headline: "5 Years in Prison, Innocent Man Home." The story was about a former Baptist Sunday School teacher who was convicted of two rapes that prosecutors now know he did not do. Two women had identified him in a police lineup as the man who raped them. Another man eventually confessed to the rapes. And finally, from the *San Francisco Chronicle* (March 5, 1981), we learn that "The Wrong Man Spent Nine Years In Prison." Eyewitnesses had positively identified Aaron Lee Owens of Oakland, California, and he was convicted of double murder. New evidence that eventually freed Owens took that many years to uncover. If nothing else, these tragic mistakes tell us there is room for improvement in our legal procedures.

Eyewitnesses can be mistaken not only about the identity of the person who committed the crime but about other facts as well. Eyewitness estimates about the passage of time can be crucial to a determination of whether a defendant acted maliciously or in self-defense. Eyewitness testimony about the color of a traffic light, whether it was red or green, can bear on the defendant's guilt in a negligent homicide case or on the issue of fault in a civil case. Witness recollections of conversations can bear on questions about premeditation, intent, and other matters. Thus in studying the problems associated with eyewitness testimony, we need to concern ourselves with the variety of such testimony that might be offered in a court of law.

Should a psychologist get involved in cases in which eyewitness testimony plays a part? That is the question we now confront. Before tackling this issue, it is worth pointing out that many prosecutions for crimes such as robbery and rape turn on identification evidence. In fact, in the absence of physical evidence or an incriminating statement from the defendant, eyewitness testimony may constitute the sole evidence linking the defendant to the crime. The accuracy of such testimony seems especially crucial when the prosecution presents but a single eyewitness and nothing more. Defense attorneys find themselves in difficult positions. Until recently, their only hope for challenging the eyewitness account was to try to find weaknesses in it and somehow get these across to the jury. All too often, they failed miserably. It's a "lawyer's nightmare," they have explained to me, "defending someone who you believe is innocent and watching that person be convicted and sent to prison." And so they began to look for another way. They looked to psychologists for help.

What should the psychologist do? As prominent forensic psychologist Lionel Haward (1981) has noted, many psychologists dislike the idea of testifying in court, and they will easily decline the invitation. They may dislike the adverse publicity that could follow, the excessive amount of time wasted, or the thought of public exposure of some aspect of their professional incompetence ("We all have our Achilles heel," says Haward, p. 174). Others accept the invitation because they feel that the psychologist, like every other citizen, has a moral duty to assist the course of justice. They feel that anyone who possesses the knowledge, experience, and skills that can contribute to the processes of the law should be prepared to make them available to those most in need of them. Finally, as Haward tells us, there are some individuals who

> rush in with gay abandon, venturing on ground where even angels fear to tread, only too anxious to savour yet another professional experience, to receive a little transitory limelight, or to save one more far-from-innocent head from today's well-padded and nonlethal block. (p. 175)

The McCloskey and Egeth message is aimed at those who are either willing or eager to testify, but especially to those who may be undecided.

THE ARGUMENT AGAINST TESTIFYING

McCloskey and Egeth (this issue [chapter 11 of this volume]) begin their article with the basic premise that any intervention in the operation of the justice system should not be undertaken lightly. They then go on to develop two major themes. First, they argue that the empirical evidence documenting the need for expert psychological testimony is weak, at best. In particular, they claim that no evidence exists to support the claim that jurors are too willing to believe eyewitness testimony. Second, even where it can be shown that jurors are fallible in the decisions they reach, it has not been shown that psychological testimony can provide much beyond the intuitions of ordinary experience. Given this sorry state of affairs, they argue, experimental psychologists may do more harm than good by premature intrusion into court proceedings.

McCloskey and Egeth's critical view of the role of experimental psychologists would have been welcome back in the early 1900s. It was then that Hugo Munsterberg, sometimes called the "father of forensic psychology" (Haward, 1981, p. 172), helped establish the role of the psychologist in American courts. It was also then that one of Munsterberg's chief antagonists said, "Experimental psychologists are no more welcome in the courtroom than Sherlock Holmes" (Moore, 1908b). By way of elaboration, this antagonist explained in a later article that experimental psychologists would get in the way by distracting attention from the real issues in the case (Moore, 1908a). McCloskey and Egeth make some similar arguments, both in these pages and in a book chapter (Egeth & McCloskey, 1983), but they are now bolstered by empirical data in a way that their predecessors were not.

At first glance, the arguments of McCloskey and Egeth appear quite persuasive. But these arguments must be scrutinized as carefully as the ideas and positions they so skillfully attack. On the positive side, these two experimental psychologists have rendered a service by providing a challenge to researchers to find a type of expert testimony that might truly have beneficial effects in our society. Their challenge has not been posed, however, by the presentation of a balanced view but, instead, by the adoption of a position that is rather one-sided. They cite cases and legal opinion that support the position they advance but ignore those that oppose their position. They use experimental evidence to support their views and yet attack those very same studies when they run counter to their prevailing view. Now it may be said that the writings of those whom they attack have been unnecessarily one-sided as well and that their current "other-sided" view is necessary to counter the confusion that others have made before them. But for the sake of the readers, especially those who have not been exposed to the history of this debate, it seems fair to provide both sides of this stormy story.

DON'T SAY "NO" JUST YET

It should be made clear at the outset that psychologists do not typically foist themselves on reluctant lawyers. Rather, the interaction begins with a request (occasionally verging on begging) by the lawyer. Since members of the legal profession initiate the interaction with psychologists, one might profitably begin by looking to the legal field for its views on whether jurors need help in evaluating the quality of eyewitness accounts and whether expert testimony can provide that help. After all, it is they who interact regularly with genuine witnesses to crimes, accidents, and other significant legal events. If one examined only the legal opinions included in the McCloskey and Egeth article, one might be left with the misimpression that the legal field doesn't want or need help with its eyewitness problem—for example, the quotation they provide from People v. Guzman:[1] "It is something that everyone knows about, the problems of identification."

But the legal view is far from one-sided; we can see this by examining the comments made by lawyers, judges, and even the justices of our highest court. Let's begin at the top.

From time to time, the U.S. Supreme Court considers the issue of eyewitness testimony, and it did so again recently in Watkins v. Sowders.[2] Briefly, John Watkins was convicted in a Kentucky court of attempting to rob a Louisville liquor store. In a separate case, James Summitt was convicted of rape. In both cases, the major evidence against the defendants was eyewitness testimony, and in both cases the defendants offered evidence that pretrial police procedures to obtain the identification were impermissibly suggestive. The cases were joined on appeal to the U.S. Supreme Court. Defense counsel argued that the trial courts should have been constitutionally obligated to conduct a hearing outside the presence of the jury to determine whether the identification was admissible. The Supreme Court decided that although it is prudent for a trial court to determine the admissibility of identification evidence out of the presence of the jury, there is no per se requirement under the due process clause of the Fourteenth Amendment.

The majority in Watkins refused to analogize to a previous decision, Jackson v. Denno,[3] in which it was held that there must be a pretrial hearing outside the presence of the jury whenever a confession was sought to be admitted and a question was raised concerning the voluntariness of the confession. Here the court required pretrial hearings for confessions, reasoning that confessions are so compelling as evidence that a jury may be unable to follow judicial instructions to ignore involuntary confessions. In contrast, the majority in Watkins presumed that juries can follow instructions to assess the reliability of eyewitness identification evidence and will be able to ignore identifications that are impermissibly suggestive. The two-person dissenting opinion in Watkins was strong: "Surely jury instructions can ordinarily no more cure the erroneous admission of powerful identification evidence than they can cure the erroneous admission of a confession." The dissent further pointed out that cross-examination in front of the jury is inadequate to test the reliability of eyewitness testimony because cross-examination may often be inhibited by a fear that rigorous questioning of hostile witnesses will strengthen the eyewitness testimony and impress it on the jury.

Although not directly concerned with the issue of expert testimony, Watkins illustrates the differences in opinion that are held on the subject of eyewitness testimony itself. Our Supreme Court justices disagree in their views on the impact of eyewitness testimony and on the ability of jury instructions or of vigorous cross-examination to cure problems in this area. The dissent seems to indicate a concern that jurors could be overly impressed with the testimony of eyewitnesses, whereas the majority in Watkins seems relatively unconcerned.

Although the Court in Watkins did not explicitly discuss the use of expert testimony, many other courts have. It cannot be denied that some legal commentators have argued strongly against the use of this expert testimony, with some of the strongest negative language being found in certain appellate opinions. Several courts, for example, have concluded that the expert testimony is not beyond the knowledge and experience of a juror and thus is not proper subject matter for expert testimony.[4] In Dyas v. U.S., the court wrote, "We are persuaded that the subject matter of the proffered testimony is not beyond the ken of the average layman nor would such testimony aid the trier in a search for the truth"(p. 832). In Nelson v. State of Florida, the court said, "We believe it is within the common knowledge of the jury that a person being attacked and beaten undergoes stress that might cloud a subsequent identification of the assailant by the victim. As such, the subject matter was not properly within the realm of expert testimony" (p. 1021). These remarks are similar to those stated by the Ontario Court of Appeals[5] as it upheld the trial judge's decision to refuse the admissibility of the expert testimony: "The same can be said of stress. Knowledge by the jury that conditions of stress affect perception by the observer would add little, if anything, to what lay persons already know" (discussed in detail by Taylor, 1980). The trial judge had refused the testimony for several reasons, one of which was lack of Canadian precedent for this type of evidence.

This negative view is far from being the dominant view held by members of the legal profession. A respectable number of lawyers (e.g., Frazzini, 1981; Stein, 1981; Woocher, 1977) and judges (Bazelon, 1980; Weinstein, 1981) have recognized the serious problems that arise because of faulty eyewitness testimony and have held that the expert testimony will be clear aid to a jury. Stein (1981) notes that the Federal Rules of Evidence (1975), especially Rule 702, will spark the use of the psychologist as an expert on this subject. The rule states:

> If scientific, technical, or other specialized knowledge will assist the trier to understand the evidence or to determine a fact in issue, a witness qualified as an expert by knowledge, skill, experience, training, or education, may testify thereto in the form of an opinion or otherwise.

In analyzing the expert testimony with respect to this rule, Stein asserts that in his view the expert testimony will certainly assist the fact finder. "Any knowledge on the subject qualifies as an assist," he says. However, he is careful to point out that there is one argument against admissibility, and it can be found in Rule 403:

> Although relevant, evidence may be excluded if its probative value is substantially outweighed by the danger of unfair prejudice, confusion of the issues, or misleading the jury, or by consideration of undue delay, waste of time, or needless presentation of cumulative evidence.

Thus even though evidence is relevant and will assist the jury on a relevant issue, it could arguably be excluded because it will confuse and mislead.

Weinstein (1981), a judge writing in the *Columbia Law Review*, considers a number of possible protections against the wrongful conviction of the innocent caused by mistaken identification. His views are clear: "Greater use of expert testimony . . . is clearly warranted" (p. 454). He goes on to note that the Federal Rules of Evidence and the rules of most of the states that follow the federal rules permit this kind of evidence. He suggests, indirectly, that some courts might hold that the government is required to provide indigent defendants with experts of this kind.

Bazelon (1981), a senior circuit judge of the U.S. Court of Appeals for the District of Columbia, has also thought a great deal about expert testimony. He states: "Within our adversarial system, our only hope lies in an informed jury. Some combination of jury instructions, lawyers' arguments, and use of expert witnesses can certainly mitigate the problem (p. 106).

Finally, Frazzini (1981) has stated:

> I believe that expert psychological testimony probably is the best way for juries to learn about the unreliability of eyewitness testimony. Prosecutor and defense counsel, in questioning the expert witness, can explain to the jury both the application and the limits of experimental research in relation to the case on trial.

He ends his article: "For innocent men and women wrongly accused because of mistaken identifications, expert psychological testimony still offers a beacon of hope" (p. xx).

In short, contrary to the impression left after reading the McCloskey and Egeth article, there are many views held by persons in the legal field regarding the eyewitness problem. Some worry more than others about the injustices that arise from mistaken testimony. Some believe that traditional methods of handling the problem such as vigorous cross-examination will be adequate; others do not. Some welcome the use of psychological expert testimony as a potential solution; others shun it. A look at the existing empirical data may shed light on the conditions in which such testimony could have real value.

EMPIRICAL DATA

Unlike many of their predecessors who objected to experimental psychologists testifying in court, McCloskey and Egeth support their position with numerous references to empirical data. One group of studies concerns the extent to which stimulated jurors are influenced by eyewitness accounts. In discussing this conflicting set of findings, McCloskey and Egeth mention several studies that showed very low conviction rates despite the positive eyewitness testimony on the part of a prosecution witness. What are we to make of these low rates? There are so many extraneous variables that influence whether simulated jurors will convict a hypothetical defendant that we cannot be sure why the conviction rates were so low in the studies cited. Perhaps it was because judicial instructions regarding the presumption of innocence and the burden of proof were given (see also Saunders, Hewitt, & Vidmar, Note 1; Saunders & Vidmar, Note 2). Perhaps it was because experimental subjects were temporarily sensitized to problems of faulty testimony by the publicity associated with cases of mistaken eyewitness testimony. Such publicity has been shown to be associated with lower conviction rates in jury simulations (Loftus, Note 3). Since we really do not know the reasons for the low acquittal rates in some studies, it seems more fruitful to view the collection of studies as indicating that there are conditions under which simulated jurors are highly believing of eyewitness testimony and other conditions under which they are not. It is the latter approach that will lead researchers to a better understanding of the types of cases in which expert testimony might be helpful and the types in which it might not.

Another type of data offered by McCloskey and Egeth to support their notion that jurors may not be overbelieving of eyewitness testimony comes from analyses of actual criminal cases. The studies they cite appear to show that positive eyewitness testimony does not increase the likelihood of conviction. The point is driven hardest by the dramatic illustration they provide of a man who was tried five times for crimes he did not commit and, even in the face of positive eyewitness testimony, was acquitted each time. Again, we have only one side of the coin. Although in this and some other cases jurors acquitted a man who was innocent, other equally dramatic cases can be found in which the innocent were convicted. It was after a careful analysis of such cases, that Lord Gardiner, speaking in the House of Lords on March 17, 1973, was moved to say:

> The danger of identification is that anyone in this country may be wrongly convicted on the evidence of a witness who is perfectly sincere, perfectly convinced that the accused is the man they saw, and whose sincerity communicates itself to the members of the jury who therefore accept the evidence. (quoted in Devlin, 1976, p. 7)

When experimental psychologists testify in court, they often describe research studies illustrating people's ability to perceive and recall complex events. Factors that may have affected the accuracy of the particular identification in the case at bar are explained to the jury. The goal is to provide jurors with additional information to better equip them to evaluate the identification evidence fully and properly (Loftus & Monahan, 1980). But McCloskey and Egeth suggest that most variables that have been listed as suitable topics for expert testimony are either not well documented by research studies or are obvious to jurors. Again, they refer to empirical work to support this claim. For example, they claim that effects of exposure duration, the wording of questions, and the cross-racial identification problem are already obvious to jurors. They claim that there is little if any empirical support for the importance of the factors of stress and weapon focus. There is thus no need for expert testimony; the defense can simply call any weakness in the identification to the attention of the jury.

It is here that McCloskey and Egeth seem especially naive about the dynamics of the courtroom trial, particularly in their suggestion that defense counsel call to the jury's attention (during opening and closing statements and in the examination of witnesses) problems in the eyewitness account. As I indicated earlier, in *Watkins v. Sowders* there was judicial recognition of the fact that cross-examination of eyewitnesses may be inhibited by a fear of its potential negative effect on the jury. This is especially problematic for the defense if the witness is also a victim. On the subject of the effectiveness of cross-examination, one law professor has explicitly said that most defense lawyers who have had to confront an eyewitness who unhesitatingly identifies the defendant as the culprit know that "even the most thoughtful cross-examination may fail to discredit the witness" (Mendez, 1980, p. 445). As for making the points during opening and closing arguments, many lawyers know that their comments are taken far less seriously than those of expert witnesses, since these remarks are perceived as being uttered in the motivated interests of a client.

But what is more troubling about their assertions is the one-sided analysis of the data. For the most part, our knowledge of what is commonly known by individuals regarding eyewitness ability comes from survey-type studies in which a variety of subjects have answered multiple-choice questions. At least seven such studies have now been conducted (see Brigham, 1981; Deffenbacher & Loftus, 1982; Brigham & Bothwell, Note 4; Brigham & Wolfskeil, Note 5; and Rahaim & Brodsky, Note 6, in addition to those studies cited by McCloskey and Egeth). In general, these studies are uniform in showing that there are areas in which many individuals do not understand how a particular psychological factor influences perception and recollection. Yet, when the studies indicate that a particular psychological factor is understood by individuals, McCloskey and Egeth accept this at face value (e.g., the factor of question-wording effects).[6] However, when the studies indicate that a particular psychological factor may be interpreted differently by subjects, or that misconceptions are widely held, then the survey item demonstrating this is invariably criticized (e.g., the factor of cross-racial identification). Some of the strongest items in terms of indicating subject misimpressions have been considerably downplayed (e.g., the accuracy-confidence relationship) or ignored altogether (e.g., the effects of violence, the measurement of lineup fairness, or the effects of photo-biased identifications).

When it comes to specific claims made by McCloskey and Egeth regarding the psychological literature, my response could go on for pages and pages. Unfortunately, space permits but a few points. First, the brief review of the literature on the effects of the retention interval is seriously misleading. The so-called run-of-the-mill retention losses are often dramatic, and even frightening, when considered in terms of changes in d'. A drop in performance from, say, 87% to 71% can represent a serious loss in d', especially when 50% represents chance performance. The importance of looking at d' changes is brought home by one study (Egan, Pittner, & Goldstein, 1977) which showed that as the retention interval increases, correct identification was not affected but false alarms increased remarkably. While on the subject of the retention interval, I am forced to mention the so-called "reminiscence effect" observed by Deffenbacher, Carr, and Leu (1981). This effect occurred only in conditions of repeated testing and this is similar to the "hypermnesia" reported by Erdelyi and Becker (1974). However, researchers have noted that these supposed improvements in memory are actually quite small (Goldstein & Chance, 1981) and in no way suggest that the memory is actually getting stronger over time.

What about the claim that there is little empirical support for many of the factors that psychologists testify about? McCloskey and Egeth have tended to look only at the literature involving experiments on recollection of realistic events. However, a psychologist's knowledge of the factors that influence eyewitness accounts comes from a large literature in cognitive, perceptual, and social psychology, as well as from experiments that attempt to mirror the eyewitness situation. I believe that there are luminance and acuity levels that make accurate perception very difficult—but this knowledge comes mostly from a vast literature on basic research in perception (see, e.g., Kaufman, 1974). I believe that people are less accurate after a longer rather than shorter retention interval because of the enormous number of memory studies that have shown this to be the case. When a occasional study comes along that fails to show a decline in memory even with a relatively long retention interval, I am interested, but it would take much more for me to completely revise my view. I believe that postevent information can modify a person's recollection of an event because of hundreds of experiments that colleagues and I have conducted that demonstrate this phenomenon in both controlled laboratory studies and in highly naturalistic simulations (see Loftus, 1979, for a review of this research, and Rodgers, 1982, for a more recent discussion). I believe that a weapon captures the attention of a witness because of recent experiments in which eye movements have been monitored while people watch crime scenes, but also because of a more traditional literature that suggests that people will fixate on unusual or highly informative objects (Antes, 1974; Loftus & Mackworth, 1978). When a lawyer says, "Please tell the jurors about the psychological research in your field," should I really refuse to do so?

Based on their analysis, McCloskey and Egeth suggest that it might be a mistake for psychologists to agree to testify on eyewitness reliability. They argue that such testimony could create underbelief on the part of jurors and that it could ultimately lead to a battle of experts that would make the profession look bad. When I reviewed their article for publication, I noted that many trials involved apparent battles of experts without any loss of scientific integrity. One bio-mechanical engineer says that a football injury was caused by the helmet striking the back of the player's neck whereas the defense expert, an equally reputable medical doctor, says it could not possibly have happened that way. In the toxic shock death case that was tried in Cedar Rapids, Iowa, a New York microbiologist testified that one component of the tampon will break down to sugar in the presence of an enzyme commonly found in the vagina. Sugar, he claimed, helps nourish a strain of bacteria that is responsible for toxic shock syndrome. On the other hand, the defense witness, a chemical engineer from Iowa State University, testified that the component cannot be broken down by the enzyme ("$300,000 Tampon Case Award," 1982). Do these confrontations lead to the detriment of the medical profession, creating or sustaining the impression of medicine as a subjective, unscientific discipline? McCloskey and Egeth say yes but that the medical profession then redeems itself by making some enormously useful medical discovery that we read about in the pages of Newsweek and Time (Egeth & McCloskey, 1983). My response at the time was that if doctors in the 1950s had been afraid to testify that they believed thalidomide caused birth defects because they feared a courtroom confrontation that would make the profession look bad, we might still have tragic limb-reduction defects occurring all over the world. My response now is that if medicine can undo the damaging effects of contradictory courtroom testimony by subsequent publicity of useful discoveries, why can't psychology do the same? In suggesting that we do not have many useful discoveries that can repair a damaged reputation, McCloskey and Egeth are perpetrating stereotypes and negative comparisons between biological and psychological fields that will indeed do us great harm.

Is a battle of the experts necessarily a bad thing? When freedom of the press is pitted against individual privacy and experts take opposing sides, are we necessarily worse off? When opposing experts battle over an issue like nuclear power, is the public worse off? Is the reputation of the field tarnished? Although there are some instances in which information might actually harm someone, it seems that as a general principle, providing information in this instance will lead to a more informed judgment.

I can conceive of some situations that might damage the reputation of psychology, and one of these has been discussed briefly by Haward

(1981). In Haward's experience, and my own, lawyers are often unaware of the difference in training between members of one branch of psychology and another. They may ask their local psychologist to testify on any psychological matter, say eyewitness reliability, even if the psychologist's specialty is the effects of crowding in prisons or the effects of different therapies. They prefer their pet psychologist to a well-trained new PhD in experimental psychology because the local one is easily available or more convenient. The chosen psychologist may be one whose background and experience are quite inappropriate to the matters at issue, and if such ill-chosen experts are made to appear inept and incompetent, they will bring discredit to themselves and their specialty. It is these sorts of cases that may be detrimental to our profession.

Although rejecting the idea that jurors have been shown to be overbelieving of eyewitness testimony, McCloskey and Egeth are kinder to the hypothesis that jurors cannot distinguish well between accurate and inaccurate eyewitnesses. They cite the studies of Wells and Lindsay (Lindsay, Wells, & Rumpel, 1981; Wells, Lindsay, & Ferguson, 1979; Wells, Lindsay, & Tousignant, 1980), which show that within a given crime situation simulated jurors were as likely to believe inaccurate witnesses as they were to believe accurate witnesses. But they go on to say that this does not mean that jurors will be more likely to convict (since believing an eyewitness does not mean that a conviction will necessarily result from that belief). Furthermore, it has not been shown that expert testimony will improve juror discrimination. They claim that the research shows that expert testimony reduces skepticism without helping the discrimination problem. And then they call for more research.

We may have struck a nice point of agreement at this juncture. With these comments, McCloskey and Egeth have invited the necessary further research that will reveal the form of expert testimony, if any, that might truly help individuals to be better judges of eyewitnesses' testimony. What type of expert testimony might improve such judgment? There are many possibilities. Expert testimony that corrected certain widely held misconceptions would seem useful. In this category we might place the research on the relationship between the accuracy of a witness about a particular detail and his or her confidence. Laypeople think there is a strong relationship (Deffenbacher & Loftus, 1982), and even the U.S. Supreme Court[7] has suggested that the confidence a witness expresses should be taken into account when evaluating that eyewitness. But a careful analysis of the literature led Deffenbacher (1980) to conclude that "this strong faith in the adequacy of certainty as a predictor of accuracy is not at all supported by the present review of 43 separate assessments of the accuracy/confidence relation in eye and earwitnesses"(p. 243).

Another possibility for future consideration is for the psychologist to serve as a friend of the court rather than to testify on behalf of one particular side or the other. Such a solution would eliminate the problem of any battle of experts and might reduce the possibility of bias in testimony. Another possibility is for the psychologist to serve as an advisor to the legal profession in ways that would not involve testimony at all. This is already a common practice (see Haward, 1981). Only future experimentation will reveal the benefits of these proposals.

In suggesting that experimental psychologists categorically stay out of the courtroom, McCloskey and Egeth have taken a rather ivory tower approach to life. When I discussed their views with colleagues in the course of preparing this reply, one theme kept recurring. "Knowledge does not have to be perfect in order for people to use it" (Malpass, Note 7). "You can't wait for a science to perfect itself" (Bolles, Note 8). In another context, philosopher Patrick Suppes made some related remarks in a keynote address he delivered in The Hague: That scientific knowledge can be made complete, he claimed, is a belief that is not only false but can lead to a misinterpretation of science and its effectiveness in society (Dillon, 1982). Compared with the views of McCloskey and Egeth, these comments reflect a strong difference of philosophy. McCloskey and Egeth seem to think that the data must be more perfect or more complete before we discuss them, whereas others say that we need not wait for perfection, especially since we are likely never to achieve it. Where one person draws his or her criterion regarding how much knowledge we should have before we tell others about it is simply a matter of personal values. But one thing is clear: To speak defensively of the probabilistic nature of the statements we can make is to reject the very essence of science.

The present controversy is an instance of a large issue. Whenever a scientific and a practical field come together, they form a mutually supportive unit in which the scientific field (in this case psychology) offers the practical field (in this case the law) some suggestions. The practical field feeds back by suggesting what the important issues are and what should be clarified and studied further by the scientific field. Psychology itself cannot operate in a vacuum or else it becomes—like the game of chess—a field completely concerned with itself. We should talk not just of the good that psychology might provide the legal system but also of the good that the law can provide psychology. My own research and teaching have been enriched considerably by interactions with the legal profession. While I am grateful to McCloskey and Egeth for encouraging me to be thoughtful about what I do and how I do it, I have no plans to abandon the enterprise altogether. I feel fortunate to be involved in an exciting area of psychological research that meshes so nicely with a practical problem and is at the same time theoretically interesting. When Paul Henderson received the Pulitzer Prize—that symbol of excellence, the prize of prizes, the award you'd want listed in your obituary (O'Donnell, 1982)—he called it "a fairy tale ending to the Titus story" (Provemza, 1982). Fairy tales are very rare in real life, but we ought not stop seeking them. When prominent members of the legal field come out and say that testimony based on psychological research offers a "beacon of hope," it makes me feel pretty good about what I'm doing.

NOTES

1. People v. Guzman, 47 Cal. App. 3rd 380, 121 Cal. Rptr. 69 (1975).
2. Watkins v. Sowders, 101 S. Ct. 654, 28 Crim. L.R. 3037 (1981).
3. Jackson v. Denno, 378 U.S. 368, 84 S. Ct. 1774 (1964).
4. See, e.g., Dyas v. U.S., 376 A.2d 827 (1977); State of Iowa v. Galloway, 275 N.W. 2d 736 (1979); Nelson v. State of Florida, 362 S.2d 1017 (1978).
5. Regina v. Audy, 34 C.C.C., 2d 231, Ont. C. A. (1977).
6. McCloskey and Egeth (this issue [chapter 11]) removed the discussion of this factor from their revised manuscript, but it still exists, as of this writing, in Egeth and McCloskey (1983).
7. Neil v. Biggers, 409 U.S. 188 (1972).

REFERENCE NOTES

1. Saunders, D. M., Hewitt, E. C., & Vidmar, N. *Discredited eyewitness testimony, judicial instructions, and juror decisions.* Paper presented at the meeting of the Canadian Psychological Association, Toronto, June 1981.
2. Saunders, D. M., & Vidmar, N. *Discredited eyewitness testimony and mock jury deliberations.* Paper presented at the meeting of the Midwestern Psychological Association, Detroit, May 1981.
3. Loftus, E. F. *Current news events can change the results of a psychological experiment: An example from juror-simulation research.* Unpublished manuscript, University of Washington, 1982.
4. Brigham, J. C., & Bothwell, R. K. *The ability of prospective jurors to estimate the accuracy of eyewitness identifications.* Unpublished manuscript, Florida State University, 1982.
5. Brigham. J. C., & Wolfskeil, M. P. *Opinions of attorneys and law enforcement personnel on the accuracy of eyewitness identifications.* Unpublished manuscript, Florida State University, 1982.
6. Rahaim, G. L., & Brodsky, D. L. *Empirical evidence versus common sense: Juror and lawyer knowledge of eyewitnesses accuracy.* Unpublished manuscript, University of Alabama, 1981.
7. Malpass, R. Personal communication, April 14, 1982.
8. Bolles, R. Personal communication, April 17, 1982.

REFERENCES

Antes, J. R. The time course of picture viewing. *Journal of Experimental Psychology*, 1974, *103*, 62-70.

Bazelon, D. L. Eyewitness news. *Psychology Today*, March 1981, pp. 101-106.

Brigham, J. C. The accuracy of eyewitness evidence: How do attorneys see it? *The Florida Bar Journal*, 1981, *55*, 714-721.

Deffenbacher, K. A. Eyewitness accuracy and confidence: Can we infer anything about their relationship? *Law and Human Behavior*, 1980, *4* 243-260.

Deffenbacher, K. A., Carr, T. H., & Leu, J. R. Memory for words, pictures and faces: Retrograde interference, forgetting and reminiscence. *Journal of Experimental Psychology: Human Learning and Memory*, 1981, *7*, 299-305.

Deffenbacher, K. A., & Loftus, E. F. Do jurors share a common understanding concerning eyewitness behavior? *Law and Human Behavior*, 1982, *6*, 15-30.

Devlin, Hon. Lord P. (Chair). *Report to the secretary of state for the home department of the departmental committee on evidence of identification in criminal cases.* London: Her Majesty's Stationery Office, 1976.

Dillon, M. Pat Suppes looks at science, society in a probabilistic way. *Stanford Observer*, April 1982.

Egan, D., Pittner, M., & Goldstein, A. G. Eyewitness identification—Photographs vs. live models. *Law and Human Behavior*, 1977, *1*, 199-206.

Egeth, H. E., & McCloskey, M. Expert testimony about eyewitness behavior: Is it safe and effective? In G. Wells & E. F. Loftus (Eds.), *Eyewitness testimony: Psychological perspectives.* London: Cambridge University Press, 1983.

Erdelyi, M. H., & Becker, J. Hypermnesia for pictures: Incremental memory for pictures but not for words in multiple recall trials. *Cognitive Psychology*, 1974, *6*, 159-161.

Federal rules of evidence for United States courts and magistrates. St. Paul, Minn.: West, 1975.

Frazzini, S. F. Review of eyewitness testimony. *The Yale Review*, 1981, *70*, xviii-xx.

Goldstein, A. G., & Chance, J. E. Laboratory studies of face recognition. In G. Davies, H. Ellis, & J. Shepherd (Eds.), *Perceiving and remembering faces.* London: Academic Press, 1981.

Haward, L. *Forensic psychology.* London: Batesford, 1981.

Houts, N. The accuracy/fallibility of eyewitness reporting. *Trauma*, 1981, *23*, 1-6.

Kaufman, L. *Sight and mind.* New York: Oxford University Press, 1974.

Lindsay, R. C. L., Wells, G. L., & Rumpel, C. M. Can people detect eyewitness identification accuracy within and across situations? *Journal of Applied Psychology*, 1981, *66*, 79-89.

Loftus, E. F. *Eyewitness testimony.* Cambridge, Mass.: Harvard University Press, 1979.

Loftus, G. R., & Mackworth, N. H. Cognitive determinants of fixation location during picture viewing. *Journal of Experimental Psychology: Human Perception and Performance*, 1978, *4*, 565-572.

Loftus E. F., & Monahan, J. Trial by data: Psychological research as legal evidence. *American Psychologist,* 1980, *35,* 270-283.

McCloskey, M., & Egeth, H. Eyewitness identification: What can a psychologist tell a jury? *American Psychologist,* 1983, *38,* 550-563.

Mendez, M. A. Memory, that strange deceiver (Review of *The psychology of eyewitness testimony* by A. D. Yarmey). *Stanford Law Review,* 1980, *32,* 445-452.

Moore, C. C. Psychology in the courts. *Law Notes,* 1908, *11,* 185-187. (a)

Moore, C. C. Yellow psychology. *Law Notes,* 1908, *11,* 125-127 (b).

O'Donnell, L. G. The reflections of a Pulitzer Prize juror. *The Wall Street Journal,* April 13, 1982, p. 24.

Provemza, N. Seattle reporter wins for series on rape case. *Seattle Post-Intelligencer,* April 13, 1982.

Rodgers, J. E. The malleable memory of eyewitnesses. *Science 82,* June 1982, pp. 32-35.

Stein, J. A. Review of eyewitness testimony. *Trial Diplomacy Journal,* 1981, *4,* 61-63.

Taylor, J. P. Eyewitness testimony: Possible legal response to the lessons from psychology on the fallibility of eyewitness identification. In J. P. Taylor (Ed.), *Recent developments in the law of evidence.* Vancouver: Butterworths, 1980.

$300,000 tampon case award. *San Francisco Chronicle,* April 22, 1982.

Weinstein, J. Review of eyewitness testimony, *Columbia Law Review,* 1981, *81,* 441-457.

Wells, G. L., Lindsay, R. C. L., & Ferguson, T. J. Accuracy, confidence and juror perceptions in eyewitness testimony. *Journal of Applied Psychology,* 1979, *64,* 440-448.

Wells, G. L., Lindsay, R. C. L., & Tousignant, J. P. Effects of expert psychological advice on human performance in judging the validity of eyewitness testimony. *Law and Human Behavior,* 1980, *4,* 275-285.

Wells, G. & Loftus, E. F. (Eds.). *Eyewitness testimony: Psychological perspectives.* London: Cambridge University Press, 1983.

Woocher, F. D. Did your eyes deceive you? Expert psychological testimony on the unreliability of eyewitness identification. *Stanford Law Review,* 1977, *29,* 969-1030.

Yarmey, A. D. *The psychology of eyewitness testimony.* New York: Free Press, 1979.

13

TESTIFYING ON EYEWITNESS RELIABILITY
Expert Advice Is Not Always Persuasive[1]

ANNE MAASS[2]
University of Kiel
JOHN C. BRIGHAM
Florida State University
STEPHEN G. WEST[3]
Arizona State University

During the past decade, much psychological research has been conducted in the area of eyewitness identification (for reviews see Clifford & Bull, 1978; Loftus, 1979; Yarmey, 1979). Eyewitnesses have objectively been found to provide rather unreliable information, while, paradoxically, potential jurors tend to believe that eyewitness identifications are highly accurate (Brigham & Bothwell, 1983; Brigham

From *Journal of Applied Social Psychology,* 1985, 15(3), 207-229. Copyright 1985 by V. H. Winston & Sons. Reprinted by permission of the publisher.

& Wolfskeil, 1983; Lindsay, Wells, & Rumpel, 1981; Sporer, in press; Wells, Lindsay, & Tousignant, 1980).

The contrast between the empirical data and the jurors' beliefs has led to the following dilemma. On the one hand, the jurors' unfounded trust in eyewitness identification implies a realistic danger that innocent suspects may be convicted by mistake. In most legal systems, such erroneous convictions are considered to be among the most serious and least desirable of all judicial errors. On the other hand, eyewitness identification constitutes an important—and in some cases the only available—source of information. It is therefore unlikely that any legal system will ever forego such evidence altogether.

One possible compromise between categorically admitting and categorically relinquishing eyewitness identification is the hearing of experts during the trial. At least in the U.S., psychological expert testimony has been considered with increasing frequency during the past few years (Loftus & Monahan, 1980; Tanke & Tanke, 1979). Such testimony, it is hoped, will make jurors aware of the shortcomings of eyewitness evidence without withholding such information altogether. A recent survey on the utility of psychological advice in Florida revealed that 75% of the public defenders thought that the psychologist's expert opinion should be considered in court "fairly often" or "routinely" when deciding the reliability of a witness's identification—quite in contrast to the state attorneys who expressed strong reservations against such testimony (Brigham, 1981).

Even though psychologists have frequently served as expert witnesses, the actual impact of their testimony is not well understood. Few studies to date have investigated this issue (Hosch, Beck, & McIntyre, 1980; Loftus, 1980; Wells, Lindsay, & Tousignant, 1980; for a summary see Hosch, 1980). Despite the differences in subject populations, methodology, and dependent and independent variables, the results of these studies have been generally consistent. Expert testimony does seem to have a reliable effect on jury deliberations, particularly on deliberation time, which increases when expert testimony is presented. Expert testimony also has a strong, though not overwhelming impact on the jurors' individual attitudes and judgments. However, the effect on jury verdict has typically been weaker. As pointed out by Hosch (1980), none of the three studies to date has investigated what type of expert testimony is more or less beneficial to jurors. The purpose of the present study is to address this question.

When considering the potential value of different forms of expert testimony to jurors, two dimensions of the testimony appear to be immediately relevant. First, the utility of expert testimony may depend on the extent to which such testimony is related to the specific eyewitness in the case, i.e., whether the testimony is *sample-based* or *person-based*. The studies reported above have differed greatly in the degree to which the testimony was related to the target case, ranging from general, sample-based research information to directly case-related information about eyewitness accuracy (Hosch et al., 1980; Loftus, 1980; Wells et al., 1980). From an applied point of view, this issue seems particularly important since various legal systems admit different types of testimony. As a case in point, expert witnesses in the U.S. are usually limited to presenting a summary of research findings in the area of eyewitness identification. They are generally not permitted to interview the witness, to administer recognition tests, or to investigate the witness's susceptibility to stress (e.g., Loftus, 1979; Hosch, 1980). In contrast, psychological experts in the Federal Republic of Germany are requested to present person-based information about the particular witness in question while normative or statistical information is generally not admissible (Jessnitzer, 1980; Roxin, 1979).

Second, the value of expert psychological testimony may depend on the extent to which it provides *causal explanations* for the inaccuracy of eyewitness identifications. Research on the "base-rate fallacy" has repeatedly demonstrated that sample base rates as well as other probabilistic information may be largely ignored when considering a specific target case (for a summary of the relevant literature, see Borgida & Brekke, 1981). One recent explanation for the base-rate fallacy claims that sample-based as well as person-based information will be uninformative as long as it is incongruent with the intuitive causal theories that a person is holding (Ajzen, 1977; Bar-Hillel, 1980; Ginosar & Trope, 1980; Tversky & Kahneman, 1980).

An excellent demonstration for this "causality heuristic" has been provided by Tversky and Kahneman (1980), who presented a series of 15 problems of differential causal relevance to their subjects. Among others, they asked them to estimate the probability that a cab of a specific cab company had been involved in an accident. Here, baseline information was treated as informative when it provided a causal link to the accident ("85% of cab accidents in the city involve green cabs and 15% involve blue cabs"), while the identical information was drastically underutilized when it was causally irrelevant ("85% of the cabs in the city are green and 15% are blue").

Since subjects tend to rely on their own causal theories, both sample-based and person-based information will be utilized only to the extent that it is either congruent with the existing causal theory or able to offer an alternative causal scheme (Tversky & Kahneman, 1980). Thus the preconceived theory will outweigh the probabilistic information as long as no new causal scheme is provided.

Applied to the eyewitness situation, the following process can be envisioned: As indicated by previous research (Brigham & Bothwell,

1983; Lindsay et al., 1981; Wells et al., 1980), potential jurors tend to believe that eyewitnesses are quite accurate when asked to identify a criminal. Apparently, their shared causal theory assumes a well-functioning memory from which the stored information can be retrieved easily and accurately. Assume that such jurors are now confronted with a psychological expert who claims that eyewitnesses have a high probability of making inaccurate identifications. Since such a statement clearly contradicts the established schema of a well-functioning human memory, subjects will most likely process the probabilistic information only when a new causal theory (e.g., human memory is highly susceptible to experiences of stress) can be provided to replace the old.

To illustrate, an expert can either report a research finding by itself (e.g., "White witnesses misidentify black faces in 40% of all cases") or provide additional causal explanations (e.g., "Because of their lack of interracial experiences, white witnesses misidentify black faces in 40% of all cases"). From a purely logical perspective, both statements should lead to the same prediction. However, from the perspective of causal heuristics, greater utilization would be expected in the second case, in which a causal link is provided.

Thus one may hypothesize that subjects will rely on expert psychological testimony only when causal explanations are offered for the inaccuracy of eyewitnesses. In contrast, noncausal information will largely be disregarded in favor of preexistent causal theories.

The following experiment was designed in order to test (1) whether expert psychological testimony would have a general impact on the deliberation and verdict of potential jurors, (2) whether jurors would be differentially affected by sample-based versus person-based information, and (3) whether such testimony was more valuable to jurors when it offered causal explanations.

METHOD

Subjects

A total of 360 students enrolled in introductory psychology classes at Florida State University participated in partial fulfillment of their course requirements. Subjects were randomly assigned to one of the twelve conditions. In all conditions there were five groups of six subjects each.

Design

A 2 × 6 factorial design was employed. The first factor consisted of two different court cases. The second factor included six information conditions. Two of the information conditions were baseline conditions that did not contain any expert testimony (case description only and case description plus eyewitness testimony). The remaining four information conditions (experimental conditions) constituted a 2×2 factorial design in which the factors were sample-based versus person-based testimony and the causal versus noncausal nature of the testimony.

Court Cases

Subjects were presented with one of two different court cases: a burglary or a convenience store robbery. Although the type of circumstances of the crime, the description of the criminal, and the criminal's alibis varied, the two descriptions shared a number of characteristics. In both cases, a black man committed the crime while a white witness observed the incident, reported it to the police, and gave a description of the criminal. Later on during the same day, the suspect was arrested by the police. He denied his involvement in the crime but was unable to produce a reliable alibi. Since the other evidence available in the case was either ambiguous or contradictory, the eyewitness identification represented a critical piece of evidence in both cases.[4] The purpose for including different court cases was to explore the generality of the findings of the information variables.

Information Conditions

Baseline conditions. Subjects in the first baseline condition (case description only condition) were asked to read the one-page description on one of two court cases and to indicate in private the probability that the suspect was guilty. In addition, the subject's certainty regarding his or her judgment was assessed. Following their private judgments, subjects were asked to discuss the case in the six-person group and to decide whether or not the offender should be convicted. If no decision had been reached, the discussion was terminated after 30 minutes. Finally, each subject's private judgment of the defendant's guilt and the associated certainty rating were remeasured following the group discussion.

Subjects in the second baseline condition (case description plus eyewitness identification) learned of the existence of a positive eyewitness identification in which the eyewitness had picked the suspect on two different occasions from a photographic lineup while expressing great confidence that his identification was correct. In all other aspects, the procedure was identical to that in the first baseline condition.

The inclusion of the two baseline conditions allowed a twofold test of the expert's impact on the jurors. It permitted a test not only of whether the expert was at all influential (comparison with baseline 2) but also of whether his impact was strong enough to compensate fully for the eyewitness testimony (comparison with baseline 1).

Experimental conditions. The same general procedure was employed in the experimental conditions. Subjects read the same court cases, including the eyewitness identification information, but expert testimony by a Ph.D. criminologist with particular expertise in eyewitness identification was added. The general tone of the testimony was that eyewitness identifications are often in error (45% chance of misidentification).

Sample- versus person-based testimony. In half of the experimental groups, subjects read an expert testimony that relied on person-based information (interviews with and tests of the eyewitness), thus resembling the policy of the German court system. In the remaining half of the groups, sample-based testimony was provided based on the results of a two-year program of research on the accuracy of eyewitness identification, reflecting the usual policy of U.S. courts.

Causal versus noncausal testimony. In addition, the testimony was varied along the causal relevance dimension. Half of the subjects in both the person-based and sample-based condition received a testimony which simply stated the probability of misidentification without providing any causal explanations for the information. The other half read a statement which offered a number of causal explanations for the low accuracy of identifications (i.e., time delay between the crime and identification, arousal, poor cross-racial identification linked to a lack of interracial experience).

Dependent Measures

Individual judgment of guilt or innocence. The most sensitive measure of the expert's impact was the individual judgment of guilt or innocence, which was assessed both before and after the group deliberation phase. Subjects were asked to indicate in private their judgment of the suspect's guilt or innocence using a seven-point Likert-type scale, ranging from "definitely innocent" (1) to "definitely guilty" (7).

Certainty. In addition, the subjects' confidence in their above judgment was assessed on a similar seven-point scale ranging from "very uncertain" (1) to "very certain" (7). This measure was included in order to investigate whether the expert testimony reduced the subjects' confidence in their decision.

Deliberation time. Deliberation time was included as an additional dependent measure, defined as the number of minutes between the beginning of the group discussion and the unanimous verdict (or termination of the discussion, respectively).

Verdict. Because of its potential relevance to actual jury decisions, the outcome of the jury deliberation (acquittal or conviction) was added to the list of dependent measures. Note that this measure provided a less powerful test of the hypotheses since it is dichotomous and based on group scores.

RESULTS

Overview of Analysis Strategy

Because of the complexity of the design, a sequential analysis strategy was adopted to investigate the effects of the information conditions. In general, the logic of the analysis requires that each previous test be significant before proceeding to the next test.

First, an overall $2 \times 6 \times 2$ analysis of variance was performed. This was followed by separate tests of the four experimental conditions (expert testimony) combined against the two baseline conditions. More molecular comparisons were also performed by contrasting each of the four experimental conditions separately with each of the two baseline conditions. The four experimental (expert testimony) conditions were then analyzed separately in order to investigate the effects of the type of testimony. These conditions were broken down into the two factors of causal versus noncausal and person-based versus sample-based testimony.

Individual judgments

Overall analysis. In order to investigate the impact of the expert testimony, a 2 (court case) $\times$ 6 (information conditions) $\times$ 2(pre-/postdeliberation) ANOVA with repeated measures on the last variable was performed on the individual judgment scores. Main effects were observed for court cases, $F(1, 348) = 35.01$, $p < .001$; information conditions, $F(5, 348) = 24.97$. $p < .001$, accounting for 36% of the between-subjects variance, $\eta^2 = .36$; and the pre- versus postdeliberation time factor, $F(1, 348) = 40.47, p < .001$. Both information conditions, $F(5, 348) = 4.37, p < .001$, and court cases, $F(1, 348) = 27.43, p$ v .001, interacted reliably with the pre-/postdeliberation variable. Finally, all of these effects were modified by a three-way interaction, $F(5, 348) = 4,87, p < .001$, which is presented in Table 1 and which will be examined more carefully in the following sections.

Expert testimony versus baselines. To test the *overall* effectiveness of the expert testimony, follow-up planned contrasts using the overall error term were performed comparing the mean of the combined expert conditions with the respective baseline conditions for either court case, using both pre- and postdeliberation scores (see Table 2). The contrasts revealed that subjects expressed significantly more lenient judgments when confronted with the expert testimony than

TABLE 13.1

Means of Individual Pre- and Postdeliberation Judgments of Guilt or Innocence in Experimental Baseline Conditions*

		Baseline 2 case plus eyewitness	Experimental conditions				Baseline 1 case only no eyewitness
			noncausal sample-b	noncausal person-b	causal sample-b	causal person-b	
PRE	burglary	4.97	3.87[ab]	4.23[ab]	3.87[ab]	3.93[ab]	3.00
	robbery	5.27	4.70[b]	4.83[b]	4.13[ab]	3.73[a]	3.43
	cases combined	5.12	4.29[ab]	4.53[ab]	4.00[ab]	3.83[ab]	3.22
POST	burglary	4.43	3.10[a]	3.57[ab]	2.53[a]	2.17[a]	2.57
	robbery	5.93	3.97[ab]	5.33[(a)b]	4.27[ab]	3.57[ab]	2.50
	cases combined	5.18	3.54[ab]	4.45[ab]	3.40[ab]	2.87[a]	2.54

a. The mean differs significantly from the respective case plus eyewitness baseline (Dunnett's test for multiple comparisons with a control group, $p < .05$).
(a). A borderline significant difference ($p < .06$).
b. A significant difference from the case only baseline.
*The means represent ratings on a 7-point scale with lower scores indicating innocence, higher scores guilt judgments.

TABLE 13.2

Comparison of Average Experimental Conditions with Respective
Baselines: Individual Pre- and Postdeliberation Judgments*

		Baseline 2 case plus eyewitness	Averaged experimental conditions	Base line 1 case only no eyewitness
PRE	burglary	4.97	3.98[ab]	3.00
	robbery	5.27	4.35[ab]	3.43
	cases combined	5.12	4.17[ab]	3.22
POST	burglary	4.43	2.84[a(b)]	2.57
	robbery	5.93	4.29[ab]	2.50
	cases combined	5.18	3.57[ab]	2.54

a. Means differ significantly from their respective case plus eyewitness baseline condition.
b. Means differ significantly from their respective case only baseline (t-tests, $p < .05$).
(b). A borderline significant difference ($p < .06$) between experimental and baseline condition.
*Averaged means of experimental conditions.

when confronted with a court case involving an eyewitness but no
expert witness. This was true for both pre- and postdeliberation scores
independent of type of court case. At the same time, the average
expert testimony conditions produced significantly more severe
judgments than the case-only baseline, indicating that the expert
witness did not compensate fully for the eyewitness identification
information.[5]

To explore these results more fully, separate Dunnett tests were
performed on the pre- and postdeliberation scores for each court case
and for the court cases combined, comparing each experimental
condition with the respective baseline conditions. The results of the
Dunnett tests are presented in Table 1. When combining the two court
cases, all experimental conditions produced significantly more lenient
judgments than the baseline condition in which eyewitness identification was provided. With one exception, judgments were more severe
than those in the baseline condition in which no eyewitness identification was presented. Only the causal, person-based testimony was able
to convince subjects to reach similar postdeliberation judgments to
subjects who had not been informed about the eyewitness. Thus all
types of testimony reduced the severity of the judgment, but only one
led subjects to discount the eyewitness information completely.

Type of testimony. Following a procedure recommended by Winer

(1962, cf. also Himmelfarb, 1975) for factorial designs with additional control groups, a 2 (court case) × 2 (sample-based versus person-based testimony) × 2 (causal versus noncausal testimony) × 3 (pre/postdeliberation) ANOVA with repeated measures on the last variable was performed; the mean squares of the effects were tested against the error term obtained from the original 2 × 6 × 2 ANOVA in order to include both the experimental and the baseline conditions in the error estimate.

The analysis revealed three effects of interest. A main effect was observed for the causality dimension, $F(1, 348) = 17.21$, $p < .001$, indicating that causal information ($M = 3.53$) had a much greater impact on the jurors' judgments than noncausal information ($M = 4.20$). This effect, however, was modified by an additional interaction with the person-based versus sample-based information dimension, $F(1, 348) = 8.23$, $p < .01$ (see also Figure 1). Follow-up t-tests revealed that the differences between the causal and the noncausal testimony occurred only when the expert based his testimony on tests and interviews of the specific witness ($M = 4.49$ for noncausal and 3.35 for causal information, $t(348) = 3.50$, $p < .01$). Causality had no impact when the expert testimony relied on sample-based information ($M = 3.91$ for noncausal and 3.70 for causal information, $t(348) = .64$, n.s.).

An additional three-way interaction with the pre-/postdeliberation dimension further suggests that the interaction between causality and person-based versus sample-based testimony was particularly pronounced after group deliberation—as can be seen from Figure 1. In fact, the difference between causal and noncausal presentation of person-based information was found to be greater in the postdeliberation phase ($M = 4.45$ for noncausal and $M = 2.87$ for causal information; $t(348) = 8.19$, $p < .001$) than in the predeliberation phase ($M = 4.53$ for noncausal and $M = 3.83$ for causal information; $t(348) = 3.63$, $p < .01$). Follow-up t-test on the postdeliberation scores further indicated that a noncausal testimony had less impact when it was sample-based than when it was person-based ($t(348) = 4.77$, $p < .001$), whereas the opposite was true for the causal testimony ($t(348) = -2.75$, $p < .01$). In other words, the sample-based information (whether causal or not) was moderately influential, while the person-based testimony had the greatest impact when providing causes but the weakest when it failed to offer causal links. Analyses on the predeliberation scores did not produce the same pattern of significant results, although the means demonstrate a similar, though much less pronounced trend.

Verdict

Similar results appeared in the group deliberation data (see Table 3). Chances for acquittal tended to be highest when the testimony was

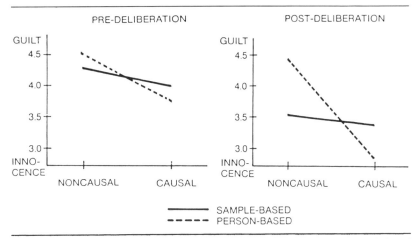

Figure 13.1   Causal and noncausal representation of person-based and sample-based information: individual judgments before and after deliberation.

both person-based and causal, lowest when it was person-based and noncausal, while an intermediate likelihood of acquittal was observed for the sample-based testimonies. However, due to the low expected frequencies, these data could not be analyzed statistically (Feinberg, 1979).

Certainty

Overall analysis. A 2 (court cases) = 6 (information conditions) = 2 (pre-/postdeliberation) ANOVA with repeated measures on the last variable was performed on the individual certainty ratings. The analysis revealed main effects for information conditions, $F(5, 348)$ = 2.83, $p < .05$ (see Table 4), explaining 4% of the between-subjects variance, $\eta^2 = .04$, and for pre-/postdeliberation, $F(1, 348) = 25.13, p <$ .001. The latter effect indicates that subjects were more certain after (M = 5.30) than before group deliberation (M = 4.87).

Expert testimony versus baselines. Overall comparison between the experimental conditions combined and the two baseline conditions revealed that subjects who had been exposed to expert testimony (M = 4.99) were less certain about their judgment than those who had been presented with the eyewitness testimony but not the expert testimony (M = 5.55, $t(348) = 2.68, p < .05$). Yet subjects who had read the expert statement did not differ in confidence from those who had received neither eyewitness nor expert information (M = 5.03).

Dunnett's tests were once again performed on the certainty scores in order to compare each experimental condition with the two baseline conditions. As indicated in Table 4, subjects who had received a *causal* expert statement felt less confident about their

TABLE 13.3
Percentage of Acquittals, Convictions, and Unsuccessful Deliberations in Experimental and Baseline Conditions

	Baseline 2 case plus eyewitness	Experimental conditions				Baseline 1 case only no eyewitness
		noncausal sample-b	noncausal person-b	causal sample-b	causal person-b	
Acquittals	30%	60%	40%	80%	90%	100%
Convictions	60%	10%	20%	20%	10%	0%
Unsuccessful deliberations	10%	30%	40%	0%	0%	0%

TABLE 13.4

Mean Certainty Ratings in the Experimental and Baseline Conditions*

	Baseline 2 case plus eyewitness	Experimental conditions				Baseline 1 case only no eyewitness
		noncausal sample-b	noncausal person-b	causal sample-b	causal person-b	
Certainty	5.55	5.03	5.26	4.79^a	$4.88^{(a)}$	5.03

a. Means differ significantly from the case plus eyewitness condition.
(a). A borderline significant difference ($p < .07$).
*The means represent certainty ratings (averaged pre- and postdeliberation scores) on a 7-point scale with high scores indicating a high degree of certainty.

judgment than those who had learned about the eyewitness but not the expert information. This was particularly true when the causal testimony was sample-based, while the difference was only borderline significant when it was person-based.

Type of testimony: causal versus noncausal, person-based versus sample-based. A subsequent 2 (court case) $\times$ 2 (causal versus noncausal) $\times$ 2 (sample-based versus person-based) $\times$ 2 (pre-/postdeliberation) ANOVA with repeated measures on the last variable revealed a main effect for pre-/postdeliberation, $F(1, 348) = 10.55$, $p < .01$, indicating, again, greater confidence after ($M = 5.16$) than before group deliberation ($M = 4.82$). No other reliable effects were observed.

Deliberation Time

Overall analysis. A 2 (court case) $\times$ 6 (information conditions) ANOVA on the deliberation time measure revealed a main effect for information conditions, $F(5, 48) =$, $p < .05$, accounting for 28% of the between-subjects variance, $\eta^2 = .28$.

Expert testimony versus baselines. A comparison between the grand mean of all experimental conditions and the baseline conditions revealed that subjects in the experimental conditions needed significantly more time to reach a decision ($M = 12.14$ min) than those the case-only baseline condition ($M = 4.15$, $t(48) = 3.22$, $p < .01$). The average deliberation time in the experimental conditions, however, did not differ significantly from the baseline in which the eyewitness information was presented ($M = 9.55$).

Dunnett's tests comparing each experimental condition with the baselines revealed that—in comparison with the case-only baseline—deliberation time increased only when subjects received a noncausal testimony (cf. Table 5). In none of the experimental conditions did the deliberation require more time than in the baseline in which an eyewitness had testified.

Type of testimony. A subsequent 2 (court cases) $\times$ 2 (causal versus noncausal) $\times$ 2 (person-based versus sample-based) ANOVA (tested against the error term from the previous 2 $\times$ 6 analysis) indicated a main effect for causality, $F(1, 48) = 6.03$, $p < .05$, suggesting that deliberation took more time when the expert failed to present causal explanations ($M = 15.55$ min compared with $M = 8.73$ min for causal testimony).

DISCUSSION

The present experiment investigated factors affecting the magnitude of impact an expert witness has when informing potential jurors about

TABLE 13.5

Deliberation Time (in Minutes) in Experimental and Baseline Conditions*

	Baseline 2 case plus eyewitness	Experimental conditions				Baseline 1 case only no eyewitness
		noncausal sample-b	noncausal person-b	causal sample-b	causal person-b	
Deliberation time	9.55	14.35[b]	16.75[b]	7.70	9.75	4.15

*Superscript b indicates that the mean differs significantly from the case only baseline condition (Dunnett's test, $p < .05$).

254

the unreliability of eyewitness recognition. In contrast to previous studies, this experiment addressed not only the general effectiveness of expert testimony, but, more specifically, the type of testimony that may have more or less impact on the juror. On theoretical grounds it had been argued that an expert witness would have an impact mainly when presenting causal explanations for his or her claim that eyewitnesses are frequently in error. A second dimension, person-based versus sample-based information, was investigated on the basis of practical considerations, since different legal systems follow different policies when defining what type of testimony is admissible.

With respect to the general impact of the expert witness, the findings of the study confirm, with some exceptions, the results typically observed in previous experiments. First, the expert's testimony convinced subjects to make more lenient individual judgments about the offender, indicating that they assigned less weight to the eyewitness information. At the same time, the results also suggest that subjects did not discount the eyewitness information completely. A similar trend was obtained from the verdict data, indicating an increase in acquittals and a decrease in convictions as a function of the expert testimony.[6]

Second, subjects exposed to the expert opinion were less confident in both their initial judgments and their judgment following a lengthy deliberation period, particularly when the expert witness provided a causal explanation. Thus the expert's claim that eyewitnesses tend to be inaccurate causes subjects to be somewhat uncertain about their decisions. The relatively high percentage of "unsuccessful" deliberations may be another indication of this insecurity: 18% of all groups who had been exposed to the expert testimony were unable to reach a decision within 30 minutes. It appears that contradicting information (eyewitness identification and the expert's claim that such an identification may be wrong) renders the deliberation more difficult and decreases the jurors' confidence in their judgment.

Third, in contrast to earlier results, expert information about the unreliability of eyewitness identifications did not significantly increase the deliberation time in comparison with the baseline in which the eyewitness but no expert testimony was presented.

In addition, judgments about the offender's innocence or guilt were found to become more lenient following the group deliberation. Although the present findings do suggest a group polarization effect, it remains unclear whether the increased leniency is due to each subject's cognitive elaboration of relevant information or to the comparison of opinions and exchange of arguments during the group interaction. In either case, the shift toward greater leniency does not represent a unique reaction to the expert's intervention since similar effects were observed in the case-only baseline.

Taken together, the results of the present study in general replicated the findings of previous experiments (Hosch et al., 1980; Loftus, 1980; Wells et al., 1980). In particular, the expert testimony appears partially, but not wholly, successful in counteracting eyewitness identifications. Yet the present study precludes an unequivocal inference about the relative contribution of eyewitness and expert testimony, since the relative impact of each type of testimony is a direct function of the strength of its manipulation. One can easily envision legal cases in which a highly credible eyewitness account may outweigh a poorly presented expert statement. Alternatively, a lengthy and convincing testimony may lead jurors to discount the eyewitness information completely.

Hence, the more important goal of the present experiment was to clarify what type of testimony may be particularly effective. The first dimension of interest was the source on which the expert based his testimony: sample-based research findings or individual tests and interviews of the particular witness. The overall results suggest that experts will have an approximately equal impact on jurors' individual judgments whether their testimony is sample-based or person-based. According to the findings obtained here, the U.S. and the West German policies on expert testimony seem equally effective in warning potential jurors about the shortcomings of eyewitness identifications.[7]

This may be somewhat surprising considering that research on the base-rate fallacy has generally found that people tend to underutilize base-rate information in favor of individuating information (cf. Borgida & Brekke, 1981). One may have suspected that the expert testimony will carry more weight when providing person-based rather than sample-based information. Two reasons may account for the fact that person-based and sample-based information had an approximately equal impact. First, it should be pointed out that both person-based and sample-based information in the present study were stated in a probabilistic manner (45% chance of misidentification) and differed only with regard to the *source* on which the statement was based. In contrast, individuating information in studies on the base-rate fallacy is frequently presented in a deterministic way. If people have only a limited capability of processing probabilistic information (Tversky & Kahneman, 1973), person-based information should be expected to be more influential only when stated in a deterministic way. This line of argument, however, does not offer a satisfactory explanation, considering the fact that many studies have observed the base-rate fallacy also in situations in which the individuating information was presented in a probabilistic way (e.g., Bar-Hillel, 1980; Tversky & Kahneman, 1973, 1980). Second, and more important, the differential impact of person-based and sample-based information may be visible only in its interaction with causality, which will be discussed in detail later.

A second dimension of interest was the degree to which the expert provided causal explanations for his claim that eyewitnesses are frequently in error. As expected, potential jurors were found to be more influenced by an expert who provided reasons for his claim that the eyewitness is likely to be wrong than by one who failed to do so. When asked individually, jurors indicated a much lower likelihood that the suspect was guilty after having been presented with a causal expert statement. Along the same line, 86% of all groups decided to acquit the offender after having listened to a causal expert statement, while only 50% of the offenders were acquitted when the expert failed to provide reasons. This is in line with the idea that probabilistic information which is incongruent with the person's preconceived theory will be utilized only when providing a new causal schema (Ajzen, 1977; Bar-Hillel, 1980; Tversky & Kahneman, 1980).

Such causal explanations, however, were only of marginal importance when the expert testimony relied on sample-based information, as is generally the case in the U.S. court system. In contrast, causal links were of great significance when the expert based his statement on tests and interviews of the particular witness, which is the typical situation in the West German court system. Interestingly, person-based information was more influential than sample-based information when a causal explanation was provided, but less influential when no reasons were presented, at least as far as the postdeliberation judgments are concerned.[8]

Two explanations may be offered for this interaction, one assuming a greater motivation to process the person-based testimony, the other assuming a greater ease to discount the sample-based testimony.

(1) Both previous research (Brigham & Botwell, in press; Lindsay et al., 1981; Wells et al., 1980) and our own observations in the baseline conditions (30% versus 100% acquittals) suggest that people rely heavily on eyewitness accounts. Apparently, they consider eyewitness testimony a trustworthy form of evidence. After all, the witness was right there observing the crime.

During the trial, this previously held belief is threatened by an expert witness claiming that eyewitnesses are frequently in error. In his statement, the expert either refers to tests and interviews of the particular witness in question or to a research program conducted on an independent sample of subjects. Research on the base-rate fallacy has generally indicated that individuating information can, for various reasons (e.g. Bar-Hillel, 1980; Borgida & Brekke, 1980; Borgida & Nisbett, 1977; Tversky & Kahneman, 1973, 1980), be processed more easily than sample-based information. At the same time, the two types of testimony imply different attributions for the unreliability of the eyewitness. The person-based testimony suggests a person attribution, whereas the sample-based statement offers a situational account of eyewitness unreliability. Research on the fundamental attribution error suggests that people prefer person-based explanations, while they have great difficulty accepting and utilizing situational explanations (Bierbauer, 1973; Jeffrey & Mischel, 1979; Ross, 1977).

Given their limited ability to process sample-based information and their relative unfamiliarity with situational accounts, potential jurors may fail to scrutinize such information carefully. Because of their general preference for person-based accounts, jurors may be more likely to process a person-based expert statement. Since the expert testimony is incongruent with the previously held beliefs, such cognitive activity may either support or oppose the expert's position (cf. Petty and Cacioppo's elaboration likelihood model, 1981). The direction of the person's cognitive activity (in support of or opposed to the testimony) may largely depend on the testimony's capacity to provide an alternative causal theory (cf. Tversky & Kahneman, 1980). If the expert's testimony is not backed by convincing causal arguments, the juror's thinking may strengthen his or her initial belief in a reliable and accurate eyewitness account. If the expert provides reasons for his or her claim, the potential juror may be convinced and willing to modify the preconceived schema. This line of argument may account for the fact that causal explanations are essential when the testimony is person-based, while they are of little interest when it relies on sample-based information.

(2) A somewhat different explanation may be offered from a cognitive conflict perspective. Kohnken (1983) has suggested that expert testimony regarding eyewitness reliability may induce a great degree of cognitive conflict. On one hand, jurors become aware of the potential inaccuracy of eyewitness identifications. On the other hand, the current law does not permit jurors (or police and courts, respectively) to forego eyewitness identification. In this situation, the potential juror can resolve the conflict only by revising his or her belief in a reliable human memory or by discounting the expert testimony as invalid or unrepresentative.

When the testimony is based on research generated from an independent sample of people, the validity of the expert statement may easily be questioned. Such testimony about eyewitnesses in general (i.e., the mean eyewitness) may or may not apply to this particular eyewitness. Thus jurors may simply reduce their conflict by considering the sample or the research situation unrepresentative or unrelated to the particular case under consideration. If the testimony is considered unrepresentative, it will be largely irrelevant whether it is backed by causal explanations or not.

Such discounting, however, is not easily possible in the situation in which a person-based testimony challenges the veracity of a particular witness. Here, the jurors will be forced to evaluate the testimony more carefully for its reasonableness and to exert a greater cognitive effort in order to reduce the experienced cognitive conflict. Whether the juror will succeed in discounting the testimony may be a function of the causal explanation offered by the expert. If the expert's statement is not backed by causal arguments, the juror will most likely be able to discount the testimony. If the expert presents cogent causal theories for his unreliability claim, the juror may be incapable of dismissing the testimony as invalid. The only way to reduce his or her cognitive conflict may be to discount the eyewitness information. In fact, the data of the present study indicate that the jurors' judgments in this situation (causal, person-based testimony) resemble closely those of the baseline condition in which the suspect had not been identified by a witness.

Although both explanations may be convincing, the observed interaction between causality and person-based versus sample-based information remains somewhat puzzling from a base-rate fallacy perspective. Bar-Hillel (1980) has convincingly argued that base-rate information will be processed correctly only when considered relevant to the case under consideration. According to Bar-Hillel, relevance can be achieved either by way of enhancing the *specificity* of the base rate (in the ideal case referring to the index case), or by enhancing the *causal relevance* of the base rate.[9] In the past, this hypothesis has received strong empirical support (cf. experiments reported in Bar-Hillel, 1980; Borgida & Brekke, 1981; Tversky & Kahneman, 1980). In support of this view, the present findings indicate the strongest impact of the expert testimony when it was both specific and causally relevant. Yet the least influential form of testimony was *not* the one that was neither specific nor causally relevant, as would be suggested by Bar-Hillel's theorizing. Rather, the expert testimony had the least impact when it was of low causal relevance, but highly specific (person-based).

A conceptual difference between the base-rate fallacy studies and the present experiment may account for this contradiction: While subjects in the typical base-rate fallacy experiments do not hold any preconceived ideas about the base rates (e.g., the percentage of blue cabs involved in accidents), prior beliefs were clearly present in this study. Both previous studies and the base-rate comparisons indicate that subjects have great confidence in the accuracy of eyewitness identifications prior to listening to an expert witness. In other words, they assume a low probability for mistaken identification.

It seems plausible that the mechanisms by which probabilistic information is processed vary depending on the existence of prior intuitive baselines. If a person has not yet developed an idea about a particular base rate, probabilistic information may be most effective when it is both causally relevant and specific to the case. If a person already holds an opinion about the probability of an event (e.g., mistaken identifications), contradicting base-rate information may constitute a threat to the prior belief and therefore be processed in a more defensive way, as has been suggested in the alternative explanations offered above.

An important issue for future research raised by the present experiment is the question of whether base-rate information is processed differently when prior base-rate beliefs exist. It appears worthwhile from both a theoretical and applied point of view to identify the differential processes that may operate when a person does or does not hold an intuitive idea about a base rate. It is possible that motivational biases add to the well-known logical biases when base-rate opinions are already formed.

NOTES

---

1. This research was supported by NSF grant BNS 77-27476 to J. C. Brigham. S. G. West was supported by a study visit grant from the Deutscher Akademischer Austausch-dienst at the University of Kiel, Federal Republic of Germany, during the writing of this article.

2. Anne Maass is now at the University of Padova, Italy.

3. Requests for reprints should be sent to Stephen G. West, Department of Psychology, Arizona State University, Tempe, AZ 85287.

4. The experimental material (case descriptions, eyewitness identification information, and expert testimony) can be obtained from the authors upon request.

5. It follows automatically that the two baseline conditions differed significantly from each other for pre- ($t(348) = 5.67, p < .001$) and for postdeliberation scores ($t(348) = 9.59, p < .001$), indicating that subjects expressed significantly more severe judgments when the suspect had been identified by an eyewitness.

6. Note, however, that the effect of expert testimony on the verdict was not tested statistically.

7. Note, however, that jurors play a somewhat different role in the West German than in the American legal system. Originally, the German court system had employed the same division of tasks that can still be found in the United States and in Britain. There, juries decide about the verdict, while the sentence is determined by the judge(s). In Germany, the status of jurors was modified considerably in 1924. Since then the court is for most trials (for exceptions, cf. Roxin, 1979) composed of one or two so-called lay judges and one to three professional judges. Lay and professional judges determine verdict and sentence in a joint deliberation and have, at least formally, the same rights and equal votes (e.g., Roxin, 1979).

8. A similar pattern was observed for the verdict data that were not submitted to statistical analyses. On the average 79% of the offenders were acquitted when subjects had access to sample-based information. For the person-based testimony, the offender was acquitted in 90% of all cases when causal explanations were provided, but only in 40% of the cases when no reasons were given. Note that these percentages closely resemble those of the two baselines (100% for case-only baseline, and 30% for case-plus-eyewitness baseline).

9. Note that causes provided by the expert (time delay, stress, cross-racial identification) were highly relevant to the cases under consideration since all of those factors were present in the case descriptions.

REFERENCES

Ajzen, L. (1977). Intuitive theories of events and the effects of base-rate information on prediction. *Journal of Personality and Social Psychology, 35*, 303-314.

Bar-Hillel, M. (1980). The base-rate fallacy in probability judgments. *Acta Psychologica, 44*, 211-233.

Bierbauer, G. (1973). *Effect of sex, perspective, and temporal factors on attribution.* Unpublished doctoral dissertation, Stanford University, Stanford, CA.

Borgida, E., & Brekke, N. (1981). The base-rate fallacy in attribution and prediction. In J. H. Harvey, W. J. Ickes, & R. F. Kidd (Eds.), *New directions in attribution research* (Vol. 3, pp. 63-95). Hillsdale, NJ: Erlbaum.

Borgida, E., & Nisbett, R. E. (1977). The differential impact of abstract vs. concrete information on decisions. *Journal of Applied Social Psychology, 7*, 258-271.

Brigham, J. C. (1981, November). The accuracy of eyewitness evidence: How do attorneys see it? *The Florida Bar Journal*, 714-721.

Brigham, J. C., & Bothwell, R. K. (1983). The ability of prospective jurors to estimate the accuracy of the eyewitness identifications. *Law and Human Behavior, 7*, 19-30.

Brigham, J. C., & Wolfskeil, M. P. (1983). Opinions of attorneys and law enforcement personnel on the accuracy of eyewitness identifications. *Law and Human Behavior, 7*, 337-349.

Clifford, B., & Bull, R. (1978). *The psychology of person identification.* London: Routledge & Kegan Paul.

Deffenbacher, K. A., & Loftus, E. F. (1982). Do jurors share a common understanding concerning eyewitness behavior? *Law and Human Behavior, 6*, 15-29.

Feinberg, S. E. (1979). *The analysis of cross-classified categorical data.* Cambridge: M.I.T. Press.

Ginosar, Z., & Trope, Y. (1980). The effects of base rates and individuating information on judgments about another person. *Journal of Experimental Social Psychology, 16*, 228-242.

Himmelfarb, S. (1975). What do you do when the control group doesn't fit into the factorial design? *Psychological Bulletin, 82*, 363-368.

Hosch, H. M. (1980). A comparison of three studies of the influence of expert testimony on jurors. *Law and Human Behavior, 4,* 297-302.

Hosch, H. M., Beck, E. L., & McIntrye, P. (1980). Influence of expert testimony regarding eyewitness accuracy on jury decisions. *Law and Human Behavior, 4,* 287-296.

Jeffrey, K. M., & Mischel, W. (1979). Effects of purpose on the organization and recall of information in person perception. *Journal of Personality, 47,* 387-419.

Jessnitzer, K. (1980). *Der gerichtliche Sachverstandige.* Koln: Hyemanns.

Kohnken, G. (1983). *Zur Wirkung von Entscheidungsdruk auf Personenidentifizierungen durch Augenzeugen: Sind Zeugen besser als ihr Ruf?* Unpublished manuscript, University of Kiel, West Germany.

Lindsay, R. C. L., Wells, G. L., & Rumpel, C. M. (1981). Can people detect eyewitness-identification accuracy within and across situations? *Journal of Applied Psychology, 66,* 79-89.

Loftus, E. F. (1979). *Eyewitness testimony.* Cambridge, MA: Harvard University Press.

Loftus, E. F. (1980). Impact of expert psychological testimony on the unreliability of eyewitness identification. *Journal of Applied Psychology, 65,* 9-15.

Loftus, E. F., & Monahan, J. (1980). Trial by data: Psychological research as legal evidence. *American Psychologist, 35,* 270-283.

Lowel, A., & Kassin, S. M. (1977). On the use of consensus information: Prediction, attribution, and evaluation. *Personality and Social Psychological Bulletin, 3,* 616-619.

Petty, R. E., & Cacioppo, J. T. (1980). *Attitudes and persuasion: Classic and contemporary approaches.* Dubuque, IA: William C. Brown.

Ross, L. (1977). The intuitive psychologist and his shortcomings: Distortions in the attribution process. In L. Berkowitz (Ed.), *Advances in experimental social psychology* (Vol. 10, pp. 173-220). New York: Academic Press.

Roxin, C. (1977). *Strafverfahrensrecht.* München: Beck.

Sporer, S.L. (in press). Allgemeinwissen zur Psychologie der Zeugenaussage: Was man weiss, oder vielleicht wissen sollte. In H. J. Kerner, H. Kury, & K. Sessar (Eds.), *Beiträge der deutschen Kriminologie.* Köln: Heyman.

Tanke, E. D., & Tanke, T. J. (1979). Getting off a slippery slope: Social science in the judicial process. *American Psychologist, 34,* 1130-1138.

Tversky, A., & Kahneman, D. (1973). Availability: A heuristic for judging frequency and probability. *Cognitive Psychology, 5,* 207-232.

Tversky, A., & Kahneman, D. (1980). Causal schemata in judgments under uncertainty. In M. Fishbein (Ed.), *Progress in social psychology* (pp. 49-72). Hillsdale, NJ: Erlbaum.

Wells, G. L., Lindsay, R. C. L., & Tousignant, J. P. (1980). Effects of expert psychological advice on human performance in judging the validity of eyewitness testimony. *Law and Human Behavior, 4,* 275-286.

Winer, B. J. (1962). *Statistical principles in experimental design.* New York: McGraw-Hill.

Yarmey, A. D. (1979). *The psychology of eyewitness testimony.* New York: Free Press.

SECTION IV

SUMMARY

Taken together the three chapters presented in section IV provide evidence of the current controversy surrounding the use of psychologists as expert witnesses in cases in which eyewitness testimony is used as evidence. Unfortunately, it may be that no clear-cut approach exists for resolving the controversy. Are judges' cautionary instructions alone adequate to familiarize the jury with the known factors affecting eyewitness accuracy? Can an expert witness provide the knowledge necessary for the jury to make an informed decision?

McCloskey and Egeth conclude that the costs far outweigh the benefits in allowing psychologists to testify on eyewitness accuracy. They maintain that there is no empirical evidence that jurors are not already aware of the problems inherent in eyewitness identifications, and, even if they are not, it is doubtful that expert witnesses would be of any real consequence in assisting them to discriminate between accurate and inaccurate witnesses. At the same time, McCloskey and Egeth do maintain that jurors need improvement in their ability to detect accuracy in eyewitnesses. It may just be that expert witnesses lead jurors to be more skeptical without improving their ability to detect accurately.

Moreover, it is assumed that the need for expert testimony relies on two assumptions: that relationships between variables and eyewitness accuracy have been identified by psychologists, and that jurors are not aware of variables that may affect accuracy. The chapter concludes that evidence fails to confirm that either of these two assumptions is correct. Further, McCloskey and Egeth feel that expert testimony may have detrimental effects on the jury by making them too skeptical.

Indeed, the research in chapter 13 may be evidence for this argument. Maass, Brigham, and West in chapter 13 did find possible evidence for additional skepticism by mock jurors, because 18% of the jurors were unable to reach a decision, possibly due to the conflicting information they had received from the expert eyewitness, leaving them skeptical of the evidence.

A final conclusion of McCloskey and Egeth centers on the "battle of experts" that might be created were psychologists to openly disagree with each other in court. They contend that although other professions have experts that disagree, these professions are able to regain their good standing by subsequently contributing new and worthwhile discoveries. They conclude that this type of disagreement between members of the psychological field would be detrimental to the field was a whole.

Loftus's chapter reveals another orientation as to how psychological research and expertise may be utilized. Specifically, she contends that expert testimony serves the function of providing jurors information with which to make more informed decisions, especially since jurors are not aware of factors (i.e., retention decrements due to time, errors in cross-racial identifications, suggestibility in questioning of witnesses) that could distort eyewitnesses' identification.

Chapter 12 also proposes that a "battle of experts" may be beneficial. The information exchanged will only make jurors more informed and knowledgeable on the issues involved in eyewitness accuracy. However, an instance is acknowledged where expert testimony may damage the profession. Soliciting of psychologists who are not experts in eyewitness research and its theories has the potential to make the profession as a whole appear incompetent, should these nonexperts testify in court.

Lastly, Loftus contends that research pertaining to eyewitness accuracy derives from many branches of psychology and has been an established body of knowledge for some time. Certainly, the perceptual processes involved in eyewitnesses' identifications and the factors affecting accuracy have been researched for most of this century. Yet, McCloskey and Egeth believe eyewitness research is not complete enough for consumption in a court of law. However, is any science ever complete? Can absolute statements ever be made, in any scientific pursuit? We think not. The nature of science demands an ever-changing, ever-growing, and never-ending pursuit of knowledge with much to understand. The application of scientific knowledge rests on the certainty that can be given current understanding in any given field.

In contrast to the conclusions of McCloskey and Egeth, there is one topic on which it appears jurors are not aware of possible inaccuracies.

This topic concerns the relationship between confidence exhibited by a witness and that witness's accuracy in identification. It has been found that subjects believe highly confident witnesses will be accurate, while low levels of confidence by a witness indicate inaccuracy (Deffenbacher & Loftus, 1982; Yarmey & Jones, 1983). Unfortunately, while subjects may hold this belief, research has found no consistent relationship between an eyewitness's confidence and accuracy of identification (Wells & Murray, 1984). Thus jurors may not be making informed decisions on verdicts when linking an eyewitness's confidence to any eyewitness's accuracy.

The courts have acknowledged the errors in eyewitness identifications, since the nineteenth century. In one case, Bryant's estate (1896), the judge noted that "there are few more difficult subjects with which the administration of justice has to deal" and that recognition or identification is "one of the least reliable of facts testified to even by actual witnesses who have seen the parties in question." More recently, the courts have cautiously tried to address the problem of eyewitnesses' inaccuracy. By 1981, five states (Alabama, Florida, Kansas, Massachusetts, and Minnesota) had adopted special cautionary instructions for juries in order to alert them to use caution in assessing eyewitness identification's accuracy (Burke, 1981). But the courts have not expressly approved the need for expert psychological testimony on the parameters of eyewitnesses' accuracy, believing the jury already possesses the appropriate knowledge for evaluation.

Maass, Brigham, and West's research demonstrates that potential jurors do not blindly follow experts' eyewitness testimony. While skeptically adopting cautionary instructions, the legal system appears to adhere to a misinformed conception that jurors will totally disregard eyewitness testimony if confronted by expert knowledge that outlines factors affecting accuracy. The legal system has acknowledged the existence of unreliability in eyewitness testimony. The next step calls for the legal system to redefine the role of psychological expert testimony and its contributions in assessing eyewitnesses' accuracy. Expert testimony could provide a means of minimizing the risk of accepting erroneous identifications and assist the legal profession in upholding the responsibilities of juries, as triers of fact.

REFERENCES

Addison, B. M. (1978). Expert testimony on eyewitness perception. *Dickinson Law Review, 83,* 465-485.

Byrant's Estate, 176 Pa. 309, 318, 35 A. 571, 577 (1896).

Burke, E. J. (1981). Eyewitness testimony: How reliable? *National Law Review, 4*, 3-4.

Deffenbacher, K., & Loftus, E. F. (1982). Do jurors share a common understanding concerning eyewitness behavior? *Law and Human Behavior, 6*, 15-30.

Freud, S. (1979). Psycho-analysis and the ascertaining of truth in courts of law. *Collected Papers, 2*, 13-24. (Originally published 1906; translated 1924)

Loftus, E. F. (1983). Silence is not golden. *American Psychologist, 38*, 564-572.

Maass, A., Brigham, J. C., & West, S. G. (1985). Testifying on eyewitness reliability: Expert advice is not always persuasive. *Journal of Applied Social Psychology, 15*, 207-229.

McCloskey, M., & Egeth, H. E. (1983). What can a psychologist tell a jury? *American Psychologist, 38*, 550-563.

Munsterberg, H. (1976). *On the witness stand.* New York: AMS Press. (Originally published 1908).

Spear, J. B. (1982). Evidence: does the eyewitness really see. *Washburn Law Review, 21*, 698-706.

Stern, W. (1939). The psychology of testimony. *Journal of Abnormal and Social Psychology, 34*, 3-20.

Wells, G. L., & Murray, D. M. (1984). Eyewitness confidence. In G. L. Wells & E. F. Loftus (Eds.), *Eyewitness testimony: Psychological perspectives.* New York: Cambridge University Press.

Yarmey, A. D. & Jones, H. P. T. (1983). Is the study of eyewitness identification a matter of common sense? In S. Lloyd-Bostock & B. R. Clifford (Eds.), *Evaluating witness evidence.* Chichester: Wiley.

SECTION V

CAMERAS IN THE COURTROOM
Introduction

Every now and then, we still see artists' drawings of trial participants on the evening news. When we do, it is because photographers were excluded from the courtroom. Until very recently, they were banned entirely. It is now common, however, to see film clips of the lawyers and witnesses on the news. Occasionally, full trials are even televised if they draw enough interest. What has changed so dramatically over the past few years, and is justice better served by this development, or not? Are trials more or less fair to the parties involved? Are jurors intimidated or distracted by cameras or simply by the awareness that they are in the public eye? Billed as the "fair trial-free press controversy," these are among the questions raised by both sides of the debate.

For years, the news media had been clamoring to gain entrance into the trial courts. And for years, their requests had been denied. The courts' aversion to the idea began in 1935 as a result of the trial of Bruno Hauptmann who was convicted for the kidnapping and murder of Charles Lindbergh's baby. The trial was described as "a Roman holiday. Photographers clambered on counsel's table and shoved their flashbulbs into the faces of witnesses. The judge lost control of his courtroom and the press photographers lost control of their senses" (Kielbowitz, 1979. p. 17).

What changed began with the U.S. Supreme Court's ruling in *Chandler v. Florida* (1981). In that case, the defendants, two Miami policemen, were convicted of burglary. At the time, the state of

Florida was experimenting with televising trials and this one was no exception. The defendants appealed their verdicts, arguing that their right to a fair trial had been compromised by the presence of cameras in the courtroom. In a decisive 8-0 decision, the Supreme Court upheld the convictions. It concluded that "no one has been able to present empirical data sufficient to establish that the mere presence of the broadcast media has an adverse impact on the judicial process."

Since the *Chandler* decision, the federal and state courts have moved in different directions. The federal judiciary has reasserted its unwillingness to open its courtroom doors to cameras, while approximately 40 states have adopted rules permitting such coverage under certain circumstances. What effect might this latter development have on the process and outcomes of jury trials? The three chapters in this section deal with that very question.

In theory, the presence of TV in the courtroom can affect a trial's outcome (and, hence, its fairness) in any number of ways. The section opens with Kassin's (1984) report of a laboratory experiment designed to explore whether jurors are distracted by the presence of cameras in the courtroom. In chapter 15, Netteburg (1980), a journalism professor, reviews the experiences reported in states that had allowed cameras in the courts. In addition, he reports on a study of a particular case in Wisconsin that had been televised. This section concludes with Swim and Borgida's (1986) study of how the public feels and is affected by the televising of rape trials. Their results are interesting and raise the possibility that TV cameras can have very general unanticipated effects on the criminal justice system.

Should cameras be allowed in the courtroom? There are many sides to this issue, and there is much armchair speculation about it. What is clear is that the answer rests largely on what we know about human behavior. The chapters in this section represent at least an initial step toward providing policymakers with the much-needed empirical answers.

REFERENCES

Chandler v. Florida, 101 S. Ct. 802 (1981).

Kielbowitz, R. B. (1979). The story behind the adoption of the ban on courtroom cameras. *Judicature, 63,* 17.

14

TV CAMERAS, PUBLIC
SELF-CONSCIOUSNESS, AND
MOCK JUROR PERFORMANCE

SAUL M. KASSIN
Williams College

The admission of cameras and other photographic equipment in the courtroom has long been a source of controversy among legal scholars and practitioners (for historical reviews, see Carter, 1981; Kielbowicz, 1979). In view of the relatively recent movement toward actually televising criminal trials, this debate has intensified dramatically

Author's Note. Portions of these data were presented at the 54th Annual Meeting of the Eastern Psychological Association, Philadelphia, April 1983. I thank Jessie W. Lenagh for her help in the preparation of stimulus materials and for her role as experimenter. I also thank Frederick X. Gibbons and Valerie P. Hans for their helpful comments on an earlier draft of the manuscript. Reprint requests should be addressed to the author at the Department of Psychology, Williams College, Bronfman Science Center, Williamstown, MA 01267.

From *Journal of Experimental Social Psychology*, 1984, 20, 336-349. Copyright 1984 by Academic Press. Reprinted by permission of the publisher.

(Barber, 1983; Fahringer, 1980; Gerbner, 1980; Goodwin, 1979; Graves, 1979; Hirschorn & Stern, 1980; Hoyt, 1980). Essentially, three arguments have been raised by its opponents—that the presence of TV cameras in court will (a) increase the impact of prejudicial publicity to which the community is exposed, (b) undermine the appearance of judicial dignity and prevent a "sober search for the truth," and (c) distract or otherwise affect the performance and behavior of the trial participants, most notably the jury.

Two U.S. Supreme Court rulings on the matter are of historical significance. In *Estes v. Texas* (1965), the defendant argued that his constitutional right to a fair trial had been impeded by the presence of TV cameras. In a 5-4 decision, the Court concurred and reversed his conviction. In the majority opinion, however, Justice Clark conceded that in the absence of "empirical knowledge," the court was forced to rely on conjecture for its decision. More recently in *Chandler v. Florida* (1981), the Court altered its previous course in a 8-0 ruling, this time *on the basis of* the fact that "no one has been able to present empirical data sufficient to establish that the mere presence of the broadcast media has an adverse impact on the [judicial] process." What, then, has changed from *Estes* to *Chandler?* In both decisions, the court lamented the absence of hard data. In the face of increasing media pressure and technological advances, however, the court essentially shifted the burden of proof on the matter. Several states, impelled by this ruling, immediately expanded their coverage rights on either a permanent or experimental basis (Abrahams, 1981).

In view of the practical importance of this problem for the judiciary and the Supreme Court's repeated plea for behavioral research on the matter, it is surprising that, to date, the only relevant data available are anecdotal case studies, public opinion surveys, and the verbal reports of those who had participated in televised trials (cf. Netteburg, 1980). The problems associated with the self-report approach are, of course, widely recognized by psychologists (Nisbett & Wilson, 1977; Weary & Arkin, 1981). Indeed its weaknesses were illustrated in a study conducted by the Florida State Supreme Court in which jurors, witnesses, and lawyers, all reported the belief that the camera had a greater effect on the other participants than on themselves (cf. Davis, 1980; Whisenand, 1978).

An inspection of the major arguments advanced by TV camera opponents reveals that their underlying concern is with the jury and its decision-making performance. Specifically, prejudice is believed to arise either directly because jurors are distracted, thereby reducing their knowledge of the evidence, or indirectly by altering the behavior of the other trial participants and the attitudes of the surrounding community. The present study was designed to test experimentally what can be called the distraction hypothesis. As Justice Clark cautioned in *Estes v. Texas* (1965), "We are all self-conscious and uneasy when being televised. Human nature being what it is, not only will a juror's eyes be fixed on the camera, but also his mind will be preoccupied with the telecasting rather than the testimony."

Should TV cameras in the courtroom have such an adverse effect and, if so, why? One possibility is suggested by self-awareness theory and the prediction that cameras, because they represent a mechanical replacement for a live, potentially evaluative audience, induce a state of self-focused attention (Duval & Wicklund, 1972; Wicklund, 1975). Several investigators have validated this hypothesis, demonstrating an increase in self-referent thoughts in the presence of a camera (Arkin & Duval, 1975; Davis & Brock, 1975; Geller & Shaver, 1976). Since conscious attention can be directed toward either salient aspects of the self *or* the environment but not both simultaneously (although attention could oscillate rapidly between the self and nonself, hence the possibility of distinguishing different degrees of self-focus over time), it follows that a state of self-awareness could interfere with the processing of non-self-related information. Experimental support for this reasoning was obtained by Vallacher (1978) who, in an impression formation study, found that subjects who believed they were being videotaped exhibited poorer discrimination among stimulus persons than those in whom the state of self-awareness was not so induced. The foregoing theory and research suggest the operational hypothesis that jurors who observe a trial while in the presence of TV cameras would exhibit decreased attention to the proceedings and therefore an impairment in their recall of the trial facts.

The extant literature, however, is limited in its applicability to the courtroom setting in one important respect—duration of exposure to the self-focusing stimulus. Over the extended life of a televised trial, one might expect a habituation effect, operationally defined by Harris (1943) to be a "response decrement as a result of repeated stimulation" (p. 385). Although this phenomenon in psychology is robust and pervasive (Thompson & Spencer, 1966; Tighe & Leaton, 1976), it has not been formally incorporated into self-awareness theory (Buss's recent treatment, 1980, of the process of audience anxiety is an exception) or specifically investigated in relevant research. Within the context of most laboratory experiments, the duration of exposure to self-focusing stimuli is typically brief, and subjects' responses are typically measured only once, so habituation effects are indetectable. The one exception was a study by Ickes, Wicklund, and Ferris (1973) who found that exposure to a recording of one's own voice lowered subjects' self-esteem, as predicted by Duval and Wicklund's (1972) theory, but that this effect diminished over time.

In order to investigate this possibility in the context of a courtroom trial, half the subjects in the camera and no-camera conditions of the present study were tested for their recall at various points during the trial presentation. It was hypothesized that the camera would impair recall in the initial stages, but that subjects would gradually adapt to its presence, redirect their attention to the environment, and show an improvement in their subsequent performance.

Finally, we explored the possibility that individual jurors would differ in their sensitivity to TV cameras in the courtroom. The personality dimension of most direct relevance is the trait of self-consciousness, as measured by Fenigstein, Scheier, and Buss's (1975) Self-Consciousness Scale. This 23-item questionnaire, designed to assess dispositional levels of self-awareness, is composed of three factors—private self-consciousness, public self-consciousness, and social anxiety. The psychometric reliability and validity of these dimensions has been reasonably well established (Carver & Glass, 1976; Turner, Scheier, Carver, & Ickes, 1978). Interestingly, several investigators have found that public self-consciousness (PSC), characterized by a concern for one's appearance, behavior, and self-presentation to others, is the dispositional analog to the state of self-awareness that is induced by an audience or a camera (Buss, 1980; Froming, Walker, & Lopyan, 1982; Scheier & Carver, 1980).[1]

In order to assess the trait × state interaction, subjects in the present study completed the Fenigstein et al. (1975) scale. Buss (1980) had advanced a "special susceptibility" hypothesis, that people who are characteristically high in public self-consciousness react more strongly to inducers of public self-awareness than those who are low on the trait. As such, it was expected that the camera would adversely affect jurors who are high rather than low in their chronic levels of PSC.

METHOD

Subjects and Design

Subjects were 51 community adults (21 male, 30 female; average age = 35) recruited through advertisement in two local newspapers and paid to serve as mock jurors. They were randomly assigned to one of eight cells produced by a 2 (camera vs. no-camera) × 2 (single vs. multiple tests) × 2(high vs. low PSC) factorial design.

Procedure

Subjects participated in small group (3-4) sessions conducted in a laboratory courtroom. Upon arrival, they completed the Fenigstein et al. (1975) Self-Consciousness Scale and a brief demographics questionnaire. They were then instructed about the experiment and shown a 95-min black-and-white videotape of *Sockett v. Alterman Transport,* a civil negligence case that had been performed in a courtroom and in the presence of a judge, an audience, and a jury, by practicing lawyers. Substantively, the plaintiff was an injured dock worker who fell from a steel plate on the loading platform because the defendant, a truck driver, had pulled away unexpectedly. The trial presentation consisted of opening statements, the examination of three witnesses, closing arguments, and judicial instructions. It was shown on a 19-in. monitor placed on the judge's bench.

In the *camera condition,* a video camera connected to a recorder was directed at the jury box from the witness stand. In order to further simulate the real-life situation in which the TV camera actually represents the potential for subsequent public exposure, subjects were additionally instructed that they were being recorded for use in a psychology class. In the *no-camera condition,* neither the video equipment nor the additional instruction was incorporated into the procedure.

Within these conditions, subjects were assigned to either a single- or multiple-testing procedure. In the *single-test condition,* subjects unknowingly received a 40-item short answer cued-recall test immediately after observing the trial. This test was carefully constructed to include questions about case facts that were explicitly revealed in testimony (e.g., "how many months after the accident did Sockett return to work?") as well as questions that required inference from the proceedings (e.g., "what was the plaintiff hoping to prove in this case?"). In addition, we attempted to sample facts that had been introduced at different points in the trial. This temporal representativeness was achieved by dividing the tape into four approximately balanced phases (opening statements, plaintiff's testimony, the remaining witnesses, closing arguments plus instructions) and selecting 10 questions per quartile. As in virtually all cases, most evidentiary facts are repeated throughout the trial. The 10 items selected for each subtest, however, were among those that had *not* previously appeared (though many did reappear at a later time). As such, questions about information appearing in the fourth subtest could not be answered correctly on the basis of knowledge obtained during the first three subtests.

Following this, subjects filled out an opinion questionnaire in which they rendered a verdict, rated their confidence in that decision, provided an award (if they voted in favor of the plaintiff), and rated the impact on their decision of each of the three witnesses. Finally, subjects rated how interesting they found the trial, how involved they were in it, how difficult it was to follow, how closely they attended, and how good their memory of the facts was. All ratings were made on 1-and 10-point scales.

In the *multiple-test condition*, the videotape was interrupted after each trial stage in order to assess subjects' midtrial recall of facts introduced therein. The four 10-item tests consisted of the same questions that constituted the overall posttrial test. Unlike the single-test condition, then, these subjects responded to each of the 40 recall questions twice—both during and after the trial.

RESULTS

Juror Decisions and Self-Report Measures

Overall, 63% of the subjects voted for the plaintiff with a mean award of $27,670. For all analyses, subjects were classified as high or low in PSC via a median split. Three scores fell at the median (18), so these subjects were eliminated, yielding $N = 48$. A 2 (camera) $\times$ 2 (PSC) $\times$ 2 (testing procedure) analysis of variance revealed no significant effects on juror verdicts, awards, confidence, or ratings of witness impact. These data are presented in Table 1.

For the self-report measures, no differences appeared in ratings of interest, involvement, attention, or memory. On the difficulty question, however, subjects in the camera condition rated the trial as somewhat more difficult to follow than did those in the no-camera condition (M's = 2.65 and 1.77, respectively; $F = 2.45, p < .10$). Closely paralleling this tendency, there was also a nonsignificant effect for high PSC subjects to rate the trial as more difficult to follow than did their low PSC counterparts (M's = 2.79 and 1.71, respectively; $F(1, 40) = 2.24, p < .15$). These results are interesting, since difficulty ratings were highly correlated with total recall performance ($r(46) = -.34, p < .01$).

Recall Performance

Subjects' responses to each recall question were assigned by a condition-blind experimenter values of 0 (if incorrect or omitted), 1 (if partially correct), or 2 (if entirely correct). Total scores could thus range from 0 to 80 (0-20 on each of the quartile tests).[2]

Camera effects. For the subjects assigned to the multiple assessment condition, a 2 (camera) $\times$ 2 (PSC) $\times$ 4 (trial stage subtest) repeated measures ANOVA on their midtrial test scores revealed that, overall, recall performance was significantly lower in the presence than in the absence of a camera (M's = 12.21 and 14.28, respectively; $F(1, 18) = 6.14, p < .03$). A significant main effect on trial stage subtests ($F(3, 54) = 5.64, p < .002$) indicated that these scores were lowest on the first subtest ($M = 11.36$), highest at the second ($M = 15.05$), and intermediate at the third

TABLE 14.1
Descriptive Statistics for Juror Decisions and Witness Impact Measures

	Camera		No Camera	
	M	SD	M	SD
Verdict-				
Confidence	6.41	2.08	6.33	2.06
Award	26.70	27.62	28.75	31.93
Witness 1	5.15	1.95	5.38	2.11
Witness 2	5.48	2.84	5.13	3.66
Witness 3	6.22	2.19	5.75	2.26

Note: All F's were < 1, p's $> .50$ ($N = 48$).

and fourth subtests (M's = 12.95 and 13.45, respectively).

Although the camera $\times$ subtest interaction did not materialize ($F(3, 54) = 1.29$, $p < .30$), the linear component of this interaction did approach significance, $F(1, 18) = 2.83$, $p < .12$. A series of specific comparisons thus revealed the predicted adaptation phenomenon, as the camera effect was due almost exclusively to a substantial difference in performance on the first subtest (M's = 9.84 and 13.20, $t(20) = 3.11$, $p < .01$). In fact, Figure 1 shows that the magnitude of this camera effect diminished gradually over time (corresponding p levels of .01, .15, .20, and .80).

On posttrial scores, a 2 (camera) $\times$ 2 (PSC) $\times$ 2 (testing procedure) $\times$ 4 (trial stage subtest) repeated measures ANOVA indicated that, overall, subjects recalled more in the multiple-test than single-test condition (M's = 14.35 and 12.29, respectively; $F(1, 40) = 12.01$, $p < .001$). This difference appeared in three of the four subtests (all at $p < .05$), demonstrating the facilitative effects of a warned-recall procedure (Taylor & Fiske, 1981) or of prior testing experience (indeed this is why a posttest-only condition was included in the design). More important, the camera manipulation did not significantly affect posttrial recall performance either alone (M's = 12.93 and 13.59 for the camera and no-camera conditions, respectively; $F(1, 40) < 1$) or in interaction with testing procedure or subsets (both F's < 1).

Taken together, the foregoing results support an adaptation hypothesis. In fact, although camera subjects' performance was relatively poor on the first *midtrial* subtest, they exhibited no impairment of recall for the same facts when subsequently presented in the first *posttrial* subtest. One possible explanation for this anomaly is that the information missed during the opening stages of the trial could have been recovered from subsequent testimony and arguments. To test this information recovery notion, items from the first subtest were

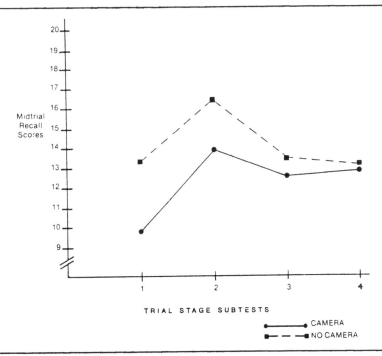

Figure 14.1 Midtrial recall scores for subjects in the camera and no-camera conditions.

divided into facts that were subsequently repeated varying numbers of times during the trial. As expected, for subjects in the camera, multiple-assessment cell, subtest 1 items that subsequently reappeared 1 (n = 3), 2 (n = 2), or 3 (n = 3) times showed performance increments (from mid- to posttest) of 18, 25, and 41%, respectively.[3]

Public self-consciousness. It is interesting to compare the effects produced by the camera to those associated with dispositional public self-consciousness. For multiple tested subjects, the 2 (camera) $\times$ 2 (PSC) $\times$ 4 (trial stage subtest) ANOVA indicated that midtrial recall was significantly poorer among the high than low public self-consciousness subjects (M's = 12.25 and 14.59, respectively; $F(1, 18)$ = 8.36, p < .01), and that this trait factor did not interact with either the camera condition or the subtest factor (both F's < 1). Moreover, in contrast to the transient effects produced by the camera manipulation, this effect for dispositional self-awareness tended to persist throughout the trial. Figure 2 illustrates the relative stability of this difference (corresponding p levels of .02, .15, .30, .02).

For the posttrial data, the four-way repeated measures ANOVA revealed that low PSC subjects performed better than those who scored as high in PSC (M's = 13.76 and 12.70, respectively; $F(1, 40)$ = 5.00,

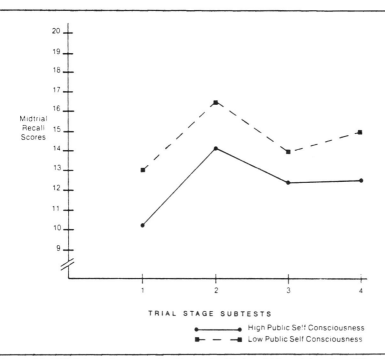

Figure 14.2 Midtrial recall scores of subjects classified as high and low in public self-consciousness.

$p < .03$). This main effect, however, was qualified by a significant interaction with the camera manipulation ($F(1, 40) = 4.08, p < .05$). Specifically, it turned out that posttrial recall was greater in the no-camera/low-public-self-consciousness group than in the remaining three cells (all at $p < .05$ via Newman-Keuls test). This pattern held for both the multiple-test and single-test conditions, $F(1, 40) = .70, p < .50$. These posttrial data, as they contrast with those of the midtrial results, are illustrated in Figure 3.

In both *Estes v. Texas* (1965) and *Chandler v. Florida* (1981), opponents of TV cameras in the courtroom had argued that the legal ideal of a "fair trial" is compromised in part because jurors are distracted, thereby reducing their use of evidence in the decision-making process. One predicted outcome of this effect would be an increase in the extent to which jurors' pretrial dispositions influence their judgments (Kaplan & Miller, 1978). The results of our study, however, showed that the presence of a camera did not systematically affect mock jurors' verdicts or evaluations of the individual witnesses or the trial as a whole. It did impair recall performance (presumably as a function of attention), but this effect was limited in two important

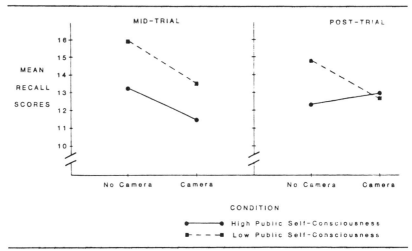

Figure 14.3 Mean midtrial (N = 22) and posttrial (N = 48) recall scores for high and low PSC subjects in the camera and no-camera conditions.

ways—(a) consistent with an adaptation hypothesis, the initial distractive effect of the camera diminished, resulting in a net posttrial loss of information that is *not* statistically significant, and (b) consistent with an individual differences hypothesis, the camera impaired the recall of subjects who were low but not high in their characteristic levels of public self-consciousness, as the latter performed poorly in both conditions.

Theoretically, these results address interesting issues concerning the trait and state of public self-consciousness and their interactive effects on attention and information processing. As noted earlier, Buss's (1980) "special susceptibility" hypothesis suggests that people who are characteristically high in public self-consciousness react more strongly to inducers of self-awareness than those who are low on the trait. Put another way, this view implies that individual differences will emerge only in situations that activate public self-awareness. Fenigstein (1979) obtained clear support for this view, finding that high self-consciousness people reacted more strongly to social rejection than those low in self-consciousness. In contrast, our midtrial data showed a simple pattern of two main effects, and the posttrial findings suggest that *either* the trait *or* the state is sufficient to disrupt attention-related performance (see Figure 3). In the latter instance, all subjects reacted to the camera, and individual differences appeared only in its absence. This interaction on the ecologically relevant, posttrial measure of recall is consistent with that obtained by Baumeister (1984) who, in a study of "choking under pressure," found that situational increases in self-focus disrupted performance on a fine motor task more among low than high PSC subjects (Experiments 3 and 4). As Baumeister reasoned, if self-attention is harmful for performance, then (a) in the absence of pressure, persons who are habitually low in self-consciousness should outperform those who are high, but (b) persons who are habitually self-conscious should be less affected by situations that produce self-focus because they are accustomed to and perhaps already performing in that state of mind.

Why do PSC and the camera manipulations show additive effects on midtrial recall, but an interactive pattern on the second, posttrial measure of performance? In Figure 3, it can be seen that the difference in patterns is attributable to a change in the relative position of one group. Although there was a small but consistent decline in recall from mid- to posttrial tests (i.e., for three of four cells, the average decrease was $-.91$), the high PSC-camera group exhibited a sharp increase ($M = +1.55$) in performance. Unfortunately, this finding is difficult to interpret because the two sets of recall data are based on different samples of respondents (the 22 multiply tested subjects represent a subsample of the 48 posttrial subjects) performing under different instructional sets (as a result of the first subtest, multiply tested subjects were led to anticipate subsequent memory assessment; such was not the case in the single-test condition).

At the very least, the foregoing results identify public self-consciousness as a potentially important, previously overlooked source of individual differences in personality and memory (cf. Kihlstrom, 1981, for a review of this literature). Apparently, people who are high in PSC, because they are characteristically self-focused in social or evaluative situations (even when they are simply members of an audience, as in the no-camera condition of the present study), are relatively inattentive to task-relevant information. Among real trial jurors, this personality variable could prove to be a particularly effective predictor of information processing, as they are often the object of others' attention.

Finally, this research leaves us with two important but yet unanswered questions. First, what competing stimulus specifically was responsible for the immediate impact of the camera? Were subjects attending to and, hence, distracted by the physical object itself or by the self-focused thoughts presumably aroused by its presence? The main effect obtained for the trait measure suggests the latter. Still, it is conceivable that in an unobtrusive camera condition (i.e., where subjects believe they are being televised without actually seeing the equipment), such an effect would not be obtained, or that in a mere physical presence condition (i.e., where the video equipment is present but subjects believe it is inoperational) such an effect would be obtained.

To explore these alternative explanations, 24 student subjects were randomly assigned to two groups (n's = 12) within the multiple-testing paradigm employed in the main experiment. In a physical distraction group, the camera and video equipment were present, but the lens was covered and subjects were told it was set up for another session. In the unobtrusive camera group, there was no equipment present, but subjects were told they were being videotaped through a camera built into a ceiling vent. Both groups watched the *Sockett v. Alterman Transport* trial and were tested for their recall of the evidence and arguments. As it turned out, subjects in the unobtrusive camera group performed somewhat poorer overall than those in the physical distraction condition (M's = 12.49 and 13.36, respectively; $p < .25$), a difference that approached statistical significance in the first subtest (M's = 9.18 and 11.86, respectively; $t(22) = -1.70$, $p < .10$). More important, a comparison of these latter scores to those obtained for the no-camera control group of the main experiment showed that although the unobtrusive camera manipulation significantly impaired subjects' initial recall ($t(22) = -2.65$, $p < .02$), the physical distractor manipulation did not ($t(22) < 1$). In short, these additional data suggest quite clearly that the immediate distractive impact of the camera is attributable to a focusing of attention on the self rather than the physical equipment.

A second important theoretical question is, was the initial impairment of recall the result of encoding or retrieval failure? Within our practical approach to the legal problem, we have assumed the former—that in the presence of a TV camera, jurors become less attentive to the trial. Yet in the procedure of our experiment, the camera was pointed at subjects not only as they watched the trial, but as they completed the recall questionnaires. It therefore remains to be seen whether the initial effect would hold if the camera were removed during testing.

In summary, this experiment addressed one of three major concerns about the effects of televising trials. From a practical standpoint, the results suggest that the presence of TV cameras does not irrevocably impair jurors' functioning. This finding is especially encouraging since it was obtained with a no-camera control group that was less on display than a real jury (Slater & Hans, 1982). It is entirely conceivable that amid the gallery of spectators, journalists, lawyers, and judges typically present at a real trial, the impact of the camera as an "observer" is superfluous. Moreover, it appears that perhaps any initial impact there is could even be prevented through the introduction of a pretrial warm-up period. Finally, the evidence for adaptation and the lack of an effect on all relevant judgmental measures suggests that the presence of TV cameras would not alter the outcome of jury deliberation.

From a practical standpoint, the present study is limited in at least two respects. First, it did not address the potential indirect effects of TV cameras on the jury, that is, those that follow from whatever effects television might have on the behavior of the trial actors or on the attitudes of and pressure from the local community (i.e., compared to trial coverage by the print media). Second, it is possible that the effects (and lack thereof) obtained here are affected by the type of case to which jurors are exposed. The *Sockett* trial was selected for this study because it is fact oriented, rather low-keyed, and nonarousing. Perhaps a more exciting or controversial case, one that more thoroughly engages and sustains jurors' attention, would not fall prey to any camera or PSC effects on recall. Further research should be directed at these important empirical questions. At this point, however, the present finding that the disruptive effect of a camera on jurors is short-lived and has no bearing on verdicts or evaluations of testimony provides at least tentative support for the *Chandler* (1981) ruling.

NOTES

1. Likewise, looking into a mirror is said to induce a state of private self-consciousness.

2. In order to establish the reliability of the scheme for coding of the recall protocol, the data from five pilot-test subjects were independently scored by both the author and the experimenter who later scored these data. Total agreement was reached on 94.2% of the items.

3. The corresponding increases in accuracy rates for the no-camera, multiple-assessment cell were -.03,. 12, and .22. Items pertaining to nonarticulated facts showed an overall improvement rate of .16.

REFERENCES

Abrahams, S. (1981). New efforts in 17 states to expand camera coverage of courts. *Judicature, 65,* 116-118.

Arkin, R., & Duval, S. (1975). Focus of attention and causal attribution of actors and observers. *Journal of Experimental Social Psychology, 11,* 427-438.

Barber, S. (1983). The problem of prejudice: A new approach to assessing the impact of courtroom cameras. *Judicature, 66,* 248-255.

Baumeister, R. F. (1984). Choking under pressure: Self-consciousness and paradoxical effects of incentives on skillful performance. *Journal of Personality and Social Psychology, 46,* 610-620.

Buss, A. H. (1980). *Self-consciousness and social anxiety.* San Francisco: Freeman.

Carter, C. A. (1981). *Media in the courts.* Washington, DC: National Center for State Courts.

Carver, C. S., & Glass, D. C. (1976). The self-consciousness scale: A discriminant validity study. *Journal of Personality Assessment, 40,* 169-172.

Carver, C. S., & Scheier, M. F. (1978). Self-focusing effects of dispositional self-consciousness, mirror presence, and audience presence. *Journal of Personality and Social Psychology, 36,* 324-332.

Chandler v. Florida, 101 S. Ct. 802, January 26 (1981).

Davis, D., & Brock, T. C. (1975). Use of first person pronouns as a function of increased objective self-awareness and prior feedback. *Journal of Experimental Social Psychology, 11,* 381-388.

Davis, N. (1980). Television in our courts: The proven advantages, the unproven dangers. *Judicature, 64,* 85-92.

Duval, S., & Wicklund, R. A. (1972). *A theory of objective self-awareness.* New York: Academic Press.

Estes v. Texas, 381 U.S. 531 (1965).

Fahringer, H. P. (1980). Cameras in the courtroom (TV or not TV?—That is the question). *Trial Diplomacy Journal, 3,* 4-6.

Fenigstein, A. (1979). Self-consciousness, self-attention, and social interaction. *Journal of Personality and Social Psychology, 37,* 75-86.

Fenigstein, A., Scheier, M. F., & Buss, A. H. (1975). Public and private self-consciousness: Assessment and theory. *Journal of Consulting and Clinical Psychology, 43,* 522-527.

Froming, W. J., Walker, G. R., & Lopyan, K. J. (1982). Public and private self-awareness: When personal attitudes conflict with societal expectations. *Journal of Experimental Social Psychology, 18,* 476-487.

Geller, V., & Shaver, P. (1976). Cognitive consequences of self-awareness. *Journal of Experimental Social Psychology, 12,* 99-108.

Gerbner, G. (1980). Trial by television: Are we at the point of no return? *Judicature, 63,* 416-426.

Goodwin, A. T. (1979). A report on the latest rounds in the battle over cameras in the courts. *Judicature, 63,* 74-77.

Graves, D. (1979). Cameras in the courts: The situation today. *Judicature, 63,* 24-27.

Harris, J. D. (1943). Habituatory response decrement in the intact organism. *Psychological Bulletin, 40,* 385-422.

Hirschorn, J., & Stern, C. (1980). Does television make a fair trial impossible?— A debate. *Judicature, 64,* 145-146.

Hoyt, J. L. (1980). Prohibiting courtroom photography: It's up to the judge in Florida and Wisconsin. *Judicature, 63,* 290-295.

Ickes, W. J., Wicklund, R. A., & Ferris, C. B. (1973). Objective self-awareness and self-esteem. *Journal of Experimental Social Psychology, 9,* 202-219.

Kaplan, M. F., & Miller, L. E. (1978). Reducing the effects of juror bias. *Journal of Personality and Social Psychology, 36,* 1443-1445.

Kielbowicz, R. B. (1979). The story behind the adoption of the ban on courtroom cameras. *Judicature, 63,* 14-23.

Kihlstrom, J. F. (1981). On personality and memory. In N. Cantor & J. Kihlstrom (Eds.), *Personality, cognition, and social interaction.* Hillsdale, NJ: Erlbaum.

Netteburg, K. (1980). Does research support the Estes ban on cameras in the courtroom? *Judicature, 63,* 467-475.

Nisbett, R. E., & Wilson, T. D. (1977). Telling more than we can know: Verbal reports on mental processes. *Psychological Review, 84,* 231-259.

Scheier, M. F., & Carver, C. S. (1980). Private and public self-attention, resistance to change, and dissonance reduction. *Journal of Personality and Social Psychology, 39,* 390-405.

Slater, D., & Hans, V. P. (1982). Methodological issues in the evaluation of "experiments" with cameras in the courts. *Communication Quarterly, 30,* 376-380.

Taylor, S. E., & Fiske, S. T. (1981). Getting inside the head: Methodologies for process analysis in attribution and social cognition. In J. Harvey, W. Ickes, & R. Kidd (Eds.), *New directions in attribution research* (Vol. 3). Hillsdale, NJ: Erlbaum.

Thompson, R. F., & Spencer, W. A. (1966). Habituation: A model phenomenon for the study of neuronal substrates of behavior. *Psychological Review, 173,* 16-43.

Tighe, T. J., & Leaton, R. N. (Eds.). (1979). *Habituation: Perspectives from child development, animal behavior, and neurophysiology.* Hillsdale, NJ: Erlbaum.

Turner, R. G., Scheier, M. F., Carver, C. S., & Ickes, W. (1978). Correlates of self-consciousness. *Journal of Personality Assessment, 42,* 285-289.

Vallacher, R. R. (1978). Objective self awareness and the perception of others. *Personality and Social Psychology Bulletin, 4,* 63-67.

Weary, G., & Arkin, R. M. (1981). Attributional self-presentation. In J. Harvey, W. Ickes, & R. Kidd (Eds.), *New directions in attribution research* (Vol. 3) Hillsdale, NJ: Erlbaum.

Whisenand, J. (1978). Florida's experiment. *American Bar Association Journal, 64,* 1860-1863.

Wicklund, R. A. (1975). Objective self awareness. In L. Berkowitz (Ed.), *Advances in experimental social psychology* (Vol. 8). New York: Academic Press.

15

DOES RESEARCH SUPPORT THE ESTES BAN ON CAMERAS IN THE COURTROOM?

KERMIT NETTEBURG

Andrews University

At a time when most Americans receive most of their news from television,[1] the question of whether cameras should be allowed in our courtrooms is a momentous one. Critics contend that cameras could disrupt courtroom proceedings, create false impressions of the judicial process and perhaps even jeopardize the defendant's right to a fair trial. Proponents remind us that the American government is committed to openness and to an informed citizenry.

The debate over cameras in courtrooms has been marked by what Karl Warden called "much heat and little light." In his 1963 article

Author's Note. This article is based upon research which the author conducted for his doctoral dissertation at the University of Minnesota. His research was funded, in part, by grants from the National Association of Broadcasters, the University of Minnesota Computing Center, and Andrews University.

From *Judicature*, 1980, 63(10), 467-475. Reprinted by permission of the author.

"Canon 35: Is There Room for Objectivity?," he called for information gathering and research to assess the impact of televised trials on the judicial process.[2] But for the most past, such investigations have never been undertaken.

A U.S. Supreme Court decision that same year, *Estes v. Texas,* effectively closed courtroom doors to cameras—and made it impossible to conduct the experiments and research Warden called for.[3] But even the Court acknowledged—somewhat to its own dismay— that it was forced to rely on conjecture and hypothesis for its decision. "[O]ur empirical knowledge of its [television's] full effect on the public, the jury or the participants in a trial, including a judge, witnesses and lawyers, is limited," said Justice Tom C. Clark, writing for the majority.[4]

For a decade television crews did not set foot inside most courtrooms. But in 1975 Alabama and Washington amended Canon 35 to allow cameras and at least 20 states have followed suit.[5] These experiments have given us a growing body of empirical knowledge about the effects of camera coverage of trials and an opportunity to test the conjecture of *Estes* against the findings of social science (see appendix, "The Results of Studies So Far").

Our purpose here is to review data that court systems and social scientists have collected on the effects of cameras on trial participants and to present the results of a survey in two Wisconsin cities of the impact of televised trials on the community. But before we do that, we should examine more closely the original basis for the Supreme Court's decision.

THE ESTES ARGUMENTS

The fundamental assumption of *Estes* was that any courtroom activity which infringes upon a defendant's right to a fair trial should be prohibited.[6] From this constitutional basis the Court offered three arguments which suggest that cameras and microphones made fair trials impossible, at least in notorious cases.

- First, the court noted the preponderance of judicial disapproval of cameras in courtrooms: At that time, 48 of the 50 states and the federal system banned all forms of camera coverage.
- Second, the court noted that cameras and microphones would be both physically and psychologically distracting to trial participants, frightening witnesses, impairing jurors' concentration, adding to the judge's duties, and impinging upon unfettered courtroom communication between counsel and client.

- Third, the court was concerned that televising trials would create such prejudice against the defendant in the community that the atmosphere would poison the proceedings.

The Court's first line of reasoning—that 49 of 51 jurisdictions have rejected cameras—is no longer valid. As many as two-thirds of the states today either allow photographing in court or are contemplating such a change.[7] The presumption, in short, now seems to favor televised trials.

Second, research has not shown a significant adverse impact of television on courtroom participants.[8] Not a single critic reported any serious misgivings about Ronny Zamora's trial.[9] Surveys of trial participants and the legal communities in Florida and Wisconsin show no serious objections to televised trials.[10] Though many questions about the effects of cameras on participants remain unanswered,[11] the growing body of empirical knowledge points in but one direction: Justice and publicity can coexist in the courtroom.[12]

This body of knowledge about courtroom effects is, however, far more extensive than our knowledge about the possibility of television's pressures toward community incitement, which formed the basis for the third *Estes* proposition.[13]

"The heightened public clamor resulting from radio and television coverage will inevitably result in prejudice," Justice Clark wrote in *Estes*.[14] But anecdotal, experimental, or survey evidence to support or refute this proposition does not exist. The results of the studies we undertook during Wisconsin's experimental year are a first attempt to develop such evidence.

GREATER FREEDOM, GREATER ABUSE?

The media enjoy greater freedom in Wisconsin courts than in almost any other jurisdiction, since they may film trials even over the objections of trial participants. In Wisconsin, judicial orders excluding broadcast or photographic coverage of the trial must show cause why such exclusion is necessary, and personal desire not to be photographed does not qualify as "cause."[15] Obviously, this greater latitude could produce greater abuse of fair trial rights and incitement of community prejudice.

In the two Wisconsin cities we selected, each with a population of about 40,000, television stations had broadcast filmed reports of trials during the experimental year. Each city is the central business district for nearby farms; each contains some light industry; and each has a branch of the University of Wisconsin with about 5,000 students. They represent stereotypical small-town America.

Our study selected 300 names randomly from telephone directories.[16] During January 1979, trained interviewers completed a 15-minute telephone survey with 258 respondents, a completion rate of 86 percent. The interviews asked for opinions about media coverage of trials and for specific knowledge about the trial most widely televised in the cities—that of Jennifer Patri. The trial occurred in a third city, miles away from the study communities; so we can assume that what people knew about the case and its participants depended on media coverage of the trial, not personal acquaintance with the facts or people.

Mrs. Patri was charged with killing her husband and with attempting to burn down their house in order to destroy his body. When the fire was not successful, prosecutors said that she buried the body behind the barn. In defense, she contended that her husband had beaten her many times, though she admitted he had not abused her in the days just before she shot him.

Every element of the crime tempted the media to be sensationalistic. Nightly courtroom film footage highlighted every Wisconsin television newscast for weeks, but courtroom decorum was never seriously threatened because both the media and the judge strictly observed Wisconsin's coverage guidelines. Thus the trial lets us focus upon the levels of community prejudice that the media may have created *outside* the courtroom.

PUBLIC OPINION ABOUT CAMERAS

A one-time survey such as this one cannot support the inference that television *causes* prejudice and such was not the purpose of this study. Instead, the study measured whether two events—camera coverage and community incitement—occurred together. Moreover, a survey of public opinion cannot establish causal inference, either; we cannot prove that TV causes prejudice simply because people believe it does. Nevertheless, this study measured public opinion because of the importance of the will of the people in the American system.

Table 1 shows the percentage of respondents who thought media coverage made fair trials easier or more difficult. We can see a reservoir of public mistrust in the media in the responses of people to traditional media coverage of trials. Fewer than 10 percent of the respondents in each category thought traditional media coverage

TABLE 15.1
Public Opinion About Cameras in the Courtroom

	Makes fair trial easier	Makes fair trial more difficult	No difference
Traditional newspaper coverage	4%	41%	54%
Traditional television coverage	8%	46%	44%
Traditional radio coverage	3%	38%	58%
TV coverage with film (broadcast during a regular newscast)	21%	26%	52%
Newspaper coverage with photos	12%	21%	67%
Live radio coverage	13%	27%	59%
Live TV coverage	13%	33%	53%

made a fair trial easier—though the Supreme Court has sometimes seen such coverage as a crucial element in several of its "public trial" decisions.[17] Between 33 percent and 44 percent felt traditional media coverage made a fair trial more difficult to achieve—a result far more consistent with the Court's latest rulings.[18]

When the respondents considered the effects of Wisconsin's new rules on trials, most of them thought the changes would make no difference, or perhaps make a fair trial even easier to achieve. Together, the "No difference" and "Easier" categories—which both indicate that no harm would come to fairness—include from 66 percent to 79 percent of the respondents, all of whom approve of cameras in the courtroom.

Public opinion does not, of course, make constitutional law. As Warden noted, "A survey of judges and lawyers on their opinion of the validity of the Pythagorean Theorem would not change its true nature."[19] Opinion must give way to fact, and propositions must be tested against reality. For that, we turn to the interview data related to the Patri trial. Three specific dimensions formed Justice Clark's community incitement theory, and each was tested by the survey data.

(1) Television can destroy the accused and his or her case in the eyes of the public. The public often considers a person *accused* of a crime *guilty* of that crime, as Richard Nixon once demonstrated when, in a slip of the tongue, he said that Charles Manson was "guilty until proven innocent."[20] To test the proposition that an accusation is itself damaging, we asked respondents if they recalled any specific trials held in Wisconsin recently. Table 2 shows that only 16 percent recalled the Jennifer Patri trial in this "Unaided recall" setting: 67 percent could remember no specific trial.

Respondents were also given a short description of the crime and asked if they remembered whether the woman charged was Jennifer Patri or Margaret Henders. (Margaret Henders was a name chosen at random in an out-of-state telephone book; only 2 percent of the

TABLE 15.2
Knowledge of the Jennifer Patri Trial

	Correct response	Incorrect response	No response
Unaided recall of Patri's name	16%	7%	77%
Aided recall of Patri's name	75%	2%	23%
Recall of murder motive	61%	10%	29%
Recall of trial outcome	5%	59%	36%
Recall of judge's name	14%	11%	75%
Recall of prosecutor's name	7%	4%	89%
Recall of defense attorney's name	15%	3%	82%

respondents chose her name.) As Table 2 shows, 75 percent correctly identified Mrs. Patri in this "Aided recall" setting. Respondents were also asked her reason for killing her husband, and Table 2 shows that 61 percent correctly named her reason.

Simple knowledge of names and facts, however, is not the same as "destroying the accused and his case." A further question, not reported in Table 2, asked those who remembered the reason Mrs. Patri gave for killing her husband whether they believed the reason. Two-thirds said they did believe her; only 18 percent did not; the others had no opinion. While many people thus knew about the defendant and her case, only a handful of those surveyed doubted the truth of her defense. The survey finds little evidence that publicity has destroyed the defendant's reputation.

(2) New trials would be jeopardized because potential jurors would have seen the original trial. Though many people recognized Jennifer Patri's name and the reason she killed her husband, 23 percent of the public could not pick Mrs. Patri's name from a list of two and 39 percent could not remember the motive for her crime.

The more devastating survey finding is that 59 percent of the respondents erroneously remembered Mrs. Patri as having been convicted of both murder and arson. Only 5 percent correctly remembered that she was *convicted* of murder and *acquitted* of arson. It is supremely disturbing that almost three-fifths of the community incorrectly reported remembering a defendant as having been convicted of a crime. Potential jurors for a retrial would not only enter the courtroom remembering "facts" about the first trial, but the facts they remember would be both incorrect and prejudicial.

One reason for that large a number of incorrect responses may have been the "unaided recall" format of the question. "In the case [of] a woman . . . charged with murdering her husband and then burning down the house in order to destroy the body," the first question asked, "[d]o you remember if the woman's name was Jennifer Patri or Margaret Henders?" Such an "aided recall" question frequently overestimates the knowledge of the respondent; since he or she has a 50-50 chance of guessing the correct answer.

The second question—"Do you remember if she was convicted or not?"—was an "unaided recall" question, which frequently *underestimates* the respondent's true knowledge. The sequence of our questions, however, eliminated this "unaided vs. aided recall" difference, since the first question clearly reminded the respondent of the two charges—murder and arson—and the second question asked the respondent if the defendant was convicted, obviously referring to both charges.[21]

Finally, it may be that in the public's mind guilty is guilty, never mind the number of charges. That, of course, presents little comfort to the defendant seeking an unprejudiced jury for retrial.

Even if such speculation is correct, however, it will not be difficult for a defendant to find unbiased retrial jurors. Once we recognize the large groups of people ignorant of the outcome of the Patri trials, we can no longer accept the *Estes* proposition that new trials will be jeopardized by televising. Although 59 percent incorrectly remembered her as guilty of both crimes and 5 percent correctly remembered her as guilty only of murder, the other 36 percent either had not *heard* of the trial or could not *remember* its outcome. (This percentage closely parallels the 39 percent who could not remember the reason given for the killing and the 25 percent who could not identify her name.) It suggests a pool of people who do not follow public affairs closely and would not carry prejudicial information into a retrial.[22]

A pool of unbiased prospective jurors—those who know little or nothing of the first trial—should thus be available. Since the Patri trial was the most widely publicized trial in Wisconsin during the experimental year, other trials broadcast less extensively could probably draw from an even larger pool of potential jurors who know nothing, or very little, of the case.

Unfortunately, the fact that only 5 percent of the respondents correctly remembered the outcome of the two trials gives little encouragement to those who argue that media publicity will create wider knowledge of the workings of the courts and inspire greater public confidence in the judicial system. The evidence in our survey suggests that the media can hardly justify their presence in the courtrooms on the grounds that they educate the public. The public simply isn't watching very closely.

(3) *The jury, defendant, lawyers, and judge would be highly publicized and widely known throughout the community.* In this survey, that simply didn't happen. When respondents were asked to identify the defendant, judge, prosecutor, and defense attorney by

choosing one of two names, they almost always failed.

Table 2 shows once again that 75 percent could correctly identify Jennifer Patri's name. However, only 15 percent could correctly identify Allen Eisenberg, Mrs. Patri's prominent Milwaukee defense attorney, known statewide for his criminal law practice. Only 14 percent could identify the judge in the case, Frederick Fink, whose handling of the camera coverage of the trial was widely discussed. And only 7 percent could identify Prosecutor Phillip Kirk.

SUMMARY

The only evidence this survey has uncovered to support *Estes* about "community incitement" is the wide knowledge of Jennifer Patri's name and, perhaps more disturbingly, the large number of respondents who incorrectly remembered her as having been convicted of *both* crimes. However, both of these findings must be seen in the context of the significant percentages of respondents who were not aware of Mrs. Patri's name or the outcome of the case. They constitute a potential pool of unbiased jurors that the *Estes* Court never imagined.

The data directly contradict the proposition that television can destroy an accused's case, since 66 percent of those who knew her reason for killing her husband believed or accepted the reason. The low name recognition rates for the judge and lawyers fail to confirm the "highly publicized" proposition. Thus none of the three elements of community incitement outlined by *Estes* could be confirmed completely by the finding.

It is disturbing to think that the majority of respondents believed Mrs. Patri was convicted of arson. Notwithstanding her acquittal, she would return to her community a convicted arsonist. The consequences here are hypothetical, of course, since she *was* convicted of murder. Nevertheless, the status of a defendant acquitted in a televised trial deserves further study.

Whatever damage to her reputation Mrs. Patri may have suffered unfairly, one still cannot infer that the public's inaccurate "knowledge" means the trial itself was unfair. Only unfairness in judicial process, not in a "court" of public opinion, can bar cameras from courtrooms according to the constitutional interpretation of *Estes*.

The research reported here finds little evidence to support the *Estes* rules that cameras and courtrooms be separated. Other research we have examined likewise fails to confirm suspicions of the detrimental effects of televising. Finally, survey data gathered in Washington,

Ohio, Florida, and Wisconsin have failed to demonstrate that trial participants are distracted by cameras.

The task now is for legal decision makers to use the findings of these studies, and others sure to follow, to create effective social policy. Social science research is not social policy, nor is it constitutional interpretation. But a careful evaluation of research data on the question of fair trials and a free press may help us see more clearly the real dangers of televised trials—and dismiss dangers that we have only imagined.

NOTES

1. Roper, Public Perceptions of Television and Other Mass Media. New York: Television Information Office, 1979.

2. Warden, Canon 35: Is There Room for Objectivity? 4 WASHBURN L. J. 211 (1965).

3. Estes v. Texas, 381 U.S. 533 (1965).

4. Id. at 541.

5. For a review of actions and proposals regarding changes in Canon 35, see White, Camera in the courtroom: a U.S. Survey, 60 JOURNALISM MONOGRAPHS 3 (1979), and Graves. Cameras in the courts: the situation today, JUDICATURE 24 (1979).

6. Estes v. Texas, 381 U.S. 533, 544-5. Bridges v. California, 314 U.S. 252 (1941). Pennekamp v. Florida, 328 U.S. 331 (1946) and other cases have established that judges can protest defendant's rights by prohibiting in-courtroom events only: what occurs outside the courtroom is outside the purview of the judge. The Estes assumption also must be limited to in-courtroom events which infringe on fair trial rights, although the court does not state that.

7. See White, supra n. 4, and Graves, supra n. 4.

8. Among the published reports are: Advances Made in Access to Courtrooms, 95 BROADCASTING 29 (August 7, 1978); Aspen, Cameras in the Courtroom: The Florida Experiment, 67 ILL. B. J. 82 (October 1978): Cameras in the Courtroom: An Update, 2 UPDATE 1 (July 1978); Hoyt, Cameras in the Courtroom: From Hauptmann to Wisconsin, paper presented to Association for Education in Journalism, 1978; Judge endorses TV presence at murder trial, 91 BROADCASTING 36 (December 20, 1976).

Also, Kaye, Documentary Draws Fire From Public Defenders, 1 THE AM. LAWYER 10 (October 1979); Lancaster, Cameras in the Courtroom: The Indiana Experience, 6 TORTFEASOR 6 (February 1978); State Courts Flirting with T.V. and Cameras, 63 A.B.A.J. 473 (1977); TV in Courtrooms, 1 UPDATE 2 (March 1978); Whisenand, Florida's Experiment with Cameras in the Courtroom, 64 A.B.A.J. 1860 (1978); Williams, The Sirhan Trial: Courtroom TV Revisited, 57 QUILL 16 (August 1969); and Verdict Is in Favor of TV in Bundy Trial, 96 BROADCASTING 29 (August 6, 1979).

9. Since the Zamora trial was the first major test of cameras in Florida, Judge Paul Baker filed an extensive report with the Florida Supreme Court: Baker. REPORT TO THE SUPREME COURT OF FLORIDA RE: CONDUCT OF AUDIOVISUAL TRIAL COVERAGE. The report was reprinted in Florida Judge Evaluates Camera Coverage of Trial, 11 EDITOR & PUBLISHER 11 (January 7, 1978).

Other reviews of Zamora are: Ayres, Influence of TV Defense Fails as Defense Plea. N. Y. TIMES (October 7, 1977), p. 18; Fretz, Cameras in the Courtroom, 14 TRIAL 28 (September 1978): Loewen, Cameras in the Courtroom : A Reconsideration, 17

WASHBURN L. J. 504 (1978); Messerschmidt, *Zamora Trial Made a Point: Public Was Eager to Watch*, MIAMI HERALD, June 30, 1978. p. 16; Stone and Edlin, *T.V. or Not T.V.: Televised and Photographic Coverage of Trials*, 29 MERCER L. REV. 1119 (1978); and *TV on Trial: Introspection by the Medium*, 94 BROADCASTING 73 (May 22, 1978).

10. See appendix, "The Results from Studies So Far," at n. 6.

11. Perhaps the most crucial question yet unanswered is whether the surveys and case studies conducted to date can be replicated with greater controls. For an example of one such replication, see Hoyt, *Courtroom Coverage: The Effects of Being Televised*, 21 J. OF BROADCASTING 487 (1977). Another question concerns what types of trials if any should be excluded from coverage: see Fretz, *supra* n. 9. Other questions would include the frequency with which courts will be covered and the long-term effects on the court system.

12. In light of the evidence, several observers suggest the same "clear and present danger" test that applies to other judicial restraints upon court reporting should be applied to the camera question. Bridges v. California. 314 U.S. 252 (1941) and Pennekamp v. Florida, 328 U.S. 331 (1946).

For example. "With the technical advances in television proceedings, it would appear that the factual basis for *Estes* fails and that the burden is now shifted to the trial court to show, in each instance, why television should be excluded." *TV in Court Seven States Approve*, 1 THE NEWS MEDIA AND THE LAW 23 (December 1977).

13. At least one commentator has suggested that the "notorious atmosphere" proposition is the only valid rationale for excluding cameras today: Fetzer, *Cameras in the Courtroom: The Kansas Opposition*, 18 WASHBURN L. J. 230 (1979).

14. Estes v. Texas, 381 U.S. 533. at 549.

15. For a discussion of the Wisconsin and Florida rules, see Hoyt, *Prohibiting Courtroom Photography: It's up to the Judge in Florida and Wisconsin*, 63 JUDICATURE 290 (December-January 1980).

16. A sample of 250 allows one to predict the population characteristics with an error estimate of ± 3 percent. Quadrupling the sample to 1,000 respondents would increase the accuracy to only slightly under 2 percent. For an excellent discussion of this topic, see Meyer, PRECISION JOURNALISM: A REPORTER'S INTRODUCTION TO SOCIAL SCIENCE METHODS. Bloomington: Indiana University Press, 1979; and Welkowitz, Ewen and Cohen, INTRODUCTORY STATISTICS FOR THE BEHAVIORAL SCIENCES. New York: Academic Press, 1971.

17. The court has noted several values to the judicial system of publicity by the media. For example, In re Oliver, 333 U.S. 257 (1948), asserted that publicity about a trial would alert prospective witnesses to come forward with their testimony.

18. Several recent decisions seem to call into question even traditional coverage. See, e.g., Gannett, Inc. v. DePasquale, 99 S. Ct. 2898 (1979) and Nebraska Press Association v. Stuart, 427 U.S. 539 (1976).

19. Warden, *supra* n. 2 at 237.

20. See, *Nixon Calls Manson Guilty. Later Withdraws Remark.* NEW YORK TIMES. August 4, 1979, p. 1.

21. Of course, one might argue that the question was somewhat ambiguous, since the respondent could not easily distinguish the conviction from the acquittal in his or her response. A respondent may thus have been led to believe that *both* trials ended in the same verdict, or even that the two charges were combined in one trial. Unfortunately, the questionnaire was developed after the murder trial and before the arson trial, but interviews were conducted after both trials.

22. The data are not reported because they do not fit into Table 2's format. Interviewers asked those respondents who could not identify Jennifer Patri's name in the "aided recall" question (see text preceding footnote 21) a follow-up question: "Have you heard anything about the trial?" Eight percent responded, "No."

The 14 percent who could not recall any specific facts about the case are in addition to the eight percent who had never heard of the case. This figure was calculated by computing the number of respondents who did not give an answer—correct or incorrect—to any of the six questions asking for recall of specific Patri trial facts, even though they said they had heard of the trial.

APPENDIX A

The Results from Studies Conducted So Far

Ronny Zamora's murder trial may be the most frequently discussed of the televised trials, but it is by no means the only one. Mob-style murders, pornography, annexation fights, wife-beating, and sexual-innuendo murders, even Department of Natural Resources civil suits have been tried under the camera's Cyclopsian eye. Discussions of these cases have filled pages with anecdote and created knowledge about a camera's impact upon courtroom decorum where before only speculation existed.

The first data on television's impact on trial participants became available when Washington state reversed its Canon 35 in 1976. The Washington Supreme Court authorized a Seattle television pool to cover a second-degree manslaughter trial as an experiment. The news stories the stations prepared were not telecast, however; they were submitted to the Washington court for evaluation of the camera's effects. When the trial was over, the presiding judge interviewed each witness, juror, and lawyer asking for an assessment of the camera experiment.[1] Reactions from trial participants were so uniformly positive that Washington now allows cameras and microphones in all its courtrooms.

Another one-time-only relaxation of Canon 35 brought cameras into a Lorain County, Ohio, courtroom, and filmed news stories from this trial were actually broadcast. When social scientist Edna Einsiedel interviewed the participants of that trial, probing for subtle distractions created by the microphones and cameras, she found none.[2]

One witness said that she was nervous about being on television, but added that she immediately forgot about the cameras when the questioning began. Four other witnesses said they were more nervous about responding to attorneys' questions than they were about being on television. Even the defense attorney, whose motions against television coverage of the case had been denied, admitted, "I felt very comfortable in this courtroom and at no time was bothered by the presence of the cameras."

Others have reported that television threatens the fairness of a trial. Judge Thomas Sholts of West Palm Beach, Florida, who presided over a murder trial televised gavel-to-gavel, notes that one witness refused to testify for fear of her life, even though she had to serve a five-month and 29-day contempt sentence. Sholts also said the court received six bomb threats and numerous leads to the "real killer."[3]

Judge Edward Cowart blasted camera coverage of the Theodore Bundy trial in Miami, Florida, in July, 1979, four months after Florida's rule allowing cameras had been made permanent. He hinted that photo coverage may have caused an unfair trial and said the news media had no business hauling their cameras into court.[4] But later he praised broadcast coverage, calling it "the most accurate reporting" he had seen.[5]

As these examples suggest, the growing body of camera-impact literature is populated with case studies, examinations of the impact of televising upon a single trial. Perhaps the best of these is the review of a Nevada Trial, *State v. Solorzano*.[6] Paul Goldman and Richard Larson received depositions from many of the trial participants, including the judge, lawyers, certain witnesses, and some jurors. Goldman and Larson concluded:

> Unlike the Supreme Court's hypothesis in *Estes* that the camera would obstruct justice, the *Solorzano* experience provides an actual empirical basis, and leads the reasonable man to conclude that the presence of the television news camera during trial is a benign—if not beneficial—influence.[7]

However, all these case studies suffer from lack of generalizability inherent in case study methodology. Simply because one trial can be conducted fairly under the camera's scrutiny does not mean that others can. Only Wisconsin and Florida have attempted statewide studies of the impact of cameras upon trial fairness, and the uniqueness of their studies make them additionally valuable.

When Florida's experiment ended in July 1978, the state supreme court commissioned a survey of witnesses, jurors, lawyers, and court officers who had participated in televised trials. The results suggest that few effects have been felt by trial participants as a result of television cameras, although attorneys showed greater reservations about televising than others did. Although the study suffered from several methodological flaws, including extreme simplicity in instrumentation and the rush which the Florida court's deadline imposed upon the researchers, the study found few reasons to bar cameras from courtrooms.[8]

Wisconsin's experiment (April 1978 to March 1979) was also evaluated through a survey, in which the Wisconsin research committee investigated a sample of *trials* instead of a sample of *participants.* This study also concluded that, with appropriate rules for media conduct, little harm would result from allowing camera coverage in Wisconsin's jurisdictions.[9]

Both Wisconsin and Florida also surveyed the trial judges of the state. In Wisconsin, 80 percent thought there was no incompatibility between televising and fair trials.[10] In Florida, 77 percent of the judges thought cameras caused no serious distraction in court.[11] Unfortunately, the response rates for judges were small, especially in Wisconsin where less than one-third of the state's judges answered the questionnaire.

While these surveys are more generalizable than case studies, they still cannot be used as evidence to draw causal conclusions. For instance, we might argue that the juror who has participated in only a televised trial has no knowledge of courtroom decorum in a nontelevised trial setting and little basis for deciding whether the new situation is more fair or unfair.

Only one study to date has employed a research design which allowed for causation to be established. University of Wisconsin Professor James Hoyt tested the effect on a witness's testimony of the knowledge that he was being filmed. Hoyt found that witnesses remembered more specific details in the televised condition than in the nontelevised condition, and that they remembered fewer wrong details. He concluded that televising trials might improve the quality of testimony, not impair it.[12]

The unique factor of all these studies is their consistent finding that the camera can coexist with justice, and that television has become so commonplace, as Justice Harlan suggested it might,[13] that it can blend into the courtroom's paneled walls.

NOTES

1. Interestingly the only permanent record of the interviews is on film. All interviews were filmed by the television pool: No court reporter made a transcript of the proceedings. The film is available from the Washington Press Association, Seattle, Washington.

2. Einsiedel. "Television in the Courtroom: An Ohio Experiment" (paper presented to the Association for Education in Journalism, August, 1978).

3. Messerschmidt, *Cameras in Court: A Year Later,* MIAMI HERALD, June 30, 1978, p. 1.

4. *Verdict Is in Favor of TV in Bundy Trial,* 96 BROADCASTING 29 (August 6, 1979).

5. Variety, February 6, 1980, p. 1.

6. Goldman and Larson, *News Camera in the Courtroom During State v. Solorzano: End to the Estes Mandate?* 10 SW. Nev. L. Rev. 2001 (1978).

7. *Id.* at 2041.

8. *A Sample Survey of the Attitudes of Individuals Associated with Trials Involving Electronic Media and Still Photography Coverage in Selected Florida Courts between July 5, 1977 and June 30, 1978,* available from the Florida Supreme Court.

Perhaps the most interesting finding of the study, unmentioned by its authors in their summary, is that jurors, witnesses, and lawyers alike felt the cameras had a greater effect on the other participants than on themselves. This finding recalls Chief Justice Warren Burger's defense of banning cameras from the U.S. Supreme Court: "Some of my brethern might posture for the cameras."

See also Buchanan, Pryor, Messke, and Strawn, *The Florida Experiment,* 15 Trial 34 (1979).

9. *Report of the Supreme Court Committee to Monitor and Evaluate the Use of Audio and Visual Equipment in the Courtroom* (April 1, 1979), available from the Wisconsin Supreme Court.

10. *Id.* at 54-55.

11. As quoted in *Report of the Supreme Court Committee, supra* n. 10, at 53.

12. James L. Hoyt, *Courtroom Coverage: The Effects of Being Televised,* 21 J. of Broadcasting 487 (1977).

13. Estes v. Texas, 381 U.S. 532, 595 (1965) (J. Harlan concurring Opinion).

16

PUBLIC OPINION ON THE PSYCHOLOGICAL AND LEGAL ASPECTS OF TELEVISING RAPE TRIALS

JANET SWIM
EUGENE BORGIDA
University of Minnesota

In 1983 a woman was gang raped in Big Dan's Bar in New Bedford, Massachusetts. The subsequent rape trial became a media event when the Cable News Network (CNN) broadcast the trail on national television. CNN's televised coverage of the trial highlighted many of the issues in the controversy over the presence of television cameras in

Author's Note. This research was supported by a faculty research grant from the Graduate School at the University of Minnesota to John Aldrich, Eugene Borgida, and John Sullivan. Janet Swim was supported in part by a University of Minnesota Graduate School Fellowship. The authors are grateful to Collette Morse for her assistance in conducting the research and to Geoff Maruyama and Patricia Frazier for their comments on an earlier version of this article. Portions of this article were presented at the 1984 meeting of the Midwestern Psychological Association, Chicago, Illinois. Requests for the courtroom. These issues can be divided into three clusters: legal and constitutional issues, psychological effects of the media on trial participants, and extended effects of media coverage on the public. The purpose of the present study was to selectively examine these issues in terms of public opinion about televising rape trials like the New Bedford case.

A consideration of public opinion about these issues is important for several reasons. First, apropos legal policy and constitutional issues, scholars have argued that the judicial process should be accountable to the public and that televising trials, even rape trials, would be consistent with this public accountability (see Lindsey, 1984, for a review). Other scholars have argued that First Amendment issues are involved. Does the public believe, for example, that freedom of the press extends to televised coverage of rape trials or, for that matter, to any courtroom proceeding?

Second, with respect to psychological effects, the public's preconceptions about electronic media coverage (EMC) may affect participants' perceptions of the effects of electronic media coverage on the trial. For example, results from a recent experimental study suggest that if a witness appears nervous during a trial, jurors may attribute the cause of nervousness to the presence of a camera (Borgida, DeBono, & Buckman, 1985). Such effects on jury decision making may well arise from public preconceptions about the effects of EMC. In the present research, public beliefs about the impact of electronic media coverage on the trial process, in general, and on a rape victim, in particular, were examined and the strength of the relationship between specific beliefs and approval of EMC were compared.

Third, televised coverage of rape trials may have extended effects on the public such as decreased reporting of rapes, increased awareness of rape, or even the provocation of more rapes. The actual extended effects of EMC in *any* kind of trial context have been virtually ignored by social scientists (Gerbner, 1980). However, beliefs about the effects of cameras inside the courtroom may be linked to beliefs about the extended effects. For instance, women may be less likely to report a rape if they believe that EMC increases a victim's trauma. Believing that EMC could increase the trauma of rape and disrupt the trial process might make prosecuting rape seem less worthwhile, which in turn may lead to decreased reporting (Feldman-Summers &

reprints should be sent to Eugene Borgida, Department of Psychology, University of Minnesota, 75 East River Road, Minneapolis, MN 55455.

From *Journal of Applied Social Psychology*, 1987, 17(5), 507-518. Copyright by V. H. Winston & Sons. Reprinted by permission of the publisher.

Ashworth, 1981). On the other hand, the public may believe that EMC would have the positive effect of raising people's awareness about rape, which could lead to increased reporting.

Thus the present investigation was conducted to fill the vacuum of public opinion data on electronic media coverage of rape cases and to examine the impact of EMC on the behavioral intention to report a rape.

METHOD

Respondents

A random probability cross-sectional sample of 138 male and female residents of the metropolitan Minneapolis and St. Paul area (N = 138) were interviewed in person for one hour as part of a more comprehensive survey. The interviews were conducted over a 2-month period from the beginning of September 1984 until the eve of the election on November 4, 1984. The refusal rate was 41%. To form the sample, households were randomly drawn from the Minneapolis and St. Paul city directories, which included a listing of all households in each city.

To ensure that respondents as well as households were selected randomly, interviewers were instructed to interview the person in the household whose birthday fell closest to the current date. If the designated individual was unwilling to participate, interviewers followed a random-walk pattern to substitute another household from the same block. The student interviewers were recruited and trained by associates in the Department of Political Science at the University of Minnesota. Approximately 20 interviewers were used over the 2-month period. Each conducted several practice interviews before going out into the field and the progress of interviewing was closely supervised.

A comparison of the demographic characteristics of the Twin Cities sample with those of the 1980 Census shows that our sample includes a slightly greater proportion of males (57% in the sample versus 46% in the population), whites (97% versus 93%), and highly educated respondents (12% versus 19% in the less than high school category, 23 versus 38% finishing high school, 28 versus 20% with one to three years of college, and 37% versus 23% with four or more years of college). The median category of income in the sample, $15,000 to $17,500, included the median income for the Twin Cities population, $15,144. Based on these comparisons, we feel that, despite an oversampling in some characteristics, the sample is fairly representative of the population from which it is drawn.

Questionnaire

Respondents were asked 10 questions about media coverage of courtroom cases as part of the Twin Cities Public Opinion survey conducted as a pretest for the Gallup Poll's 1984 Presidential Election survey. Appendix A lists the questions asked of the respondents for the present research. The first questions were designed to assess respondents' general opinion about EMC in the courtroom. The next six items inquired about respondents' opinions about specific issues related to EMS. The first two are related to constitutional and legal issues: the media's First Amendment rights and the public's right to be informed. The next two tap potential effects inside the courtroom: the victim's trauma and disruption of the trial process. The last two items represent possible extended effects of EMC on reporting, public awareness, and incidence of rape. The final question assessed whether or not EMC would affect female respondents' behavioral intention to report a rape.[1]

RESULTS

Descriptive Analysis

A descriptive analysis of responses to the 10 items was conducted first. For each question, three response categories were created by collapsing scale points 1-3 and 5-7 and by treating the neutral point (4) as a separate category.

When asked whether they agreed or disagreed with the statement that court cases should be televised, 60.2% of the respondents disagreed. However, disagreement increased to 84.8% when asked about televising rape cases. When asked about *constitutional and legal policy issues,* the majority of respondents believed that the media did not have the right to televise rape cases (71.3%), and that the public's right to keep informed about the justice system did not extend to watching televised rape cases (80.2%). With regard to *issues inside the courtroom,* most respondents believed that the victim's trauma would increase (90.8%) and that cameras would disrupt the trial process (68.2%). Responses to the extended psychological *effects outside the courtroom* were more ambiguous. Most, 68.0%, believed that televising rape trials would reduce reporting, 42.7% believed that televised rape trials would raise awareness, and 35.2% believed that televising rape trials would encourage more rapes. When asked how knowledge that some rape trials were televised in Minnesota would affect their reporting, 7.9% of the women said they would be more likely to report a rape, 28.9% said they would be unaffected, and 63.2% said they would be less likely to report a rape.[2]

Regression Analyses

Multiple regression analyses were done to determine which beliefs were related to approval of televising rape trials and behavioral intentions to report a rape.[3] The first dependent variable, approval of televising rape trials, was measured by respondents' degree of agreement with the statement "In general, rape cases should be allowed to appear on television." The first regression analysis examined whether any demographic variables should be included in the regression equation for this first dependent variable. Of these variables, sex of the respondent (unstandardized coefficient = .63, p = .03) was significantly related to approval, with women more likely to disapprove, but education (unstandardized coefficient = –.13, p = .16), age (unstandardized coefficient = .01, p = .18) and income (unstandardized coefficient = .04, p = .37) were not significantly related to approval. (These coefficients have df = 1, 123.) Hence, for the next regression sex of respondent was entered into the equation. The significance of the regression equation is .06, $F(4, 123) = 2.33$, and the adjusted R^2 = .04 (see Weisberg, 1980, p. 188, on adjusted R^2, which adjusts for the number of predictor variables).

Correlations between the issue questions were examined to determine if any were above .60; if so, they were not entered as separate variables in the final equation. For this reason the questions on legal policy and constitutional issues (i.e., Questions 3 and 4 in the appendix) were combined to form one variable (r = .65, $p < .001$). Zero order correlations for these variables are presented in Table 1.

For this first dependent variable, six variables were entered hierarchically into the equation. Results for the final equation reflect the order in which these variables were entered in the equation. People who believed that legal and constitutional issues of public rights and media rights did not justify televising rape trials were more likely to disapprove of televising rape trials (unstandardized coefficient = .24, $p < .001$). People who felt that television would disrupt the trial process (unstandardized coefficient = .17, p = .04) and increase trauma of the rape victim were more likely to disapprove of televising rape trials (unstandardized coefficient = .29, p = .01). Opinions about the extended effects of raising awareness about rape (unstandardized coefficient = –.02, p = .76), encouraging more rapes (unstandardized coefficient = .04, p = .56), and reduced reporting (unstandardized coefficient = .09, p = .18) were not significantly related to approval (these coefficients all have df = 1, 114). The significance of the regression equation is $p < .001$, $F(7, 114) = 11.77$, and the adjusted R^2 = .38.

The second dependent variable was women's behavioral intention to report a rape if they knew other women's trials had been televised.

TABLE 16.1
Zero Order Correlations

		1	2	3	4	5	6	7	8	9	10
Approval of EMC	Q1-all cases										
	Q2-rape cases	.46**									
Rights and policy Issues	Q3-Media	.34*	.56**								
	Q4-Public access	.42**	.56**	.65**							
Effects Inside Courtroom	Q5-Trauma	.17*	.43**	.33**	.50**						
	Q6-Disrupt	.42**	.40**	.36**	.30**	.34**					
Effects Outside Courtroom	Q7-Report	.08 p=.18	.13 p=.08	.28**	.30**	.40**	.12 p=.09				
	Q8-Aware	.28**	.16*	.15*	.30**	.07 p=.20	.19*	.08 p=.19			
	Q9-More Rapes	.05 p=.29	.14 p=.05	.03 p=.37	.13 p=.07	.12 p=.08	.22*	.16*	.18*		
Behavioral Intention	Q10-Likelihood of reporting (Females only)	.33**	.25*	.42**	.50**	.40**	.19*	.38**	.28*	.18 p=.06	

Note: N for questions 1 to 9 ranges from 127 to 132; N for question 10 ranges from 81 to 82.
*p < .05; **p < .001.

303

Again demographic variables were examined to determine if they should be included in the regressions on this second dependent variable. Of the demographic questions, education was marginally significant (unstandardized coefficient = .23, p = .06) and age (unstandardized coefficient =–.01, p = .41) and income (unstandardized coefficient = .05, p = .34) were not significant (the coefficients have df = 1, 78). The education variable, therefore, was entered into the next regression equation. The regression equation was not significant, $F(3, 78)$ = 1.30, p = .28, adjusted R^2 = .011.

Three questions were chosen to be regressed hierarchically on the behavioral intention measure because they reflected issues women might consider when trying to decide about reporting a rape. Again, the order in which the variables are presented reflects the order in which they were entered in the equation. Women who felt televising rape trials would not increase a victim's trauma were more likely to report a rape (unstandardized coefficient = .50, p = .001). Women who felt that televising rape trials would raise awareness about rape were more likely to report a rape (unstandardized coefficient = .22, p = 02). The question about disruption of the trial process was not significantly related (understanding coefficient = .02, p = .82). (The coefficients have df = 1, 76.) The significance of the regression equation is p = .001, $F(4, 76)$ = 5.51, and the adjusted R^2 = .18.

DISCUSSION

The two primary dependent variables examined in the present study were approval of televising rape trials and women's behavioral intention to report a rape. The descriptive results suggest that *both men and women support the ban on televised rape trials*. The regression analysis relating various beliefs to approval of televising rape trials showed that disapproval was most closely related to respondents' reluctance to extend freedom of press guarantees to televising rape trials and to granting unrestricted public access to the justice system. The second and third most important reasons for disapproval of televising rape trials were concern about effects inside the courtroom, specifically disruptions of the trial process, and an increase in the victim's trauma. Opinions about extended effects were not significantly related to approval.

Beliefs about legal and constitutional effects may have been most predictive because of a general tendency to evaluate public policy decisions on the basis of symbolic beliefs rather than instrumental responses. Symbolic beliefs reflect politico-social attitudes, while instrumental beliefs reflect personal concerns. For instance, Tyler and Weber (1982) found that symbolic political and social beliefs were more predictive of support for the death penalty than instrumental concerns related to decreasing crime (see also Tyler, 1984). In the present study, it could be argued that responses to the legal policy and constitutional issues represent respondents' symbolic beliefs about the rights of the media and the participants in the trial, while beliefs about effects inside the courtroom and beliefs about extended effects represent more instrumental reasons for not supporting EMC of rape trials.

One explanation for why beliefs about the effects of EMC inside the courtroom were more significantly related to approval than beliefs about extended effects may be respondents' greater ability to imagine the former than the latter. Sherman, Cialdini, Schwartzman, and Reynolds (1985), for example, had subjects imagine either having a disease with easily imaginable symptoms such as low energy levels, muscle aches, and frequent severe headaches, or having difficult-to-imagine symptoms such as a vague sense of disorientation, a malfunctioning nervous system, and an inflamed liver. After imagining the diseases, subjects rated how likely it was that they would contract the disease. Subjects who imagined the concrete symptoms judged the disease as more likely to occur than subjects who imagined the less concrete symptoms. In the present study it was probably easier to imagine the effects of an increase in rape victim trauma and a disruption of the trial process than to imagine the extended effects of an increased number of rapes, decreased reporting of rapes, and increased public awareness of rape. Furthermore, courtroom effects may be more easily imagined because there is a seemingly more direct causal relationship between EMC and effects inside the courtroom than between EMC and the relatively more amorphous extended effects. That is, respondents may be more capable of imagining television cameras effects *inside* the courtroom, but the causal impact *outside* the courtroom is clearly not as straightforward because of the number of intervening variables to consider.

When analyzing the second dependent variable, the descriptive results indicate that if women knew that other rape trials had been televised, they would be less likely to report a rape. The regression results show that believing that television coverage of a rape trial would cause a rape victim even more trauma was the variable most highly related to women's behavioral intention to report a rape. The televising of the rape trial in New Bedford, for instance, may have had this effect. The number of rapes reported to the police dropped from 30% in New Bedford to 0% during the televising of the trial (E. Bennett, personal communication, March 14, 1985). Even today, according to a women's rape crisis center in New Bedford, women are hesitant about reporting rape because they fear media coverage.

Support for the finding that beliefs about victim trauma was the variable most highly related to behavioral intentions to report rape also comes from Feldman-Summers and Ashworth's (1981) study on factors that affect behavioral intentions to report. Normative expectations and perceived outcomes of respondents from four ethnic groups (Asian, Black, Hispanic, and Caucasian) were regressed on respondents' behavioral intention to report a rape. For all ethnic groups, the perceived likelihood that reporting the rape "would result in my feeling calm, safe and better having talked to someone about the rape" was the best predictor. The other 23 predictors included perceived outcomes such as "would result in adequate medical attention"; "a trial in which I would have to testify"; "gathering the necessary evidence that could be used in court"; "nothing being done to help me"; and "my being treated as an immoral person."

If women were better informed about their state laws, however, viewing a televised rape trial might not affect their reporting rates. Indeed, in most states that permit EMC, a rape trial would not be televised if the victim opposed televised coverage. As of January 1985, 5 states prohibit coverage of rape trials, 6 require consent from the victim, and in 6 states, if a victim submits an objection, the objection automatically will be upheld. In only 6 states is a victim's objection not automatically upheld, and in 7 states the decision is left only to the judge. The other 20 states and the District of Columbia do not allow televised coverage of criminal courts (National Center for State Courts, 1985). It is unlikely, however, that more than a minority of rape victims know the law in their state prior to reporting rape.

Therefore, public education efforts aimed at informing women about changes in how the legal system treats victims of sexual assault should be expanded. In the absence of such educational efforts about victim rights, the present results suggest that preconceptions about media effects may be perpetuated and may, in turn, reduce the likelihood of rape reporting.

APPENDIX A

Survey Questions

Respondents were asked to rate their degree of agreement on a 7-point scale from *strongly agree* (7) to *strongly disagree* (1) for the following two statements:

(1) In general, court cases should be allowed to appear on TV.
(2) In general, rape cases should be allowed to appear on TV.

After the following questions were 7-point scales with the two opposing opinions described in the question as endpoints. Respondents were asked to choose the number that best represented their opinion. (For the analysis, the response least favorable to EMC was coded as a 1 and most favorable as 7.)

(3) Some people argue that the media should be allowed to televise rape trials because the media has a right to report on courtroom proceedings. Others argue that the media does not have this right. Where would you place yourself on this scale?

(4) Some people believe that rape trials should be televised because the public has a right to be informed about the criminal justice system. Others believe that this right does not justify televising rape trials. Where would you place yourself on this scale?

(5) Some people think that televising rape trials would increase a rape victim's trauma. Others think that televising rape trials would not increase a victim's trauma. Where would you place yourself on this scale?

(6) Some people feel that televising rape trials would disrupt the trial process. Others feel that televising rape trials would not be disruptive. Where would you place yourself on this scale?

(7) Some people think that televising rape trials would reduce the likelihood that a woman would report a rape to the police. Others think that televising rape trials would not reduce the likelihood that a rape would be reported. Where would you place yourself on this scale?

(8) Some people think that TV coverage of rape trials would raise public awareness about rape. Others think that TV coverage of rape trials would have no such effect. Where would you place yourself on this scale?

(9) Some people feel that televising rape trials would encourage even more rapes. Others feel that televising rape trials would not encourage more rape. Where would you place yourself on this scale?

(10) (Women only) If you were a rape victim and you knew that some rape trials were televised in Minnesota, do you think that you'd be more likely to report the rape, less likely to report the rape, or unaffected?

NOTES

1. Five other general questions about rape and physical assault were also asked. But because none dealt with EMC issues these questions were not included in our analysis. Respondents were also asked four questions about the New Bedford trial. However, so many respondents had not seen the broadcast (78.8%) that the inclusion of comparisons

between these respondents and those who had seen the coverage would not have been meaningful.

2. Space limitations on the questionnaire prevented us from asking respondents to directly compare the effects of television coverage with the effects of other forms of the news media such as newspaper coverage, or to gauge effects in nonrape cases. A sample of 249 undergraduates, however, was asked questions that compared the effects of television coverage with newspaper coverage. The frequencies resemble the results found in the present study. For instance, while 27.8% felt that reading about a rape trial in a newspaper would discourage reporting, 54.1% felt that seeing a rape trial on television would discourage reporting even if the victim had consented to being televised. Similarly, 81.9% believed that the presence of television cameras would cause more trauma for victims than the presence of newspaper reporters.

3. Because of the sample size and some skewed frequencies, the regression results should only be interpreted as a description of the present sample.

REFERENCES

Borgida, E., DeBono, K. G., & Buckman, L. A. (1985). The effects of electronic media coverage on witness testimony in a criminal trial. Unpublished manuscript, University of Minnesota.

Feldman-Summers, S., & Ashworth, C. D. (1981). Factors related to intentions to report a rape. Journal of Social Issues, 37, 53-70.

Gerbner, G. (1980). Trial by television: Are we at the point of no return? Judicature. 63(9), 416-426.

Lindsey, R. P. (1984). An assessment of the use of cameras in state and federal courts. Georgia Law Review, 18, 389-424.

National Center for State Courts. (1985). (Ref. No. RIX 85.241). Williamsburg, VA.

Sherman, S. J., Cialdini, R. B., Schwartzman, D. F., & Reynolds, K. D. (1985). Imagining can heighten or lower the perceived likelihood of contracting a disease: The mediating effect of ease of imagery. Personality and Social Psychology Bulletin, 11, 118-127.

Tyler, T. R. (1984). The influence of citizen satisfaction with police behavior upon public support for increases in police authority. Law and Policy, 6, 329-338.

Tyler, T. R., & Weber, R. (1982). Support for the Death Penalty; Instrumental response to crime, or symbolic attitude? Law and Society Review, 17, 21-45.

Weisberg, S. (1980). Applied linear regression. New York: Wiley.

SECTION V

SUMMARY

As the chapters in this section illustrate, TV cameras in the courtroom can have any number of effects on the behavior of trial participants, juries, and the public at large.

The section opened with Kassin's (1984) report of a mock jury experiment, and the finding that although cameras were distracting during the opening moments, subjects rapidly adjusted to their presence. Considering the fact that juries in real trials are already on public display (that is, amid a gallery of spectators, journalists, lawyers, and the judge), it seems safe to conclude from this result that TV cameras do not pose a direct threat to the jury's decision-making process. As Kassin noted, however, this finding does not address the potential for indirect effects on the jury—namely, how TV cameras influence their verdicts by affecting (a) the behavior of the trial actors (for example, do witnesses testify differently?) or (b) the attitudes of pressure from the jurors' community. Might juries be affected in indirect ways by televised coverage of their case?

In response to that question, Netteburg (1980) reviewed the experiences reported in states that had allowed cameras in the courts. In addition, he described a study of a particular trial in Wisconsin in which a survey of public opinion suggested that the trial participants, including the defendant, were generally unharmed by their exposure on TV. But was that the case? It turned out that nearly 60% of the respondents surveyed erroneously believed that the defendant was convicted of both murder and arson. In fact, she was found not guilty on the arson charge. The problem is, how do we know what the public would have believed if their exposure to the case had been limited to what they read in the newspapers? The answer is, we do not. Moreover, how do we know that there isn't a potential for harm in certain identifiable types of trials? With this study focused on a single trial, again we do not know.

This section concludes with Swim and Borgida's (1986) study of how the public feels and is affected by the televising of rape trials. Interestingly, these investigators found that most people, male and female alike, do not think rape trials should be televised. Also, many women indicated that because of the threat of a televised trial, they might be personally reluctant to report a rape to the authorities. This finding is important. It leads us to question whether televising trials might not have far-reaching and undesirable ramifications for other aspects of the criminal justice system. Indeed, as Swim and Borgida pointed out, there is reason to believe that after the gang-rape trial in New Bedford, Massachusetts, the number of rapes reported in that area dropped sharply.

Should cameras be allowed in the courtroom? The chapters in this section represent a first step toward defining what the relevant questions are for policymakers. Unfortunately, this research is just that—a first step. Mock-jury research can address part of the problem, such as whether jurors or witnesses behave differently in the presence of TV cameras. Similarly, public opinion surveys can offer suggestions about other, less direct problems. But there are limits to what can be concluded about the *actual* effects of cameras on the behavior of real trial participants simply by testing laboratory subjects or by asking people how they *think* they were affected. At this point, there is a clear need for controlled research conducted within the courts (see, for example, Slater & Hans, 1982). As long as the empirical issues are well defined, the answers are lacking, and judges are willing to experiment with the procedure, this need can be fulfilled.

REFERENCES

Slater, D., & Hans, V. P. (1982). Methodological issues in the evaluation of "experiments" with cameras in courts. *Communication Quarterly, 30,* 376-380.

About the Editors

Lawrence S. Wrightsman is Professor of Psychology at the University of Kansas, where he served as department chairperson from 1976 to 1981. For the academic year 1981-1982 he was Intra-University Visiting Professor at the University of Kansas School of Law. He received a B.A. and an M.A. from Southern Methodist University and Ph.D. in social psychology from the University of Minnesota. The author or editor of 10 books (including, with Saul M. Kassin, *The Psychology of Evidence and Trial Procedure,* Sage, 1985) and numerous journal articles, he has also served as President of the Society for the Psychological Study of Social Issues (SPSSI) and the Society of Personality and Social Psychology (Division 8 of the American Psychological Association). He currently directs the Kansas Jury Research Project and teaches a course on jury decision making to law students there.

Cynthia E. Willis is currently a doctoral student in the Department of Psychology at the University of Kansas. She holds a B.A. degree from Washburn University and an M.A. degree from the University of Kansas. She has prepared affidavits for appeals to the Kansas Supreme Court and has taught a psychology-and-the-law course at the U.S. Penitentiary in Leavenworth, Kansas. Her interests concentrate on jury decision making, especially jurors' reactions to the testimony of eyewitnesses.

Saul M. Kassin is Associate Professor of Psychology at Williams College. He received his Ph.D. in personality and social psychology at the University of Connecticut after which he served as a postdoctoral research fellow at the University of Kansas and on the faculty at Purdue University. He is the author of numerous journal articles and book chapters, and has coedited three other books, including *The Psychology of Evidence and Trial Procedure* (Sage, 1985). Interested in various aspects of jury decision making and trial procedures, he has recently held a Judicial Fellowship at the U.S. Supreme Court (1984-1985) and an NIMH Postdoctoral Research position at Stanford University (1985-1986).